TM

References for the Rest of Us!

BESTSELLING BOOK SERIES

Are you intimidated and confused by computers? Do you find that traditional manuals are overloaded with technical details you'll never use? Do your friends and family always call you to fix simple problems on their PCs? Then the For Dummies® computer book series from Hungry Minds, Inc. is for you.

For Dummies books are written for those frustrated computer users who know they aren't really dumb but find that PC hardware, software, and indeed the unique vocabulary of computing make them feel helpless. For Dummies books use a lighthearted approach, a down-to-earth style, and even cartoons and humorous icons to dispel computer novices' fears and build their confidence. Lighthearted but not lightweight, these books are a perfect survival guide for anyone forced to use a computer.

> *"I like my copy so much I told friends; now they bought copies."*
>
> — **Irene C., Orwell, Ohio**

> *"Quick, concise, nontechnical, and humorous."*
>
> — **Jay A., Elburn, Illinois**

> *"Thanks, I needed this book. Now I can sleep at night."*
>
> — **Robin F., British Columbia, Canada**

Already, millions of satisfied readers agree. They have made For Dummies books the #1 introductory level computer book series and have written asking for more. So, if you're looking for the most fun and easy way to learn about computers, look to For Dummies books to give you a helping hand.

Hungry Minds™

1/01

by Barbara Assadi and Galen Gruman

Hungry Minds™

Best-Selling Books • Digital Downloads • e-Books • Answer Networks • e-Newsletters • Branded Web Sites • e-Learning

New York, NY ◆ Cleveland, OH ◆ Indianapolis, IN

QuarkXPress® 5 For Dummies®

Published by
Hungry Minds, Inc.
909 Third Avenue
New York, NY 10022
www.hungryminds.com
www.dummies.com

Library of Congress Control Number: 2001097472

ISBN: 0-7645-0643-9

Printed in the United States of America

10 9 8 7 6 5 4 3 2 1

1B/SQ/QS/QS/IN

Distributed in the United States by Hungry Minds, Inc.

Distributed by CDG Books Canada Inc. for Canada; by Transworld Publishers Limited in the United Kingdom; by IDG Norge Books for Norway; by IDG Sweden Books for Sweden; by IDG Books Australia Publishing Corporation Pty. Ltd. for Australia and New Zealand; by TransQuest Publishers Pte Ltd. for Singapore, Malaysia, Thailand, Indonesia, and Hong Kong; by Gotop Information Inc. for Taiwan; by ICG Muse, Inc. for Japan; by Intersoft for South Africa; by Eyrolles for France; by International Thomson Publishing for Germany, Austria and Switzerland; by Distribuidora Cuspide for Argentina; by LR International for Brazil; by Galileo Libros for Chile; by Ediciones ZETA S.C.R. Ltda. for Peru; by WS Computer Publishing Corporation, Inc., for the Philippines; by Contemporanea de Ediciones for Venezuela; by Express Computer Distributors for the Caribbean and West Indies; by Micronesia Media Distributor, Inc. for Micronesia; by Chips Computadoras S.A. de C.V. for Mexico; by Editorial Norma de Panama S.A. for Panama; by American Bookshops for Finland.

For general information on Hungry Minds' products and services please contact our Customer Care Department within the U.S. at 800-762-2974, outside the U.S. at 317-572-3993 or fax 317-572-4002.

For sales inquiries and reseller information, including discounts, premium and bulk quantity sales, and foreign-language translations, please contact our Customer Care Department at 800-434-3422, fax 317-572-4002, or write to Hungry Minds, Inc., Attn: Customer Care Department, 10475 Crosspoint Boulevard, Indianapolis, IN 46256.

For information on licensing foreign or domestic rights, please contact our Sub-Rights Customer Care Department at 212-884-5000.

For information on using Hungry Minds' products and services in the classroom or for ordering examination copies, please contact our Educational Sales Department at 800-434-2086 or fax 317-572-4005.

For press review copies, author interviews, or other publicity information, please contact our Public Relations Department at 317-572-3168 or fax 317-572-4168.

For authorization to photocopy items for corporate, personal, or educational use, please contact Copyright Clearance Center, 222 Rosewood Drive, Danvers, MA 01923, or fax 978-750-4470.

Hungry Minds™ is a trademark of Hungry Minds, Inc.

About the Authors

Barbara Assadi is co-founder and principal of BayCreative, a San Francisco-based marketing services agency. She was formerly editor-in-chief of Oracle Corporation's Web site in Redwood Shores, California. She managed Quark, Inc.'s Editorial Services department, overseeing the creation of documentation, training materials, and marketing collateral. Barbara has reviewed desktop and online publishing software for *Macworld, Publish,* and *InfoWorld* publications, and has co-authored several other books on desktop publishing, including the *QuarkXPress Bible* (Hungry Minds, Inc.), and was editor of *The Official Adobe Electronic Publishing Guide* (Adobe Press).

Galen Gruman is the editor at *M-Business* magazine, and previously was executive editor at both *Upside* and *Macworld,* as well as West Coast bureau chief of *Computerworld*. A pioneer user of desktop publishing in professional magazine production, Galen adopted the technology in 1986 for a national engineering magazine, *IEEE Software*. He covered desktop publishing technology for the trade weekly *InfoWorld* for 12 years, as well as for other publications. Galen is co-author with Deke McClelland of several *PageMaker For Dummies* books, with Barbara Assadi the series of *QuarkXPress For Dummies* and *QuarkXPress Bible* books, and with Kelly Anton and John Cruise the *Adobe InDesign 1.0 Bible,* all from Hungry Minds, Inc.

Dedications

Barbara Assadi: To my sister Dawn, a kindred spirit.

Galen Gruman: To my brothers Stephen and Darius.

Authors' Acknowledgments

We want to thank Brad Jones for his assistance in updating the book. We also thank Kelly Kordes Anton for reviewing the content and for her support in developing example files. Special thanks to Christine Berman for editing this book and also to everyone on the Hungry Minds Editorial and Production staffs for their contributions.

We also thank Amy Hethcoat, Caleb Gilbert, and Arne Hurty for their support and encouragement, and Tim Banister for his technical review of the content. Special thanks to Fred Ebrahimi and Glen Turpin of Quark, Inc.

Publisher's Acknowledgments

We're proud of this book; please send us your comments through our Hungry Minds Online Registration Form located at www.dummies.com.

Some of the people who helped bring this book to market include the following:

Acquisitions, Editorial, and Media Development

Associate Project Editor: Christine Berman
 (*Previous Edition: Kathleen M. Cox and Kathy Simpson*)

Acquisitions Editor: Bob Woerner

Copy Editor: Amy Pettinella

Technical Editor: Tim Banister

Editorial Managers: Leah Cameron, Constance Carlisle

Media Development Manager: Laura VanWinkle

Media Development Supervisor: Richard Graves

Editorial Assistant: Amanda Foxworth

Production

Project Coordinator: Maridee Ennis

Layout and Graphics: Joyce Haughey, Jackie Nicholas, Jacque Schneider, Betty Schulte, Jeremey Unger, Mary J. Virgin, Erin Zeltner

Proofreaders: John Greenough, Andy Hollandbeck, Susan Moritz, Dwight Ramsey, TECHBOOKS Production Services

Indexer: TECHBOOKS Production Services

General and Administrative

Hungry Minds Technology Publishing Group: Richard Swadley, Vice President and Executive Group Publisher; Bob Ipsen, Vice President and Group Publisher; Joseph Wikert, Vice President and Publisher; Barry Pruett, Vice President and Publisher; Mary Bednarek, Editorial Director; Mary C. Corder, Editorial Director; Andy Cummings, Editorial Director

Hungry Minds Manufacturing: Ivor Parker, Vice President, Manufacturing

Hungry Minds Marketing: John Helmus, Assistant Vice President, Director of Marketing

Hungry Minds Production for Branded Press: Debbie Stailey, Production Director

Hungry Minds Sales: Michael Violano, Vice President, International Sales and Sub Rights

Contents at a Glance

Cartoons at a Glance

By Rich Tennant

"Oh, that's Jack's area for his paper crafts. He's made some wonderful US Treasury Bonds, Certificates of Deposit, $20's, $50's, $100's, that sort of thing."

page 335

"QuarkXPress does a lot of great things. I'm not sure running a word processing program sideways without line breaks on butcher's paper is one of them."

page 373

"It says, 'Seth - Please see us about your idea to wrap newsletter text around company logo. Production.'"

page 83

Poet e.e. cummings makes his last service call.

page 7

"I APPRECIATE YOUR COMPUTER HAS 256 COLORS, I JUST DON'T THINK THEY ALL HAD TO BE USED IN ONE BOOK REPORT."

page 213

"What I'm looking for are dynamic Web applications and content, not Web innuendoes and intent."

page 289

"You might want to adjust the value of your 'snap distance' function."

page 265

Cartoon Information:
Fax: 978-546-7747
E-Mail: richtennant@the5thwave.com
World Wide Web: www.the5thwave.com

Table of Contents

Introduction

• •

A man walks down the street when he comes upon a construction site where a group of three brick masons are busily at work. He stops to talk to the first brick mason and asks, "What are you doing?" The brick mason answers, "I'm putting bricks on top of other bricks."

The man continues down the sidewalk until he comes to the second brick mason. Again he asks the same question, "What are you doing?" The second brick mason answers, "I'm putting some bricks together to make a wall."

The man then walks on until he comes face-to-face with the third brick mason. The man poses the same question to the third brick mason: "What are you doing?" The third brick mason answers, "I'm building a beautiful cathedral."

Is QuarkXPress Too High-End for Me?

Right now, you may be wondering why on earth we are telling this story as part of the introduction to a book on QuarkXPress. Good question. But, when you think about it, the people who use QuarkXPress are a lot like those brick masons, and QuarkXPress is a lot like the mortar and bricks used by those brick masons to do their work.

What we are saying is this: There are all kinds of users of QuarkXPress. Some do very simple, one-color documents. Some do moderately challenging documents, which include photos, illustrations, and complex charts. With Version 5, some even create Web pages. Still others — like the third brick mason who was building a cathedral — use QuarkXPress to create high-end, highly designed and illustrated works of art.

QuarkXPress — like the mortar and bricks used by the brick masons in our story — is a *tool*. Nothing more, nothing less. It works for the world's most-celebrated graphic designers. It also works for people who create simpler documents, such as school newsletters.

The point is, QuarkXPress can never be too high-end for you, or for anyone else, because you pick and choose which parts of this tool you need to use. Also, keep in mind that if you create *any* type of document, you can benefit from the program's features. Sure, it's true that if your documents are simple, you won't need to use all the sophisticated features in QuarkXPress. But, when you think about it, isn't it nice to know that these features are available when and if you ever need them? And that you won't outgrow the program as you become more proficient with document design? We think so.

How to Use This Book

Although this book has information that any level of publisher needs to know to use QuarkXPress, this book is also for those of you who are fairly new to the field, or who are just becoming familiar with the program. What we try to do is to take the mystery out of QuarkXPress and give you some guidance on how to create a bunch of different types of documents. Here are some conventions used in this book:

- ✔ **Menu commands** are listed like this: Style⇨Type Style⇨Bold.

  If we describe a situation in which you need to select one menu and then choose a command from a secondary menu or list box, we do it like this: Choose File⇨Get Picture (or press ⌘+E on Mac or Ctrl+E in Windows). After the first mention, we drop the platform reference. This shorthand method of indicating a sequence of commands is often followed by the keyboard shortcut, as shown in this example.

- ✔ **⌘:** This is the Macintosh's Command key — the most-used shortcut key. Its Windows equivalent is **Ctrl.**

- ✔ **Key combinations:** If you're supposed to press several keys together, we indicate that by placing plus signs (+) between them. Thus Shift+⌘+A means press and hold the Shift and ⌘ keys, and then press A. After you've pressed the A key, let go of the other keys. (The last letter in the sequence does not need to be held down.) We also use the plus sign to join keys to mouse movements. For example, Option+drag means to hold the Option key when dragging the mouse.

- ✔ **Panes:** QuarkXPress has an interface feature, tabbed panes, that you may have seen in other applications. This is a method of stuffing several dialog boxes into one dialog box. You see tabs, like those in file folders, and by clicking a tab, the options for that tab come to the front of the dialog box in what is called a *pane.*

- ✔ **Pointer:** The small graphic icon that moves on the screen as you move your mouse is a pointer (also called a cursor). The pointer takes on different shapes depending on the tool you select, the current location of the mouse, and the function you are performing.

✔ **Click:** This means to quickly press and release the mouse button once. On most Mac mice, there is only one button, but on some there are two or more. All PC mice have at least two buttons. If you have a multi-button mouse, click the leftmost button when we say to click the mouse.

✔ **Double-click:** This means to quickly press and release the mouse button twice. On some multi-button mice, one of the buttons can function as a double-click. (You click it once, the mouse clicks twice.) If your mouse has this feature, use it; it saves strain on your hand.

✔ **Right-click:** A Windows feature, this means to click the right-hand mouse button. On a Mac's one-button mouse, hold the Control key when clicking the mouse button to do the equivalent of right-clicking in programs that support it. On multi-button Mac mice, assign one of the buttons to the Control+click combination.

✔ **Dragging:** Dragging is used for moving and sizing items in a QuarkXPress document. To drag an item, position the mouse pointer on the item, press *and hold* down the mouse button, and then slide the mouse across a flat surface.

How This Book Is Organized

We've divided *QuarkXPress 5 For Dummies* into seven parts, not counting this introduction. Each part has anywhere from two to five chapters, so you don't have to wade through too much explanation to get to the information you need. Note that the book covers QuarkXPress on both Macintosh and Windows platforms. Because the application is almost identical on both, we only point out platform-specific information when we need to, or when we remember to, or both.

Part I: Getting Started

Designing a document is a combination of science and art. The science is in setting up the structure of the page: How many places will hold text and how many will hold graphics? How wide will the margins be? Where will the page numbers appear? And so on. The art is in coming up with creative ways of filling the structure to please your eyes and the eyes of the people who will be looking at your document.

In this part, we tell you how to navigate your way around QuarkXPress using the program's menus, dialog boxes, and tabbed panes. We also show you how to set up the basic structure of a document and then how to begin filling the structure with words and pictures. We also tell you how to bring in text and graphics created in separate word processing and graphics applications.

Part II: Adding Style and Substance

Good publishing technique is about more than just getting the words down on paper or Web page. It's also about tweaking the letters and lines — and the space between them — to make your pages shine. This part shows you how to do all that and a lot more, including tips on using Required Components and XTensions to get more out of QuarkXPress and how to get your document out of your computer and onto some other medium, such as film or paper or the Web. We give you some solid suggestions on how to work with all those other people in the world who know how to help you get the job done.

Part III: The Picasso Factor

Let's be honest. Pablo Picasso didn't become famous for realistically portraying people. His claim to fame is based on how he took facial features and then skewed, slanted, stretched, and shrunk them into new forms. Some folks loved his work; others found it hard to figure out. But you had to admire the fact that it was unique.

We named this part of the book after the famous artist because it tells not only how to use QuarkXPress as an illustration tool, but also how to take normal-looking text and graphics and distort them. Why would you want to do this? Good question. The answer could be that, like Picasso, you want to present ideas in a visually interesting way. Either that, or you want to see how your relatives might look with their faces rearranged. QuarkXPress lets you manipulate text and art in interesting ways, and we show you how.

Part IV: Going Long and Linking

QuarkXPress includes features that help you keep track of figure numbers, table numbers, index entries — well, you get the idea. In fact, crafting long documents with QuarkXPress is a piece of cake. In this section, we show you how to handle long documents of all flavors, including those that link together several smaller documents into a whole.

Part V: Taking QuarkXPress to the Web

It used to be that QuarkXPress was the tool for print documents. Now QuarkXPress 5 has features that let you build Web pages — and when it comes to building Web pages, a lot of the regular QuarkXPress rules don't apply. We show you how to use the new Web features to make some snazzy pages for online use.

Part VI: Guru in Training

After you master the basics, why not pick up some of the tricks the pros use? In this part, we show you how to customize QuarkXPress so that it fits you like a comfortable easy chair. We also explain how QuarkXPress works on PCs that use Windows and on Macs.

Part VII: The Part of Tens

This part of the book is like the chips in the chocolate chip cookies; you could eat the cookies without them, but you'd be missing a really good part. It's a part of extremes, of bests and worsts. It's like a mystery novel that's hard to put down until you read the very last word. In fact, you might even be tempted to start reading here and then go back to Chapter 1, but don't. The concepts in this book will make more sense to you if you read the other six parts of the book first.

Icons Used in This Book

So that you can pick out parts that you really need to pay attention to (or, depending on your taste, to avoid), we've used some symbols, or *icons* in this book.

When you see this icon, it means we are pointing out a feature that's new to Version 5 of QuarkXPress.

This icon points out features that behave a bit differently on Windows machines and Macs.

This icon alerts you to a valuable nugget of information you should store in your memory.

If you see this icon, it means that we're mentioning some really nifty point or idea that you may want to keep in mind as you use the program.

If you skip all the other icons, pay attention to this one. Why? Because ignoring it could cause something really, really bad or embarrassing to happen, like when you were sitting in your second-grade classroom waiting for the teacher to call on you to answer a question, and you noticed that you still had your pajama shirt on — backwards. We don't want that to happen to you!

Sometimes things work a certain way for no apparent reason. When you see this icon, it means you are about to read about some QuarkXPress mystery. But don't worry: We tell you how to solve it.

This icon tells you that we are about to pontificate on some remote technical bit of information that might help explain a feature in QuarkXPress. The technical info will definitely make you sound impressive if you memorize it and recite it to your friends.

Where to Go from Here

QuarkXPress is an extremely versatile publishing tool. The time you take to become familiar with Quark's many capabilities will be amply repaid in your ability to create the types of documents you want and need, from the most basic to the most bizarre. QuarkXPress can take you anywhere you want to go in print or online publishing. So get going!

Part I
Getting Started

Poet e.e. cummings makes his last service call.

In this part . . .

Getting off to a great start with QuarkXPress is what this part is about. We take you from a blank screen to a text-filled document, helping you navigate your way around QuarkXPress using the program's menus, dialog boxes, views, and tabbed panes. And we explain the basics about how to get QuarkXPress to do what you want it to: First you build a box and then you start to fill it with text or graphics. All this just to get you on your way.

Chapter 1

Introducing QuarkXPress

In This Chapter

▶ Getting familiar with menus, dialog boxes, and keyboard shortcuts

▶ Exploring QuarkXPress's Tool palette and Measurements palette

*W*hen the first personal computer shipped in the early 1980s, a quiet revolution began. The turning point in that revolution was the introduction of desktop publishing in the mid-1980s, which let anyone anywhere become a publisher. Soon, anyone with a message could get it out to the world. That revolutionized much of business and society. You, too, are a revolutionary. And by buying QuarkXPress and this book, you have taken up the cause.

Over the years, QuarkXPress has become the best desktop publishing tool around. Professionals know that, which is why they have made QuarkXPress the corporate standard for magazine, newspaper, and catalog publishing. It is also an effective book-publishing tool, thanks to its capability of index documents and creating tables of contents and multichapter books. Now the folks at Quark have upped the ante again with the release of QuarkXPress 5. In addition to hosting a boatload of new desktop-publishing features (including the long delayed, though very welcome inclusion of a table-making tool), 5 boasts an entire suite of publishing tools for the World Wide Web, including tools for creating forms, radio buttons, hyperlinks and "hot spots." In short, if ever you wanted to limit your publishing options to just one or two applications, you certainly can't go wrong choosing QuarkXPress 5 to be among them.

You may feel a little daunted by QuarkXPress. Relax. Throughout this book, we walk you through the program to familiarize you with all it has to offer. You may be a bit intimidated by the vast layers of panes, palettes, tools, and menus you see before you. Don't be. Working with QuarkXPress is like working with a new person at the office — things may be awkward at first, but after you get to know each other, you find you can do great things together.

A Familiar Interface

First, you'll no doubt notice that the QuarkXPress interface bears a strong resemblance to the features used by other Windows and Macintosh programs. If you use other programs, you already know how to use QuarkXPress components such as file folders, document icons, and the set of menus at the top of the document window.

You create a document by choosing File➪New➪Document or open an existing document by choosing File➪Open➪Document. The program displays a window similar to the ones shown in Figure 1-1.

This book is for both Windows and Macintosh users. We use both Windows and Mac screen shots throughout the book — unless the two platforms' versions of QuarkXPress have significant differences. In those cases we show screens from both.

When you display a document in either Windows or Macintosh, you'll notice a few visual elements:

- ✔ The *ruler origin box* lets you reset and reposition the ruler origin, which is the point at which the side and top rulers are 0 (zero).

- ✔ The name of the open document appears on the *title bar,* located below the menu bar on the Mac and above the menu bar in Windows. You can move the document window around in the screen display area by clicking and dragging the title bar.

- ✔ If you have reduced or enlarged a document, clicking the *zoom box* on the Mac or the *restore box* in Windows, at the top right corner of the document window, returns it to its previous size.

- ✔ You can make a document all but disappear by minimizing it (in Windows) or turning it into a window shade (on the Mac). To minimize a document, click the minimize box in the document's title bar. To make a document into a window shade, double-click its title bar or click its WindowShade box on the Mac.

- ✔ The *vertical* and *horizontal rulers* on the left and top of the window reflect the measurement system currently in use.

- ✔ The *pasteboard* is a work area around the document page. You can temporarily store text boxes, picture boxes, or lines on the pasteboard. Items on the pasteboard do not print.

- ✔ QuarkXPress displays a shadow effect around the document page. The shadow indicates the edges of the document.

- ✔ If you select Automatic Text Box in the New dialog box (which you access by selecting New Document from the File menu), a text box appears on the first page of the new document.

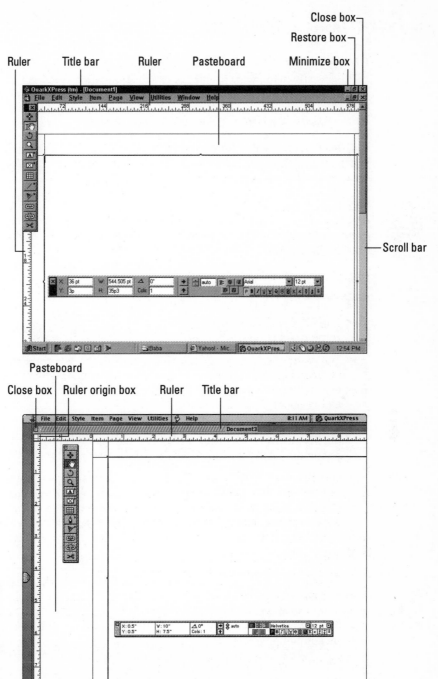

Figure 1-1:
The Quark-
XPress
document
window.

✔ Clicking and dragging the *size box* on the Mac resizes the document window as you move the mouse. In Windows, you can drag any side of the window to resize it.

✔ The *View Percent* field shows the magnification level of the page that's currently displayed. To change the magnification level, enter a value between 10 and 800 percent in the field; then press the Return key or click elsewhere on the screen. Press Control+V on the Mac or Ctrl+Alt+V in Windows to highlight the View Percent field.

✔ Switch pages using the *page pop-up*.

✔ Use the *scroll bars, boxes,* and *arrows* to shift the document page around within the document window. If you hold down the Option or Alt key while you drag the scroll box, the view of the document is refreshed as it "moves."

✔ Close a document by clicking its *close box*. On the Mac, you can also use the shortcut ⌘+W; in Windows, use Alt+F4.

Menus

The menu bar appears across the top of the document window. To display a menu on a Mac, click the menu title and, if you're using an older version of operating software, hold down the mouse button. (In Windows or Mac OS 9 or later, just click the menu title; you don't need to hold down the mouse button.)

From the menu, you can select any of the active menu commands. QuarkXPress displays inactive menu commands with dimmed (grayed-out) letters. When commands are dimmed, it means that these commands are not currently available to you — they're inactive.

To select one of the active menu commands, hold down the mouse button as you slide through the menu selections. (As you get used to the program, you can avoid using menus by using the keyboard equivalents for menu selections instead. Keyboard equivalents are displayed to the right of the command names in the menu.)

If an arrow appears to the right of a menu command, QuarkXPress displays a second, associated menu when you choose that command. Sometimes this secondary menu appears automatically when you highlight the first menu command; other times, you must continue to hold down the mouse and slide it to the submenu name in order to activate the menu. This may sound a little confusing on paper. But go ahead and try it. You'll find it's no big deal. (Again, in Windows or Mac OS 9 or later, you don't need to hold down the mouse button; just click the arrow to make the submenu appear.) Figure 1-2 shows the Style menu and the secondary menu that appears when you select the Font menu command.

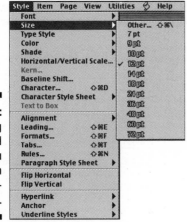

Figure 1-2:
Selecting
menu and
submenu
items in
Quark-
XPress.

Dialog boxes

Some menu commands are followed by a series of dots called an ellipsis (. . .).
If you choose a menu command whose name is followed by an ellipsis, a dialog
box appears. Figure 1-3 shows a dialog box. Dialog boxes give you a great deal
of control over how QuarkXPress applies specific features or functions to your
document.

Some dialog boxes also contain submenus. If a menu has a submenu associated with it, an arrowhead appears to the right of the menu entry. In addition
to submenus, QuarkXPress includes several pop-up menus, which appear
when you make certain selections in a dialog box. Figure 1-3 shows a pop-up
menu for text justification.

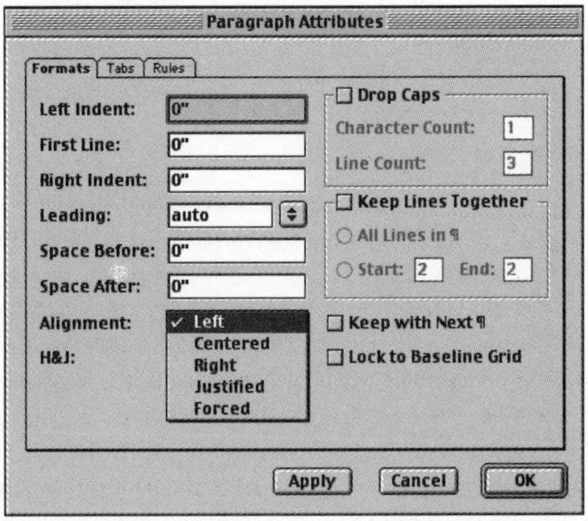

Figure 1-3:
The
Paragraph
Attributes
dialog box,
showing the
Alignment
pop-up
menu on the
Formats tab.

Working with contextual menus

All versions of Windows since 1995, as well as Mac OS 8 and later, use a technique called contextual menus to save you time. By right-clicking an item in Windows, or Control+clicking on the Mac, you got a menu of options just for that item. This saves you time going through menus, dialog boxes, and palettes. QuarkXPress 4, unfortunately, really skimped when it came to context menus. That has changed in QuarkXPress 5. Now you can use context menus in relation to virtually everything in and around a QuarkXPress document. To do so, simply press and hold the appropriate keyboard command, and then click on the object you want to modify.

On the Mac, the default keyboard command to launch a context menu is Control+click. You can, however, change this keyboard command to Control+Shift+click by clicking Zoom in the Control Key area of the Preferences dialog box (Edit➪Preferences➪Interactive). If you have a multibutton mouse, you can set the right-hand mouse button to be the Control+click or Control+Shift+click command.

To display a context menu in Windows, just right-click on the object you want to modify.

Context menus are available for a document's pasteboard, rulers, empty space on a document page, picture boxes, text boxes and text paths, lines, tables, and even many of the palettes. Because they require less mouse movement and menu searching, and require less brain power (something we all want to conserve on!), context menus may soon replace keyboard shortcuts as the beeline of choice among QuarkXPress users.

QuarkXPress uses tabs, a semi-new kind of dialog box that merges several dialog boxes into one. In fact, you'll often see six or seven of these tabs — similar to what you see on a file folder in an office cabinet — in a single dialog box. Like the file folders in an office cabinet, these tabs keep a large amount of stuff organized in one tidy spot. Click the tab, and it comes to the forefront, showing you the options for that tab (refer to Figure 1-3). You simply work with each tab you want within the dialog box.

Keyboard shortcuts

You can select some QuarkXPress functions through pull-down menus, some through palettes, some through keyboard shortcuts, and some through all three options. Most new users begin by using menus because menus are so readily available and familiar. But as you become more comfortable using the program, you may want to save time by using the other options as well, particularly the keyboard shortcuts.

Suppose that you want to move from page one of a document to page three. You can change pages by choosing Go To from the Page menu, or you can use the keyboard shortcut: Press and hold the Command key (⌘) or Ctrl key while you press the J key. In this book, we write this key combination as follows: ⌘+J (Macintosh shortcut) or Ctrl+J (Windows shortcut). The Macintosh shortcut appears first, followed by the Windows shortcut. If the two platforms use the same shortcut, we list the shortcut just once.

In most cases, the Mac's ⌘ key and the Windows Ctrl key are the same, as are the Mac's Option key and the Windows Alt key. Shift is the same on both, whereas the Control key exists only on the Mac and has no Windows equivalent. On both platforms, the Return key is the same as the Enter key (some keyboards use one word whereas some keyboards use the other); in neither case do we mean the Enter key that appears on the keyboard's numeric keypad at the far right of the keyboard. (To avoid confusion, we say "Return" for the key that inserts a new paragraph or activates a command, and we say "keypad Enter" when we mean the key on the numeric keypad.)

The Tool and Measurement Palettes

One of the coolest features of the QuarkXPress interface is its palettes, which let you perform a wide range of functions on an open document without having to access pull-down menus. Like context menus and keyboard shortcuts, palettes are huge time-savers, and you'll undoubtedly find yourself using them all the time. Without a doubt, the Tool palette (see Figure 1-4) and the Measurements palette are the most commonly used. In fact, you'll probably keep these two palettes open all the time. You can find both palettes by choosing View⇨Tools⇨Show Tools, and View⇨Show Measurements. The following list describes the contents of the two palettes.

Figure 1-4:
The Quark-
XPress Tool
palette.

To use a tool on the palette, you first need to activate the tool. To activate a tool, just click it. Depending on which tool you select, the cursor takes on a different look to reflect the function the tool performs (see "A Myriad of Mouse Pointers" later in this chapter). When you click the Linking tool, for example, the cursor looks like links in a chain.

Throughout the book, we explain in greater detail many of the functions you can perform with the Tool palette. But, for now, the following sections give brief descriptions of each tool.

Item tool

The Item tool controls the size and positioning of items. In other words, when you want to change the shape, location, or presence of a text box, picture box, or line, you use the Item tool. We discuss text boxes, picture boxes, etc. in detail later in this book. For now, just keep in mind that the Item tool lets you select, move, group, ungroup, cut, copy and paste text boxes, picture boxes, lines and groups. When you click the Item tool on a box, the box becomes *active,* which means that you can change or move the box. Sizing handles appear on the sides of the active box; you can click and drag these handles to make the box a different size.

Content tool

The Content tool controls the *internal* aspects of items on a page. Functions that you can perform with the Content tool include *importing* (putting text into a text box, or putting a picture into a picture box), cutting, copying, pasting, and editing text.

To edit text in a text box, select the Content tool. Then select the areas of text you want to edit by clicking and dragging the Content tool to highlight the text or by using different numbers of mouse button clicks, as follows:

- ✔ **To position the cursor:** Use the mouse to move the I-beam pointer (it looks like a large capital *I*) to the desired location and click the mouse button once.

- ✔ **To select a single word:** Use the mouse to move the pointer within the word and click the mouse button twice.

- ✔ **To select a line of text:** Use the mouse to move the pointer within the line and click the mouse button three times.

- ✔ **To select an entire paragraph:** Use the mouse to move the pointer within the paragraph and click the mouse button four times.

- ✔ **To select the entire document:** Use the mouse to move the cursor anywhere within the document and click the mouse button five times.

When the Content tool cursor changes to a hand shape, you can use the tool to move the contents of the picture box around the inside the picture box. You can also use it to manipulate the picture's contents, such as applying shades, colors, or printing effects. Again, we discuss the in and outs of text boxes and picture boxes in more detail later in this book. For now, just keep in mind the Content — and the aforementioned Item tool — go hand-in-hand with these boxes.

Rotation tool

Use the Rotation tool to rotate items on a page. You can click a text box, picture box or line, and rotate it by dragging it to the angle you want. You also can rotate items on a page in other ways, which include using the Measurements palette and the Modify command in the Item menu.

Zoom tool

You may want to change the magnification of a page on-screen. For example, you may be making copy edits on text that is set in 8-point type; increasing the displayed size of the text makes it easier to see what you are doing as you edit. The Zoom tool lets you reduce or enlarge the view you see in the document window. When you select the Zoom tool, the cursor looks like a small magnifying glass; when you hold the cursor over the document window and click the mouse button, QuarkXPress increases or decreases the magnification of that section of the screen in increments of 25 percent. (To increase magnification, choose the Zoom tool and click on your document. To decrease magnification, choose the Zoom tool, hold the Option or Alt key, and click on your document.)

Another way to change the magnification of the page is to enter a percentage value in the bottom-left corner of the document window (refer to Figure 1-1); when a page is displayed at actual size, the percentage is 100. QuarkXPress lets you select any viewing percentage, including those in fractions of a percent (such as 49.5 percent), as long as you stay within the range of 10 to 800 percent.

Text Box tools

QuarkXPress needs to have a text box on the page before it lets you type text into your document or import text from a word processor file. You can instruct QuarkXPress to create text boxes on each page of the document automatically, or you can create a text box manually — which you do by using the Text Box tools. We discuss Text Box tools more in Chapter 3.

To create a text box, select the desired Text Box tool and place the cursor where you want the box to appear. Click the mouse button and hold it down as you drag the box to size. More on this in Chapter 3.

Notice the arrow to the right of the Text Box tool's icon: This arrow indicates that if you click and hold down on the Text Box tool, a pop-up menu appears to show alternative Text Box tools. Select any of these alternative tools, and it becomes the default tool shown in the Tool palette. The seven Text Box tools (see Figure 1-5) function as follows:

✔ **Rectangle Text Box tool:** Produces the standard rectangles in which most text is placed. The Rectangle Text Box tool should be the default tool for most users. To get a perfectly square text box, hold down the Shift key while drawing.

✔ **Rounded-Rectangle Text Box tool:** Produces text boxes with rounded corners. You can adjust the degree of rounding, called the *corner radius,* in the Modify Section of the Tools Preferences dialog box. Access the Modify section by choosing Edit⇨Preferences⇨Tools⇨Modify. To get a perfectly square text box, hold down the Shift key while you draw it.

✔ **Oval Text Box tool:** Produces an ellipse. To create a perfect circle, hold down the Shift key while drawing your oval.

✔ **Concave-Corner Text Box tool:** Produces boxes that are "notched out" in the corners. You can adjust the degree of "notching," technically referred to as the corner radius, in the Modify Section of the Tools Preferences dialog box. Hold down the Shift key while drawing to get a perfect square.

✔ **Beveled-Corner Text Box tool:** Produces boxes that have beveled corners as if they've been sheared off by diagonal lines. You can adjust the degree of "shearing," also referred to as the *corner radius,* in the Modify Section of the Tools Preferences dialog box. To get a perfectly square beveled text box, hold down the Shift key while you're drawing the box.

✔ **Bézier Text Box tool:** Named after the renowned French engineer, Pierre Bézier, this tool lets you produce polygons (shapes composed of a series of flat sides) and polycurves (shapes composed of a series of curves), as well as shapes that combine both sides and curves. This tool works differently than the other Text Box tools: Rather than holding down the mouse, you click and release at each corner (or *node,* in graphics-speak). When you want to complete the box, return to your first node and click on it. (*Hint:* You know the tool is working when the pointer changes into a circle from the normal cross.) If you click and drag a little at each desired node, you'll see the Bézier control handles appear. These are the handles that let you create a curve. You can have both straight and curved sides based on how you use the mouse at each node. The best way to learn to use Bézier curves (unless you are Bézier himself) is to experiment with them, and get a feel for how they work. (If you want to convert a straight side to a curve, you can do so, as we describe in Chapter 4.)

✔ **Freehand Text Box tool:** Produces curved shapes — shapes composed of a series of curves. The box takes shape as you move the mouse, as if your mouse were a pen tracking on paper. To complete the box, you usually bring the mouse back to the origin point and then release the mouse button. (Notice how the pointer changes to a circle from the normal cross.) If you release the mouse button before you return to the origin point, QuarkXPress automatically draws a straight line from where you released the mouse to the origin point. Using this tool, too, requires practice — not to mention a steady hand.

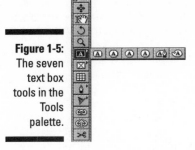

Figure 1-5:
The seven
text box
tools in the
Tools
palette.

Picture Box tools

Picture boxes hold graphics that you import from graphics programs. As with text, QuarkXPress needs a box — in this case a picture box — on the page before it can let you import and manipulate a graphic on a page. You can create a picture box manually, using one of four of QuarkXPress's Picture Box tools. These tools work very much like the Text Box tools. You choose the Picture Box tool you want to use from the Picture Box pop-up menu in the Tool palette, place the cursor where you want the box to appear, click and hold the mouse button, and drag the box to size. (We talk more about this in Chapter 3.) The following list describes the Picture Box tools in detail:

 ✔ **Rectangle Picture Box tool:** Produces the standard rectangles that most pictures are placed in. This should be the default tool for most users. To get a perfectly square text box, hold down the Shift key while you draw.

 ✔ **Rounded-Rectangle Picture Box tool:** Produces text boxes with rounded corners. You can adjust the degree of rounding, called the *corner radius,* in the Modify Section of the Tools Preferences dialog box. To get a perfectly square text box, hold down the Shift key while you draw.

 ✔ **Oval Picture Box tool:** Produces an ellipse. To create a perfect circle, hold down the Shift key while drawing your oval.

 ✔ **Concave-Corner Picture Box tool:** Produces boxes that are "notched out" in the corners. You can adjust the degree of "notching," technically referred to as the corner radius, in the Modify Section of the Tools Preferences dialog box. Hold down the Shift key while drawing to get a perfect square.

 ✔ **Beveled-Corner Picture Box tool:** Produces boxes with beveled corners, as if they've been sheared off by diagonal lines. You can adjust the degree of "shearing," also referred to as the *corner radius,* in the Modify Section of the Tools Preferences dialog box. To get a perfectly square beveled text box, hold down the Shift key while you draw.

 ✔ **Bézier Picture Box tool:** Produces polygons (shapes composed of a series of flat sides) and polycurves (shapes composed of a series of curves), as well as shapes that combine both sides and curves. This tool works differently than the other Picture Box tools: Rather than holding down the mouse, you click and release at each corner (or *node,* in graphics-speak). When you want to complete the box, return to your first node and click on it. (*Hint:* You know the tool is working when the pointer changes into a circle from the normal cross.) If you click and drag a little at each desired node, you'll see the Bézier control handles appear. These are the handles that let you create a curve. You can have both straight and curved sides based on how you use the mouse at each node. The best way to learn to use Bézier curves (again, unless you are Bézier himself) is to experiment with them, and get a feel for how they work. (If you want to convert a straight side to a curve, you can do so, as we describe in Chapter 4.)

✔ **Freehand Picture Box tool:** Produces curved shapes — shapes composed of a series of curves. The box takes shape as you move the mouse, as if your mouse were a pen tracking on paper. To complete the box, you usually bring the mouse back to the origin point and then release the mouse button. (Notice how the pointer changes to a circle from the normal cross.) If you release the mouse button before you return to the origin point, QuarkXPress automatically draws a straight line from where you released the mouse to the origin point.

The Table tool

Longtime QuarkXPress users worldwide breathed a collective sigh of relief when Quark announced it would include a Table tool with QuarkXPress 5. And understandably so. Despite the tons of sophisticated features QuarkXPress has amassed in the last decade and a half, a tool for creating tables quickly and efficiently has been conspicuously absent. Now, however, those same-said users have cause to celebrate, because directly below the Picture Box tool in the Tools palette, they will find the Table tool — the answer to their publishing prayers.

The Table tool lets you organize data into rows and columns — a "table," if you will. Creating a table is very much like creating a text or picture box. You simply choose the Table tool in the Tool palette, place the cursor where you want the table to appear, click and hold the mouse button, and drag it until the table is the approximate size you want. The Table Properties dialog box appears, asking you the number of rows and columns you want to include in your table, and whether you want to fill the individual spaces of the table, called "cells," with text or picture boxes. After you create your table, you can adjust it by choosing Item⇨Modify and selecting options in the Modify dialog box and/or choosing Item⇨Table and selecting options in the Table pop-up menu that appears. We discuss creating and modifying tables in more detail in Chapter 8.

The Line tools

The four Line tools in the Line Tools pop-up palette let you draw — you guessed it — lines. After you draw a line, you can change its thickness (called "weight") and/or style. A line style is, for example, a dotted line — like the ones people sign in movies all the time.

✔ **Orthogonal Line tool:** Produces straight lines that are completely horizontal or vertical.

 ✔ **Diagonal Line tool:** Produces straight lines at any desired angle. If you hold down the Shift key while drawing diagonal line, the line is constrained to be perfectly horizontal, perfectly vertical, or at a perfect 45-degree angle. (Note that the QuarkXPress manual simply calls this the Line tool, but we use the name Diagonal Line tool so that you don't mix it up with the other three Line tools.)

✔ **Bézier Line tool:** Produces both straight and curved lines, much like the edges created with the Bézier Text box and Bézier Picture Box tools. A section of a line will be straight or curved, depending on how you use the mouse at each node.

 ✔ **Freehand Line tool:** Produces curved lines that follow the motion of your mouse — similar to drawing with a pen on paper.

As with the Text Box and Picture Box pop-up palettes, you can change the arrangement of the Tool palette's Line tools to suit your style.

To use any of the Line tools, click the tool to select it and position the cursor at the point where you want the line to begin.

✔ For the Diagonal Line, Orthogonal, and Freehand Line tools, click and hold down the mouse button as you draw the line. When the line is approximately the length you want, release the mouse button.

✔ For the Bézier Line tool, click at each point, as described for the Bézier Picture Box and Text Box tools. If you click and drag for a little bit at each desired node, you see the Bézier control handles appear that let you create a curve. You can have both straight and curved sides based on how you use the mouse at each node — again, it is suggested you play around with this tool to get the hang of it. After you draw a line, use the Measurements palette to select the line weight and line style.

Text Path tools

In QuarkXPress 5.0, you can draw four kinds of text paths — lines that text will follow — to create text that flows in any direction, instead of being confined within a text box. The four Text Path tools work much like the Line tools, and like the line tools, they reside in their own pop-up palette in the Tool palette. They are:

 ✔ **Freehand Text Path tool:** Produces curved text paths that follow the motion of your mouse — similar to drawing with a pen on paper.

 ✔ **Orthogonal Text Path tool:** Produces straight text paths that are completely horizontal or vertical.

 ✔ **Bézier Text Path tool:** Produces both straight and curved text paths, much like the edges created with the Bézier Line tool. A section of a line will be straight or curved, depending on how you use the mouse at each node.

✔ **Line (or Diagonal) Text Path tool:** Produces straight text paths at any desired angle. If you hold down the Shift key while drawing, the paths are constrained to be perfectly horizontal, perfectly vertical, or at a perfect 45-degree angle. (Note that the QuarkXPress manual calls this simply the Text Path tool, but we use the name Line [or Diagonal] Text Path tool so that you don't mix it up with the other three Text Path tools.)

Linking and Unlinking tools

Directly beneath the Tool palette are the Linking tool (above) and the Unlinking tool (below). The Linking tool lets you link text boxes together so that extra text flows from one text box into another. The Unlinking tool lets you break the link between text boxes. Linking is particularly useful when you want to "jump" text — for example, when a story starts on page one and jumps to (continues on) page four. We cover linking and unlinking text boxes in-depth in Chapter 3.

Scissors tool

Introduced in QuarkXPress 4.1, the Scissors tool lets you "cut" lines you have created with the Text Box, Picture Box, or Line tools. For example, you can use the Scissors tool to split a single line into two separate lines, or to remove the corner of a box. This tool also comes in handy when you want to edit a shape you've created with the Freehand Text Box, Freehand Picture Box, or Freehand Line tool. You can cut lines made with the Text Path tools, too, although any text on the text path will remain linked — even if it is split into two entirely separate parts.

The Measurements Palette

The Measurements palette was first developed by Quark and is now widely imitated by other software developers. This palette is one of the most significant innovations to take place in the evolution of desktop publishing, and (honest!) you'll use it all the time. The Measurements palette gives you precise information about the position and attributes of any selected page element, and it lets you enter values to change those specifications. If you want to see the Measurements palette, you need to have a document open as you choose View⇨Show Measurements, or press F9.

The information displayed in the Measurements palette depends on the element currently selected. When you select a text box, the Measurements palette displays the text box position coordinates (X: and Y:), size (W: and H:), amount of rotation, and number of columns (Cols:), as shown in Figure 1-6. By clicking the up and down arrows on the palette, you can modify the leading of the text box (or you can simply type a value in the space next to the arrows); click the right and left arrows to adjust kerning or tracking for selected text. (If you're unfamiliar with these typographic terms, check out Chapter 5.)

Figure 1-6:
The
Measure-
ments
palette
when a text
box is
selected.

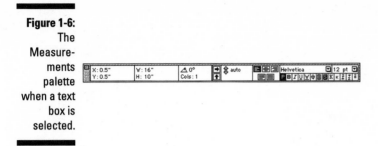

Specify text — left, center, right, or justified — by using the alignment icons. In the type section of the palette, you can control the font, size, and type style of selected text.

For a picture box, the Measurements palette displays different information. In Figure 1-7, the Measurements palette shows the position of the box (X: and Y:), its size (W: and H:), the amount it is rotated, its corner radius, its reduction or enlargement percentage (X%: and Y%:), its repositioning coordinates (X+: and Y+:), the amount of picture rotation within the box, and the amount of slant.

Figure 1-7:
The
Measure-
ments
palette
when a
picture box
is selected.

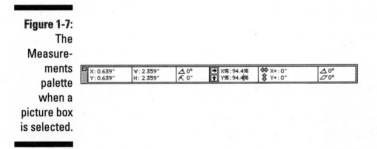

For a line or text path, the Measurements palette (see Figure 1-8) displays the location coordinates (X: and Y:), line width, line style, and endcap (line ending) style. The line style pop-up menu lets you select the style for the line. Note that if you select a freehand or Bézier line, the Endpoints section of the Measurements palette will be replaced with an icon that controls the line's rotation.

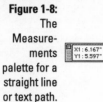

Figure 1-8:
The
Measure-
ments
palette for a
straight line
or text path.

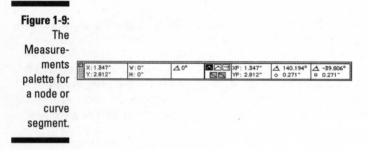

If you select a Bézier or freehand element's node or curve, you get controls for the nodes, as shown in Figure 1-9. Chapter 11 explains what the controls do.

Figure 1-9:
The
Measure-
ments
palette for
a node or
curve
segment.

Chapter 2

Have It Your Way

Do you ever wonder how sitting in front of a computer all those hours is affecting your eyesight? Do you find yourself hunched over, nose to screen, trying to read the really small print? Well, you're not alone. And those nice people who brought you QuarkXPress are doing their part to save your eyes by providing some nifty ways for you to change how documents appear onscreen. For example, you can zoom in to make things larger or create thumbnail pages so you can see how well (or in some case, not so well) your page layouts work together. Another set of time-saving features in the program's interface, *palettes,* lets you perform a wide range of functions without having to access pull-down menus.

This chapter helps you get up close and personal with QuarkXPress. We begin by giving you tips on taking control using the View menu.

Creating Your First Document

To change the way you view a document in QuarkXPress, you must first have a document to view. Follow these steps to create a document:

1. **Choose File➪New.**

   A pop-up menu appears, listing things like Library and XML, for example. Don't panic! We talk about that stuff later.

2. **Select Document from the menu.**

   The New Document dialog box appears (see Figure 2-1), offering you a whole bunch of other options.

3. **Click OK.**

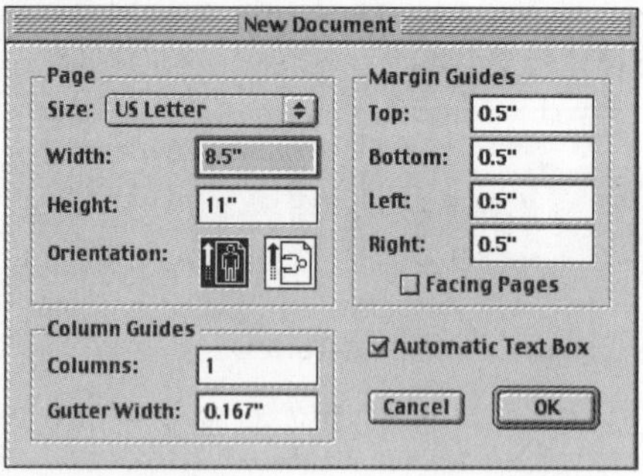

Figure 2-1:
The New
Document
dialog box.

Congratulations! You've just given birth to your first QuarkXPress document.
Here, have a cigar.

The View Menu

After you create a document, the View menu gives you a number of preset
options through which to view it. The View menu (see Figure 2-2) lets you
control the display of items onscreen.

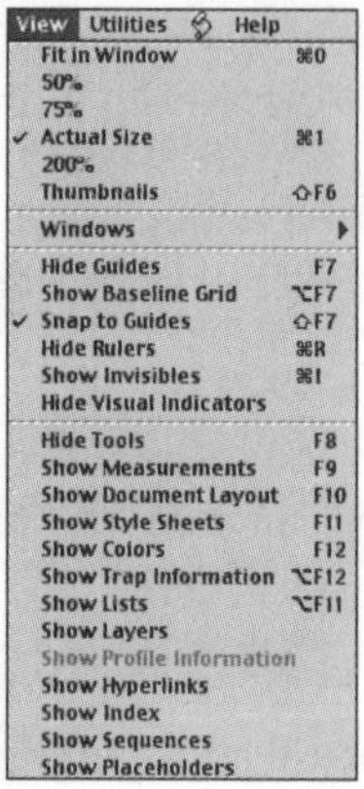

Figure 2-2:
The View
menu.

This menu has four sections:

> ✔ The first section of the View menu contains the view option commands
> (covered later in this section under "Using the preset options").

✔ The second section of the View menu lets you control how multiple documents are displayed. It also lets you switch among several open documents. (This section is actually a whole different menu — the Window menu — in the Windows version of QuarkXPress.)

   • The Tile Documents option is particularly useful if you are lucky enough to have multiple monitors, which give you enough room to see several documents at the same time. (In Windows, you can choose Tile Horizontally or Tile Vertically.)

   • The Stack Documents option simply keeps the windows offset slightly so that all the document names are visible.

   In QuarkXPress for Windows, the tile and stack options are in a separate menu — the Window menu — which also has a handy option that closes all open windows.

✔ The third section of the View menu provides commands that control the display of positioning aids: guides, baseline grid, rulers, and invisibles (tabs, returns, and so on). You can toggle features on and off; if a command is active, a check mark appears next to its name.

✔ The final section of the View menu contains commands that display or hide QuarkXPress palettes. You can toggle features on and off; if a palette is open, its option changes from Show to Hide. We explain palettes in Chapter 1.

Using the preset options

The preset view options in the View menu are menu commands that scale the document view to a set of sizes preset by QuarkXPress. The preset view options in the View menu are:

✔ **Fit in Window (⌘+0 [zero] on the Macintosh, Ctrl+0 [zero] in Windows):** Fits the page into the area of the document window.

✔ **50%:** Displays the document page at half its actual size.

✔ **75%:** Displays the document page at three-fourths of its actual size.

✔ **Actual Size (⌘+1 or Ctrl+1):** Displays the document page at actual size (100%), which may mean that you can see only part of the page on screen.

✔ **200%:** Displays the document page at twice its actual size.

✔ **Thumbnails (Shift+F6):** Displays miniature versions of the document pages. Figure 2-3 shows a thumbnail view.

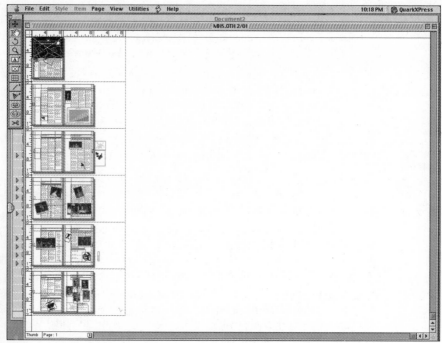

Figure 2-3:
A thumbnail
view of a
document.

View-Changing Tips and Tricks

In addition to the present view commands mentioned in the previous section, QuarkXPress offers some alternative ways of changing views. We find the following methods to be particularly useful:

✔ To increase the page view in 25-percent increments, select the Zoom tool. (It looks like a magnifying glass.) When you place the mouse pointer in the document with the Zoom tool selected, the pointer changes to a magnifying glass. Each time you click the mouse button, the view increases in 25-percent increments, up to a maximum of 800 percent. To decrease the page view in 25-percent increments, hold down the Option or Alt key as you click the mouse button.

✔ To increase the view by 25 percent, an even easier method is to hold down the Control key and click the mouse. This works only on the Mac.

✔ To zoom in on a specific area, click the Zoom tool, select a corner of the area you want to zoom in on, hold down the mouse button, drag to the opposite corner of the specified area, and release the mouse button.

✔ Another easy way to change your view is to use the keyboard shortcut (Control+V or Ctrl+Alt+V). This highlights the view percentage in the bottom-left corner of your QuarkXPress window. Just enter the new percentage (you don't need to enter the % symbol) and then press Enter or Return. If you want to go to the thumbnail view, enter **T** instead of a percentage.

You can change the increment for all these Zoom-tool options from its default of 25 percent to any other amount by making changes in the Tool pane of the Document Preferences dialog box. Access the dialog box by choosing Edit➪ Preferences➪Document, or by pressing ⌘+Y or Ctrl+Y.

See Chapter 21 for information about changing default document and application preferences to gain still more control over the way QuarkXPress handles your documents.

Palettes: Here, There, Everywhere!

In Chapter 1, we introduce you to the Tools palette and the Measurements palette — the palettes you use most often in QuarkXPress. But the program comes with a slew of other palettes, including palettes for color management, page layout, style sheets and, with the introduction of Web pages in QuarkXPress 5, a palette for creating hyperlinks. The following sections give you the lowdown on all these palettes and how they can help you with page layouts as you become more adept with the program.

The Document Layout palette

In the Document Layout palette, shown in Figure 2-4, you can create, name, delete, move, and apply master pages. Master pages are important because they hold page elements such as graphics and margins that QuarkXPress can apply automatically to new pages, much as a style sheet works to apply standardized formatting to text. You also can add, delete and move document pages. To display the Document Layout palette, choose Show Document Layout from the View menu, or press F10.

The Style Sheets palette

The Style Sheets palette, shown in Figure 2-5, lists the names of the style tags attached to selected paragraphs and also lets you apply style sheets to paragraphs. To display the Style Sheets palette, choose View➪Show Style Sheets or press F11. We cover Style sheets in depth in Chapter 6.

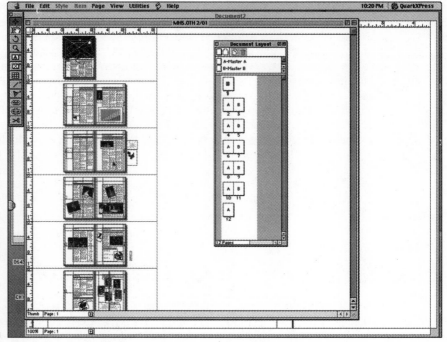

Figure 2-4:
The
Document
Layout
palette
shows a
thumbnail
view of the
document's
master
pages.

Figure 2-5:
The Style
Sheets
palette
displays the
names of
style tags
attached to
paragraphs.

The Colors palette

The Colors palette lets you designate the color and shade (percentage of color) you want to apply to text, pictures, and backgrounds of text and picture boxes. You also can produce color blends, using one or two colors, to apply to box backgrounds. To display the Colors palette, shown in Figure 2-6, choose Show Colors from the View menu, or press F12.

In QuarkXPress, you can create both process and spot colors effortlessly — and both display in your Colors palette just fine. Previously, after they were displayed in your palette, there was no way of knowing which colors were the spot colors and which were the process; if you wanted to find out, you had to return to the Edit Colors dialog box by choosing Edit⇨Colors. Frankly, it was kind of a hassle. That's not the case anymore, however. In QuarkXPress 5, spot and process colors are distinguished by the Spot Color and Process Color buttons. This new feature makes it easier to keep your document's color palette organized.

Figure 2-6:
The Colors
palette.

The Trap Information palette

One of the features that has made QuarkXPress the program of choice among professional publishers is one that you never have to worry about: trapping. *Trapping* refers to the technique of extending one color so that it slightly overlaps an adjoining color, preventing the gaps between two abutting colors that sometime result from misalignment of plates on a printing press. In the Trap Information palette, you can set or change trapping specifications for selected items. To display the palette, choose View⇨Show Trap Information or press Option+F12 or Alt+F12.

Don't use the Trap Information palette unless you know what you're doing. This palette is considered an expert feature, and using it inexpertly can produce uneven results when you print your document.

The Lists palette

QuarkXPress lets you create lists based on paragraph styles that you can use to build tables of contents, tables of figures, and so on. In the Lists palette, you can set or change list settings. To display the palette, use Show Lists from the View menu or press Option+F11 or Alt+F11. Chapter 17 covers list creation in detail.

The Layers palette

The Layers palette is new to QuarkXPress 5. This palette, shown in Figure 2-7, lets you create layers, or "tiers" of QuarkXPress documents, thus enabling you to isolate certain items in a document that otherwise might cause unnecessary clutter. If, for example, you have items that need to be in a document, but that should not print, such as crop marks or output instructions, you can place them on a "hidden" layer — completely separate from the document to be printed. To display the palette, choose View⇨Show Layers.

Figure 2-7:
The Layers palette is a new addition to Quark-XPress 5.

The Profile Information palette

Another expert feature is the Profile Information palette, used to set or change color profiles for selected items. Color profiles make slight adjustments to an object's colors to compensate for differences among color input and output devices. Most users don't have to worry about this feature, and if they do, their service bureau will let them know when to worry about it. To display this palette, choose View⇨Show Profile Information.

Don't use the Profile Information palette unless you know what you're doing. The Profile Information palette is another expert feature of QuarkXPress, and using it without knowing precisely what you need to use it for can produce uneven results when you print your document.

The Hyperlinks palette

Hyperlinks are at the core of Web documents. That being the case, it only makes sense that the new, Web-friendly QuarkXPress 5 would sport a Hyperlinks palette (see Figure 2-8). For those of you unfamiliar with Webspeak, a "hyperlink," is an item in a Web page (or PDF file) that you can click to perform a specific action — like jumping to another page for example.

This item can be a word or phrase, a picture, or even a portion of a page or picture. You can think of them as "the things people click on." In QuarkXPress, you can create, update, and maintain hyperlinks at will. To display this palette, choose View➪Show Hyperlinks. Find out more about hyperlinks in Chapter 18.

Figure 2-8:
The
Hyperlinks
palette.

The Index palette

QuarkXPress now lets you create indexes based on words that you specify in this palette, described in more depth in Chapter 17. To display the palette, choose View➪Show Index.

The Web Tools palette

The Web Tools palette, shown in Figure 2-9, contains tools for creating and editing Web documents, including form control and image map tools. You can open the Web Tools palette using Show Web Tools in the Tools pop-up menu (View➪Tools➪Show Web Tools). Note that this pop-up menu isn't available when you are working with a print document — you can access it only when a Web document is displayed, or when no document is displayed. We cover the Web Tools palette in Chapter 19.

Figure 2-9:
The Web
Tools
palette.

Library palette

QuarkXPress lets you store layout elements (text or picture boxes, lines, or groups) in one or more library palettes. To use this feature, select the element that you want to store from the document or the pasteboard, and drag it into an open library palette. Because you can have several library palettes, you can group items into specific libraries, such as one for each project or, for example, one for logos and one for employee photos. You then can use items stored in the library in other documents. To create a library palette, choose File⇨New⇨Library.

A Myriad of Mouse Pointers

Just as many palettes exist in QuarkXPress, you'll find a bunch of mouse pointer icons as you begin working with the program's features. Basically, these pointers are visual hints about what tool you're using. For example, when you choose the rotation tool, you find that the pointer, or "cursor," becomes the "oration pointer." Here are the various mouse pointers you can expect to see in QuarkXPress:

 ✔ **Standard pointer:** Appears as you move through dialog boxes, menus, and windows, and as you move over non-selected elements. The standard pointer is the most common pointer.

 ✔ **Creation pointer:** Appears if you have selected a box or line tool. Use this pointer to draw boxes and lines.

 ✔ **Sizing pointer:** Appears if you select one of the handles on a text or picture box (with either the Item or Content tool selected) or on a line. You can resize the item by holding down the mouse button and dragging the handle.

 ✔ **Item pointer:** Appears if the Item tool is selected and you have selected a box or line. You can move the selected item by holding down the mouse button and dragging the item.

 ✔ **Lock pointer:** Appears if the Item tool is selected and you have selected a locked text box, picture box, or line. The lock pointer indicates that the box will not move if you try to drag it (you can move it, however, by changing the coordinates in the Measurements palette or by choosing Item⇨Modify).

 ✔ **I-beam (text) pointer:** Appears if the Content tool is selected and you select a text box. If the cursor is blinking, any text you type inserts where the cursor appears. If the cursor is not blinking, you must click at the location in the text box where you want to edit text.

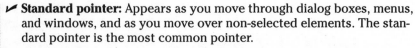

✔ **Grabber pointer (also known as the page-grabber hand):** Appears if the Content tool is selected and you have selected a picture box containing a graphic. You can move the graphic within the box by holding down the mouse button and dragging the item.

 ✔ **Rotation pointer:** Appears if you select the Rotation tool in the Tools palette. After you select the tool, hold down the mouse button and drag the pointer until the object is rotated to the angle you want. You can actually see the object rotating as you drag the pointer across the page.

 ✔ **Zoom-in pointer:** Appears if you select the Zoom tool and click the mouse button (clicking the mouse button zooms in on the image by the predefined amount, which by default is 25 percent). You can also select an area to zoom into by clicking one corner of the area of interest, holding down the mouse button, dragging the mouse to the opposite corner, and then releasing the button.

 ✔ **Zoom-out pointer:** Appears if you select the Zoom tool and hold down the Option or Alt key while clicking the mouse button (clicking the mouse button zooms out by a predefined amount, which by default is 25 percent).

 ✔ **Link pointer:** Appears if you select the Link tool. Click the pointer on the first text box and then on the second text box in the chain of boxes through which you want text to flow. If there are more boxes, repeat the process (for example, link box two to box three, then box three to box four, and so on). You can switch pages while this tool is active to flow text from one box to another across pages.

 ✔ **Unlink pointer:** Appears if you select the Unlink tool. Click the pointer on the first text box, then on the second text box in the chain of boxes that have the link that you want to break. If there are more boxes to unlink, repeat this process for each pair of boxes to be unlinked. You can switch pages while this tool is active to unlink text flow across pages.

Chapter 3

Boxes and Text Unite!

In This Chapter

▶ Creating text boxes

▶ Getting text into text boxes

▶ Importing text from your word-processing application

*L*et's face it — when you think of a flat piece of paper or a Web page with words and pictures on it, you don't intuitively know that those words and pictures are held in boxes, right? Not if you're like most people we know. And the boxes that we're talking about now are not your typical supermarket boxes. In fact, they are unlike any three-dimensional boxes that you may be familiar with. About the only way in which QuarkXPress boxes are similar to those you're familiar with is that they also hold stuff — but the stuff in QuarkXPress boxes is two-dimensional text and pictures.

Surprised? You're not alone. It never fails to amaze brand-new QuarkXPress users that just about everything on a page produced in this program must be placed into a box. QuarkXPress boxes may not be able to hold a great deal of memorabilia, but they are pretty powerful just the same; they serve as the placeholders for the text and pictures that you use to build a page. These boxes not only define the layout of a page by controlling the size and placement of pictures; they also delineate the white space between an illustration and its caption, and they identify the portion of a page's real estate that is covered with words.

Yes, these boxes do a lot. And if you spend any time at all working with QuarkXPress, you'll get comfortable with its text boxes and picture boxes in no time flat. This chapter focuses on creating text boxes. In Chapter 4, we concentrate on building and modifying picture boxes.

Revisiting Text Box Tools

Composing a page in QuarkXPress involves arranging and rearranging the program's basic building blocks, among them *text boxes*. In Chapter 1, we show you the QuarkXPress Tool palette. The fact that the Tool palette contains seven box-related tools (the Rectangle Text Box tool, the Rounded-Corner Text Box tool, the Oval Text Box tool, the Concave-Corner Text Box tool, the Beveled-Corner Text Box Tool, the Bézier Text Box tool and the Freehand Text box tool) reflects how important they are to page design in QuarkXPress.

As you probably guessed by now, you use these seven tools to make text boxes (see Figure 3-1). (You also can tell QuarkXPress to create a single text box on each page automatically, which we describe in the section, "Making a box automatically," later in this chapter.) After you create a text box, you can enter text directly into it by typing on your computer's keyboard, or you can import text from a word processor file.

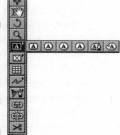

Figure 3-1:
QuarkXPress
offers seven
tools for
creating text
boxes.

Building Text Boxes

To create a text box, you just choose one of the tools in the Text Box Tools palette and use the mouse to draw the box. Later, you can change things about the box, such as its size, its placement on the page, and the width of its margins.

Creating a text box is easy. Just follow these steps:

1. **Select the Rectangle Text Box tool from the Tools palette.**

   (In case you forgot, the Rectangle Text Box tool looks like a little rectangle with a capital A in its center.)

   Notice that when you move the mouse pointer into the document page, the mouse pointer changes to look like a crosshair.

2. **Hold down the mouse button and drag the mouse across your document until you've drawn a text box the size you want.**

3. **Release the mouse button.**

Now step back and admire your work. It doesn't get any easier than that.

Active and inactive boxes

If you draw a text box and decide that it's too small and too high on the page, what can you do? Do you scrap the box and start over, hoping for better luck the next time you create it?

No, you know that deleting the box and drawing it again takes too long, plus (to be honest about it) it would mean that you're chickening out. Be brave! You can fix that box, and we show you how in the section, "Taming the wild text box," later in this chapter. But before you can do anything to the box, you have to *activate* it.

As we tell you in Chapter 1, *selecting* an item using the Content tool or the Item tool is the same as activating it. Before you can make changes in a text box — or any item, for that matter — you must select it, or activate it, so that QuarkXPress knows what part of your document to work on next.

Figure 3-2 shows two boxes. The box on the left is inactive, or unselected. The box on the right is active, or selected. Activating the box enables you to modify it in many ways. As you can see, determining that a box is active is easy because little black boxes, called *sizing handles,* appear on its sides and corners.

Taming the wild text box

You probably know at least one person who can be called a control freak. You know — the friend who goes berserk when he finds that a piece of paper on his desk is rotated at an angle, instead of being perfectly aligned with the pencil box; the hostess who follows you around her house, carrying a towel to wipe everything you've touched; or the boss who insists on reading every word you write and knowing where you are each minute of the day (they like to call it micromanaging).

Generally, being a control freak isn't something to be proud of. You won't find it on many résumés (although you may run across "micromanager" from time to time). However, when you get into desktop publishing, taking control is a necessary and highly-valued trait. Striving to make things perfect takes over even if you aren't a control freak, and soon you find yourself spending hours tweaking each little element on a document.

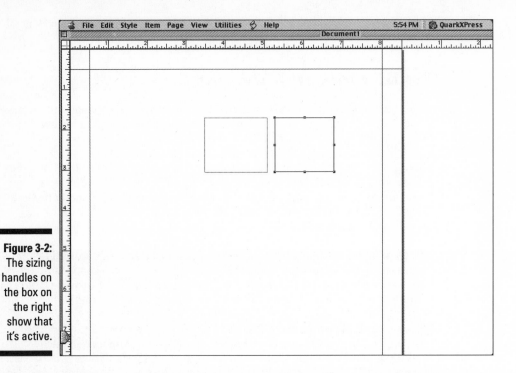

Figure 3-2:
The sizing
handles on
the box on
the right
show that
it's active.

So relax. When you're building a page, being a control freak is perfectly okay. Honestly, half the fun of using QuarkXPress is the unbelievable amount of control it gives you over everything in a page layout.

Text boxes are one of the things you have complete control over when you use QuarkXPress. After you create a text box, you can exercise that control by using the Modify dialog box.

Here's how you make the Modify dialog box appear:

1. **Make sure that the text box is active. (Look for the sizing handles around it.)**

   You can activate it by using either the Content tool or the Item tool.

2. **Choose Item⇨Modify to display the Modify dialog box for text boxes, as shown in Figure 3-3, or press ⌘+M (for Macintosh) or Ctrl+M (for Windows) as a shortcut.**

The four panes of the Modify dialog box enable you to tweak a text box to your heart's content. By entering values, choosing items from pop-up menus, checking or unchecking boxes, and so on, you can modify the appearance of the box and set other box properties.

The Box pane lets you adjust the position and appearance of a text box, including the following:

✔ The box's size and position on the page

✔ The angle of the box's rotation

✔ The *skew angle* (or slant) of the box and the text within

✔ The amount of roundness applied to the box's corners

✔ The color — or colors, in the case of a two-color blend — and shade applied to the box's background

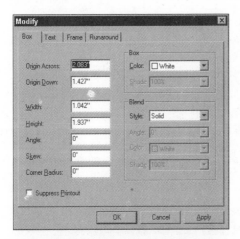
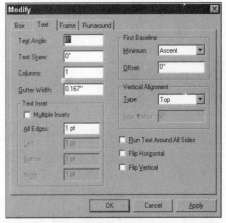
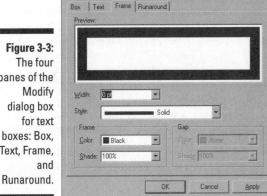
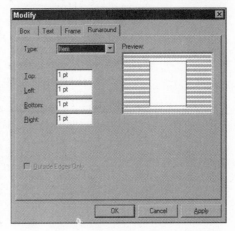

Figure 3-3:
The four panes of the Modify dialog box for text boxes: Box, Text, Frame, and Runaround.

The Text pane lets you adjust the placement and appearance of the text in the box, including the following:

- The number of columns and the space between columns
- The distance between the edge of the box and the text within
- The angle of the lines of text within the box
- The skew angle of the text
- The placement of the first line of text relative to the top of the box
- The vertical alignment of the text
- How text flows within the box when an item is placed in front of the box
- The option to flip the text within a box along a vertical and/or horizontal axis

The Frame pane (explained in detail in Chapter 13) lets you apply a frame around a text box and to specify the style, width, color, and shade of the frame, as well as the color and shade applied to the gap between dotted, dashed, and multiple-line frames.

The Runaround pane (we cover this in Chapter 5) lets you control the flow of text in a box in relation to another box. If you want text in a text box to flow around the edge of a picture, for example, you go to the Runaround pane to do it. We explain how to work with many of these modifications in Chapter 5. For now, just be aware that they exist.

Creating irregular text boxes

In addition to the four Text Box tools that allow you to create text boxes based on rectangles, QuarkXPress offers two tools — the Bézier Text Box tool and the Freehand Text Box tool — for creating irregular boxes that have straight or curved edges. You also have the option to convert any box shape into any other shape (we explain this in Chapter12). Be careful, though. If you create a document full of irregularly shaped text boxes, the visual effect can at best be described as hodgepodge. In other words, don't make your document ugly just because you can, okay?

Figure 3-4 shows two text boxes created with the Bézier Text Box tool: A straight-edged box and a curved-edge box.

Figure 3-4:
A straight-
edged box
and a
curved-
edge box
created with
the Bézier
Text Box
tool.

Follow these steps to create a straight-edged (polygon) Bézier text box by using the Bézier Text Box tool:

1. **Select the Bézier Text Box tool.**

2. **Click and release the mouse button to establish the first point of your box.**

3. **Move the mouse to where you want to establish the next point; then click and release the mouse button.**

4. **Continue to establish the points of your box by moving the mouse and then clicking and releasing the mouse button.**

5. **Close the box by clicking on the first point that you created. You can also close a box by double-clicking anywhere to create a final point.**

    When you double-click, a final point is created, and a final segment is automatically drawn back to the first point.

To create a curved-edged Bézier text box by using the Bézier Text Box tool, follow these steps:

1. **Select the Bézier Text Box tool.**

2. **Hold down the mouse button as you drag the mouse in the direction of the next point; then release the mouse button.**

You don't have to drag the mouse all the way to the next point; you can release the mouse button after you drag the mouse a short distance in the general direction. The first point, along with two control handles that indicate the curve slope, is established.

3. **Move the mouse to where you want to establish the next point, drag a short distance in the direction of the following point, and then release the mouse button.**

4. **Continue to establish the points of your box by moving the mouse and then clicking, dragging, and releasing the mouse button.**

5. **Close the box by clicking the first point that you created or double-clicking anywhere.**

   If you double-click, a final point is created, and a final segment is automatically drawn back to the first point.

Here's how to create a curved-edged Bézier text box with the Freehand Text Box tool:

1. **Select the Freehand Text Box tool.**

2. **Hold down the mouse button and then drag the mouse, using it like a pencil to create any shape you want.**

3. **Close the box by dragging the crosshair mouse pointer back to the first point and releasing the mouse button.**

   You can also release the mouse button at any time to have QuarkXPress create the final segment by drawing a line from the current position of the crosshair mouse pointer to the point of origin.

Keep in mind that you can create shapes that contain straight edges and curved edges by combining the techniques for creating straight-edged and curved Bézier boxes. After you create a Bézier box, you can adjust it by clicking and dragging points and edges. Before you try to adjust a Bézier box, make sure that a check mark appears before the Shape command in the Item⇨Edit submenu. If Shape is not checked, you can adjust the height and width of a Bézier box, but you can't move its points or edges. (An easier shortcut is to press Shift+F4 on the Mac or F10 in Windows to switch between editing the box's shape and changing its dimensions or position.) Here are a few things to keep in mind when you change the shape of a Bézier box:

✔ If Shape is checked when you click anywhere on or within a Bézier box, the entire box becomes active, and all points are displayed. You can then drag the point or segment that you want to move.

✔ To move multiple points at the same time, hold down the Shift key and click the points; then drag any of the selected points.

✔ If you want drag the points in a straight, perfectly even line — in other words, if you want to "constrain" the direction you are dragging the points — continue to hold down the Shift key as you drag them.

✔ If you pause a moment before dragging a point or segment, QuarkXPress redraws the contents of the box as you drag.

✔ To add new points, hold down the Option or Alt key and click a segment at the place where you want the point to appear.

✔ To delete a point, hold down the Option or Alt key and click on the point.

Bézier boxes can contain three kinds of points (corner points, smooth points, and symmetrical points) and two kinds of segments (curved and straight). You can change any kind of point or segment into any other kind. In addition, you can split a segment into one or more segments by using the Scissors tool. Chapter 11 explains how to change the shape of Bézier boxes by cutting and changing points and segments.

Making a box automatically

Howie is a desktop publisher. He likes to tinker with page layout to see exactly how everything works. He has no problem spending hours in front of the computer, getting all his layout ducks in a row, luxuriating in the depth and breadth of controls offered by QuarkXPress.

Pamela, on the other hand, is always rushed. In her job, she's responsible for producing two newsletters every week. She works at top speed, collecting QuarkXPress shortcuts the way that some kids collect baseball cards.

Howie is perfectly comfortable with manually creating every text box that appears in his document. Pamela, who would go crazy at the very thought of such a time-consuming approach, has found a way to make QuarkXPress automatically and precisely create a text box for her on every page. She uses the program's Automatic Text Box feature each time she creates a new document.

Suppose that Pamela is going to create a two-page flyer, and she wants the text to appear on each page in two columns. She starts a new document (by choosing File⇨New⇨Document, or by pressing ⌘+N or Ctrl+N), which causes the New Document dialog box to appear (see Figure 3-5). In the Column Guides area, she specifies two columns. She also makes sure that the Automatic Text Box check box is checked.

That's all Pamela has to do. QuarkXPress takes care of the rest, automatically creating a two-column text box on each page of the document.

What's more, when Automatic Text Box is checked, QuarkXPress can automatically insert new pages when text overflows in an automatic text box. Each of these new pages will, in turn, have their own automatic text box.

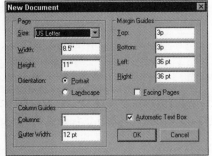

Figure 3-5:
You create
automatic
text boxes in
the New
Document
dialog box.

It's important to remember, though, that if you want QuarkXPress to insert new pages automatically, you must first go to the Auto Page Insertion option in the General section of the Preferences dialog box and make sure it's set to End of Story. To display this dialog box, choose Edit⇨Preferences⇨ Preferences (or press Option+Shift+⌘+Y or Ctrl+Alt+Shift+Y), and choose General in the scroll list to the left. If you don't check Automatic Text Box, you have to draw all the Text boxes manually and link them before you can bring text into them.

This, of course, leads to the obvious question: "What the #%@# is linking?" Hold your horses. We cover that next.

Linking and unlinking text boxes

Automatic text boxes are great for creating multipage documents in which text automatically flows from page to page. In other situations, however, text must flow not from one page to the next page, but from one page to a different, nonconsecutive page or from one box to another within a single page. A newsletter layout, for example, may require a story that begins on page 1 to finish on page 4. How do you make this *jump* (or "continued on" instance) happen? You link the two boxes.

An easy way to remember linking in QuarkXPress is to think of text boxes as being links in a chain, just like a metal chain that has links connected to other links. The only difference is that in QuarkXPress, you're linking boxes that hold text. Because you can't link a text box to another box that already contains text, however, you need to do your linking before you fill the boxes with text. Here's how you link empty text boxes:

1. **Open the document to the page that contains the first text box that you want to use in the linked chain of text boxes.**

2. **Click the Linking tool (the third tool from the bottom of the Tool palette; it looks like a piece of chain) to select it.**

3. **Position the mouse pointer anywhere inside the text box that will be the first box in the chain.**

   Notice that the mouse pointer changes to look like a chain link.

4. **Click the mouse button.**

   Notice that the text box has a moving dashed line around it, a *marquee* to be exact, which tells you that this box is the start of the link.

5. **Go to the page that contains the text box that will be the next box in the chain.**

   To get to that page, choose Page⇨Go to (or press ⌘+J or Ctrl+J).

6. **Position the mouse pointer in the next text box that you want to use in the chain; then click the mouse button.**

   The second text box is now linked to the first. If you enter or import more text into the first box than it can hold, the overflow text continues in the second box, even if the two text boxes are separated by several pages. As text is entered or imported, it flows to the next box in the text chain until there is no text left over.

7. **Repeat Steps 2 through 6 until all the text boxes that you want to use in the chain are linked.**

How do you know whether two text boxes are linked? Simply activate either of the boxes; then select the Linking tool and look for the large gray arrow pointing to or from the next box in the chain. Figure 3-6 shows you what this linking arrow looks like.

As nice as it is to link text boxes, being able to change your mind about how the text flows or doesn't flow is also nice — meaning that you want to be able to unlink two or more linked text boxes, too. Here's how:

1. **Open the document to the page that contains the text box that you want to unlink from a chain.**

2. **Click the Unlinking tool (the tool that is second from the bottom in the Tool palette) to select it.**

3. **Position the mouse pointer in the text box, hold down the Shift key, and then click the mouse button.**

   This step unlinks the selected text box from the chain while retaining links between the preceding box in the chain and the following box in the chain. If you want to break the chain entirely, click the arrowhead on the top-left side of the box. If you want to take it one step further, click the arrow's tail feathers on the bottom-right corner of the first box; this breaks the link to the following box as well. (In this instance, holding down the Shift key isn't necessary.)

4. **To unlink additional text boxes, repeat Steps 2 and 3.**

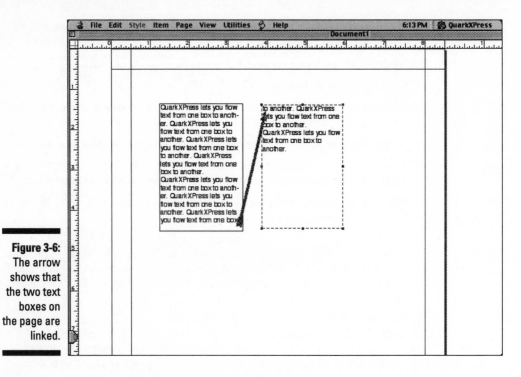

Figure 3-6:
The arrow
shows that
the two text
boxes on
the page are
linked.

As you spend more time using QuarkXPress, you find that being able to link and unlink boxes is very useful.

Filling the Text Box with Text

Okay, here comes the part that you've been waiting for. After you create a QuarkXPress document, add text boxes, and link the text boxes the way you want them, you're ready to fill those boxes with some text!

As we mention earlier, you can fill text boxes in one of two ways: You can use the built-in QuarkXPress word processor to type text (you simply activate a text box; select the Content tool; click inside the activated box; and start typing). Or, you can import text from a word processor into the text box. Follow these steps to import the text:

1. **With the QuarkXPress document open, select the Content tool.**

2. **Click (or activate) the text box into which you want to import the text.**

   If the text box is empty, the flashing I-beam pointer appears in the top-left corner.

If the text box already contains text, simply click where you want the imported text to begin; text is always imported wherever the I-beam pointer is flashing. Importing text does not remove the text already in the text box; it simply bumps the text that follows the I-beam pointer to the end.

3. **Choose File⇨Get Text (or press ⌘+E or Ctrl+E) to display the Get Text dialog box.**

4. **Select the text file that you want to place in the text box.**

5. **Check the Convert Quotes check box if you want QuarkXPress to automatically change typewriter-type double dashes, straight quotation marks, and apostrophes to their more sophisticated typographic equivalents.**

If you want to include the style sheets used in the word processor, check the Include Style Sheets box. We talk much more about style sheets in Chapter 6.

6. **Click OK.**

The text flows into the text box or the linked chain of text boxes.

It doesn't get any easier than that. Unfortunately, as is the case with most things in life, importing text files into QuarkXPress isn't always as cut and dried as the preceding steps may suggest. There can be snags. The good news is, if you make a few adjustments to your text files before you import them, you should be able to import text with minimum brain damage.

More about Word-Processor Files

You can import a whole bunch of different kinds of word-processor files into QuarkXPress. However, QuarkXPress 5 doesn't necessarily read the latest versions of Word or WordPerfect. The latest versions supported are Word 97/2000 (Windows) or 98/2001 (Mac) and WordPerfect 6 (Windows) or 3.5 (Mac). If you have a later version of Word or WordPerfect, either save your files in a supported version or see whether Quark has an updated import filter on its Web site (www.quark.com). If you use those newer programs, you need to save your files in a previous format supported by QuarkXPress: Windows Word 97/2000 (8.0), 95 (7.0), or 6.0; Mac Word 98/2001, 6.0, 5.*x*, 4.0, or 3.0; Windows WordPerfect 6.*x* and 5.*x*; and Mac WordPerfect 3.*x*. QuarkXPress 5 can also import Rich Text Format (RTF), Hypertext Markup Language (HTML), and text-only (ASCII) files.

The Macintosh version of QuarkXPress no longer imports files created in WriteNow 3.0 and higher, Microsoft Works 1.1 and higher, or any version of Claris MacWrite Pro and MacWrite II. But it now imports RTF files.

Because word processors are updated according to their manufacturers' schedules — which don't necessarily coincide with Quark's — there is no guarantee that QuarkXPress will import files easily from a particular updated version of one of these packages. If your word processor is not in the preceding list, it's a good idea to test the "importability" of your text to see how everything works before you get into a production or deadline situation. If you run into problems, try saving the word-processor file as one of the text file formats that QuarkXPress supports. Most word processors allow you to do this.

If a test shows you're stuck, don't despair. Some manufacturers of word processors offer import/export filters for QuarkXPress. We suggest that you check Quark's Web site at www.quarkxpress.com for new and updated filters.

Getting text ready to import

Suppose that you're already familiar with how to format text within the word processing program that you have on your computer. That is, you know how to create text, flow it into two columns, add a header and footer, and italicize and bold selected sections of text. Doing as much as possible within the word processing file and then importing the text into QuarkXPress may seem to be a good thing to do.

But is this a good thing to do? No way. The fact is that, unless you plan ahead, you risk losing some of the work that you did in the word processor after you import the text into QuarkXPress. Now why would you want to waste your valuable time?

Keeping it simple: All you need is text

Here's a good guideline: When using a word processor to create a file that you intend to import into QuarkXPress, remember that you'll be importing only *text,* not a polished document. If you keep that thought in mind, you'll resist the temptation to do more formatting than necessary in the word processor. To make the most of your investment, use the power of QuarkXPress for your *document* formatting. With that said, what word-processing features should you go ahead and use?

If you tell QuarkXPress to keep style sheets from Microsoft Word and WordPerfect when you import text into a text box, they'll come across, along with their associated text. Figure 3-7 shows the Get Text dialog box that appears when you import text from a word processor. Be sure to check Include Style Sheets when you import your text; otherwise your style sheets won't import along with the text. We explain more about style sheets in Chapter 6.

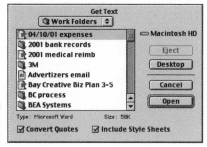

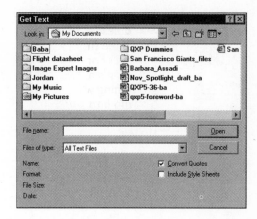

Figure 3-7:
The Get Text
dialog box
for Mac and
Windows.

One key to successfully importing text into QuarkXPress is to avoid using the graphics and layout features of the word processor. Limit your word-processor text formatting to the kind that enhances the reader's understanding or that places emphasis, such as boldfacing, italicizing, and varying type styles.

If you use Microsoft Word and Corel WordPerfect, by far the most popular word processors in use today, rest assured that these formats import into QuarkXPress:

✔ Boldfaced, outlined, italicized, and shadow characters

✔ Underlining (in Word, all underlining changes to a single underline)

✔ Color

✔ Font changes

✔ Varied point sizes

✔ Small caps

✔ Strikethrough characters

✔ Subscript

✔ Superscript

✔ Special characters

If you use a different word processor supported by QuarkXPress, these same features should import, but there's no guarantee — so do a test before using a format other than Word or WordPerfect. After QuarkXPress takes care of the characters in your text, you can deal with issues on a bigger scale — tables, headers and footers, and more that you may have included in your word-processor files. Can any of them be saved? The sections that follow let you know what to expect.

Tables: Don't bother

If you decide to create a table in a word-processor file and then import the file into QuarkXPress, be forewarned that the table will disappear. Ergo, take heed: If you like tables in your documents, wait until you're using QuarkXPress to format them — especially now that QuarkXPress 5 has its own table-making tool, a feature we discuss in Chapter 8.

On the other hand, if you format a table with tabs (whether or not you make the tabs line up properly using style sheets), you can import the table into QuarkXPress along with the rest of the text in the file and can then modify the styles in QuarkXPress as needed. Just be sure to check the Include Style Sheets check box in the Get Text dialog box. Basically, to create a table that can imported by QuarkXPress, you need to separate each column with a tab and each row with a paragraph return. If your word processor uses style sheets, make sure the table text uses a unique style so you can set up the tabs in QuarkXPress just once (in that table text's style) and have all the table text use those tabs automatically. (Chapter 6 covers style sheets in depth.)

If you create a table in a spreadsheet or database program (such as Lotus 1-2-3, Microsoft Excel, or FileMaker Pro), you can import the table into QuarkXPress, but not smoothly. You need to choose between saving the files as tab-delimited ASCII text or as graphics. If you save the files as tab-delimited ASCII text, you need to do some work inside the QuarkXPress document, setting tab stops to line up everything (just as you would with tabbed text imported from a word processor). If you save the files as graphics, you won't be able to change any of the data in QuarkXPress.

Headers and footers: Forget it

In case you don't know, *headers* are pieces of information, such as the name of the current chapter, that appear at the tops of pages in a document. *Footers* appear at the bottoms of pages and usually include information such as the current page number and the name of the document.

As a QuarkXPress user, you need to get into the habit of thinking about headers and footers as layout issues rather than text issues. Because these elements are layout issues, you should wait until you're working on your document in QuarkXPress before you worry about them. For one thing, your document will invariably paginate differently in QuarkXPress; if it does, the page elements in your headers and/or footers will be useless, even if they did import into QuarkXPress (which they don't).

Footnotes: Nope!

Several word processors include a footnoting feature that lets you do two things: (1) mark certain spots in text with a number and (2) have the number and some corresponding text appear at the bottom of the page containing the footnote.

Word-processing mistakes to avoid

After you figure out that QuarkXPress does a good job of importing text from your word processor, be careful not to fall victim to the temptation of using all the features of the word processor simply because they exist. Here are some pointers to keep in mind:

✔ **Don't spend too much time doing extensive formatting in your word processor.** A word processor's style sheets are always much less sophisticated, with fewer options than the effects you can achieve in QuarkXPress. Avoid using any layout-related features in the word processor, such as page numbers, headers and footers, and multiple columns — QuarkXPress simply ignores them.

✔ **Don't use the word processor as though it were a manual typewriter.** In other words, don't press the Return or Enter key at the end of each line of text — only at the end of a paragraph. If you forget to skip this old-standby task, you'll spend considerable time in QuarkXPress removing all the unnecessary returns, which can clutter an otherwise tidy document. Also, don't use two spaces between sentences; professional typesetters never do this. Of course, you can fix many of these sorts of mistakes within QuarkXPress by using the find-and-replace feature, but it's better not to make the mistake in the first place.

✔ **Don't try to use multiple word spaces or multiple paragraph returns to align words or lines of text on-screen.** Use QuarkXPress to tweak the spacing of words and characters; it's easier and much more precise.

✔ **Notice the version number of your word processor.** If your word-processing program is a couple of versions older or newer than those QuarkXPress supports, you may have trouble when you import your text file. If in doubt, create a test text file using all the features that you're likely to use and import it into a text box in a test QuarkXPress document. You may find that you need to make adjustments to the list of word processing features that you can use with QuarkXPress.

✔ **Don't use the fast-save option on files that you plan to import into QuarkXPress.** This note of caution applies if your word processor has a fast-save option (an option that writes information about what's been changed in a text file at the end of the file, instead of rewriting the entire file each time you do a save). Microsoft Word has this feature, and it's active by default. The fast-save option can cause problems with the text file when you import it. We suggest that you turn off the fast-save feature for files that you plan to import into QuarkXPress. With today's super-speedy hard drives, the time that you gain by using fast-save is barely noticeable anyway.

The point of all these points is this: If you want to use a separate word processor, use it. But you should limit what you do in that program to plain old text entry, saving the fancy stuff for when you import the text into QuarkXPress.

If you import a word-processor file that contains footnotes into QuarkXPress, the footnotes no longer appear on the same page as the text that they reference. Instead, all the footnotes for the document appear at the end of the imported text. Also, the superscript or subscript footnote indicators in the body of the document may not import correctly.

In-line graphics: Difficult but not impossible

Most Macintosh and Windows word processors support *in-line graphics* — pictures that you import into your word processor and associate with certain sections of text. In most cases, QuarkXPress can import the in-line graphics with your text, particularly if they were formatted in Microsoft Word or WordPerfect. You may need to experiment a bit if you use another word processor that allows in-line graphics.

The embedded graphics in your word-processor document that use the Mac's Publish and Subscribe feature or OLE (a Mac and Windows Publish and Subscribe–like feature from Microsoft) do not import into QuarkXPress.

In-line graphics import into QuarkXPress in the form of their previews, not as their original formats — when they import at all. Because of this quirk, the versions of the in-line graphics that end up in your QuarkXPress document probably will have a lower resolution in your QuarkXPress layout than they had in their original word-processor file. To get them back to their proper resolution, you have to "re-link" them in the Pictures pane of the Usage dialog box (choose Utilities⇨Usage). (We cover linking picture files in more detail in Chapter 5.)

Style sheets: Absolutely, positively!

Okay, now for the good news. QuarkXPress allows you to import styles created in Microsoft Word and WordPerfect *if* you check the Include Style Sheets check box in the Get Text dialog box — but only if you remember to check the Include Style Sheets Box *before* you import the text. (To display this dialog box, choose File⇨Get Text, or press ⌘+E or Ctrl+E.) In fact, even if you don't always use style sheets in your word processor, checking the Include Style Sheets box when you import text is a good idea; you may end up saving important text formatting you forgot you'd even applied.

We tell you more about style sheets in Chapter 6.

XPress tags: Your secret code

Are you keen on secret codes? QuarkXPress has them in the form of a nifty, although tough to learn, feature that allows you to insert tags into text that you're preparing to import into QuarkXPress. These secret codes are referred to as *XPress tags;* you can use them to give QuarkXPress instructions on how to format text that's being imported into a QuarkXPress document. XPress tags are actually ASCII (text-only) text containing embedded codes that tell QuarkXPress which formatting to apply. XPress tags are similar to macros, and you embed them in the text that you create in your word processor.

Chapter 4

A Picture Is Worth . . .

*O*kay, we admit it: Many documents don't need graphics. But any document that you would go to the trouble of laying out probably does. The graphic may be as simple as a logo or as complex as a series of annotated photos. When all is said and done, graphics are integral parts of publications, and you'll use them in your layouts. But how do you get those graphics ready for use in QuarkXPress, and how do you get them on the page after they're prepped? That's what this chapter's all about.

Building Boxes for Pictures

If you know how to create text boxes, you've probably already made a thousand or two of them (or maybe just five or six). But when you look at a page with nothing but text boxes on it, you start to realize that it looks . . . well, kind of *boring*. What you need is a picture or two.

Pictures, or graphics, do more than just add visual interest to a page. A well-designed graphic actually can convey more information than a block of text. As the old saying goes, "A picture is worth a thousand words," and a photo, drawing, or chart truly can convey some very meaningful ideas.

Okay, you're convinced. It's time to start adding some pictures to the page. You do this by creating picture boxes and filling them with pictures.

First, you need to select one of the seven picture-box tools in the Tools palette. As we mention earlier in the book, the picture box tools found in the Picture Box palette are the same kind as those found in the Text Box palette: Rectangle, Rounded-Corner, Beveled-Corner, Concave-Corner, Oval, Bézier, and Freehand.

Follow these steps to create a picture box:

1. **Open the document to the page on which you want to draw the picture box.**

2. **Click a picture box tool to select it.**

3. **Position the crosshair mouse pointer at the location where you want one of the corners of the picture box to appear.**

4. **Hold down the mouse button and drag the mouse to shape the picture box.**

5. **Release the mouse button.**

To draw a perfectly square picture box, hold down the Shift key as you draw the box with the Rectangle Picture Box tool. To create a perfect circle, use the Oval Picture Box tool and hold down the Shift key while dragging.

Congratulations! You have now mastered the fine art of picture-box making. Really, it isn't all that different from making text boxes. Nor are the boxes all that different looking. In fact, the only real way to tell the difference between a picture box and a text box is that a picture box has a big "X" inside of it, and a text box doesn't. If you turn off the guides in the View Menu (choose View⇨Hide Guides), the "X" disappears, and there is really *no* way of telling one from the other. But don't fret too much about getting the two types of boxes mixed up; QuarkXPress won't allow you to put text inside a picture box or a picture inside a text box. You can, however, change a picture box into a text box (and vice versa) by choosing Item⇨Content and then choosing Text (or Picture) from the Content submenu.

Setting picture box specifications

Just as it does with text boxes, QuarkXPress allows you to be pretty darned picky about every part of a picture box. To establish a bunch of parameters for your picture box, use the five panes of the Modify dialog box for picture boxes. Figure 4-1 shows the Picture, Runaround, and Clipping panes (The Box and Frame panes are identical for text boxes and picture boxes. See Chapter 3). The Modify dialog box enables you to size and position a picture box precisely, rotate it, scale it and add color to its background, and skew (slant) it. In these ways, the picture box options in the Modify dialog box are pretty similar to those of the text box options. One thing you can do to a picture box that you can't do to a text box is position or crop the image inside the picture box. More about that later.

If you specify custom values in the Picture pane of the Modify dialog box before you import a graphic into it, the settings are applied to the imported graphic. But if, for some reason, you reimport the graphic (or any other) into the picture box, QuarkXPress ignores the custom settings and uses the default settings. In other words, you must re-enter your settings all over again.

Changing the size and position of a picture box

After you draw a picture box, you can tweak it in many ways. The most common way is by using the options in the Measurements palette, where you can change the size of the box by entering different W (width) and H (height) values. You also can change the position of the box by entering different X (vertical) and Y (horizontal) coordinates. You can make the same changes in a Bézier picture box, and when you activate an individual point (the "corners" connecting the sides of the Bézier bar) by clicking it, the Measurements palette lets you adjust the point and its control handles.

Actually, QuarkXPress gives you a rich selection of ways to change the size and position of a picture box:

✔ **The Measurements palette.**

- Enter different values in the X and Y fields to position the picture box.

- Enter different values in the W and H fields to resize the box.

- Enter a different value in the Angle field to rotate the box.

- Press Return or Enter to exit the palette and apply the new values.

This method is our favorite because it lets you see the result of your work as it happens.

✔ **The Box pane of the Modify dialog box.** To display the Modify dialog box, shown in Figure 4-1, choose Item⇨Modify or press ⌘+M or Ctrl+M:

- Enter values in the Origin Across and Origin Down fields to control the position of the box.

- Enter values in the Width and Height fields to control the size of the picture box.

- Enter values in the Angle and Skew fields to rotate and slant the picture box, and so on (see Chapter 5).

To see the results of changed values, click the Apply button.

Although it works fine, we aren't enthusiastic about this method because the Modify dialog box takes up a great deal of space, which can make it difficult to see what's happening to the picture box as a result of the new values you're entering.

✔ **The Item tool.** Use this tool to drag the box into position, and then grab the handles of the box to resize it.

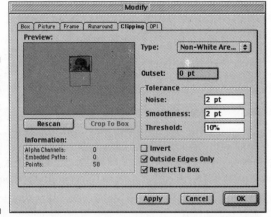

Figure 4-1:
The Modify
dialog box
for picture
boxes:
Picture,
Runaround,
and Clipping
panes.

Creating odd shapes

On occasion, to add visual interest to a page, you may want to import a graphic into a nonrectangular picture box, such as an oval, a circle, a straight-edged polygon, or a curved shape. But as with irregular text boxes, we recommend that you use this trick sparingly. More than that, we recommend that you *not* use irregular boxes unless you are using them for a well-reasoned and well-planned effect. Okay, okay, you've heard the lecture. Now exactly how *do* you create irregular picture boxes? Exactly the same way that you create irregular text boxes:

- The Rounded-Corner, Beveled-Corner, and Concave-Corner Picture Box tools provide alternatives to square-cornered boxes, and the Oval Picture Box tool enables you to create both ovals and a perfect circle (by holding down the Shift key as you drag).

- With the Bézier Picture Box tool, you can create straight-edged boxes, curved-edge boxes, and boxes that have both straight and curved edges.

- The Freehand Picture Box tool lets you create Bézier boxes by using the mouse as a freehand drawing tool.

As with Bézier text boxes, you can adjust the shape of Bézier picture boxes by clicking and dragging points and edges. (***Remember:*** Before you try to adjust a Bézier box, make sure that a check mark appears before the Shape command in the Item⇨Edit submenu). Here's a list of things to keep in mind as you change the shape of a Bézier box:

- If Shape is checked when you click anywhere on or within a Bézier box, the entire box becomes active, and all points are displayed. You can then drag the point or segment that you want to move.

- To move multiple points at the same time, hold down the Shift key and click the points; then drag any of the selected points.

- If you want drag the points in a straight, perfectly even line — in other words, if you want to "constrain" the direction you are dragging the points — continue to hold down the Shift key as you drag them.

- If you pause a moment before dragging a point or segment, QuarkXPress redraws the contents of the box as you drag.

- To add new points, hold down the Option or Alt key and click a segment at the place where you want the point to appear.

- To delete a point, hold down the Option or Alt key and click on the point.

Like Bézier text boxes, Bézier picture boxes can contain three kinds of points (corner points, smooth points, and symmetrical points) and two kinds of segments (curved and straight). And like Bézier text boxes, you can change any kind of point or segment in a Bézier picture box into any other kind point or segment. You can also split the segments into one or more segments by using the Scissors tool. (See Chapter 11.)

Pick a Format, Any Format

Okay, despite our sage design advice, you may have created a rather "unique," seashell-shaped picture box using the Bézier Picture Box tool. You've resized it and reshaped it about a million times, and now you're ready to import a picture. Right? Well, not exactly. QuarkXPress is designed to handle a slew of graphics types, including some that you may not have heard of. We suggest that you take some time to get acquainted with these file formats before you begin importing anything:

- **BMP (Windows Bitmap).** The bitmap format introduced with Windows is popular for lower-end programs, such as Microsoft Publisher. On a PC, look for the file name extensions .BMP and .DIB.

- **CT (Continuous Tone).** Continuous tone is created by high-end photo-retouching systems, such as Scitex. On a PC, look for the extension .CT or .SCT.

- **DCS (Document Color Separation).** This variant of EPS (see the following bullet) includes color-separation files, so it's actually five files— one for each of the four publishing colors (cyan, magenta, yellow, and black — known as the CMYK color system), plus a file that contains a preview image and instructions on how to combine the four color files. On a PC, look for the extensions .EPS and .DCS. (DCS Version 2.0 can have more than the four standard publishing colors, so you could find more than five component files.)

- **EPS (Encapsulated PostScript).** EPS is the publishing standard for drawings created by programs such as Adobe Illustrator, Macromedia FreeHand, and CorelDraw. Except for Illustrator, you need to export files to this format from the drawing program's native format (Illustrator's native format *is* EPS). On a PC, look for the extensions .EPS and .AI.

- **GIF (Graphics Interchange Format).** This bitmap format, developed for the CompuServe online service, is generally used for Web pages.

- **JPEG (Joint Photographic Experts Group).** This bitmap format uses file compression to make large files of photos and other scanned images into files of reasonable size. The trade-off is that the compression can make the image lose some detail. To import JPEG files, make sure that the JPEG Import filter is in your XTension folder. On a PC, look for the extension .JPG. (See Chapter 9 for more about XTensions.) Along with the GIF, this format is the most popular graphics format used on the World Wide Web.

- **MacPaint.** This bitmap format supports only black and white, which means that it's pretty much a goner in today's color marketplace. QuarkXPress for Windows does not support this format.

- **PCX (PC Paintbrush).** This bitmap format is the reigning bitmap format on PCs; it even predates Windows. High-end users junked it for TIFF because only recently did PCX add support for high-color (16-bit and 24-bit) images. If you're using the Macintosh version of QuarkXPress, make sure that the PCX Import filter is in your XTension folder. On a PC, look for the .PCX extension.

- **Photo CD.** This format was developed by Eastman Kodak for its corporate attempt to move consumers from film to CD for picture processing. That gambit didn't work, but it did create a standard for photo libraries that is rapidly taking over the publishing industry as the medium for storing stock photos. If you want to import Photo CD files, make sure that the Photo CD Import filter is in your XTension folder. On a PC, look for the extension .PCD.

- **PICT (Picture).** This Mac format is actually two formats: a drawing format and a bitmap format. In both cases, QuarkXPress imports the format. On a PC, look for the extension .PCT.

- **PNG (Portable Network Graphics).** This new bitmap image format from Adobe is aimed primarily at Web site creators. On a PC, look for the extension .PNG.

- **RLE (Run-Length Encoded).** The bitmap format used by OS/2 is a variant of BMP. On a PC, look for the extension .RLE.

- **TIFF (Tagged Image File Format).** Probably the most popular format for designers on the Mac (and fairly popular on the PC, too), this format is the standard for many scanners and photo-editing programs, because it supports 24-bit images (with millions of colors). PC TIFF and Mac TIFF are slightly different, but QuarkXPress reads them both. On a PC, look for the extension .TIF. For Macintosh users, the LZW Import filter must be in your XTension folder if you want to import LZW-compressed TIFF graphics. For QuarkXPress for Windows, the LZW-XT filter must be installed.

- **Windows Metafile.** This drawing format is similar to the Mac's PICT in that it is the native format for the operating system. On a PC, look for the extension .WMF.

If you've tried to import any of the preceding formats, only to have QuarkXPress refuse your attempt, QuarkXPress probably thumbed its nose at you for one of two reasons. One possible explanation is embarrassingly obvious: The file may not be in the format that you think it's in (or it may be corrupt). The other explanation isn't so obvious: The right import filter may not be installed in your XTension folder, one that's necessary for QuarkXPress to handle that file type. Filters for several popular file formats are installed automatically when you install QuarkXPress, but others are not.

If you're not accustomed to using any of these formats, don't sweat it. You can probably convert whatever formats you've been using to a format that QuarkXPress can handle. If you're doing your illustration work in FreeHand or CorelDraw, for example, you'll find that these programs can save or export in one or more of the previously listed formats.

Although QuarkXPress supports all these file formats, we recommend that you stick to just two formats for your graphics — TIFF and EPS (including DCS) — because they offer the most flexibility and the best output results. Runners-up are PCX, Photo CD, PICT, and Windows Metafile. If you're creating a Web page, we recommend that you stick to JPEG and GIF files exclusively. As for the rest, use them if you have them, but ask your artists (or the person who buys your clip art and stock photos) to convert the images into one of the formats recommended earlier.

Why only these few formats? QuarkXPress offers a slew of controls for TIFF files (see Chapter 12 for details) that it doesn't provide for other formats. As for EPS files, they provide the best-quality output, they allow you to embed fonts, and they support color separations better than any other drawing format. The only downside to EPS files is that they require a PostScript printer to print at high resolution, and many Windows users may not have such a printer (the PCL printer format is popular in Windows). PCXs, PICTs, Photo CDs, and Windows Metafiles are good second choices simply because they're so common, but their formats don't offer the same capabilities for high-end output that TIFF and EPS do.

If you're building a Web page in QuarkXPress, there really isn't much to debate. GIFs and JPEGs are the only reliable graphics file formats available. The Web doesn't recognize any of the other file formats mentioned, and although more and more Web applications are supporting the PNG format, still not enough do.

Pouring in the picture

After you check out the picture you want to use in your QuarkXPress document, you're ready to import it. Follow these steps:

1. **Open the document to the page that holds the picture box that you want to fill with a picture; then click the picture box to activate it.**

2. **Click the Content tool if it's not already selected.**

3. Choose File⇨Get Picture (or press ⌘+E or Ctrl+E).

The Get Picture dialog box appears, as shown in Figure 4-2.

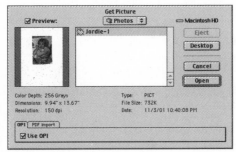

Figure 4-2:
The Get
Picture
dialog box in
Mac and
Windows.

4. Navigate the folders and drives until you find the image that you want to import.

If the Preview box is checked, QuarkXPress displays a thumbnail version of the image when you click the filename; this preview is meant to help you see whether it's the one you want. The preview may take a few moments to display after you select an image.

5. Click Open.

The picture appears in the active picture box. In some cases, QuarkXPress takes a few moments to load the file, particularly if it is more than 200K, has millions of colors, or is a compressed file (such as JPEG or Photo CD).

QuarkXPress treats objects differently, depending on what tool is selected. If you select the Content tool, you can work with the contents of a box — the text or graphics.

If you click the Item tool, you can work with the box itself. Thus, to move an image within its box, click the Content tool; to move the box and the image inside it, select the Item tool.

In addition to importing pictures into picture boxes, you can copy a picture from one box and paste it into another. You can also copy a picture onto the Clipboard from an image-editing or illustration program, switch to

QuarkXPress, and paste the picture into a picture box. You should avoid using this method, however, because the original image file is not used when the document is printed.

Making the Graphics Fit

What if you import an image and find that the image doesn't fit the box? What's going on?

When QuarkXPress imports a graphic, it does so at the graphic's original size. If the original is 6 inches square, QuarkXPress makes the image 6 inches square, no matter the size of the box that it's being placed in.

Following are a couple of ways to get your graphic to fit:

- ✔ Just drag the handles to resize the picture box to fit the image.

- ✔ If you want the graphic to fit the box's current size, make sure the Content tool or the Item tool is selected; then press Shift+Option+⌘+F or Ctrl+Shift+Alt+F. That finger-wrenching keyboard shortcut makes QuarkXPress resize the image so that it fits the box. Make sure that you press all four keys.

  If you miss the Option or Alt key and press just Shift+⌘+F or Ctrl+Shift+F, you get a distorted version of the image; it will be resized differently along the length than along the width. (No, we don't know why the more common option has the harder-to-use key combination.) The difference? The first shortcut keeps the image's original proportions, whereas the second makes the image fit the size of the box, distorting it if necessary. Figure 4-3 shows what happens when you use each option.

Sounds ugly, doesn't it? Fear not! You can now avoid this conundrum entirely, thanks to some new menu options that have been added to the Style menu in QuarkXPress 5.

- ✔ The Fit Picture to Box (Proportionally) command (Style⇨Fit Picture to Box [Proportionally]) lets you resize an image so that it fits in a box without distortion.

- ✔ If you want the picture to fit the size of the box, distortion and all, you can choose Fit Picture To Box in the Style Menu command (Style⇨Fit Picture to Box).

  In QuarkXPress 5, you can now resize the picture box to the size of the picture with the Fit Box To Picture command (Style⇨Fit Picture to Box). This option adjusts the picture box to fit around the picture instead of vice versa.

Another keyboard shortcut — Shift+⌘+M or Ctrl+Shift+M — centers a graphic within the box. This shortcut won't resize your image, so you'll still likely use Option+ Shift+⌘+F or Ctrl+Alt+Shift+F to make your image fit in the box.

In addition to taking advantage of QuarkXPress's automatic controls, you can manually reposition, or "crop," a graphic within a box. The easiest way to reposition a graphic manually is to start with the Content tool active. Then just click the graphic and move it. The pointer becomes a hand (called the grabber hand) when you position it over the graphic. Hold down the mouse button and move the mouse — you'll see the graphic move within the box. Release the mouse button when you're done.

You also can specify how much you want the image to move within the box. QuarkXPress uses a floating palette — the Measurements palette — that allows you to control text attributes, graphics attributes, and box attributes. Figure 4-4 shows the Measurements palette with the settings for the picture box that's in the top-left corner of the page.

The X% and Y% values show the amount of scaling (see Figure 4-4); you can change those values by typing new ones in the boxes and then pressing Enter or Return.

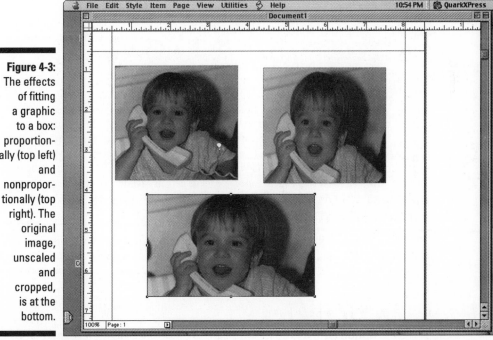

Figure 4-3:
The effects of fitting a graphic to a box: proportionally (top left) and nonproportionally (top right). The original image, unscaled and cropped, is at the bottom.

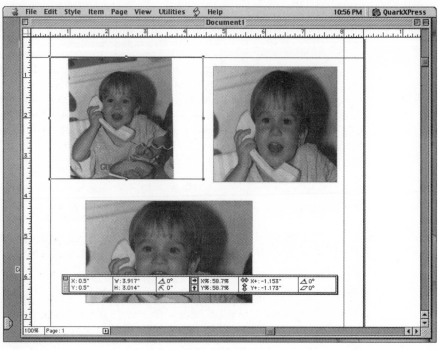

Figure 4-4:
The
Measure-
ments
palette
allows you
to resize
and
reposition
graphics
within a
picture box.

You also can change the position of a graphic by changing the X+ and Y+ values. A positive number moves the image to the right for X+ and down for Y+. Another method is to click the arrows to the right of the X+ and Y+ boxes. These arrows nudge the image up, down, left, or right, depending on which arrow you click. (Hold down the Option or Alt key to nudge an image in tiny steps: 0.001 unit of the current measurement, such as inches or picas.) You can, of course, use a combination of these techniques. Use the grabber hand to roughly position the graphic and then fine-tune the placement by clicking nudge arrows and/or changing the X+ and Y+ values manually. Another option is to choose Item⇨Modify (or press ⌘+M or Ctrl+M) and then click the Picture tab to get to the Picture pane of the Modify dialog box. There, you can change the Scale Across, Scale Down, Offset Down, and Offset Across values. That method is too much work, though.

When your graphics are placed in the box, sized, and positioned the way you like them, you can move on to using graphics as embellishments.

Managing Graphics

Getting pictures into your QuarkXPress documents is easy, but only part of the job. You also have to keep track of your imported pictures throughout the production process to make sure that everything goes smoothly when it's time to output final pages.

You may not know it, but when you import a picture into QuarkXPress, you don't actually import the entire picture file. If QuarkXPress added imported picture files to documents when you imported a picture, the size of the documents would get out of hand. A few high-resolution scans could easily produce a QuarkXPress document that exceeds 50MB. So instead of importing entire graphic files, QuarkXPress imports only a low-resolution version of each image. This image is what you see when you rotate, crop, resize, or otherwise alter a picture. When you print the picture, the original file is sent to the printer.

Dealing with modified pictures

After you import a picture, you should be aware of several pitfalls. First, if somebody modifies a picture that you imported into a QuarkXPress document, you want to re-import the picture before you print it. If you don't update a picture that's been modified, QuarkXPress warns you when you print it and gives you a chance to update the graphic. If you do update the graphic, however, you won't get to see the modified graphic before it's printed, and you may be in for a surprise. You have two options for updating modified pictures:

✔ You can update individual pictures manually in the Pictures pane of the Usage dialog box. (To display this dialog box, choose Utilities➪Usage and then click the Pictures tab. See Figure 4-5.) The scroll list displays information on an imported TIFF file that was modified after it was imported. If you click the More Information button, QuarkXPress displays additional information about the picture whose name is highlighted in the scroll list. To update a modified picture, click its name and then click Update. Hold down the ⌘ or Ctrl key when you click to update multiple pictures.

✔ You can have QuarkXPress update modified pictures for you automatically. The Auto Picture Import list in the Preferences dialog box provides two choices — On and On (Verify) — that automatically update modified pictures when you open a document. (To display the Preferences pane, choose Edit➪Preferences➪Preferences and choose General from the list at the left, or press ⌘+Y or Ctrl+Y.) If you choose On or Verify, QuarkXPress displays a dialog box when it updates a modified picture.

Dealing with moved pictures

Sometimes, pictures get modified after you import them; other times, they get moved from their original locations. When you import a picture, QuarkXPress records its storage location so that it knows where the picture file is located when it's time to print. But if you move a picture file after you import it, QuarkXPress won't be able to find it. If this happens, QuarkXPress warns you when you try to print the picture and provides you the option of re-establishing the link to the missing file.

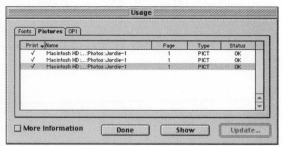

You can also re-establish links to missing pictures via the Pictures pane of the Usage dialog box. To update a missing picture, click it and then click Update. QuarkXPress displays a standard Open dialog box that allows you to locate and select the missing file. Sorry — you have to do this part yourself; QuarkXPress isn't smart enough to figure out the location of missing picture files.

Keeping track of picture files is particularly important if you use a printer pre-press house to produce final output. In addition to providing your QuarkXPress documents to your printer, you must provide all imported pictures for those documents. If you don't include picture files, your service provider can still output your documents, but the low-resolution previews will be used instead of the original high-resolution picture files. Not a pretty picture.

Collecting pictures for output

In documents that contain many pictures, keeping track of all the pictures can be tricky, but collecting them all manually in preparation for output could challenge your sanity. Fortunately, QuarkXPress does this job for you. Just choose File⇨Collect for Output. In addition to collecting picture files, QuarkXPress generates a report that contains printing-related information about the document, including a list of fonts used, XTensions required for output, and the document's page size.

In QuarkXPress 5, the Collect for Output feature also lets you pick and choose which pictures you want QuarkXPress to collect, as well as fonts and ICC color profiles. Previous versions of QuarkXPress only collected picture files; you had to collect the other items yourself. For more about QuarkXPress 5's new Collect For Output feature, see Chapter 11.

Chapter 5

Getting Tricky with Boxes

• •

• •

*Y*ou've conquered the text box. You've uncovered the hidden secrets of the picture box. You've even dabbled with XPress tags (okay, if you skipped XPress tags, we won't hold it against you). Now it's time get creative! Let your hair down!

In this chapter, we show you some cool things to do with text and picture boxes. After all, you bought QuarkXPress to become a desktop publisher, right? And no self-respecting desktop publisher would be caught without a bag of layout tricks. These tricks are as necessary to a desktop publisher as flies to a frog, slop to a hog, or biscuits to a dog. Discovering how to create some tricky effects with text and picture boxes is definitely worth your while.

For example, QuarkXPress lets you flow text inside boxes shaped like letters. Or, you can flow text around those letter-shaped boxes. You can even wrap text around the contours of a picture. All these layout tricks help you establish a relationship or solidify the relationship between form and content in your designs.

Keep in mind that this chapter covers just a small part of what you can do with text and pictures in QuarkXPress — indeed, entire books have been written about manipulating (and remanipulating) documents in QuarkXPress. You have to go a long way to truly unleash the powers of this program. But that doesn't mean you can't have some fun now. Start filling up that bag of tricks.

Running Around

In Chapter 3, we introduce the Runaround pane as part of the Modify dialog box. This section covers the Runaround pane in more detail.

In QuarkXPress, when text wraps around the edges of something — for example, a picture box, another text box, or something within a picture — it's called a *runaround*. You may know this effect as a text wrap, so try to adjust your vocabulary to runaround when using QuarkXPress. Keep these factors in mind when you create a runaround:

- ✔ You need two things — some text in a box (or on a text path) and an "obstructing item." The obstructing item is the item the text runs around.

- ✔ The obstructing item must be in front of the text box in the page's stacking order. To bring an item in front of a text box, choose Item➪ Bring to Front. (See Chapter 11 for more information about adjusting the stacking order of items.)

Text runaround actually occurs by default any time you place an item in front of a text box. This default text runaround can easily be turned on or off to meet your needs, so you need to know how to create a runaround and how to adjust it.

Follow these steps to create a runaround:

1. **Create a text box on the page and fill it with text.**

2. **Create an additional item for the text to wrap around — this is the obstructing item. Alternately, select an item on the page and choose Item➪Bring to Front to be sure it's in front of the text box.**

3. **Choose Item➪Modify and then click the Runaround tab. (Or press ⌘+T or Ctrl+T to open the Runaround tab shown in Figure 5-1.)**

   Make sure Item is selected from the Type menu. (If you're trying to turn Runaround off, of course, you would choose None.)

4. **Enter point values in the Top, Bottom, Left, and Right fields to specify how much white space to leave between the item and text runaround.**

   If the item is not rectangular, you'll be able to specify only a single runaround value in the Offset field. If the obstructing item has any holes in it (for example, a box shaped like the letter "O"), the Outside Edges Only option will be available. If you check it, text cannot flow into and out of the holes.

5. Look in the Preview area and click the Apply button to see whether you like the runaround. When you're satisfied, click OK.

QuarkXPress gives you two runaround options for text boxes, three options for lines and text paths, and several options for picture boxes. You choose an option by selecting it in the Type list in the Runaround pane of the Modify dialog box. After you choose an option, look in the Preview window to see how the text will flow. Here are the choices for flowing text around text boxes and boxes with no content:

✔ **None.** QuarkXPress flows the text behind the active box as though no item appeared there. Figure 5-2 shows the overprinting of text that occurs when you choose a runaround type of None for a text box.

✔ **Item.** Flows the text around the edges of the item as shown in Figure 5-3. Notice that you can determine how far away from the box the text will flow by entering values in the Top, Left, Bottom, and Right fields of the Runaround pane. In the figure, we set this amount as 6 points.

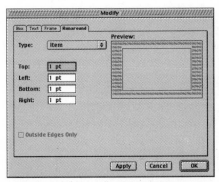
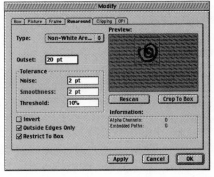

Figure 5-1:
The Runaround pane of the Modify dialog box lets you specify how text wraps around an item placed in front of it.

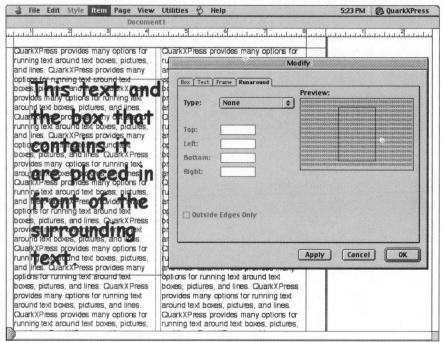

Figure 5-2:
Selecting
None as the
Type for a
text-box
runaround
creates this
effect.

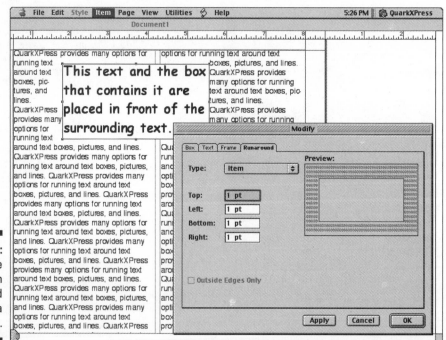

Figure 5-3:
An example
of the Item
runaround
for a
text box.

You can choose among three options for lines and text paths:

✔ **None.** Flows the text behind the active line or text path.

✔ **Item.** Flows text around the active line or text path. Note that if the active item is a text path, the runaround text behind is not affected by the text on the path — only by the path itself. As a result, the text on the path can overlap and obscure the text that's behind.

✔ **Manual.** Flows text around the image as it does when you choose Item. Enter a value in the Outset field to specify the distance between the line or text path and the runaround text.

If you choose Manual, QuarkXPress creates an editable shape, called a *runaround path*, around the active line or text path. If you activate the line or text path, you can edit the runaround by choosing Item⇨Edit⇨Runaround (or pressing Option+F4 or Ctrl+F10) and then dragging points, control handles, and segments.

Here are the choices for picture boxes:

✔ **None.** Flows the text behind the active picture box and picture.

✔ **Item.** Flows text around the active box.

✔ **Auto Image.** Creates a runaround path around the image within the box and flows text around the runaround path. Figure 5-4 shows an Auto Image runaround.

✔ **Embedded Path.** Creates a runaround path based on a picture-embedded path, drawn in Adobe Photoshop, and runs text around this path.

✔ **Alpha Channel.** Creates a runaround path based on an alpha channel built into a TIFF image by a photo-editing application, and runs text around this path. (An *alpha channel* is an invisible outline picture used to edit the image to which it is attached.) If you have more than one alpha channel embedded in your image, QuarkXPress lets you choose the alpha channel you want to run the text around.

✔ **Non-White Areas.** Creates a runaround path based on the picture's contrast. If you choose Non-White Areas, the Outset and Tolerance controls allow you to customize the runaround path.

✔ **Same as Clipping.** Runs text around the clipping path specified in the Clipping pane of the Modify dialog box. (A clipping path is a shape, created in an image-editing program, that isolates a portion of a picture.)

✔ **Picture Bounds.** Creates a runaround path based on the rectangular shape of the imported graphic. The runaround area includes the white background of the original picture file.

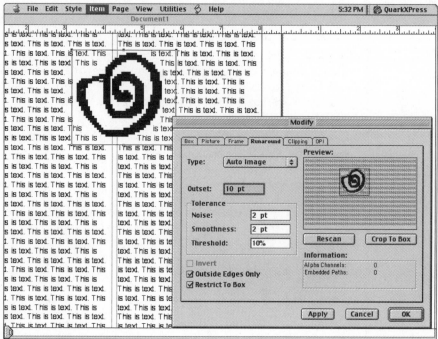

When you select a picture box, you get additional runaround controls, including Outset, Tolerance, and Invert options. To use the extra controls you need to be familiar with sophisticated image-editing techniques, so we don't cover them here. (If you use these options, watch how the preview window shows the effects of your settings.)

The Outside Edges Only check box in the lower left corner of the Runaround pane should normally be checked because it prevents text from getting inside a shape's interior gaps (for example, inside the hollow part of a doughnut shape).

The Restrict to Box check box, also in the lower left corner of the Runaround pane, should normally be checked too. If unchecked, your text would wrap around any part of the image cropped by the box. (In other words, if your picture is larger than the picture box containing it, the part visible in the box is the cropped portion. The rest of the picture still exists but won't display or print. If Restrict to Box is not checked, QuarkXPress assumes you want the text to wrap around the entire picture, not just the part visible in the picture box. Although at times you may want such a "ghost wrap," those times are rare.)

If you run text around an item that's placed in front of a single column of text, by default QuarkXPress runs text on only one side of the item — whichever side can hold more text. If you want the text to run around both sides of an obstructing item, you must select the box that contains the runaround text, display the Text pane of the Modify dialog box (choose Item⇨Modify, or press ⌘+M or Ctrl+M), and check the Run Text Around All Sides check box.

Rotating Boxes

You can rotate both text boxes and picture boxes in QuarkXPress. If used effectively, rotated boxes can provide additional spark to the appearance of a page. For example, you might rotate a "sale" banner to splash it diagonally across an advertisement. Again, as with the other layout tricks, use rotation sparingly for best results.

Figure 5-5 shows a text box rotated at 45 degrees and 90 degrees.

You can control the rotation of selected text boxes, picture boxes, or no-content boxes in three ways:

✔ **Option 1.** Choose Item⇨Modify (or press ⌘+M or Ctrl+M) to display the Modify dialog box. If necessary, click the Box tab, then enter a rotation amount between 360 (degrees) and –360 in the Angle field.

To rotate the box clockwise, use a negative value in the Angle field; to rotate the box counterclockwise, use a positive value in the Angle field.

✔ **Option 2.** Click the Rotation tool in the Tool palette to select it. Position the mouse pointer at the point around which you want to rotate the box (click the center of the box if you want to rotate it around its center, for example); then hold down the mouse button and move the mouse pointer away from the point where you clicked. Continue to hold down the mouse button as you drag in a circular direction — clockwise or counterclockwise.

✔ **Option 3.** Enter a rotation value in the Angle box of the Measurements palette.

No single, correct way exists to rotate boxes. Experiment with all three options to see which method is most comfortable for you.

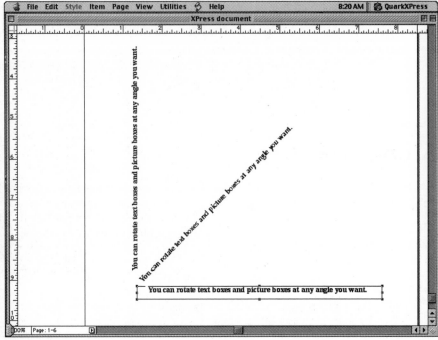

Figure 5-5:
Rotated text
boxes are
useful for
such things
as photo
and
illustration
credit lines,
product
packaging,
and
coupons.

Skew, too!

The Box pane of the Modify dialog box also lets you enter an amount in another field called the Skew field. Not to be confused with the Angle box, which deals strictly with the rotation of a box, the Skew box applies an actual "slant" to the shape of the box, much like the one shown in Figure 5-6.

To skew a box, do the following:

1. **Open the document to the page that holds the text box or picture box that you want to slant.**

2. **Click the box to make it active.**

3. **Choose Item⇨Modify (or press ⌘+M or Ctrl+M).**

   The Modify dialog box appears.

4. **Click the Box tab if it's not already selected.**

5. **In the Skew field, enter a value between 75 and –75.**

   A positive number slants the box to the right; a negative number slants the box to the left.

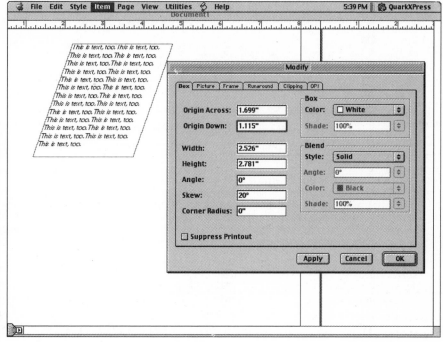

Figure 5-6:
The slanted text box in this example was achieved by entering a value of 20 in the Skew field in the Box pane of the Modify dialog box.

If you apply a skew value to a box, any text or picture within the box is also slanted. You can also specify a skew value for only the contents of the box — text or picture — by displaying the Text or Picture pane of the Modify dialog box and entering a value in the Skew field.

Anchoring boxes within text

Fifteen years ago, in the old days of publishing, graphic designers used wax or spray mount and a rubber roller to adhere galleys of text and halftones to paste-up boards. QuarkXPress not only frees you from such manual drudgery, but also enables you to do something that wasn't possible before the advent of electronic publishing. You have the option to anchor picture boxes and text boxes, as well as lines and text paths, within text so that the boxes move with the text if editing causes the text to reflow. This feature is great if, for example, you create catalogs that contain product pictures. You can paste a picture box within each product description. If the text is subsequently edited, you don't have to worry about having to reposition all the pictures, because the pictures have been anchored and flow right along with the text.

Anchoring an item within text isn't difficult, but it requires a sequence of actions — including switching tools — that's a little bit tricky. Follow these steps to anchor a box:

1. **Click the Item tool if it's not already selected.**

2. **Click the box that you want to anchor within text.**

3. **Choose Edit⇨Copy (or press ⌘+C or Ctrl+C).**

   You can also choose Edit⇨Cut (or press ⌘+X or Ctrl+X). You won't need the original box after you anchor it so, in the long run, cutting it probably is easier.

4. **Click the Content tool to select text.**

5. **Click within a text box at the point in the text where you want to paste the copied/cut box.**

6. **Choose Edit⇨Paste (or press ⌘+V or Ctrl+V).**

You can anchor any box, including Bézier boxes and boxes that have been rotated or skewed. After you anchor a box within text, you can modify the contents of the box the same way that you modify the contents of an unanchored box. One thing that you can't do, however, is move an anchored box with the Item tool, because QuarkXPress treats an anchored box in much the same way as a character within text. To delete an anchored box, click to its right with the Content tool to place the cursor next to it; then press Backspace or Delete. You can also delete an anchored box by highlighting it as you would a text character and then pressing Backspace or Delete.

If you click an anchored box, a pair of small icons appears on the left edge of the Measurements palette. If you click the top button (Align with Text Ascent), the top of an anchored box aligns with the top of the characters on the line that contains it; if you click the bottom button (Align with Text Baseline), the bottom of an anchored box aligns with the baseline of the line that contains it. The Box pane of the Measurements palette also enables you to specify the alignment of an anchored box, and it offers an Offset box that enables you to adjust the position of baseline-aligned anchored boxes.

A few pitfalls exist when you anchor boxes within text. Here are some things to look out for:

✔ If the item that you're anchoring is wider than the column you're pasting it into, the item won't fit. When you paste, you create a text overflow. To avoid this problem, make sure that the item you're anchoring is narrower than the column that will contain it.

✔ If the item that you're anchoring is taller than the leading of the paragraph that you paste it into, the anchored item can cause uneven leading or obscure some of the surrounding text.

✔ If you want to anchor a box that's taller than the leading of the paragraph that will contain it, the safest practice is to anchor the box at the beginning of the paragraph (that is, make the anchored box the first character of the paragraph).

✔ In previous versions of QuarkXPress you couldn't anchor grouped items — pictures or otherwise. That's changed in QuarkXPress 5.0. You can now anchor any and all grouped items, including grouped pictures, grouped text boxes and any combination thereof.

In Figure 5-7, the picture boxes in the left and right margins have been anchored in a two-column text box. The anchored box in the left column is a simple rectangle. The box was pasted at the beginning of the paragraph; the top of the box is aligned with the top of the first line. The anchored box on the right is aligned with the baseline of the first line of a paragraph. The box was rotated and slanted before it was anchored (although you can apply rotation and skew to a box after you anchor it, too).

QuarkXPress also allows you to anchor lines into text; anchoring lines works just like anchoring boxes.

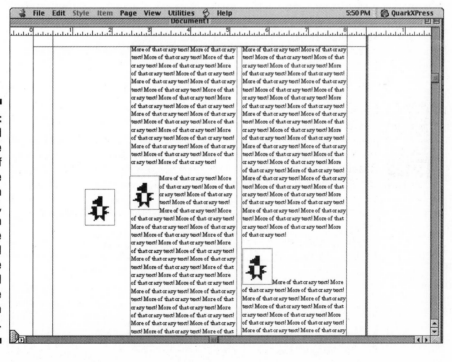

Figure 5-7: Anchored boxes, like the pair of picture boxes within the text, flow with the text. The anchored boxes were created from the original in the margin.

Part II
Adding Style and Substance

The 5th Wave   By Rich Tennant

"It says,' Seth - Please see us about your idea to wrap newsletter text around company logo. Production.'"

In this part . . .

Good publishing technique is about more than just
getting the words down on paper. It's also about
tweaking the letters and lines — and the space between
them — to make your pages shine. This part shows you
how to do a lot, including how to get your document out
of your computer and onto some other medium, such as
film or paper (later on in the book, we show you how to
put pages on the Web). We tell you how to use XTensions,
plug-ins to the program that beef up its capabilities. We
also give you some solid suggestions on printing and
working with all those other people in the world who
know how to help you get the job done.

Chapter 6

You've Got Real Style

In This Chapter

▶ Using style sheets to format paragraphs in your documents

▶ Creating, changing, and applying styles

▶ Importing style sheets from other documents

*A*lthough you've heard about them, you've probably never really been into *style sheets*. Yet you know some people who use them on every single document. Still, something inside you says, "Style sheets? Document formatting? Whoa! Save it for the big-time publishers!" We think you should reconsider. Surely you must realize by now that half the fun of desktop publishing is being able to automate some of the tasks that used to take so long. QuarkXPress makes setting up styles for your documents easy. Best of all, using style sheets saves you tons of time and helps you keep your formatting consistent throughout a document.

Style sheets are just about the best invention since the snooze alarm. They define basic specifications for your text: typefaces, type sizes, justification settings, and tab settings. If you select a paragraph and apply a style sheet to it, the paragraph automatically formats itself to the font and size specified in the style sheet. Even better, in QuarkXPress, you can apply styles to any text selection, not just whole paragraphs.

Just think of all the time automatic styling saves you. Instead of applying each attribute to text individually, you can just tell QuarkXPress that you want particular swaths of text to take on all the formatting attributes established in a style tag. Then — with one click of the mouse — you send QuarkXPress on its merry way to format your document quicker than you can take a sip of coffee.

Like many features of publishing, style sheets come with their own jargon, which would be helpful for you to know:

✔ **Style sheet:** The group of formatting attributes (styles) in a document. It's called a *sheet* because, in times before electronic publishing, typesetters had typewritten sheets that listed the formatting attributes they had to apply to specific kinds of text, such as body copy and headlines. QuarkXPress treats style sheets as part of the document.

✔ **Style or style tag:** These two terms refer to a group of formatting attributes that you apply to one or more paragraphs or to selected text. You name the group, or style, so that you can apply all the attributes to the document at once. For example, in text styled Body Text, you may indicate the typeface, type size, leading, and so on, as part of that Body Text style. The word *tag* means that you "tag" selected paragraphs or selected text with the style you want to apply. Because the word *style* also sometimes refers to a character attribute, such as italics or underline, many people use *style tag* to refer to the group of attributes. This distinction helps you avoid confusing the two meanings. (Note that QuarkXPress uses the phrase *style sheet* for what we call a style or style tag; we decided it was better to use the industry-standard term than to go with Quark's term.)

Styles work in two places: You can apply them to selected paragraphs or text in your QuarkXPress document, or to paragraphs (but not selected text) in the word processing text you plan to import. We explain how to do it both ways in the sections that follow.

Paragraph versus Character Styles

Until QuarkXPress Version 4, you could use paragraph styles to save attributes for entire paragraphs only. If you needed to format individual words, you had to do that manually. So Quark added an amazing new feature in QuarkXPress 4: character styles that let you save the attributes for selected characters as well.

Paragraph and character styles are not an either/or proposition. You can use both interchangeably:

✔ The time-saving part about paragraph styles is that you apply them to whole paragraphs. For example, first-level heads might have a Header 1 style, captions a Caption style, bylines a Byline style, body text a Body Text style, and so on. Specifying a style for all paragraph types that you often use is a great idea. With a paragraph style, all the text in the paragraph receives the same settings: fonts, size, leading, alignment, hyphenation, and so on.

✔ The beauty of the character styles feature is that you can ensure consistent typography throughout your document. A paragraph style does that for entire paragraphs, but documents often have pieces of text that always get the same formatting. For example, drop caps might always use a specific font and be compressed, or the first few words after a bullet might always appear bold and be in a different font. By creating a character style named Drop Cap with the settings for those specific characters, you can ensure that you always apply the correct settings. Think about it: Before character styles, you had to apply each setting yourself — font, size, perhaps even baseline shift — and hope that you both remembered and used the correct settings each time. With character styles, QuarkXPress remembers for you. And as with paragraph styles, if you change the style sheet's settings, all the text using the style automatically updates throughout your document. Cool!

To help you distinguish between paragraph and character styles, QuarkXPress precedes the names of styles with either a ¶ to indicate a paragraph style or an **A** to indicate a character style. You see these symbols in the Style Sheets dialog box (see the following section, "Styling Your Style Sheets."), in the Append dialog box (see the section, "Copying styles between documents"), and in the Style Sheets palette (also covered in "Making styles happen," later in this chapter).

Styling Your Style Sheets

We promised you it would be easy. You find the keys to creating, changing, and applying styles in one spot — the Style Sheets dialog box, which you access by choosing Edit⇨Style Sheets or by pressing Shift+F11 (see Figure 6-1).

Figure 6-1:
You can do almost anything you want to style sheets from within the Style Sheets dialog box.

Learn it once, use it twice

You can always apply character and paragraph formatting to selected text in your QuarkXPress document, whether or not you use style sheets. The good news is that after you understand the dialog boxes used to set formatting for style sheets, you know the dialog boxes and menus needed to locally format text outside of style sheets. QuarkXPress uses the same system for both kinds of formatting:

✔ The Style menu's Font, Size, Type Style, Color, Shade, Horizontal/Vertical Scale, Track, and Baseline Shift menu options are the same as the formatting options in the Edit Character Style Sheet dialog box.

✔ The Character Attributes dialog box (Style⇨ Character or Shift+⌘+C or Ctrl+Shift+C) is the same as the Edit Character Style dialog box.

✔ The Style menu's Alignment and Leading menu options are the same as the same-name options in the Formats pane of the Edit Paragraph Style Sheet dialog box.

✔ The Formats pane (Style⇨Formats, or Shift+⌘+F or Ctrl+Shift+F), Tabs pane (Style⇨Tabs, or Shift+⌘+T or Ctrl+ Shift+T), and Rules pane (Style⇨Rules, or Shift+⌘+N or Ctrl+Shift+N) of the Paragraph Attributes dialog box are the same as those in the Edit Paragraph Style Sheet dialog box.

So you see, by knowing how to format text through style sheets, you can format any kind of text in QuarkXPress.

Oops! We almost forgot a couple of style-related functions that you set outside the Style Sheets dialog box:

✔ Set hyphenation controls in the H&Js dialog box by choosing Edit⇨H&Js, or by pressing Option+⌘+H or Ctrl+Shift+F11.

✔ Control character and space scaling by accessing the Character tab in the Preferences dialog box (choose Edit⇨Preferences⇨Preferences, or press Option+Shift+⌘+Y or Ctrl+Alt+Shift+Y).

We cover style-related functions in more detail in Chapter 8. If you're new to this style sheet business, give yourself some time to experiment. After all, you can always delete any style sheet you dislike by simply highlighting the style in the Style Sheets dialog box and clicking the Delete button.

We *told* you it was easy!

Delving into the Style Sheets dialog box

The Style Sheets dialog box, shown in Figure 6-1, gives you several choices for editing style sheets. Your choices are as follows:

✔ **New.** Lets you create a new style from scratch or create a new style based on an existing style. Note that the New button is a drop-down button — if you click it, it becomes a pop-up menu with two choices: ¶ Paragraph and **A** Character. You need to tell QuarkXPress whether you want to create a paragraph or character style.

Suppose that you just spent 15 minutes defining text settings through the Style menu or Measurements palette. Can you turn these settings into a style? You bet. All you need to do is position your text cursor anywhere on the text that has the desired settings. Then open the Style Sheets dialog box and choose New. All settings automatically appear in the new style you create. Alternatively, you can Control+click or right-click any style name in the Style Sheets palette (open it by choosing View➪Show Style Sheets or by pressing F11) to get a pop-up menu that shows the New command.

✔ **Edit.** Lets you make changes to an existing style. Alternatively, you can Control+click or right-click any style name in the Style Sheets palette (open it by choosing View➪Show Style Sheets or by pressing F11) to get a pop-up menu that shows the Edit command.

✔ **Duplicate.** Makes copies of all the attributes of an existing style and gives the duplicate style the name Copy of style. You then can change any attribute settings, including the style name.

✔ **Delete.** Lets you delete existing styles. A dialog box asks you to confirm the deletion if you applied the style to text in the current document. Any text using a deleted style retains the style's attributes, but the Style Sheets palette and style menu show these paragraphs as having No Style. Alternatively, you can Control+click or right-click any style name in the Style Sheets palette to get a pop-up menu that has the Delete command in it. Note that if you delete a style sheet that you applied to text, QuarkXPress asks you which style sheet to apply instead. You can choose No Style, which leaves the text formatting untouched while removing the style sheet, or pick another style sheet and apply it to the text.

✔ **Append.** Lets you copy a style from another QuarkXPress document.

✔ **Save.** Saves all the style changes you make in the Style Sheets dialog box. If you forget to save styles when leaving the dialog box, the changes won't take effect, so try to remember to save, okay?

✔ **Cancel.** Makes the program ignore all style changes you made in the Style Sheets dialog box since you last saved changes.

Notice how QuarkXPress shows you the settings for the selected paragraph or character style in the Description area at the bottom of the Style Sheets dialog box? Reading this area is a great way to double-check your settings.

Examining the Edit Character Style Sheet dialog box

The best place to start creating styles for a document is with character styles. Why? Because paragraph styles use character styles to format their paragraphs' text. Even if a paragraph uses a particular character style, you can use that same character style for selected text. Doing this saves you effort when you're creating paragraph styles because you can create several similar paragraph styles that all use the same character style; you define the text formatting once in the character styles and just change the paragraph formatting (such as indentation or space above) in the various paragraph styles based on it. We talk about editing paragraph styles in the next section.

The default setting for Normal is left-aligned, 12-point Helvetica with automatic leading. To change any attributes of the Normal style, close all open documents, choose Edit⇔Style Sheets or press Shift+F11, and edit the Normal style as we describe in the following two sections. These settings become the new defaults for all future new documents. Any style tag created without a document open becomes part of the default style sheet for all new documents.

Figure 6-2 shows the Edit Character Style Sheet dialog box, where much of the action of setting up styles happens.

Figure 6-2: The Edit Character Style Sheet dialog box.	![Edit Character Style Sheet dialog box showing fields for Name (Drop Cap), Keyboard Equivalent, Based On (Normal), Font (Helvetica), Size (12 pt), Color (Black), Shade (100%), Scale (Horizontal 100%), Track Amount (0), Baseline Shift (0 pt), and Type Style options including Plain (checked), Bold, Italic, Underline, Word U-line, Strike Thru, Outline, Shadow, All Caps, Small Caps, Superscript, Subscript, Superior, with Cancel and OK buttons]

Following are explanations of the fields in the Edit Character Style Sheet dialog box:

> ✔ **Name** shows the name of an existing style you're editing; the field is empty if you're working on a new style.

✔ **Keyboard Equivalent** lets you set up key shortcuts that make it easier to quickly apply styles to text. To enter keyboard equivalents, press the actual function key (F1 through F15) you want to use, including any combinations with Shift, Option, ⌘, Alt, or Ctrl.

QuarkXPress includes a keyboard template that lists function-key equivalents for often-accessed commands. You can override the original commands by assigning function keys to style sheets, but, if you do, you lose the ability to access the commands assigned to those keys.

✔ **Based On** lets you build a group of styles by basing the group on another style. Then, if you decide to change the group, you only need to change the original base style and those changes automatically apply to the rest of the group. For example, if you had five body text styles created using the Based on option and using the same font, instead of altering all five style sheets to change your body text font, you merely edit the base style, and the remaining styles in the group reflect the font change.

✔ **Font** is where you choose the typeface. The pop-up list shows all the fonts installed in your system, as shown in Figure 6-3. If you type the first few letters of a font's name, the menu automatically scrolls to the first font whose name begins with those letters.

QuarkXPress for Windows adds a code before each font name — T1, O, or TT — to indicate whether a font is a Type 1 PostScript font (best when outputting to film), the new OpenType format (fine for laser and inkjet printers), or a TrueType font (fine for laser and inkjet printers).

✔ **Size** lets you pick the type size in points (the standard measurement for text size, of which there are 72 to an inch). You can pick from the pop-up list's sizes, or simply type any size you want in the Size field. (You can specify type size to three decimal places, such as 12.123 points. If you enter more decimal places than that, QuarkXPress ignores them.)

✔ **Color** lets you choose the color for text. Any color defined in the document (see Chapter 15) appears in this list.

✔ **Shade** lets you determine how dark the selected color (including black) appears. You can pick from the pop-up list's percentages or enter your own figure (up to three decimal places).

✔ **Scale** lets you scrunch type either horizontally (width) or vertically (height); pick which you want from the pop-up menu. Then enter a percentage value for how much you want to expand (widen) or condense (compress) the size — values less than 100% condense the type; values greater than 100% expand the type.

✔ **Track Amount** adjusts the spacing between all characters, moving them closer together (a negative number) or farther apart (a positive number). See Chapter 8 for more on tracking and its cousin, kerning.

✔ **Baseline Shift** lets you move text up or down relative to other text on the line (the baseline is the imaginary line that type rests on). A positive number moves the text up; a negative number moves it down.

✔ **Type Style** is where you set the typeface settings. Check all the appropriate boxes. Note that some settings disallow others: Underline and Word Underline override each other, as do All Caps and Small Caps, and Subscript and Superscript. Selecting Plain deselects everything else.

QuarkXPress dialog boxes often include pop-up menus to help you make selections faster. For example, in the Edit Character Style Sheets dialog box, Font, Size, Color, and Shade all offer pop-up menus. You also can enter the value you want directly into the box.

When you finish selecting the character formatting for your new or edited character style sheet, click OK. You return to the Style Sheets dialog box (refer to Figure 6-1).

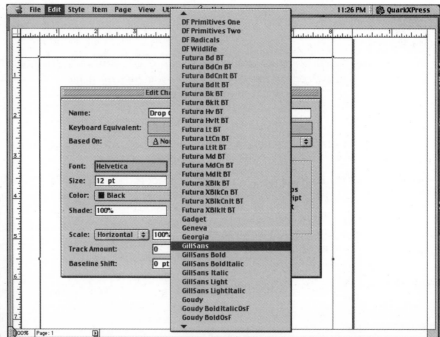

Figure 6-3:
The Font pop-up menu in the Edit Character Style Sheet dialog box.

Checking out the Edit Paragraph Style Sheet dialog box

After you work with character styles, you can create or edit the paragraph style sheet. In the Style Sheet dialog box, use the New button to create a new paragraph style sheet. To change an existing paragraph style, click the style and then click the Edit button. The Edit Paragraph Style Sheet dialog box, shown in Figure 6-4, appears. In the sections that follow, we cover the four panes of Edit Paragraph Style Sheet dialog box in order. You can use these Edit Paragraph Style Sheet features in any order and ignore the ones that don't apply to the current style.

The General pane

The default pane is the General pane (see Figure 6-4).

The first two options are the same as their counterparts in the Edit Character Style Sheet dialog box:

- ✔ **Keyboard Equivalent** lets you assign a shortcut key to a paragraph style.

- ✔ **Based On** lets you make the paragraph style use a previously created style sheet's settings (and update the current style sheet if the style sheet it's based on is changed in the future).

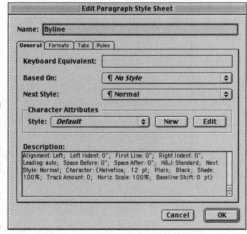

Figure 6-4:
The General pane of the Edit Paragraph Style Sheet dialog box.

The other settings are unique to the Edit Paragraph Style Sheet dialog box:

✔ **Next Style** lets you establish linked styles. For example, suppose you specify that a headline style always be followed by a byline style, which will always be followed by a body text style. If you choose Next Style, here's what happens after you enter a headline: As you type text into the QuarkXPress page, every time you enter a paragraph return after typing a byline, the style automatically changes to the Body Text style. If your style is used on paragraphs typically followed by other paragraphs using the same style, such as body text, leave Next Style set to Self.

✔ **Style** tells QuarkXPress which character style to use in this paragraph style (that's why we suggest that you create the character styles first). If you want to create a new character style, you can do so by clicking the New button. You can also edit an existing character style by picking it from the Style pop-up menu and then clicking the Edit button.

The Formats pane

Most of the work that goes into creating a paragraph style occurs in the Formats pane. Figure 6-5 shows this pane.

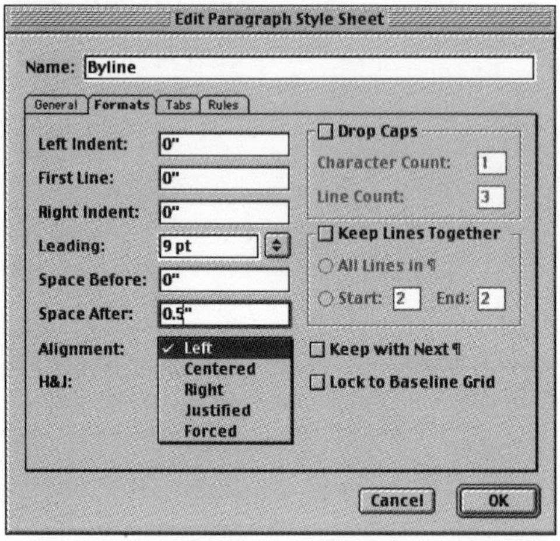

Figure 6-5:
The Formats pane of the Edit Paragraph Style Sheet dialog box.

Here are the options:

✔ **Left Indent** indents the entire paragraph's left margin by the amount you specify.

✔ **First Line** indents the first line of a paragraph — a common thing to do with body text. A typical setting makes the indent the same as the text's point size (equal to an em space).

✔ **Right Indent** indents the entire paragraph's right margin by the amount you specify.

You don't have to use the same measurement system in this — or any — dialog box. The Left Indent and Right Indent could appear in inches whereas the First Line could appear in picas and points. For example, if you want the first line to be an em space, which is the same as the point size, you can enter 0p9, which means 0 picas and 9 points, instead of figuring out its equivalent in inches. You could easily enter 9 pt to indicate 9 points.

✔ **Leading** sets the space between lines. Enter the leading you want, type **auto** to apply the Auto settings specified in the Preferences dialog box's Document Paragraph pane (choose Edit⇨Preferences⇨Preferences or press Option+Shift+⌘+Y or Ctrl+Alt+Shift+Y), or use the pop-up menu to select Auto.

✔ **Space Before** lets you insert a fixed amount of space before the paragraph. Note that this space is not inserted if the paragraph happens to start at the top of a page, column, or text box. An example of when to use this setting is for headlines within a story. You typically want some space between the text and the headline. Add it here.

✔ **Space After** is like Space Before, except it adds space after a paragraph. It's pretty rare that you use both on the same paragraph.

✔ **Alignment** tells QuarkXPress whether to align the text to the left margin, to align the text to the right margin, to center the text, or to align the text against both margins (justified). Note that Force Justify makes the last line of a paragraph align against both margins (rarely used), while the regular Justify option leaves the last line aligned only to the left.

✔ **H&J** is where you pick the hyphenation and tracking settings for the paragraph. You create such H&J sets by choosing Edit⇨H&Js or by pressing Option+⌘+H or Ctrl+Shift+F11. Chapter 8 covers this in detail.

We recommend that you always create an H&J set called None that has hyphenation disabled. For several kinds of text, such as headlines and bylines, you won't want the text to be hyphenated, so you need such an H&J set.

✔ **Drop Caps** lets you make the first character(s) in a paragraph large and dropped down into the text, as shown in Figure 6-6. This is a popular technique for introductions and conclusions. Use the Character Count box to indicate how many characters are to be oversized and dropped down (1 is typical); use Line Count to determine how deep the drop is (2, 3, and 4 are typical). We think drop caps are more effective if you boldface the dropped character(s) or change the font, as we did in the last two examples in Figure 6-6. If you have a huge drop cap, as in the bottom of the figure, you may not need a bold drop cap — it's a question of judgment and taste.

Including a drop cap in a different font than the rest of the paragraph is a common technique in publishing, so it's puzzling to see that QuarkXPress still can't set the paragraph style to make this font change for you. That means you need to create a drop cap character style and then, after you've applied the drop cap paragraph style, apply the character style to the dropped cap letter itself manually each time. (You could change the drop cap's font each time by using the Measurements palette or by choosing Style⇨Character [Shift+⌘+D or Ctrl+Shift+D], but using the character style ensures that every drop cap will have exactly the same settings.)

✔ **Keep Lines Together** ensures that a paragraph's lines are kept together, rather than split at a column break or page break. You can set this field so that all lines are kept together by selecting the All Lines in ¶ button. Another way to keep lines together is to specify how many lines in the beginning and end of a paragraph must be kept together by entering the desired values in the Start and End boxes and clicking the button next to the Start box.

Many typographers hate orphans and widows — not people who are orphaned or widowed, but text isolated from the rest of its paragraph. An orphan is the first line of text in a paragraph that is at the bottom of a column or page, isolated from the rest of its paragraph (on the next column or page); a widow is the last line of a paragraph that is by itself at the top of a page or column (see Figure 6-7). To prevent these typographic horrors, the typographically correct sector likes to set the Start and End fields to 2 to force QuarkXPress to avoid such lonely lines. However, incorporating those settings means that the bottoms of your columns may not align, because QuarkXPress may have to move text from the bottom of a column to prevent a widow or an orphan.

We agree that widows are a bad thing when it comes to printing, but we think orphans are just fine, so we recommend that you leave Start at 1 and set End at 2. To avoid the uneven column bottoms that result when QuarkXPress moves widowed text, add a few words to each of your documents' shorter columns — QuarkXPress puts back a line of text at the bottom of each column so all of your text aligns properly. (*Note:* If you read other typography publications, you may find definitions of widows and orphans that vary from those described above. We suggest that you stick with the *For Dummies* definitions which match those used in the QuarkXPress documentation and by most professional publishers. Understanding consistent instructions is easier.)

✔ **Keep with Next ¶** ensures that a paragraph does not separate from the paragraph that follows. For example, you wouldn't want a headline at the bottom of a column or page; to make sure the headline doesn't separate from the body text that follows, check Keep with Next ¶ in your headline paragraph style.

✔ **Lock to Baseline Grid** ensures that all text aligns to the baseline grid that you set up in the Paragraph pane of the Preferences dialog box (access the dialog by choosing Edit➪Preferences➪ Preferences, or by pressing Option+Shift+⌘+Y or Ctrl+Alt+Shift+Y). Figure 6-8 shows this pane and highlights the part that sets the baseline grid. Locking a paragraph to the baseline grid means that QuarkXPress ignores the leading specifications if needed to ensure that text aligns from column to column. If you use this feature, make sure you set the Increment amount the same as your body text's leading, so you don't get awkward gaps between paragraphs.

The Tabs pane

The Tabs pane lets you set up tabs in your paragraphs — handy for creating tables and aligning bullets and the text that follows them. Figure 6-9 shows the Tabs pane.

In the Tabs pane, you can't help but see a ruler that you use to set your tabs. Under the ruler you see buttons for each kind of tab: left-aligned, center-aligned, right-aligned, decimal-aligned, comma-aligned, and character-aligned (Align On). (If you choose Align On, enter the character you want the tab to align to in the Align On field.) The text aligns to the tab's location based on the type of alignment you choose. Figure 6-10 shows examples of all six types of alignments.

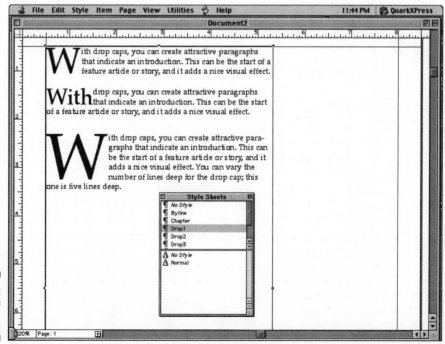

Figure 6-6:
Examples of
drop caps.

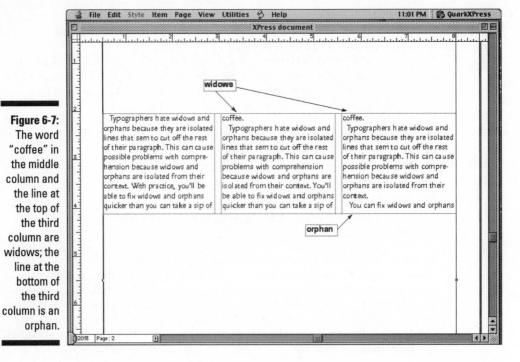

Figure 6-7:
The word "coffee" in the middle column and the line at the top of the third column are widows; the line at the bottom of the third column is an orphan.

Click the button for the alignment you want; then click the ruler where you want that tab to appear. If you miss the exact spot you want, just click the tab location and, holding down the mouse button, move the mouse to the left or right as needed until you get to the desired location. Notice how the Position box shows the current location.

Figure 6-8:
Set the baseline grid amount in the Preferences dialog box.

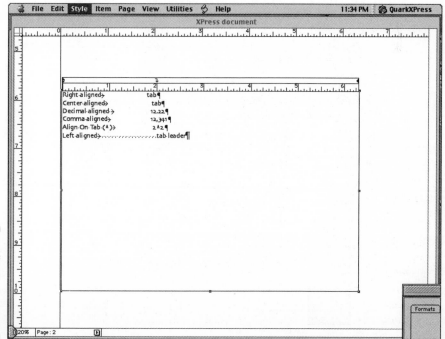

Figure 6-9:
The Tabs
pane of the
Edit
Paragraph
Style Sheet
dialog box.

If you prefer to be exact, you can just click the button for the alignment you want and then enter the position you want in the Position box. Enter a new number to change its position if you got it wrong the first time. When the new tab is where you want it, click the Set button to tell Quark you're done and ready to enter a new position for a new tab. You can alter a tab's position by clicking it in the ruler and entering a new value in the Position box.

Figure 6-10:
Examples of
the six tab
alignments
plus a tab
leader.

Either way you set the position, you can change the alignment by selecting the tab and clicking a new alignment button.

If you create several tabs and want to get rid of them all, just click the Clear All button. To delete an individual tab, select it with the mouse, hold down the mouse button, and drag the tab outside of the ruler. Release the mouse button, and the tab disappears. Or select the tab and press the Backspace key or the Delete or Del key.

When creating a tab, you may want a *leader* or *fill* character. For example, to get a series of dots between text in a table of contents and its page number, you'd have a tab between the text and the number. By giving that tab a fill character of a period (.), you get your row of dots. You can enter two fill characters in QuarkXPress; the tab alternates the two characters. For example, entering += as the fill characters results in a leader like +=+=+=+=+=+=+=. More commonly, you would have a period and a space as your two leader characters, so the periods are not packed too tightly together.

The Rules pane

Using the Rules pane, you can insert ruling lines above and/or below your paragraphs (see Figure 6-11). This feature is handy especially for underlining kickers (small-print text that appears below headlines), headlines, and other such elements. You can use the underline settings in the Edit Character Style Sheet dialog box, but those settings give you no control over the type of underline, its position, color, or pattern. In the Rules pane, you set the rules for these rules.

Figure 6-11:
The Rules pane of the Edit Paragraph Style Sheet dialog box.

First, decide whether you want the rules above and/or below your paragraph. Check the Rule Above and Rule Below boxes as appropriate. You can set the two rules independently, which is why you see the exact same specifications twice, once for each rule. You're not seeing double — QuarkXPress is simply giving you identical controls for each rule. Here's what you have control over:

- ✔ **Length** lets you choose between Text, which makes the rule the same width as the text (if the paragraph has multiple lines, the length of the rule will match the top line if you use Rule Above; the length of the rule will match the length of the last line of text if you use Rule Below) or Indents, which makes the rule a specific length.

- ✔ **From Left** tells QuarkXPress how far from the column's left margin to start the rule, if you selected Index in the Length pop-up menu.

- ✔ **From Right** tells QuarkXPress how far from the column's right margin to end the rule, if you selected Index in the Length pop-up menu.

- ✔ **Offset** is tricky. You can enter a percentage from 0% to 100% to move the rule away from the text, but the difference between 0% and 100% is just a point or two. Or you can enter a value like 1.0" or –9 pt to position the rule relative to the text. Larger positive numbers move the rule above the text's baseline; a value of 0 puts the rule at the baseline, while a negative number moves the rule below the baseline. (The maximum and minimum values depend on the point size and leading; QuarkXPress tells you when you exceed the specific text's limits.) You simply have to experiment with these settings until you get what you want.

- ✔ **Style** lets you select the rule style. The pop-up menu displays any rules defined in the Dashes & Stripes dialog box (Edit➪Dashes & Stripes); Chapter 12 covers this in detail.

- ✔ **Width** is the rule's thickness. Choose from the pop-up menu's sizes or enter your own in the field.

- ✔ **Color** lets you select a color for the rule. Any color defined in the document (see Chapter 15) appears in this list.

- ✔ **Shade** lets you set the percentage of the color selected (including black). Choose from the pop-up menu's sizes or enter your own in the field.

The QuarkXPress Style Sheets dialog box has a nifty feature that makes style management incredibly simple. In the Show pop-up menu, you can choose which style sheets you want to display: All Style Sheets, Paragraph Style Sheets, Character Style Sheets, Style Sheets in Use, and Style Sheets Not Used. Those last two come in really handy.

Making styles happen

You can apply a style in three ways (two of which — Options 1 and 2 — appear in Figure 6-12):

- **Option 1:** Use the Paragraph Style Sheet and Character Style Sheet menu options.

- **Option 2:** Use the Style Sheets palette (at the right side of Figure 6-12) by choosing View⇨Show Style Sheets or by pressing F11. This option is our favorite way to apply styles in most cases.

- **Option 3:** Use the keyboard shortcut, if you defined one in the Style Sheets dialog box. (In Figure 6-12, we did not invoke a shortcut key.) Although this option is the fastest method, use it only for very commonly used styles because you need to remember the keyboard shortcuts that you assign.

If you aren't convinced that style sheets can save you a great deal of time, we suggest you take a few minutes and give them a try, and then compare formatting a document with them to formatting a document without them. Most desktop publishers find style sheets to be terrific time-savers, and we think you will, too.

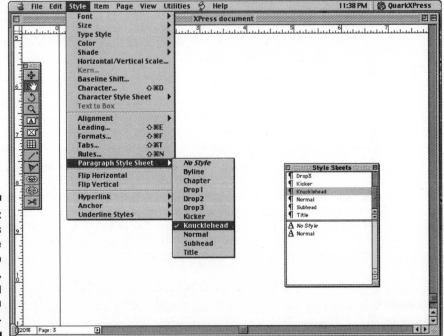

Figure 6-12:
QuarkXPress offers three ways to apply style, including menus and a palette.

Altering Styles

Decisions, decisions. Just when you think you've created a great style, you think again and decide to make some little changes to make it even better — you know, add half a point to the size of your headline, make your byline italic, change the leading on your body copy.

Again, you can make changes to a style easily: Simply open the Style Sheets dialog box, select the style sheet you want to change, and click Edit. You then can change attributes as you want. You also can use this approach to create new styles based on current ones or to create duplicate styles and modify them to make new ones.

If you want to compare two styles, QuarkXPress has a great feature that makes comparing easy. Select two styles in the Style Sheets dialog box (⌘+click or Ctrl+click the second style so that the first style remains selected as well). Then hold down the Option or Alt key and watch the Append button become the Compare button. Click Compare, and a dialog box like the one shown in Figure 6-13 appears. With this Compare feature, you can now determine quickly how styles differ, making it easier for you to identify the styles that you need to alter to ensure typographic consistency in your document.

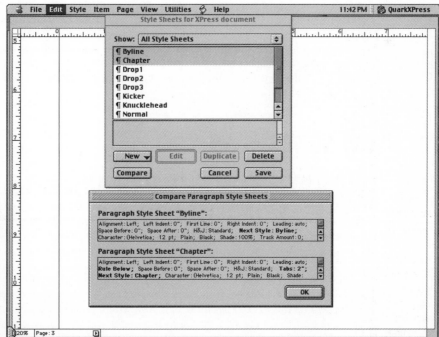

Figure 6-13:
The Compare option shows the differences between two styles.

Based-on styles

When you create styles for a document, you probably want several similar styles, perhaps with some styles even being variations of others. For example, you may want both a Body Text style *and* a style for bulleted lists that's based on the Body Text style.

No problem. QuarkXPress uses a technique called *based-on formatting* in its styles. By selecting the Based On option in the Edit Character Style dialog box, you can tell QuarkXPress to base the Bulleted Text character style on the Body Text character style (in which you defined typeface, point size, leading, justification, hyphenation, indentation, tabs, and other attributes). You then modify the Bulleted Text character style to accommodate bullets — by changing the indentation, for example. The great thing about based-on formatting is that if you later decide to change the typeface in Body Text, the typeface automatically changes in Bulleted Text and in all other character styles that you created or edited based on Body Text. Think of it as a shortcut that saves you a great deal of work in maintaining consistent styles.

Duplicating styles

Another nifty way to change an existing style or create a new one is to duplicate an existing style and then edit the attributes in that duplicate.

Duplicating a style is similar to creating a based-on style, except that the new style does not automatically update if you modify the style it is duplicated from — unless you base the style that you duplicated or edited on another style.

Replacing styles

Did you know that you can replace style sheets in your document as easily as you can change text? In fact, you use the same method — choose Edit➪Find/Change, or press ⌘+F or Ctrl+F. When you use this feature, you may wonder how you can replace style sheets because you see no obvious option to do so. The trick is to uncheck the Ignore Attributes check box; doing so enlarges the dialog box to make room for new options (see Figure 6-14).

To replace one style sheet with another, check the Style Sheet check boxes in the Find What and Change To sections of the Find/Change dialog box and then use the pop-up menus to specify which style sheet should replace another. When you do this, make sure you're at the beginning of your document or story — QuarkXPress only searches from the text cursor's location, ignoring text before it. (A *story* is the QuarkXPress term for text in the current text box and any text boxes linked to it.) To replace the style throughout the document, make sure that the Document check box is selected; to replace the style only in the current story, make sure the Document check box is unchecked.

Click the Find Next button to find the first occurrence of the style you want to replace. Then click Change All to have QuarkXPress replace all occurrences of that style from that point on, or click Change Then Find to replace the found text's style and look for the next occurrence, or click Change to change the found text's style, but not look for the next occurrence.

Figure 6-14:
The Find/
Change
dialog box
with the
Style Sheet
option
checked.

Note that replacing a style sheet does not get rid of that style sheet — it simply retags all the text that uses the original style sheet with the new style sheet.

Importing Styles

Sometimes you find yourself in a situation where you already have style sheets in one QuarkXPress document that are *just right* for what you need in another one. Have no fear — you don't need to start the process all over again. Just copy styles from one document to another.

Copying styles between documents

You copy styles between documents by clicking the Append button in the Style Sheets dialog box to open the Append Style Sheets dialog box (see Figure 6-15). This dialog box is similar to the dialog box for opening a QuarkXPress document. You can change drives and directories as needed to select the QuarkXPress document that has the style sheet you want. You can also append style sheets through the Append dialog box (choose File⇨Append), which also lets you append other settings, such as color definitions.

To append a style (or styles), simply select the names of individual styles you want to copy. If a style you select to append has the same name as one already in the current document, you get to choose whether to override the current style with the one you want to copy, cancel the appending of that style, or append the style anyhow but give it a new name.

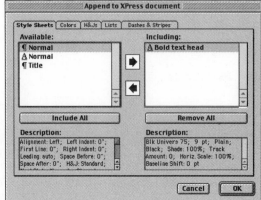

Figure 6-15:
The Append
Style Sheets
dialog box.

Importing styles from a word processor

Some people create text right inside the text boxes of a QuarkXPress document (using the QuarkXPress built-in text editor). Others prefer to use a separate word-processing program for drafting the text, and then import the text into QuarkXPress later. Either way works fine, and both methods let you take advantage of style sheets.

QuarkXPress lets you import paragraph styles created in Microsoft Word and Corel WordPerfect. To make the process of importing text files that include style sheets work smoothly, we suggest that you first put a check mark in the Include Style Sheets box at the bottom of the Get Text box (see Figure 6-16).

You also use the Include Style Sheets option if you want to import text saved in the XPress Tags format. Although the purpose of the XPress Tags format is to embed style tags and other formatting information in your text, you still must remind QuarkXPress to read those tags during import. Otherwise, QuarkXPress imports your text as an ASCII file and treats all the embedded tags as regular text without acting on them. (If you want to find out more about XPress Tags, refer to the Appendix of the QuarkXPress documentation.)

If you check the Include Style Sheets check box for word-processor formats that have no style sheets, QuarkXPress ignores the setting. Thus, if you typically import style sheets with your text, get into the habit of always checking this box; checking the box causes no problems when importing other text formats.

Figure 6-16:
Check the
Include
Style Sheets
option when
you import
a word-
processor
document
that has
style sheets
associated
with it.

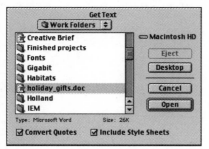

One final point: If the imported style sheet has a style tag that uses a name already in use by the QuarkXPress document, you have the option of renaming the imported style tag or ignoring it and using the existing QuarkXPress style tag in its place. Resolving style conflicts so easily is nice, and this capability is just one more reason to use style sheets.

As you can tell, we are style-sheet fans to the core. Style sheets are a cool invention. They save you time. And saving time saves you money. And we all know that saving money is a good thing.

Chapter 7

Working with Special Characters

● ●

In This Chapter

▶ Generating typographic quotes and dashes automatically

▶ Understanding ligatures

▶ Simplifying use of accents and international characters

▶ Using special hyphens and spaces

▶ Working with bullets

▶ Adding dingbats

▶ Using special symbols

● ●

*B*efore desktop publishing, you could distinguish homegrown publications from the professionally produced kind by the difference in typography. Homegrown publications were typewritten and either dittoed, mimeographed, or photocopied; professional publications were typeset. Anyone could spot the difference: Homegrown publications, for example, contained two hyphens (- -) as a dash, whereas professional publications used the (—) character. Not to mention the fact that professionally-produced publications also generally featured accents on letters, different styles of characters, a whole slew of symbols, and even characters of different sizes.

Then came desktop publishing. Soon anyone with a Mac or PC had access to the same typeset characters. The only problem was that most people didn't know how to use these characters. You could use all sorts of keyboard commands get these characters, but who could remember them all? So you kept seeing (- -) and (') and (") in documents that looked professional; you could tell that the documents had come off of someone's laser printer because of those telltale typewriter characters.

But working with special characters soon became simpler with QuarkXPress. At first, Quark would convert the typewriter dashes and quotes into typographic dashes and quotes automatically — but only when you imported text. Later, Quark added the ability to generate those quotation characters as you typed text. Automating the quotes goes a long way toward helping your publications look professionally produced. Today, it's nearly impossible to tell by the characters alone whether a publication is professional or nonprofessional.

Unfortunately, you still have to type in em dashes the hard way — by using special keyboard commands. We're mystified that Quark hasn't added this obvious feature by now. It's further mystifying that the Microsoft Word for Windows automated feature to convert hyphens to an em dash uses an en dash instead, and when QuarkXPress for Mac imports Word for Windows files, these dashes are often replaced with the æ character. We recommend that you turn off the AutoFormat as You Type feature in Word for Windows (choose Tools⇨AutoCorrect) so the two hyphens stay as two hyphens. QuarkXPress will properly convert those to em dashes during file import.

Typographic Characters

Your otherwise-humble authors are typographic snobs, so we think everyone should use the curly quotes and the long-line dash instead of the typewriter symbols. Why? Because professional typographers always use them, and they've become synonymous with professionalism. And besides, they're so easy to use that you have no excuse not to use them. Table 7-1 shows the typographic versus typewriter characters that you'll care about most often. It also shows shortcuts for quotes and dashes in Windows and on a Mac.

Table 7-1	Typographic versus Typewriter Characters	
Character	*Typographic Character*	*Typewriter Character*
Em dash	—	-- (two hyphens)
En dash	–	- (single hyphen)
Apostrophe	'	'
Single quotes	' '	'
Double quotes	" "	"

Quotes and dashes

One of the first things you should do in QuarkXPress is configure it to type in the professional characters for you automatically. In addition, make sure QuarkXPress is set to convert quotes and double hyphens on import.

Entering curly quotes

To do so, choose Edit⇨Preferences⇨Preferences, or press Option+Shift+⌘+Y (or Ctrl+Alt+Shift+Y) to activate the Interactive pane on the left side the Preferences dialog box (see Figure 7-1). You can ignore most of the dialog box for now; only the options highlighted in the middle affect typography. Make sure that the Smart Quotes option is checked: Smart Quotes converts quotes as you type (sorry, as we said, it *still* won't do dashes). Smart Quotes should be checked by default.

If you're not publishing in English, you can select a different set of quote characters through the Format pop-up menu, shown in Figure 7-1.

TIP

For many preferences, to make them affect all QuarkXPress documents, you have to make sure that no document is open before you change the preferences. Otherwise, the changed preferences will apply only to that document. But any preferences set in the Interactive pane of the Preferences dialog box affect all documents, whether or not a document was open when you set those preferences. Here's a case where you can lower your guard and not worry about whether documents are open or not.

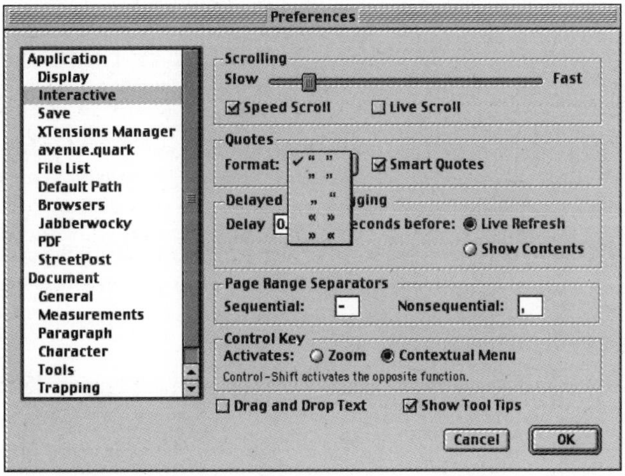

Figure 7-1:
The Interactive pane lets you set up automatic conversion of keyboard quotes into their typographic equivalents.

Preferences

Application
  Display
  Interactive
  Save
  XTensions Manager
  avenue.quark
  File List
  Default Path
  Browsers
  Jabberwocky
  PDF
  StreetPost
Document
  General
  Measurements
  Paragraph
  Character
  Tools
  Trapping

Scrolling
Slow ———————————— Fast
☑ Speed Scroll   ☐ Live Scroll

Quotes
Format: ☑ Smart Quotes

Delayed ... ging
Delay 0. ...conds before: ⦿ Live Refresh
                           ○ Show Contents

Page Range Separators
Sequential: [-]   Nonsequential: [,]

Control Key
Activates: ○ Zoom ⦿ Contextual Menu
Control-Shift activates the opposite function.

☐ Drag and Drop Text   ☑ Show Tool Tips

[Cancel]   [OK]

Converting quotes and dashes

In text files that you import, you can ensure that QuarkXPress converts the quotes and, yes, even the double hyphens to dashes, by checking the Convert Quotes box in the Get Text dialog box. You can access the Get Text dialog box by choosing File⇨Get Text, or by pressing ⌘+E or Ctrl+E. Actually, you don't even have to check the Convert Quotes check box; QuarkXPress leaves the box checked for all future imports until, of course, you uncheck it. Figure 7-2 shows how the Preferences dialog box looks with the Convert Quotes box checked.

When double hyphens convert to em dashes, you get *breaking em dashes.* A breaking em dash is one that can separate from its preceding text and appear as the first character in a line. Most editors prefer not to start a line with a dash, so they manually enter nonbreaking em dashes. See Table 7-2 for the keyboard shortcuts for nonbreaking em dashes.

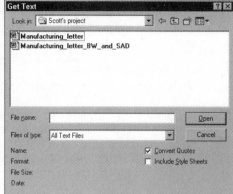

Figure 7-2:
When
importing
text, check
the Convert
Quotes
box to
automatic-
ally convert
keyboard
dashes and
quotes.

The Mac has many built-in shortcuts for special characters and symbols, and QuarkXPress adds some of its own. Windows also supports many symbols, although it uses special codes for most, rather than keyboard shortcuts. When you use keyboard shortcuts, keep the following conditions in mind:

- Not all keyboard shortcuts are available in all programs. This is truer in Windows than on the Mac, because Windows programs are generally less consistent than Mac programs.

- Not all symbols are supported in all fonts; for symbols listed as *not supported,* you may be able to find a symbol or pi font that includes the symbol (as used here, *not supported* means that the symbol is not available in standard fonts).

- To use the Windows codes, press and hold the Alt key and enter the four-digit numeral code from the numeric keypad, not from the numbers on the keyboard (above the letters). The Mac doesn't use an equivalent numeric system; instead, all characters are accessible through some shortcut combination.

Table 7-2 shows shortcuts for quotes and dashes in Windows and on a Mac.

Table 7-2	Shortcuts for Quotes and Dashes	
Character	*Mac Shortcut*	*Windows Shortcut*
Open double quote (")*	Option+Shift+[	Shift+Alt+[*or* Alt+0147
Close double quote (")*	Option+Shift+]	Shift+Alt+] *or* Alt+0148
Open French double quote («)*	Option+\	Ctrl+Alt+[*or* Alt+0171

Character	Mac Shortcut	Windows Shortcut
Close French double (»)*	Option+Shift+\	Ctrl+Alt+] *or* Alt+0187quote
Open single quote (')*	Option+[	Alt+[
Close single quote (')*	Option+]	Alt+]
Breaking em dash (—)**	Option+Shift+ - (hyphen)	Ctrl+Shift+= *or* Alt+0151
Nonbreaking en dash (–)	Option+- (hyphen)	Ctrl+= *or* Alt+0150
Nonbreaking em dash (—)	Option+⌘+=	Ctrl+Shift+Alt+=

Ligatures (only for Macs)

Ligatures are linked-together characters in many higher-end publications where you find the combination of *f* and *i* typeset not as *fi* but as *fi*. Such a combination avoids having the dot on the *i* get in the way of the top curve or the bar of the *f*. In QuarkXPress, you have automatic access to an *fl* ligature, an *ffi* ligature, and an *ffl* ligature.

Figure 7-3 shows some ligatures. Other ligatures than these occur in some fonts, but QuarkXPress automatically handles only these four. For others (assuming that the font supports other ligatures), you have to enter the ligature code manually (a process we describe in Table 7-3).

To use ligatures consistently in all your publications, first make sure no documents are open. Then, go to the Character pane in the Preferences dialog box (Edit⇨Preferences⇨Preferences or Option+Shift+⌘+Y). Here, you set up the treatment of ligatures, which are special forms of characters that are linked together. Figure 7-4 shows the appropriate pane, with the ligature section highlighted.

Windows doesn't support ligatures. When you open a Mac file that has ligatures into QuarkXPress for Windows, QuarkXPress translates the ligatures back to regular characters. If you move the file back to the Mac, the ligatures reappear. There's a slight chance that such translations could affect the line length of your document, so double-check to make sure you don't gain or lose a line or two if you try this. In general, if you're working in a cross-platform publishing environment, you should not use ligatures.

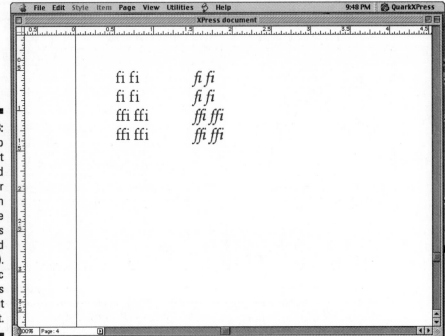

Figure 7-3:
Ligatures up close (first column) and the regular version of the characters (second column). Italic versions appear at the right.

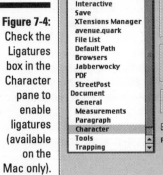

Figure 7-4:
Check the Ligatures box in the Character pane to enable ligatures (available on the Mac only).

Now you see them, now you don't

If you use ligatures, you may find that sometimes the combined characters appear as a ligature and sometimes they don't. Ligatures vary because of the spacing computations used by QuarkXPress.

Ligatures make sense when characters are close together, because that's when pieces of the characters may overlap (which is the problem that ligatures were designed to solve). But when text is spaced more widely, the characters won't overprint; in such a case, you have no reason to combine them. In fact, if you

did combine them, your document would look weird because most letters would have space between them *except for* the ligatures.

QuarkXPress automatically figures out when the characters should be combined into ligatures and when they shouldn't, so don't worry about it. In fact, QuarkXPress is so smart that if you did a search for the word *first* and the *fi* was a ligature in your text, QuarkXPress would find the ligature even though you entered *fi* in the Find dialog box.

Table 7-3	Shortcuts for Ligatures	
Character	*Mac Shortcut*	*Windows Shortcut*
fi	Option+Shift+5	*not supported*
fl	Option+Shift+6	*not supported*
ffi	*no shortcut*	*not supported*
ffl	*no shortcut*	*not supported*

When you use the codes in Table 7-3, you actually enter the ligature character manually; when QuarkXPress generates the ligatures for you, it remembers the actual letters in your document but substitutes the ligature characters for them both onscreen and when printing. Note that these coded ligature characters may appear in your Find palette as a square. That's okay: QuarkXPress still searches for the actual character. Also note that using codes to generate ligatures, rather than using the QuarkXPress automatic ligature feature, causes the spelling checker to flag words with the coded-in ligatures as suspect words. The bottom line: Don't code in ligatures. It's not worth the hassle.

Accented and Foreign Characters

You don't have to use accents for words like *café* that came to English from another language. *Cafe* is quite acceptable. But adding the accent to the *e* gives the word a bit more sophistication (plus it helps people pronounce it *ka-fay* rather than *kayfe!*). Of course, if your publication is international or multilingual, you want to use the international characters and accents.

First, decide how you want to treat accents on capital letters. If you use accents, you always use them on lowercase letters, but you have an option for uppercase letters — as long as you're consistent and either always use the accents on capitalized letters or never use them within the same publication. QuarkXPress lets you make consistent decisions on accents with ease.

If you select the Accents for All Caps option in the Character pane of the Preferences dialog box, all accented letters keep their accents when capitalized. If you don't select that option, the accent is removed when the letters are capitalized and reinstated when the letters are lowercased. With this option, you can always add the accents as you type and then have QuarkXPress take care of handling the uppercase letters.

So how do you get the accents in the first place? Table 7-4 shows the various codes. (Windows supports hundreds of more special characters and accented characters, available through Word's Insert Symbol feature, but we don't include these because they don't have special codes and aren't supported in QuarkXPress (Windows or Mac) unless you have fonts with those characters. Table 7-4 shows symbols that work in QuarkXPress with most common fonts.) Note that the Mac and Windows platforms handle accents and foreign characters differently, as we explain in the next two sections.

Table 7-4	Shortcuts for Accents and Foreign Characters	
Character	*Mac Shortcut*	*Windows Shortcut*
acute (´)*	Option+E *letter*	' *letter*
cedilla (ç)*	*see Ç and ç*	' *letter*
circumflex (^)*	Option+I *letter*	^ *letter*
grave (`)*	Option+` *letter*	' *letter*
tilde (~)*	Option+N *letter*	~ *letter*
trema (¨)*	Option+U *letter*	" *letter*
umlaut (¨)*	Option+U *letter*	" *letter*

Character	Mac Shortcut	Windows Shortcut
Á	Option+E A	' A *or* Alt+0193
á	Option+E a	' a *or* Alt+0225
À	Option+' A	` A *or* Alt+0192
à	Option+' a	` a *or* Alt+0224
Ä	Option+U A	" A *or* Alt+0196
ä	Option+U a	" a *or* Alt+0228
Ã	Option+N A	~ A *or* Alt+0195
ã	Option+N a	~ a *or* Alt+0227
Â	Option+I A	^ A *or* Alt+0194
â	Option+I a	^ a *or* Alt+0226
Å	Option+Shift+A	Alt+0197
å	Option+A	Alt+0229
Æ	Option+Shift+`	Alt+0198
æ	Option+`	Alt+0230 *or* Ctrl+Alt+Z
Ç	Option+Shift+C	` C *or* Alt+0199
ç	Option+C	` c *or* Alt+0231 *or* Ctrl+Alt+,
Ð	*not supported*	Alt+0208
ð	*not supported*	Alt+0240
É	Option+E E	' E *or* Alt+0201
é	Option+E e	' e *or* Alt+0233
È	Option+` E	` E *or* Alt+0200
è	Option+` e	` e *or* Alt+0232
Ë	Option+U E	" E *or* Alt+0203
ë	Option+U e	" e *or* Alt+0235
Ê	Option+I E	^ E *or* Alt+0202
ê	Option+I e	^ e *or* Alt+0234
Í	Option+E I	' I *or* Alt+-205

(continued)

Table 7-4 *(continued)*

Character	Mac Shortcut	Windows Shortcut
í	Option+E i	' i *or* Alt+0237
Ì	Option+` I	` I *or* Alt+0204
ì	Option+` i	` i *or* Alt+0236
Ï	Option+U I	" I *or* Alt+0207
ï	Option+U i	" I *or* Alt+0239
Î	Option+I I	^ I *or* Alt+0206
î	Option+I i	^ I *or* Alt+0238
Ñ	Option+N N	~ N *or* Alt+0209
ñ	Option+N n	~ n *or* Alt+0241
Ó	Option+E O	' O *or* Alt+0211
ó	Option+E o	' o *or* Alt+0243 *or* Ctrl+Alt+O
Ò	Option+` O	` O *or* Alt+0210
ò	Option+` o	` o *or* Alt+0242
Ö	Option+U O	" O *or* Alt+0214
ö	Option+U o	" o *or* Alt+0246
Õ	Option+N O	~ O *or* Alt+0213
õ	Option+N o	~ o *or* Alt+0245
Ô	Option+I O	^ O *or* Alt+0212
ô	Option+I o	^ o *or* Alt+0244
Ø	Option+Shift+O	Alt+0216
ø	Option+O	Alt+0248 *or* Ctrl+Alt+L
Œ	Option+Shift+Q	Alt+0140
œ	Option+Q	Alt+0156
Þ	*not supported*	Alt+0222
þ	*not supported*	Alt+0254
ß	*not supported*	Ctrl+Alt+S or Alt+0223
Š	*not supported*	Alt+0138

Character	Mac Shortcut	Windows Shortcut
š	*not supported*	Alt+0154
Ú	Option+E U	' U or Alt+0218
ú	Option+E u	' u or Alt+0250 *or* Ctrl+Alt+U
Ù	Option+` U	` U or Alt+0217
ù	Option+` u	` u or Alt+0249
Ü	Option+U U	" U or Alt+0220
ü	Option+U u	" u or Alt+0252
Û	Option+I U	^ U or Alt+0219
û	Option+I u	^ u or Alt+0251
Ý	*not supported*	` Y or Alt+0221
ý	*not supported*	` y or Alt+0253
Ÿ	Option+U Y	" Y *or* Alt+0159
ÿ	Option+U y	" y *or* Alt+0255
Spanish open exclamation (¡)	Option+1	Ctrl+Alt+1 *or* Alt+-0161
Spanish open question (¿)	Option+Shift+/	Ctrl+Alt+/ *or* Alt+0191
French open double quote («)**	Option+\	Ctrl+Alt+[*or* Alt+0171
French close double quote (»)**	Option+Shift+\	Ctrl+Alt+] *or* Alt+0187

* On the Mac, enter the shortcut for the accent and then type the letter to be accented. For example, to get é, type Option+E and then the letter e. In Windows, if the keyboard layout is set to United States-International — via the Keyboard icon in the Windows Control Panel — you can enter the accent signifier and then type the letter (for example, type ' and then the letter e to get é). To avoid an accent (for example, if you want to begin a quote — such as "A man" rather than have Ä man") type a space after the accent character — for example, " then space then A, rather than " then A.

** Automatically generated if you select the Smart Quotes option in the Preferences dialog box and the French quotes in the Quote pop-up list, also in the Preferences dialog box.

Pretty daunting, you say? Relax. It's not as bad as it looks. Just follow the advice in the following two sections.

Because the process for using accents and foreign characters on Windows differs significantly from the Mac, we cover the procedures for the two platforms separately.

Foreign characters in Windows

For the six most common accent marks — the grave (`), the acute (´), the circumflex (^), the tilde (~), the cedilla (¸), and the umlaut or trema (¨) — you can have Windows automatically generate the accented character by first entering a character that invokes the accent you want and then the letter you want it applied to. Table 7-4 shows these characters: ' for grave, ' for acute and cedilla, ^ for circumflex, ~ for tilde, and " for umlaut (or trema). Thus, ' followed by an *o* results in *ó*. If you type a combination and get two characters, rather than an accented character, it means that font doesn't support that particular accented letter.

For Windows to generate these accented characters, you need to set it to use the US-International keyboard layout. Figure 7-5 shows the sequence.

First, you go to the Windows Control Panel, in which you click the Keyboard icon. (The Control Panel usually resides in the Start button's main menu, so you can usually access it via Start⇨Settings⇨Control Panel, unless it was moved elsewhere.) That opens up the Keyboard dialog box also shown in the figure. Go to the Language pane (in Windows 2000, this is called Input Locales), where you click the Properties button to change the Keyboard Layout option from United States to United States-International.

Sometimes when you set Windows to use the United States-International keyboard layout, you get frustrated. You type along, minding your own business, and all of a sudden you get an accented character instead of the quoted text you wanted. For example, you type *"A man...* but get *Ä man...* a instead. What to do? Get into the habit of typing a space after the ', ", and ' characters. Allowing for that extra measly space prevents unintended, spontaneous accents. Why? Because typing a space after those specific characters — or, for that matter, after the ^ and ~, too — tells Windows to type those characters rather than prepare for the possibility of adding an accent to the next character.

For some foreign characters, you have to enter a specific code. For example, no accent code exists to generate the *hacek* used in eastern European languages (such as for š), so you have to enter, for example, the code Alt+0154 (using the numerals on the numeric keypad, not the numerals above the letter keys) to get lowercase s with a hacek or Alt+0138. In some cases, you use keyboard shortcuts to get these foreign characters, such as Ctrl+Alt+Z to get the diphthong (æ) character. Table 7-4 shows these codes and shortcuts. You also can use these shortcuts if you don't use the United

States-International keyboard layout. Note that some programs may use the shortcuts for something else, in which case you can't use them to generate the foreign character.

What do you do in those cases? Read on.

A few visual options can help you as well. You can use the Character Map software that comes with Windows. (It should be in the Accessories group — accessed via Start➪Programs➪Accessories — unless someone moved it; if this is the case, run the Windows setup and select it for installation.) We move Character Map to our Startup group so that we always have it available in the Start menu as a minimized icon. Figure 7-6 shows the Character Map.

Figure 7-5:
By changing your keyboard layout to United States-International, you can have Windows automatically create accented characters.

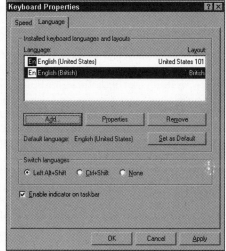

Figure 7-6:
The Character Map utility lets you select special characters for use in your document.

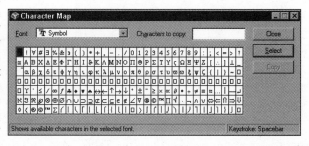

Notice how the Character Map magnifies the character that your pointer is currently on? It also displays the code for the selected character and lets you select and copy characters to the Windows Clipboard so that you can paste them into your text. You can even change fonts if the character you want is available in a different font than your text uses. (A choice of fonts comes in very handy when inserting foreign characters, like Greek or Cyrillic, not available in standard fonts.) We change fonts all the time and suspect that you may, too.

If you close Character Map, you have to relaunch it from the Accessories or Startup group (or whatever group you put it in). Unfortunately, you can't easily prevent this, so try to get in the habit of minimizing.

When you create your text, you can also use the special symbol features that come with your favorite word processor. Whether you use Microsoft Word 6 or up (via Insert⇨Symbol) or WordPerfect 6 or up (Insert⇨Character, or Shift+F11), you have an option to insert special characters from a Character Map-like list. Figure 7-7 shows two columns. Word lets you assign your own shortcuts for symbols and foreign characters (for use within Word only); WordPerfect ships with TrueType fonts in several character sets (including Greek, Cyrillic, Japanese, Hebrew, Arabic, mathematical, and phonetic).

QuarkXPress 5 necessarily reads the latest versions of Word or WordPerfect. The latest versions supported are Word 97/2000 (Windows) or 98/2001 (Mac) and WordPerfect 6 (Windows) or 3.5 (Mac). If you have a later version of Word or WordPerfect, either save your files in a supported version or see if Quark has an updated import filter on its Web site (www.quark.com).If you use those programs, you need to save your files in a previous format: Windows Word 97/2000 (8.0), 95 (7.0), or 6.0; Mac Word 2001/98, 6.0, 5.*x*, 4.0, or 3.0; Windows WordPerfect 6.*x* and 5.*x*; and Mac WordPerfect 3.*x*.

Figure 7-7:
The Insert Character options in Word and Word-Perfect (Mac versions) let you select special characters for use in your document.

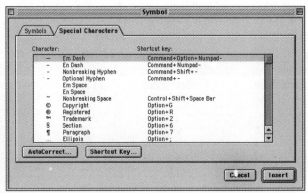

Finally, if the foreign character you want simply is not available in your font, you may need to buy a version of the font that has the characters you want. Generally, you can find Cyrillic, Greek, eastern European, Hebrew, Arabic, Thai, Kanji, and other character sets for popular fonts like Times and Helvetica; in a pinch, you can use one of these characters with a similar font like Palatino or Universe. But if you use decorative or other less-universal fonts, you may not be able to get a version with the special characters you need. And keep in mind that the Symbol font that comes with Windows includes most Greek letters.

Foreign characters on the Mac

For the five most common western European accent marks — the *grave* (`), the *acute* (´), the *circumflex* (^), the *tilde* (~), and the *umlaut* or *trema* (¨) — you can have the Mac automatically generate the accented character by first entering the code for the accent you want and then the letter you want it applied to. You'll see these codes in Table 7-4: Option+' for grave, Option+E for acute, Option+I for circumflex, Option+N for tilde, and Option+U for umlaut (or trema). Thus, Option+E followed by an *o* results in ó. If you type a combination and get two characters (rather than an accented character), you've just discovered that the font you're using doesn't support that particular accented letter.

For some characters, you have to enter a specific code. For example, no accent code exists to generate the *cedilla* in ç, so you have to enter the code Option+C to get the whole character. Table 7-4 shows these characters as well.

A few specific visual options help you as well. For example, you can use the Key Caps software that comes with the Mac, shown in Figure 7-8. (You can find the KeyCaps software under the Apple menu or, if you removed the software or never installed it, you'll find it with your Mac OS installation software.) The Key Caps utility shows you keyboard layouts and lets you select the characters you want; it also displays the shortcuts for the characters. To find a character in KeyCaps, hold the Option, ⌘, and other keys to see what's available for keyboard combinations using them. The Mac-only PopChar Pro utility ($29, from Uni Software Plus at www.unisoft.co.at) is a great character-selection program that takes KeyCaps to a whole new level.

When you create your text, you can also use the special symbol feature that comes with Microsoft Word 6.0 and up (Insert⇨Symbol). The symbol feature in Word has an option to insert special characters from a KeyCap-like list. Also, Word lets you assign your own shortcuts for symbols and foreign characters (for use within Word only). Figure 7-9 shows the Symbol dialog box used in Word.

Figure 7-8:
The Key
Caps utility
lets you
select
special
characters,
including
accents.

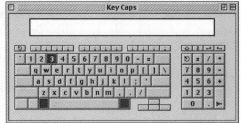

Finally, if the foreign character you want simply is not available in your font, you may need to buy a version of the font that has the characters you want. Generally, you find Cyrillic, Greek, eastern European, Hebrew, Arabic, Thai, Kanji, and other character sets for popular fonts like Times and Helvetica; in a pinch, you can use one of these characters with a similar font like Palatino or Universe. But if you use decorative or other less-universal fonts, you may not be able to get a version with the special characters you need. And keep in mind that the Symbol font that comes with the Mac includes most Greek letters.

Figure 7-9:
The Symbol
dialog box in
Microsoft
Word lets
you assign
shortcuts
for symbols
and foreign
characters.

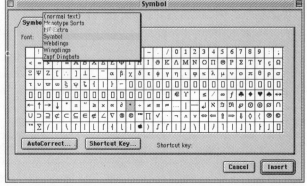

Special Punctuation

"What's the deal with punctuation?" you may ask. "That's what grammar books are for." True enough, but you can use some tricks to access special punctuation in addition to the typographic versions of quotes and dashes we talk about earlier in this chapter. You can't automate the other punctuation you may need — QuarkXPress won't substitute, for example, an ellipsis (...) when you type three periods (. . .). Besides, you may not even know how to access these characters because they're not on your computer. The sections that follow show you how to get those characters. Table 7-5 shows the shortcuts to get them into your document.

Table 7-5	Shortcuts for Other Punctuation	
Character	*Mac Shortcut*	*Windows Shortcut*
Ellipsis (...)	Option+; (semicolon)	Ctrl+Alt+. (period) *or* Alt+0133
En bullet (•)	Option+8	Shift+Alt+8 *or* Alt+0149
Nonbreaking hyphen (-)	⌘+=	Ctrl+Shift+hyphen
Discretionary (soft hyphen (-))	⌘+- (hyphen)	Ctrl+-(hyphen)
Nonbreaking en dash (–)	Option+- (hyphen)	Ctrl+= *or* Alt+0150
Nonbreaking space	⌘+spacebar	Ctrl+spacebar
Breaking en space	Option+spacebar	Ctrl+Shift+6
Nonbreaking en space	Option+⌘+spacebar	Ctrl+Shift+Alt+6
Breaking punctuation space	Shift+spacebar	Shift+spacebar
Nonbreaking punctuation space	Shift+⌘+spacebar	Ctrl+Shift+spacebar
Breaking flexible space	Option+Shift+ spacebar	Ctrl+Shift+5
Nonbreaking flexible space	Option+⌘+spacebar	Ctrl+Shift+Alt+5

Bullets (all nonlethal)

A *bullet* is a form of punctuation that starts an element in a list. On a typewriter, you use an asterisk (*) to indicate a bullet. But in desktop publishing (and in modern word processing), you have the real thing: the character that typographers call an *en bullet* (•).

You can find *many* more bullets than the en bullet that we all know and love. First, bullets don't even have to be round. They can be any shape — squares, stars, arrows, or triangles. They can be hollow or solid. They can be a small version of a corporate logo. They could be some other symbol — anything that clearly demarcates the start of a new item. Take a look at the symbol characters in Table 7-6 and also look at what symbols come with the Symbol and Zapf Dingbats fonts on most computers. (A *dingbat* is a symbol that ends a story or serves as a graphical embellishment for a certain type of text. It's sort of like a bullet — one that you can use at the beginning of each byline, for example, at the beginning of a continued line, or at the end of the text so that you know a story is over.) While you're at it, check out the Wingdings fonts that ships with Windows and with the Mac version of Microsoft's Word and Office software. Figure 7-10 shows some example bullets.

You can use tons of symbols as bullets. For now, though, just make sure that you don't use an asterisk when you can use a bullet — it would be too tacky for words.

You can set Word for Windows to use a shortcut for the bullet character. Choose Insert⇨Symbol, then select the bullet character from the palette of special characters. Click the Shortcut Key button, enter your preferred shortcut in the Press New Shortcut Key field (we prefer Alt+8 for the bullet), then click the Assign button. Close the dialog boxes to return to Word.

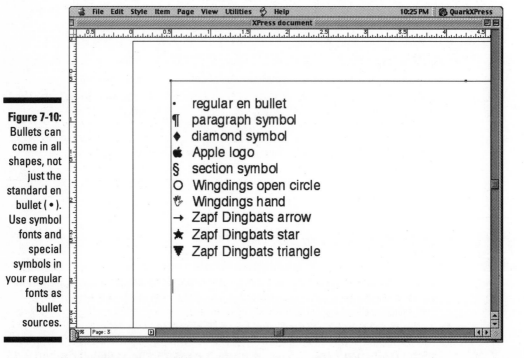

Figure 7-10: Bullets can come in all shapes, not just the standard en bullet (•). Use symbol fonts and special symbols in your regular fonts as bullet sources.

Ellipses

On a typewriter, you use three periods — some people put spaces around them, others don't — to indicate an *ellipsis,* the character (...) that indicates missing text, particularly in quoted material. You can also use it to indicate that a speaker trailed off when talking.

The nice thing about using the actual ellipsis character is this: As text moves within a column, some of the periods won't appear at the end of one line with the rest at the beginning of the next line. Of course, you can get around that design *faux pas* by typing the three periods with no spaces, which would make QuarkXPress see them as a single "word." But, if you do that, then the spacing within the ellipsis could be too tight or too loose, because it would be stretched or compressed like the other words on the line by the QuarkXPress justification feature. If you use the ellipsis character, the space between its constituent dots can't change, so the ellipsis always looks like, well, an ellipsis.

If you just don't like the look of three consecutive periods *or* a font's ellipsis character, you have a third option: Use nonbreaking spaces between the periods. Spaces are covered later in this chapter in the "Spaces" section.

Hyphens

Normally, a hyphen's a hyphen, right? Not always. If you want to hyphenate two words to a third, such as in "*Star Trek*–like," the proper typographic style, according to the World Typography Police, is to use an en dash instead of a hyphen (compare "*Star Trek*–like" to "*Star Trek*-like"). But using a regular hyphen is still no crime. You can also use variants of the hyphen, which Chapter 8 describes in more detail. These variants control the positioning of the hyphen; to a reader, a hyphen looks like a hyphen and an en dash looks like an en dash.

Spaces

A space is one of those characters you take for granted. So many people who get into desktop publishing wonder what all the fuss is about concerning different kinds of spaces. As with hyphens, the basic reason to use different kinds of spaces is to affect positioning. What you need to know is that you can use several fixed-size spaces that come in really handy when you try to align numbers in a table. An *en space* is the width of most numerals, and a *punctuation space* (also called a *thin space*) is the width of a comma or period. (In some popular fonts, like New Century Schoolbook, use an en space for punctuation as well as for numerals. And in a few decorative fonts, the numerals and punctuation don't correspond to any of the fixed spaces' widths.) So, if you try to decimal-align *10,000* and *50.12* against the left margin, you'd put three en spaces and a punctuation space in front of *50.12*. Figure 7-11 shows the results.

Another type of fixed space is called the *flexible space,* or *flex space* for short. The user defines this space in the Flex Space Width field of the Character pane of the Preferences dialog box, which you access by choosing Edit⇨ Preferences⇨Preferences, or by pressing Option+Shift+⌘+Y or Ctrl+Alt+ Shift+Y. You enter its value in terms of the percentage of an en space. To get a punctuation (thin) space, you'd enter 50%; to get an em space, you'd enter 200%. Or you can create your own type of space and enter another value from 1% to 400%.

Unfortunately, you can't use these fixed spaces when right-aligning text. Suppose that you want to decimal-align *10,000* and *50.12* against the right margin. Based on the preceding example, you'd expect to put a punctuation space and two en spaces after the *10,000* before right-justifying the two numbers. But that doesn't work. QuarkXPress ignores spaces at the end of a line when it right-aligns (it does see them when centering, however). To get Quark to space correctly (rather than just space out) when you right-align, you have to use the tab feature in QuarkXPress instead, as we explain in Chapter 8.

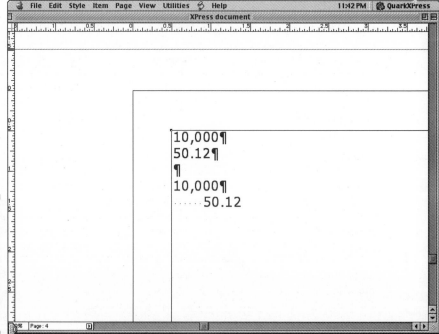

Figure 7-11:
By using en
spaces and
punctuation
spaces, you
can align
numbers
easily.

Working with Symbols

We're amazed at the number of special characters. You get more than 100 with each regular font, and scores if not hundreds of fonts (called symbol or pi fonts) contain nothing but symbols. Some people use symbols all the time; others rarely. Your own use of symbols depends on the kind of text you work with. Table 7-6 shows the shortcuts for the symbols that most Mac and Windows fonts offer. For symbol and pi fonts, you have to use the documentation that came with the font or a keyboard-character program (like the Mac's Key Caps utility, the $29 PopChar Pro shareware program for Macs, or the Windows Character Map utility) to see what's available. The section, "Accented and Foreign Characters," earlier in this chapter covers these programs in more detail.

Table 7-6	Shortcuts for Symbols	
Character	*Mac Shortcut*	*Windows Shortcut*
Legal		
Copyright (©)	Option+G	Shift+Alt+C *or* Ctrl+Alt+C *or* Alt+0169
Registered trademark (®)	Option+R	Shift+Alt+R *or* Alt+0174
Trademark (™)	Option+2	Shift+Alt+2 *or* Alt+0153
Paragraph (¶)	Option+7	Shift+Alt+7 *or* Ctrl+Alt+; *or* Alt+0182
Section (§)	Option+6	Shift+Alt+6 *or* Alt+0167
Dagger (†)	Option+T	Shift+Alt+T *or* Alt+0134
Double dagger (‡)	Option+Shift+T	Alt+0135
Currency		
Cent (¢)	Option+4	Alt+0162
Euro (€)	Option+Shift+2	Alt+Ctrl+5
Pound sterling (£)	Option+3	Alt+0163
Yen (¥)	Option+Y	Ctrl+Alt+- (hyphen) *or* Alt+0165

(continued)

Table 7-6 *(continued)*

Character	Mac Shortcut	Windows Shortcut
Measurement		
Foot (')	*not supported**	Ctrl+'
Inch (")	*not supported**	Ctrl+Alt+"
Mathematics		
One-half fraction (½)	*not supported*	Ctrl+Alt+6 *or* Alt+0189
One-quarter fraction (¼)	*not supported*	Ctrl+Alt+7 *or* Alt+0188
Three-quarters fraction (¾)	*not supported*	Ctrl+Alt+8 *or* Alt+0190
Infinity (∞)	Option+5	*not supported*
Multiplication (×)	*not supported*	Ctrl+Alt+= *or* Alt+0215
Division (÷)	Option+/	Alt+0247
Root (√)	Option+V	*not supported*
Greater than or equal (≥)	Option+>	*not supported*
Less than or equal (≤)	Option+<	*not supported*
Inequality (≠)	Option+=	*not supported*
Rough equivalence (≈)	Option+X	*not supported*
Plus or minus (±)	Option+Shift+=	Alt+0177
Logical not (¬)	Option+L	Ctrl+Alt+\ *or* Alt+0172
Per mil (‰)	Option+Shift+R	Alt+0137
Degree (°)	Option+Shift+8	Alt+0176
Function (f)	Option+F	Alt+0131
Integral (∫)	Option+B	*not supported*
Variation (∂)	Option+D	*not supported*
Greek beta (β)	Option+S	*not supported*
Greek mu (μ)	Option+M	Alt+0181
Greek Pi (Π)	Option+Shift+P	*not supported*
Greek pi (π)	Option+P	*not supported*
Greek Sigma (Σ)	Option+W	*not supported*
Greek Omega (Ω)	Option+Z	*not supported*

Character	Mac Shortcut	Windows Shortcut
Miscellaneous		
Apple logo (🍎)	Option+Shift+K	*not supported*
En bullet (•)	Option+8	Shift+Alt+8 *or* Alt+0149
Light (¤)	*not supported*	Ctrl+Alt+4 *or* Alt+0164
Open diamond (◊)	Option+Shift+V	*not supported*

*To get these characters, turn off the Smart Quotes feature in the Interactive pane of the Preferences Dialog box by choosing Edit⇨Preferences⇨Preferences, or by pressing Option+Shift+⌘+Y or Ctrl+Alt+Shift+Y. However, note that the next time you open the document in QuarkXPress, you may find these characters have been translated into their typographic-quote equivalents.

Why dingbats are smart

When you hear "dingbat," you may think of Edith Bunker, of Archie Bunker, Meathead, and *All in the Family* fame. But in publishing, a dingbat is no dummy. A dingbat is a visual marker. And, as with bullets, you have a whole host of choices available to you. Take a look at the symbols in Figure 7-10 and in Table 7-5 of the regular text for some dingbat ideas. Many people use a square (hollow or solid), but you can be more creative than that. Maybe you can use a version of your company or publication logo. Or you even could use a stylized letter: *Macworld* and *M-Business* magazines, for example, use different stylized *M's*.

When you use dingbats, remember that you have choices in how you use them. For dingbats that end a story, you usually have the dingbat follow the last of the text, with an en space or em space separating them (see Table 7-4). If your text is justified against both margins, it's common to have the dingbat flush right in the last line of the story. To make it flush right, you set up a tab stop equal to the width of your column. So if your column is 21/2 inches wide, you would set up a right-aligned tab at 21/2 inches. (Chapters 6 and 8 cover how to set up tabs.) A shortcut is to use Option+tab or Shift+tab, which sets up a right-aligned tab at the right edge of the column.

You would use the same techniques to place, say, a square before the text *Continued on page 14* or perhaps place a hollow square before a byline.

Chapter 8

Devil in the Details

● ●

In This Chapter

▶ Finding and replacing text and text attributes

▶ Setting tabs

▶ Creating and modifying tables

▶ Getting copy to fit

▶ Using the spelling checker

▶ Adding words to the spelling and hyphenation dictionaries

▶ Controlling hyphenation and spacing

▶ Changing kerning and tracking (and what they mean)

● ●

*P*robably everyone's least favorite part of publishing is the proofreading and attention to small text details, whether setting tabs so they align on a decimal or remembering to use italics whenever appropriate. Details get missed. In practically every magazine you read, there's a typo. No matter how many people look at a story, errors amazingly get through.

Although there's no magic cure for these errors, you can substantially reduce them. Old-fashioned proofreading by a fresh pair of eyes — not the author's, not the editor's, and not the layout artist's — is the first and best line of defense so that all concerned have a chance to find and replace incorrect text, fix spelling errors, and fit copy. A close second is setting exacting typographic controls over hyphenation and justification; these settings often catch errors of both grammar and ease of reading. And, although technically not a mistake, poor spacing and justification can lead the reader to misread text — called a "reado," which is as bad as a typo because it causes a problem for the reader.

But buck up. It's not all doom and gloom. Follow the advice in this chapter, and you'll minimize — and maybe on a good week even eliminate — imprecision and errors.

Replacing and Correcting Text

One of the most-used text editing features is correcting text by replacing a word or a chunk of text with another word or chunk of text. Sometimes you want to replace just one instance of a word or phrase; other times, you want to replace a word or phrase every time it occurs in the document.

For example, imagine that you're working on the brochure for courses that teach people about traveling to Indonesia. You decide that you need to change each instance of the word "Bali" to "Indonesia." What's the best way to do this?

You have a couple of choices:

✔ You can go back to your original word processor document, make the changes there, reimport the text into your QuarkXPress document, and then redo any formatting you've already done. (We don't like this method simply because it involves too many steps!)

✔ You can use QuarkXPress's built-in replace function, which you access through the Find/Change palette by choosing Edit⇨Find/Change (or by pressing ⌘+F on Macintosh or Ctrl+F in Windows), shown in Figure 8-1.

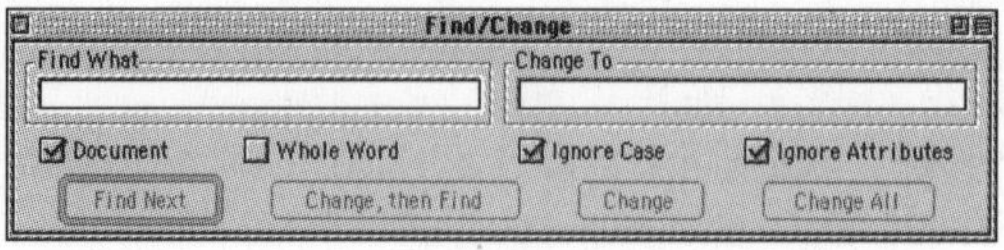

Figure 8-1:
The Find/Change palette.

As you can see, the QuarkXPress replace function works like the standard search and replace tool found in most word processing programs. You can search for whole words or for words whose capitalization matches the words or characters you type in the Find What field.

The Find/Change palette lets you choose whether QuarkXPress should look for a whole word — such as Quark as a standalone but not inside QuarkXPress. (If the Whole Word box is unchecked, the program finds the string of characters wherever it appears — such as Rob inside the name Robert.) You can also have the program search and replace a word — regardless of its capitalization — by checking Ignore Case. If the Document box is checked, the replace affects all stories and text in your document. The other buttons, such as Find Next, work as they do in word processing programs.

Even if you check Document, QuarkXPress doesn't search text on master pages while it searches text on document pages. So if you need to change the date in the folio for a newsletter, for example, start by displaying the master pages in the document window. To do so, choose Page⇨Display⇨Master). This searches the text on master pages.

Changing text attributes

The Find/Change palette has another incredibly cool function. You can find and replace text attributes, typefaces, and sizes. You can also find and replace text that's set according to a specific paragraph or character style.

These Find/Change capabilities can be useful if, for example, you want to change all instances of 12-point Helvetica in a document to 11.5-point Bookman.

To access these options, uncheck Ignore Attributes in the Find/Change palette. When Ignore Attributes is deselected, the palette expands and offers you attribute-replacement options, as shown in Figure 8-2.

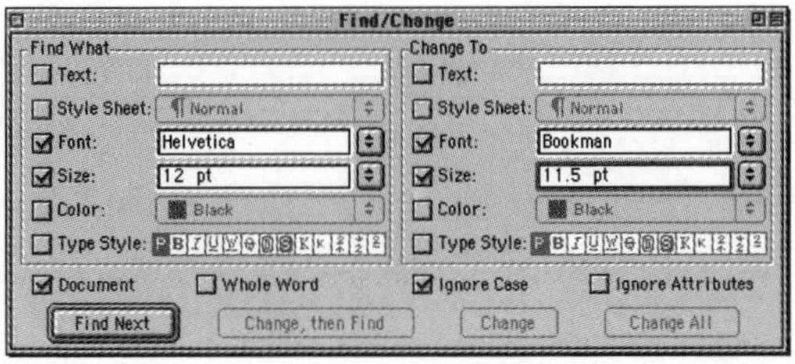

Figure 8-2:
The expanded Find/Change palette lets you search for specific text attributes.

Figure 8-2 shows text set in 12-point Helvetica about to be replaced with 11.5-point Bookman text.

You can select specific text, typeface, and styles for both the search and replace functions by checking the Text, Style Sheet, Font, Size, and Type Style check boxes in the Find What and Change To columns of the dialog box.

The Type Style area of the palette has several controls:

✔ Click an attribute box once to make it gray — this means you don't care about the attribute in your search — for example, if QuarkXPress finds italic text, it leaves it italic.

✔ Click an attribute box again to reverse it out — this turns the attribute on, meaning you want to find text with that attribute (on the Find What side) or apply that attribute (on the Change To side).

✔ Click an attribute box yet again to turn it off — this means that you don't want to find text with this attribute applied (on the Find What side) or that you want to remove it (on the Change To side).

Another new cool feature added to the Find/Change palette is its capability of finding and replacing colors.

Removing carriage returns

It's not uncommon for QuarkXPress users to receive text files for typesetting that have several extra carriage returns entered between paragraphs. The Find/Change feature in QuarkXPress gives you an easy way to remove these unwanted carriage returns.

You can use Find/Change to find and delete extra carriage returns, but you can't do it by simply typing in a carriage return in the Find/Change palette field because pressing the Return key activates the Find button. Instead, you need to enter the symbol for a new paragraph: \p.

Enter two consecutive return symbols, \p\p, in the Find What field and then enter one return symbol, \p, in the Change To field. Figure 8-3 shows what the Find/Change palette should look like when you are about to begin removing unwanted carriage returns, which are also referred to as *hard returns*.

Figure 8-3:
Automatically stripping extra hard returns from a file by entering the symbol for two returns (\p\p) with the symbol for a single return (\p).

If the text you're working with has multiple carriage returns between paragraphs, you may need to repeat this Find/Change procedure a number of times.

What do you do if a hard return exists at the end of each line of text, in addition to the extra hard returns between paragraphs? If you simply delete all the hard returns by using a Find/Change procedure similar to the one shown in Figure 8-3 (where you would search for \p and replace it with nothing), you would lose all paragraph breaks. So you need to follow a two-step procedure:

1. **Search for paragraph breaks that are marked by two hard returns, \p\p, and replace the paragraph breaks with a string of characters that's not used in the document, such as #!#.**

2. **Search for all hard returns and replace them with nothing (enter \p in the Find what field and leave the Change to field blank).**

After you delete the hard returns, you need to reinsert the paragraph breaks. To do this, enter the character(s) you used to replace the paragraph breaks (#!# in our example) in the Find What field, and enter \p in the Change To field and perform Find/Change again. See Chapter 21 for a list of codes that you can use to find noncharacter items, such as new lines and tabs.

Setting Tabs

Use tabs when you want to line up text into columns to create lists, tables, and other columnar data. QuarkXPress provides six paragraph tab options: Left, Center, Right, Decimal, Comma, and Align on. Tabs can be tricky, and using them effectively takes some practice.

If you've ever used a typewriter, you're familiar with typewriter tabs, which are left-aligned only: You press the tab key, and the carriage moves to a new left margin. But QuarkXPress offers a wide variety of tabs, which are available through the Paragraph Attributes pane, which you access by choosing Style⇨Tabs (or by pressing Shift +⌘+T or Ctrl+Shift+T). Each type of tab has its own mark on the tab ruler, which appears when you set tabs. Figure 8-4 shows the Paragraph Attributes pane.

Copy in an open document can be set with six different tab settings, all of which are described in Chapter 6. The tab settings are as follows:

✔ **Decimal.** Numbers with a decimal (.) that are typed after the tab will align on the decimal. This tab setting is useful if you have columns of numbers that include decimal places.

✔ **Comma.** Numbers with a comma (,) that are typed after the tab will align on the comma. This tab setting is handy if you have some numbers with decimal places, such as 31.001, and some without, such as 2,339.

✔ **Align on.** With this option, you select which character you want the text to align on. In the example in Figure 8-4, we aligned a column of numbers with the closing parenthesis.

✔ **Left.** Text typed after the tab will align to the tab as if the tab were a left margin. This is, by far, the most popular tab setting.

✔ **Center.** Typed text will be centered, with the tab stop serving as the center of the text.

✔ **Right.** Text typed after the tab will align to the tab as if the tab were a right margin. The right tab setting is often used with tables of numbers because the numbers align with all of their rightmost digits in a row.

The default for tabs is one left tab every half inch. If you want to apply different tab settings that you can use throughout the document, choose Edit➪Style Sheets (or press Shift+F11), and then select the Tabs pane. If you're working on a specific paragraph or want to override a style for one paragraph, choose Style➪Tabs (Shift+⌘+T or Ctrl+Shift+T) to access the Paragraph Attributes pane.

You can place thousands of tabs in a paragraph (in earlier versions of QuarkXPress, you were limited to 20 tabs), and you can use any printing character to fill the space between tabs.

Specifying your own tabs

After you access the Paragraph Attributes pane, here's how you set your own tabs:

1. **Select the Alignment you want (Left, Center, Right, Decimal, Comma, Align On).**

2. **Type the numeric position for the tab in the Position box or move your mouse to the Tab ruler and click to set the position of the tab.**

You can also specify tabs for a selected paragraph or range of paragraphs by choosing Style➪Formats (Shift+⌘+F or Ctrl+Shift+F) and selecting the Tabs pane, and then clicking on the ruler displayed above the box or column.

As we mention earlier, setting tabs in QuarkXPress is simple, but the process can be tricky if you've never done it before. For example, it takes time to learn how using tabs with the various Alignment options we mention earlier affects your document. We recommend that you take a few minutes to practice ting some tabs so that you'll be comfortable with the process. And nowh. can aligning these tabs be more difficult than when you create a table.

Using leader characters in tabs

A leader character, also known as a *tab leader,* is a series of characters that runs from text to text within tabular material. An example of a tab leader is the series of dots (periods) that you sometimes see between a table-of-contents entry and its corresponding page number. A tab leader guides the reader's eye, especially across the width of a page.

QuarkXPress calls a tab leader a *fill character.* To define a leader, enter up to two characters in the Fill Character box in the Paragraph Attributes pane. If you enter two characters, they alternate to fill the space between the defined tab stop and the place where you pressed the Tab key. Figure 8-4 shows a space and a period as the two fill characters.

Note that in Figure 8-4, we've left the Paragraph Attributes pane open so that you can see the entries we made. You can see the resulting tab leaders at the left side of the open document, above the Paragraph Attributes pane.

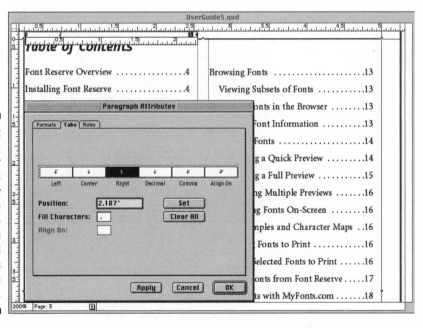

Figure 8-4: Setting leader characters for tabs by entering up to two characters in the Fill Characters field in the Tabs pane.

Making tables in QuarkXPress

Version 5 adds a Table tool that's not only easy to use — it's flexible and efficient, as well. The Table tool can handle both text and pictures. (This capability comes in incredibly handy when you create Web sites. See Chapter 25 for more details.)

Before you start drawing tables, you need to consider what you're going to fill the table with. If you fill the table with text, you need to figure out what format the text is currently in. If you're going to enter the text into the QuarkXPress table, go ahead and draw the table. But if the table already exists, for example, in a word processing file, you'll be much better off importing the text into a text box, then converting it into a table. See the section, "Converting text to a table and vice versa," later in this chapter for more information.

Creating a table

Creating a table in QuarkXPress is much like creating a picture or text box in QuarkXPress. You simply click the Table tool and use the mouse to draw a table. After you draw a table, the Table Properties dialog box appears, asking you how many rows and columns you want in your table, as well whether you want the table to contain text or picture boxes. Because this chapter focuses on tweaking text, we focus for now on text. Click the Text Cells button and then click OK. There you go: instant table.

Of course at this point the table looks a bit empty. You need to put some text in it. No problem. A table works pretty much like a text (or picture) box — in fact it is basically just several text (or picture) boxes joined together. So the first thing to do is type some text into the first box, or "cell." From there you apply all the attributes you can apply to standard text box — leading, ascent, color, and even text skew. Then you click in the next cell and do the same. Some boxes may be more time-consuming than others, depending on the number of cells involved. Nevertheless, the results will be stunning (see Figure 8-5).

A table in QuarkXPress is essentially a kind of box. That means it won't flow with the rest of your text. If you want the table to move with your text, treat it like any other box you want anchored in text. Select the table with the Item tool; cut it and then switch to the Content tool. Click within text where you want to insert the table box and paste the box.

Modifying a table

To modify tables, QuarkXPress provides several commands in the Table submenu of the Item menu:

- Insert Rows adds horizontal rows to the selected table.
- Insert Columns adds vertical columns to the selected table.

✔ Delete removes the current selection, whether you have the entire table, rows, or columns selected. To delete entire rows or cells, just select all the cells in the row or column (Shift click the cells, or with the Item tool, select the row / column).

✔ Combine Cells merges selected cells into a single cell. Use the Content tool to select the cells first.

✔ Convert Table to Text extricates text from the table so you can use it in another format.

As with other boxes in QuarkXPress, the Modify dialog box gives you a lot of power over tables. The Table pane controls the width, height, and placement of the table on the page, the Cell pane controls the width and height of the cells and their background colors, and the Text pane controls how text is placed within the cells.

In addition to modifying cells, QuarkXPress gives you control over the lines between the cells (called *gridlines*). Select the gridlines using the Gridlines submenu of the Item menu: Select Horizontal, Select Vertical, Select Borders, or Select All. Then, choose Item⇨Modify. The Grid pane appears and you can do all kinds of designy things to your gridlines.

Figure 8-5:
A table
of prices
created
with the
Quark-
XPress
Table tool.

Veuve Clicquot "Yellow Label" Brut	Cost to You
Argonaut Price	$44.49
Restaurant Menu Price	Cost to You
Del Frisco's	$90
Zenith	$90
Tante Louise	$85
Vasil's Euro Grille	$84
Bravo!	$84
Bloom	$80

One key feature about the Table tool is its capability of containing pictures in addition to text. Of course, looking at the Table Properties dialog box, you'd think that you choose either text or pictures. And because this chapter focuses on text, it just doesn't seem right to get into the whole picture thing right now (we do that in Chapter 25). But the truth is you don't have to choose between one format or the other. As is the case with picture boxes and text boxes, you can actually change the content of a particular cell at will. It works basically the same way as it does with other boxes. Just put the cursor in the cell you want to change, choose Item⇨Content, and change the text cell to a picture cell or vice versa. Who knows? You may want to drop a picture into your otherwise tedious text chart to grab some attention. This feature lets you do it!

Converting text to a table and vice versa

Creating a table from scratch is fine if it's a new element. But what if that table already exists, either in your text document or in an older QuarkXPress document as a series of tabbed text? Quark thought of that, too.

Just select a set of text — with the elements you want in cells separated by tabs, spaces, paragraphs, or commas — then choose Item⇨Convert Text to Table, as shown in Figure 8-6. In that dialog box, you have several options, although the default works for tabbed text:

- ✔ You can specify in the pop-up menus what separates rows and columns. Your options are Commas, Tabs, Spaces, and Paragraphs. Almost always, you'd choose Paragraphs as the separators for rows. For columns, you'd typically choose either tabs or commas. Most people use tabs in Word and QuarkXPress to set up tables, and when you save Excel files to text, tabs are used as well. But a common format exists for separating data called CSV (comma-separated value) which uses commas instead. Spaces are also used, however we don't recommend your using this option because distinguishing a space separating two cells from a space used with a cell's text can be hard. In the Separate Columns With pop-up menu, simply select whatever separates the data in your source text.

- ✔ The Rows and Columns options change based on what you select in Separate Rows With and Separate Columns With. If you type in different values, QuarkXPress creates extra cells or skip some cells, depending on whether the values are greater or less than the actual "cells" in your source text.

- ✔ Cell Fill Order tells QuarkXPress how to determine how the source text maps to your intended table. The default is to read from left to right for a row's column contents and then to the next line (paragraph return) for the next row. That's the option that looks like a Z. But you could select the other options to change the table's appearance. For example, selecting the reversed Z essentially puts the first piece of data in your source text's first "row" at the end of the table's row. Selecting the option that looks like an N would essentially swap the columns and rows, which may be a more efficient way to convert the source text into a table.

You can also convert a QuarkXPress table to text. Choose Item⇨Table⇨ Convert Table to Text, which reveals a dialog box almost like the Convert Text to Table dialog box. Specify how columns and rows should be exported (separated by tabs, commas, and so on), what order the data should be extracted in, and whether the original table should be deleted. That's it!

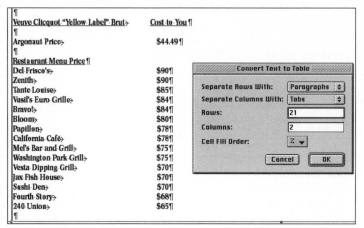

Figure 8-6:
Quark-
XPress lets
you control
how text
being
converted to
a table is
handled.
This lets you
convert
most
popular
forms of
source data
into a table.

Getting Copy to Fit

Copy fitting is just what it sounds like — The process of fitting text into the layout. Sometimes you feel as if you're trying to squeeze 20 pounds of lemons into a five-pound bag. If your original, unmodified text fits the layout the first time through, consider it a stroke of luck because that's not what usually happens.

Copy fitting, when done well, can make your document look very professional. It can also save you money. For example, imagine that you have the budget to produce an eight-page document. You flow in your text and find that you have 8¼ pages to deal with. By doing a good job of copy fitting, you can make the text fit into eight pages and save yourself the expense and hassle of adding an additional signature to your booklet.

You can make copy fit onto a page or within a column in a number of ways. Sometimes you can use just one method; sometimes you have to use a combination of methods to make text fit in the available space.

Having more text than space is common. Therefore, the following tips assume that the goal is to shorten text. But you can use the same procedures in reverse to expand text. *Note:* Use the last two tips only if you can't make text fit using the first few.

✔ **Edit text** to remove extra lines. Watch for lines at the end of a paragraph that have only a few characters. Getting rid of a few characters somewhere else in the paragraph may eliminate these short lines, reducing the amount of page space needed while keeping the amount of text removed to a minimum.

- ✔ **Adjust the tracking of the text** so that the text occupies less space and, especially, so that short lines are eliminated.

- ✔ **Tighten the leading** by a half or quarter point. Because this is such a small change, the average reader won't notice it; it may even save you a few lines per column, which can add up quickly.

- ✔ **Reduce the point size** by a half point. This action saves more space than is first apparent, because it lets you place a few more lines on the page and put a bit more text in each line. You can change point size in the style sheet or select text and use the type-size controls in the Measurements palette.

- ✔ **Reduce the horizontal scale** of text to a slightly smaller percentage (perhaps 85 percent) to squeeze more text in each line by entering a percent value in the Horizontal Scale field (with the text selected, choose Modify from the Item menu).

- ✔ **Vary the size of columns** by setting slightly narrower column gutters or slightly wider margins.

Winning the Spelling Bee

Many people dread spelling; that's why word processors and publishing programs come with spelling checkers. But there's a catch: Spelling checkers work by being based on lists of words. Sure, spelling dictionaries sometimes contain 500,000-odd words (QuarkXPress's has a "mere" 120,000), but industry-specific terms like *PowerPC* or people's names rarely show up in these dictionaries. So you can't completely automate spell-checking. Sorry, but you need to have another dictionary somewhere around for referral.

Although you can't automate spell-checking, you can make it a part of your routine. You should spell-check your text in the word processor before laying it out in QuarkXPress. You also should spell-check it again in QuarkXPress after you finish your layout but before you print it. You'll be surprised how much text gets added or changed in the layout, after the stories are officially "done."

QuarkXPress provides an internal spelling checker, which you can access by choosing Utilities➪Check Spelling, as shown in Figure 8-7. Check Spelling has three submenus: Word, Story, and Document. You can jump directly to these options by pressing ⌘+L or Ctrl+W for Word, Option+⌘+L or Ctrl+Alt+W for Story, and Option+Shift+⌘+L or Ctrl+Alt+Shift+W for Document. Chances are that you'll use the Story and Document options the most — the ones with the hardest-to-remember shortcuts. (A story is all text in the current text box and in all text boxes linked to that text box. A story is usually the contents of an imported text file.)

To access the Story or Word options, you have to have the Content tool active and the text pointer on a piece of text. You don't have to select a word to spell-check it; just have the text pointer somewhere on the word. If you select multiple words and use the Word spell-checking option, QuarkXPress spell-checks only the first word in the series. You can't spell-check a high-lighted range of words.

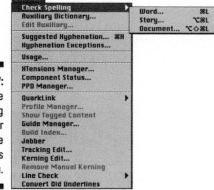

Figure 8-7: Access the spelling checker through the Utilities menu.

Running the spelling checker

If you spell-check an entire document or the current story, you see the dialog box shown in Figure 8-8.

Figure 8-8: Quark-XPress reports how many words it checked and how many it didn't recognize.

Click OK to continue, which displays the dialog box shown in Figure 8-9.

Figure 8-9:
Quark-
XPress
shows
you each
suspect
word in turn.

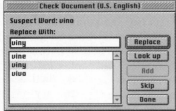

If you spell-check a single word, skip to the dialog box shown in Figure 8-10, which is a more compact version of the previous dialog box.

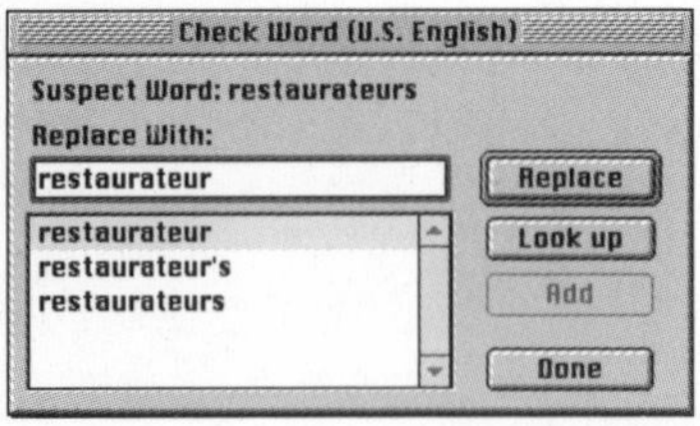

Figure 8-10:
When spell-
checking
a single
word, go
directly to
this version
of the
dialog box.

The dialog boxes shown in Figures 8-9 and 8-10 differ in several ways:

- ✔ The Check Word dialog box has no capability of moving on (when you click the Skip button) to the next suspect word (an option that doesn't make sense for one-word spell-checking), as the Check Story or Check Document dialog boxes do.

- ✔ The Check Word dialog box automatically looks for possible correct words to replace the suspect word; the other dialog boxes require that you click the Lookup button to get a list of possible replacements. If one of those words is the correct one, just click it and then click Replace, or just double-click the word in the list.

- ✔ The Check Word dialog box has no Add button, which lets you add words to your personal dictionary (explained a little later in this section).

In all three dialog boxes, you can select a new word and click the Replace button to ask QuarkXPress to make the replacement. If the word appears several times, QuarkXPress tells you how many times the word is used and replaces all instances when you click Replace.

You can also use this feature in QuarkXPress 5's new spell-check Selection dialog box, which you access by choosing Utilities⇨Check Spelling⇨Selection.

Setting up your personal dictionaries

If you've experimented with QuarkXPress's spelling checker, you probably noticed that the Add button stays gray. So what's it there for? For the Add button to become active, you need to set up an auxiliary dictionary — a personal dictionary of words that QuarkXPress's own dictionary (the file XPress Dictionary on the Mac and the file XPress Dictionary.DCT in Windows) doesn't know about.

To set up an auxiliary dictionary, choose Utilities⇨Auxiliary Dictionary, which displays the dialog box shown in Figure 8-11. Any existing dictionaries in the current folder are displayed. You can select one of them, move to a different directory to select a different dictionary, or click the New button to create a new auxiliary dictionary.

Figure 8-11: You create or switch to a different auxiliary spelling dictionary by using the Auxiliary Dictionary dialog box.

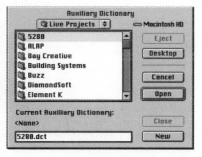

In Figure 8-11, we had set up an auxiliary dictionary for the current document previously, so the name of that dictionary is displayed in the Current Auxiliary Dictionary field.

The Windows QuarkXPress Auxiliary Dictionary dialog box looks a little different than its Mac counterpart because it follows the Windows conventions for an Open or Save dialog box. But it has all the same features and buttons. You need to know one other thing about the auxiliary dictionaries in Windows QuarkXPress: Although the main dictionary (XPress Dictionary.DCT) uses the extension .DCT, the auxiliary dictionaries use the extension .QDT (such as Computer.QDT).

After you create the auxiliary dictionary, you have to add words to it. Actually, you don't have to add them right then — you just add words as you find them in the spelling checker by clicking the Add button when you come across a word like *PowerPC* that is correct but unknown to QuarkXPress. Or, if you already know some of the words you want to add, you can choose Utilities⇨Edit Auxiliary to invoke the dialog box shown in Figure 8-12. You also can use this dialog box to remove incorrect words (maybe someone was too fast on the trigger and clicked Add by accident).

Figure 8-12:
Adding
spelling
variations
to the Edit
Auxiliary
Dictionary
dialog box
lets you
modify the
spelling
dictionary
on a
document-
by-
document
basis.

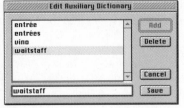

Be sure to click the Save button after making changes to your auxiliary dictionary. Otherwise, the changes won't be saved.

Notice as you add words that case doesn't matter. If you enter *PowerPC,* it will display as *powerpc.* The use of only lowercase ensures that the word won't be flagged as incorrect if it were typed in all caps. Or, for a word like *uninstall,* which is not in QuarkXPress's own dictionary file, this use of only lowercase ensures that the word isn't flagged if the first letter is capitalized at, for example, the beginning of a sentence or in a title — *uninstall, Uninstall,* and *UNIN-STALL* are all considered to be the same to QuarkXPress's spelling checker, which just keeps the form *uninstall* in its dictionary file.

But this lowercase-only approach means that you can't set QuarkXPress to flag incorrectly capitalized words (for example, some people refer to Quark Xtensions, when the correct capitalization is *XTensions*). Your word processor probably has case-sensitive (which means it looks at the capitalization of words, not just at the sequence of letters in them) spell-checking, but QuarkXPress doesn't. That's another reason to do a spell-check in your word processor before importing the text into QuarkXPress.

Because auxiliary dictionaries are just files, you can share them over a network, which is a great way to maintain spelling consistency among several users. You also can have different dictionaries for different projects (if your work involved very different types of audiences). But one thing you can't do is share dictionaries between Windows and Macintosh users. The two dictionary formats aren't compatible, and no way exists to translate either dictionary into the other's format.

By maintaining an up-to-date spelling dictionary and spell-checking at key points in the editing and layout process, you can greatly reduce typographical mistakes. Some typos (for example, words that are spelled correctly but are actually the wrong word) won't be caught this way, however, so you still need a person to proofread. But at least the obvious mistakes will have been caught by the time a proofreader sees your text.

Hyphenating the Right Way

You can make or break the look of every line and paragraph of text — whether in a letter, a two-column newsletter, or a design-intensive ad with text wrapping around items and images — with good or bad hyphenation settings. For example, if you have justified text without hyphenation, you can get big gaps in text. Or, if you wrap text around the edges of an item, you may need hyphens to improve the wrap.

But hyphenation is even harder for many people than spelling. Where do you break a word? Between two consonants? After a syllable? You can follow rules, but the English language is so full of exceptions that you may think it's hardly worth learning the rules unless you're a copy editor.

As it does for spell-checking, QuarkXPress offers automatic hyphenation. In fact, the hyphenation is so good that you'll rarely need to add words to its exception dictionary — although you can if you want. Before you do that, however, you need to know how to specify hyphenation, which we cover in the next section.

Creating hyphenation sets

Any ink-stained newspaperman (or woman) can tell you what an H&J set is. But in case you don't have an ink-stained newsperson nearby, we'll clue you in: An H&J set is newspaper lingo for a hyphenation and justification set — the specifications for how words are divided across lines and how the text in each line is spaced. We cover some of the spacing features later in this chapter.

To set up hyphenation settings, choose Edit⇨H&Js (Option+⌘+H or Option+ Shift+F11 on a Mac, Ctrl+Shift+F11 in Windows) to display the H&Js dialog box, shown in Figure 8-13. When you first open this dialog box, you see just one listing in the H&J list: Standard. Edit this listing first so that you can establish the hyphenation settings you want as the default for your text styles. After you edit Standard to your liking, you can create additional H&J sets for other needs. For example, you may want an H&J set called No Hyphen for text (like headlines and bylines) that should have no hyphenation.

Figure 8-13:
The H&Js
dialog box is
your
gateway to
hyphenation
control.

As is true for other global preferences, QuarkXPress works differently if no document is open than if one is. If you create or change H&J sets when no document is open, QuarkXPress uses that H&J set for all future documents (until you change the dictionary again). If a document is open, the H&J set is created or changed just for that document. You can tell whether the H&Js are being edited globally for all new documents or locally for the currently opened one: If the dialog box says Default H&Js (as shown in Figure 8-14), you're changing the global settings; if it says H&Js for *document name,* you're changing the settings locally for whatever *document name*'s real name is (the real name will display in the title, not *document name*).

Figure 8-14:
The Edit
Hyphenation
&
Justification
dialog box
contains
hyphenation
controls at
the left side
of the
screen.

To edit an existing H&J set, select its name from the list and double-click it. To create an H&J set, click the New button. Either way, you get the Edit Hyphenation & Justification dialog box shown in Figure 8-14. The fields at the left are the ones that affect hyphenation.

Take a close look at the values in Figure 8-1; compare them to the values in your copy of QuarkXPress. Our values differ from yours because we edited the Standard settings in our copy of QuarkXPress to work best in multicolumn layouts such as newsletters, newspapers, and magazines. Here's how each setting works:

- **Name.** If you clicked New, enter the name for the H&J set here. (H&J sets are named, just as style sheets are.) If you clicked Edit to edit the Standard H&J set, you won't be able to edit the name.

- **Auto Hyphenation.** If this box is checked, hyphenation is turned on for any style sheet that uses this H&J set. If the box is unchecked, hyphenation is turned off for any style sheet that uses this H&J set.

- **Smallest Word.** This field tells QuarkXPress to ignore words with fewer characters than that field's value. The default is 6, so any word of five or fewer characters won't be hyphenated. The default value of 6 is a good choice because few words of six or fewer letters are unable to fit on a line with other text or will look good if they are split across two lines, so there's little reason to change this default value. (One possible instance to change it would be if you had wide columns — for example, 6 inches or more — in which case there's plenty of room for words so a value of 8 would be fine.)

- **Minimum Before.** This field tells QuarkXPress how many characters in the word must precede a hyphen. Thus, if you leave the value set to the default of 3, QuarkXPress will not hyphenate the word *Rolodex* as *Ro-lodex,* even though that's a legal hyphenation for the word. The first place that QuarkXPress will hyphenate would be after the *l,* but that's an incorrect hyphenation point, so QuarkXPress would insert the hyphen after *Rolo.*

- **Minimum After.** This field is like Minimum Before, except that it tells QuarkXPress the minimum number of characters in a word that must follow the hyphen. The default is 2, although many people change that to 3 so QuarkXPress won't hyphenate verbs before the *-ed,* as in *edit-ed.* Many publishers think that looks tacky. It's a personal choice.

- **Hyphens in a Row.** The default is Unlimited, which means that theoretically every line could end in a hyphen. Having too many end-of-line hyphens in a row makes the text hard to read because it's hard to keep track of what line to move to next. We suggest 3 as a good setting, although 2 and 4 are fine, too. The smaller the number, the greater the chance that QuarkXPress will have trouble spacing text in a line; a line that could really use a hyphen wouldn't have one just because it happened to come after that maximum number of consecutive hyphenated lines. (For example: If you set Hyphens in a Row to 2 and a particular paragraph turns out to have two hyphens in a row somewhere, even though the third line needs a hyphen to avoid awkward spacing, QuarkXPress won't hyphenate that line.)

When you confront this spacing situation, don't despair — and don't change the settings in your H&J set. Just type a regular hyphen followed by a space. (If you try to use the soft hyphen — ⌘+hyphen or Ctrl+hyphen — to create a break on that third line, QuarkXPress won't add the hyphen because soft hyphens respect the Hyphens in a Row setting.) But add a regular hyphen and space only when everything else in the layout is finished — if your text were to reflow, you might find a hyphen and space in the middle of a word in the middle of a line. Oops! This cheat lets you get around the H&J limitations without changing a standard that works most of the time. And, if you're unsure where to hyphenate a word (and no dictionary's handy), just click on the word and choose Utilities⇨Suggested Hyphenation (⌘+H or Ctrl+H) to have QuarkXPress show you where hyphens may be added.

✔ **Break Capitalized Words.** This box does just what it says. Some typographers frown on hyphenating proper names, like *Macworld* or *Alexander.* We think it's a silly prohibition, so make sure this box is checked. Better a broken name than awkward spacing around it.

✔ **Hyphenation Zone.** For text that is left-aligned, right-aligned, or centered, this box tells QuarkXPress how far from the outside margin to look for opportunities to hyphenate. Hyphenation Zone helps you prevent awkward gaps — something that looks like a kid's smile with no front top teeth — because a word happened to hyphenate halfway into the line. Set the zone to at least 10 percent of the column width (15 percent is better), but to no less than 0.2 inches. Thus, for a 1.5-inch-wide line, a good setting would be 0.225 inch (although you can round that to 0.2 or 0.25); that's 1.5 (inches) times 0.15 (percent). For justified or force-justified text, this setting has no effect, however, because all the text is aligned to both the left and right margins, which means that the text has no possible gaps for you to worry about.

When you click the New button, the new H&J set takes the attributes of the Standard H&J set, so it's best to edit Standard to your liking before creating new sets. That way, attributes that you've specified in several sets (such as checking Auto Hyphenation and Break Capitalized Words) are automatically copied into the new sets. If you want to duplicate an H&J set and then make slight modifications to it (perhaps two sets are identical except for the Hyphenation Zone settings), select one of the sets in the H&J dialog box and click the Duplicate button; then modify (and rename) that duplicate set.

Figure 8-15 shows the effects of different hyphenation settings. The figure shows really skinny columns because thin columns emphasize the differences between hyphenation settings. The wider the columns, the less noticeable the differences because QuarkXPress has more text to play around in while adjusting spacing.

The harvest brings a bounty of beauty from artist Jack Pine's glass garden. This new Lakewood-based glassblower creates hundreds of one-of-a-kind pumpkins. Just like the real things, Pine's pumpkins come in a range of shapes and sizes. And these gourds don't just come in orange.

The harvest brings a bounty of beauty from artist Jack Pine's glass garden. This new Lakewood-based glassblower creates hundreds of one-of-a-kind pumpkins. Just like the real things, Pine's pumpkins come in a range of shapes and sizes. And these gourds don't just come in orange.

Click OK when you're done creating or modifying an H&J set (or click Cancel if you want to abort those settings). QuarkXPress displays the H&Js dialog box, from which you can create or edit other sets. When you're done, be sure to click Save to save all the work you've done — if you click Cancel, your work's toast.

If you created H&J sets in another document, you can import those sets into the current QuarkXPress document by using this mini-procedure: Click the Append button (it really should be named Import — Append makes it sound like it will copy the current H&J set to another set, not *from* it); then navigate the dialog box to find the document you're importing from.

Remember that *all* H&J sets in that document will be imported into your current document with one exception: If both documents have H&J sets with the same name, importing sets into the current document will not affect its H&J set. For example, suppose that the current document has the H&J sets Standard and No Hyphen, while the other document has the H&J sets Standard and Masthead. When you import H&J sets from the other document, Masthead will be copied into the current document but Standard won't be copied, and the current document's Standard H&J set will remain unaffected.

If you want to copy H&J sets from another document and make them the default for all future documents, make sure that no document is open in your copy of QuarkXPress before you import H&J sets from that other document. This is a great way to copy standards from a client's system to your system, or from a master document to a new employee's copy of QuarkXPress.

After you set up your H&J sets — many documents will have just two: Standard and No Hyphen — edit your style sheets so that each style uses the appropriate H&J set. Headlines, bylines, and other categories of display type usually are not hyphenated, while body text, bios, captions, and sidebars usually *are* hyphenated. You also can apply an H&J set to a selected para-graph (or several selected paragraphs) in the Paragraph Attributes pane. Choose Style⇨Formats (or press Shift+⌘ +F or Ctrl+Shift+F) and change the H&J value to the H&J set you want to apply.

Personalizing your hyphenation

As with spelling dictionaries, you can create your own personal hyphenation dictionaries, in which you tell QuarkXPress how to hyphenate words it doesn't know about. You also can set personalized hyphenation to change the default hyphenation of words that are hyphenated differently based on their pronunciation (such as the verb *pro-ject* and the noun *proj-ect*) or what dictionary they appear in.

To add your own hyphenation, choose Utilities⇨Hyphenation Exceptions. The dialog box shown in Figure 8-16 appears. (Looks a lot like the dialog box for spelling exceptions, doesn't it?)

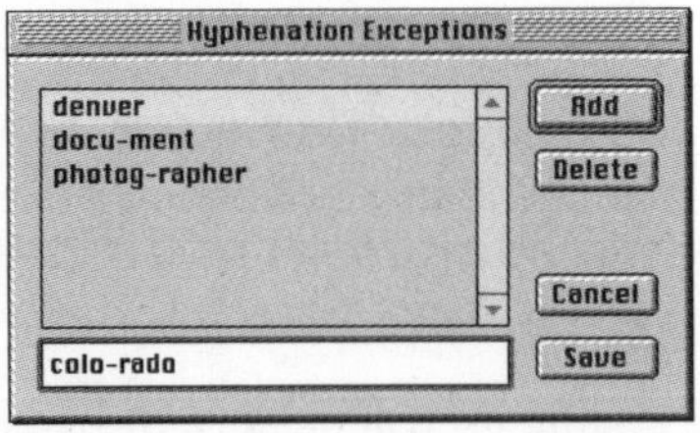

Figure 8-16:
The
Hyphenation
Exceptions
dialog box.

Hyphenation Exceptions
denver	Add
docu-ment	
photog-rapher	Delete
	Cancel
colo-rado	Save

Just enter into the Hyphenation Exceptions dialog box the word whose hyphenation you want to personalize, include hyphens where it's okay for QuarkXPress to hyphenate the word, and click Add. (If you want to prevent a word from being hyphenated, enter it with no hyphens.) To delete a word, select it from the list and click Delete.

After you're done, click Save. Clicking Cancel wipes out any changes you made.

Preventing "Reados"

The other half of the H&J set — the J, or justification — controls the spacing of text. It's easy to overlook this aspect of typography and just go with the defaults. But you don't want to do that. How you set your spacing has a subtle but important effect on readability. QuarkXPress assumes that you're doing single-column-wide documents, which is fine for reports and price lists. But, for multicolumn documents, the default settings can result in spacing that leaves awkward gaps between words and can make the space between characters in words open enough that you may not be sure whether the characters make one word or two.

Default spacing

With the help of expert typographers, Quark set the default spacing in the Edit Hyphenation & Justification dialog box to work for most basic columns of text. (Although, basically the settings for spacing rely on the typeface, size, column width, and other factors in use.) Nonetheless, you can improve on the defaults, as shown in Figure 8-17.

Using the settings shown in Figure 8-17, the results are that the characters in a word are closer together and no unsightly gaps remain between words. You can experiment with the values, but, before you do that, read on to find out what those values mean.

All settings for justification are in the section of the dialog box labeled Justification Method. At the top are six fields that determine how your text is spaced between characters and words; the spacing of text between characters and words is called letter spacing and word spacing, respectively. The first row determines the space between words; the second row controls the space between characters within a word. Generally, you want tighter space within a word than between words so that words look unified and the space between them is easily discernible. The three columns determine the rules by which QuarkXPress spaces characters and words.

The spacing columns may not make sense at first because they behave differently depending on how the text is aligned. If text is left-aligned, right-aligned, or centered, QuarkXPress always uses the Opt. (optimum, or target) values. If the text is justified or force-justified, QuarkXPress tries to meet the Opt. values; if it can't meet those values, it uses a value in the range between the Min. (minimum) and Max. (maximum) values. If that doesn't work, it uses a value greater than the Max. value. QuarkXPress *never* uses less than the Min. Settings.

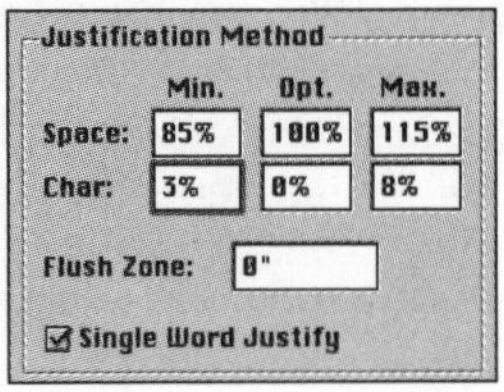

Figure 8-17:
The
justification
half of the
Edit
Hyphenation
&
Justification
dialog box
contains the
authors'
preferred
settings.

Justification Method

	Min.	Opt.	Max.
Space:	85%	100%	115%
Char:	3%	0%	8%

Flush Zone: 0"

☑ Single Word Justify

Because of how QuarkXPress applies spacing, setting the Opt. values to 100% for words and 0% for characters works best. Those particular Opt. values tell QuarkXPress to use the defaults from the font's internal spacing specifications. (Presumably, the font's designers picked those specs for a good reason.)

For the Min. settings, we prefer 85% for words and –3% for characters. That prevents words and letters from getting too close, but it also helps balance any spaced-out text with slightly cramped text, keeping the overall average closer to the Opt. values. For Max., we allow a greater difference from Opt. than we do from Min., because the human eye can handle extra space better than it can too little space.

Local space controls: Tracking and kerning

But wait, there's more! You can override the spacing settings for selected text or even with a style sheet. But, pray, why would you do this? Consider these scenarios:

✔ Some text is too spacey, or you know that if some text were just a little closer together, you'd get the text to rewrap and take one line less. Here's where you would use QuarkXPress's tracking feature to tighten (or loosen) the space among characters in a selected block of text.

✔ Standard H&J set's justification settings work fine for your body text but not for your headlines. Rather than create a new H&J set for headlines, you just adjust the tracking settings in your Headlines style sheet to compensate for the difference.

✔ Only a few characters don't quite mesh. Here and there, a couple of letters in a word seem to be too close or too far apart. Just use the QuarkXPress kerning feature to adjust the space between those two characters.

Tracking and kerning are pretty much the same thing — ways to adjust the spacing between characters. So what's the difference? The scope of the adjustments they make. *Kerning* adjusts spacing between just two characters, while *tracking* adjusts spacing between all characters selected. QuarkXPress uses the same menus for these two features because they really are just variations of the same feature. Thus, you see the Kern command in the Style menu if your text pointer happens to be between two characters, but it's replaced by the Track command if you select several characters. Similarly, the horizontal arrows on the Measurements palette adjust kerning if the pointer is between two characters, and they adjust tracking when several characters are selected.

Figure 8-18 shows the Character Attributes pane, which appears when you choose Style➪Kern or Style➪Track. Figure 8-19 shows how you can modify kerning or tracking from the Measurements palette.

Using the keyboard shortcuts or the Measurements palette to adjust tracking and kerning is best because you can see the effects of your changes as you make them. (Otherwise, you need to make the greater effort of opening a dialog box, entering a value, closing the dialog box, seeing the result, reopening the dialog box to further adjust the spacing, and so on.) Press Shift+⌘+]or Ctrl+ Shift+], to increase spacing in ⅟₂₀ increments and Shift+⌘+Option+] or Ctrl+Alt+ Shift+] to increase spacing in ⅟₂₀₀ increments. To decrease spacing, press Shift+ ⌘+[and Option+Shift+⌘+[on the Mac and Ctrl+Shift+[and Ctrl+Shift+[and Ctrl+Alt+Shift+[in Windows.

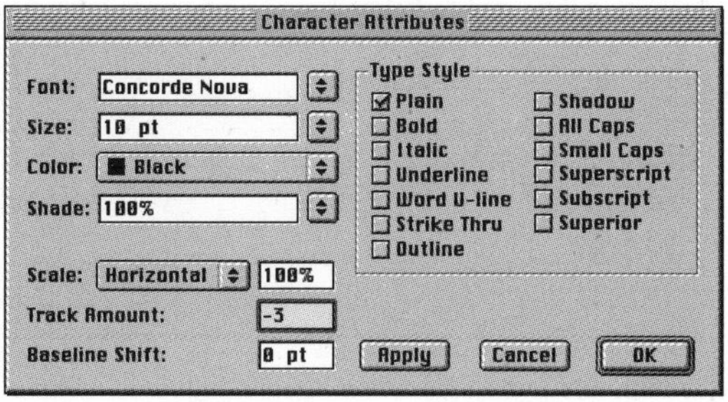

Figure 8-18:
To open the Character Attributes dialog box with the Kern Amount or Track Amount field highlighted, choose Kern or Track from the Style menu.

Character Attributes

Font:	Concorde Nova
Size:	10 pt
Color:	■ Black
Shade:	100%

Type Style
- ☑ Plain
- ☐ Bold
- ☐ Italic
- ☐ Underline
- ☐ Word U-line
- ☐ Strike Thru
- ☐ Outline
- ☐ Shadow
- ☐ All Caps
- ☐ Small Caps
- ☐ Superscript
- ☐ Subscript
- ☐ Superior

Scale: Horizontal 100%
Track Amount: -3
Baseline Shift: 0 pt

[Apply] [Cancel] [OK]

Figure 8-19:
You also can specify kerning and tracking in the highlighted field in the Measurements palette.

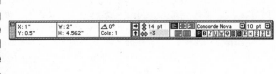

The values QuarkXPress uses for tracking and kerning are not percentages, as they are for the H&J sets' spacing options. Instead, for tracking and kerning QuarkXPress uses a unit of measurement called (of all things) a *unit* — a handy little length that measures all of ¹⁄₂₀₀ of an em space. An em space is as wide as a font is high; thus, an em space for 9-point type is 9 points wide. That means that a unit is ⁹⁄₂₀₀ of a point for 9-point type, ⁸⁄₂₀₀ (or ¹⁄₅₀) of a point for 8-point type, and so on. As you can see, a unit really is another way to express a percentage: 0.05% (that's the decimal way to represent ¹⁄₂₀₀). That's a pretty small value. So, in the Measurements palette, QuarkXPress jumps in 10-unit increments when you click the left and right arrows to adjust tracking or kerning. Of course, you can select your own precise values by entering a number. A positive number adds space; a negative number removes it.

Chapter 9

A Touch of Color

In This Chapter

▶ Understanding how colors work in printing

▶ Using the Color Management System in QuarkXPress

▶ Importing colors into QuarkXPress

▶ Applying colors to items in your documents

olor is tricky. It's everywhere, so we take it for granted. We don't usually spend much time thinking about color theory or color physics. (And we don't spend much time on those topics in this chapter, either.)

In the wonderful world of computers, color has become the rule rather than the exception. You can get high-quality color inkjet printers for as little as $100, and they're great for limited-run output (for a few dozen copies or for use in a color copier). You can also buy more expensive color printers (for $5,000 to $20,000) that use technologies with intimidating names, such as *dye sublimation* and *thermal wax*. These printers are for professional publishers who perform color proofing of publications, such as magazines and catalogs, which will be reproduced at a commercial printing plant. Or you can have your work printed by a commercial printer that does color work, in which case, your lowly grayscale laser printer is merely a proofing device for your text and image placement.

The color tools in QuarkXPress are aimed at professional color publishers. (Check out *QuarkXPress 5 Bible* — by the authors of this book and also published by Hungry Minds — which delves into professional color in detail.) But that doesn't mean that you can't benefit from color as well. After all, who can resist using color, especially if you have one of those inexpensive color inkjet printers? But before you can make the best use of color, you need to understand a bit about how color happens — and that process is a lot more complicated than you may think.

Heading off to Color Class

Prepare to see all sorts of acronyms when you explore color. Color theory is like the military — capital letters and confusion everywhere.

RGB versus CMYK

As far as desktop publishing is concerned, color comes in two basic types: RGB (red, green, and blue) and CMYK (cyan, magenta, yellow, and black). Computer monitors use RGB, whereas printers use CMYK. Because the color types differ, what you see on-screen usually looks different from what your printed output looks like. (Sometimes you don't even receive a close match.) These types of color schemes are called *color models;* the model is the physics behind the colors.

RGB (red, green, and blue), for example, is composed of the three colors of light that a monitor or television uses to create all colors. As a kid, you probably played with prisms, which split white light into its constituent colors. White light goes in one side of the prism, and a rainbow comes out the other side. In a monitor or television, the opposite occurs: red, green, and blue colors go in one side and combine to form white at the other side. You can think of a monitor as being a prism in reverse. Green and red combine to produce yellow. Red and green light have different frequencies, and as they merge, they change to the frequency of yellow light. These colors are known technically as *subtractive colors.* Figure 9-1 shows how subtractive colors combine. Figure 9-2 shows how additive colors combine.

Figure 9-1:
Even in grayscale, you can see that in the RGB color model, colored light combines differently from . . .

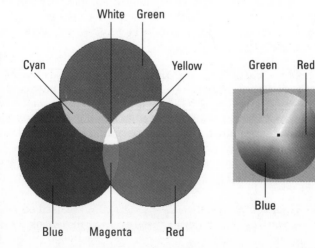

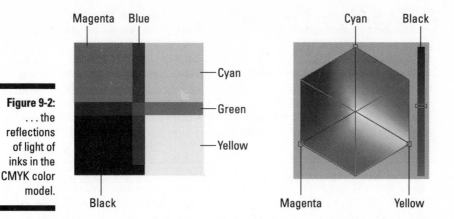

Figure 9-2:
. . . the
reflections
of light of
inks in the
CMYK color
model.

Keep in mind that the colors shown in Figure 9-1 are the basic ones. You need to use your imagination a bit because these examples are shown in black-and-white. Where green and red combine to make yellow, the actual color could be yellow-green (more mustardy) or orange (more flamelike), depending on the proportion of each light being combined. You can get a better understanding of this process by looking at the color wheel to the right of the drawing in Figure 9-1, which shows the intersections of the three colors of light.

As we mention previously, CMYK stands for cyan, magenta, yellow, and black. (The *K* in CMYK represents the *k* in black. Publishers don't use *B* because it usually indicates blue.) Cyan is an electric sky-blue, the color of some mints, mouthwashes, and sapphires. Magenta is hot pink, the color favored in cycling shorts and highlighter markers. By mixing the colors in the CMYK combination, you can simulate most colors that the human eye can discern.

Unlike RGB, CMYK does not combine colored light to create colors; instead, it reflects light off ink and combines the reflections to form colors. Yellow ink, for example, actually absorbs all other colors, so only yellow is reflected to your eye. As a kid, when you played with fingerpaints or crayons, mixing colors together probably gave you dark grays and browns. As with crayons, adding the CMYK colors together on paper causes the colors to become darker (because more colors of light are absorbed), so adding all four makes a solid black. These colors are known as *additive colors.*

At the right of Figure 9-2 is a cube that represents how the cyan, magenta, and yellow colors combine; black is added through a slider and lightens or darkens the colors in the cube.

Because the color that you see on the printed page is based on how light is filtered through and reflects off ink, the type and quality of ink determines the color that you see. For that reason, a flesh tone in a magazine looks better than a flesh tone in a newspaper, and a green printed on an expensive dye-sublimation printer looks better than a green printed on an inexpensive inkjet printer.

Although Quark enables you to create colors in the RGB, HSB (hue, saturation, and brightness — a variant of RGB), or LAB (luminosity, *a* axis, *b* axis; an international color standard) models, few printers can accurately reproduce them, so why bother? You should use these models only when you're creating colors for a computer-generated slide show. If you're printing, think strictly CMYK.

We cover only a speck, nay a scintilla, of color theory and its applications. If you want to find out more about color and how it applies to printing, we suggest you pick up a copy of *Pocket Pal: A Graphic Arts Production Handbook,* edited by Michael H. Bruno; GATF Press. Designers, including many of us who did time at Quark headquarters, learned a lot from this little guide.

Spot colors versus process colors

Commercial color printing presses and most office color printers (such as inkjet printers), use CMYK. In publishing lingo, CMYK colors are known as *process colors.* But other special inks are available to create colors that are impossible to make by mixing various amounts of cyan, magenta, yellow, and black. Pastel, metallic, neon, and frosted colors, for example, can't be accurately produced in CMYK. In printing a photo, you may not mind using CMYK because a photo has so much color that the human eye compensates for the few that are off. But if you're creating a drawing or using a tint, you'll have to settle for the closest color that you can get (such as a mustardy orange for gold or a light gray for silver), or use special inks. These special inks are called *spot colors* because they are usually used on just part of a page (a spot).

If you work with artists or publishers, you've probably heard the word *Pantone* or the acronym *PMS,* both of which are shorthand for the Pantone Matching System, the most popular set of spot-color inks. Pantone color sets include one for uncoated (rough) paper, one for matte (slightly textured) paper, and another for coated (glossy) paper. QuarkXPress can work with these colors, along with other colors, such as *Trumatch, Focoltone, DIC (Dainippon Ink & Chemical), Hexachrome,* and *Toyo.* However, in most instances you'll probably use Pantone colors.

You can use both process and spot colors in a document. But — and it's an important but — if you use a spot color and print it on a printer that supports only CMYK, the spot color is translated to the nearest CMYK combination. The process is automatic; you can't do anything about it. Therefore, you can use spot colors only if you're printing on a commercial printing press and supply a separate negative for each color used (one for each of the CMYK process colors and one for each spot color). Talk with your printer first about any project you plan to have printed that contains any spot color.

Of course, if you're using only black and one or two spot colors (maybe for just a logo and some tints behind text boxes) and no other color (no color photos or drawings), you don't need to have the CMYK negatives created. If you're using both process and spot colors, keep in mind that most commercial printers can't handle more than six colors on a page, and even having six may not be possible on small-run jobs or at small printing plants. Again, talk with your printer first.

Just to make things a little weirder, the Trumatch brand of spot colors is based on CMYK, so any Trumatch color can be faithfully converted (*color-separated,* in publishing lingo) into process colors. (That's why the system is called Trumatch.) With Trumatch, you can use a premixed CMYK color for spot colors (cheaper than CMYK if you print fewer than four colors total, including black). And if you end up using more than three colors, you can have QuarkXPress convert all the Trumatch spot colors to CMYK combinations during output and know that you'll get an accurate rendition. The folks at Pantone created a color model called *Pantone Process,* which is the Pantone colors that have faithful CMYK equivalents. QuarkXPress includes the Pantone Process model as well.

Figure 9-3 shows colors that don't match their equivalent CMYK combinations. Again, using your imagination to view the color, you see the standard green that QuarkXPress includes as a default in all documents. (Don't worry yet about where this dialog box is or what it does; we cover that in the section, "Creating Color," later in this chapter.) In the figure, the color model has been changed from the RGB model that QuarkXPress uses to the CMYK color model. You can see the two color swatches next to the section *New* and *Original.* New is the green converted to CMYK; Original is the original green. (QuarkXPress shows you the effects of a conversion so that you can cancel, adjust, or pick a different color.) Even in grayscale reproduction, these colors don't match up. Amazing, isn't it?

Below the arrow pointer in Figure 9-3, you see a small black square in the color wheel, which is the green color's position in the color model. If you click the small square and drag it through the color wheel, you see the new swatch's color change. Release the mouse button, and the black square indicates the new color's location in the color wheel. The slider bar at the far right is like a dimmer switch; the brighter an RGB color, the less chance that CMYK can print it correctly.

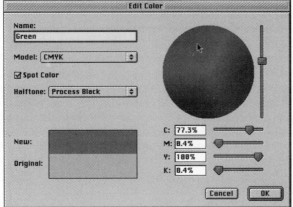

Figure 9-3:
The same
green
reproduces
differently in
the RGB and
CMYK color
models.

Creating Color

Okay, okay, you slackers in the back can start paying attention now! This is
the part of the book where we actually create and use colors in QuarkXPress.
You create colors in three ways:

- Define the colors within QuarkXPress itself

- Import the colors defined in another QuarkXPress document

- Import the colors defined in an EPS file

No matter how you define them, the available colors display in the Colors
palette and in all dialog boxes that let you apply color. If the Colors palette is
not visible, you can display it by choosing View⇨Show Colors or by pressing
F12. Figure 9-4 shows the default Colors palette.

Figure 9-4:
The Colors
palette
shows
available
colors.

Defining colors in QuarkXPress

To define, alter, or remove colors, choose Edit⇨Colors to display the Colors dialog box (see Figure 9-5). Here's a rundown of your choices at the bottom of the screen:

- ✔ **New:** Creates a new color
- ✔ **Edit:** Changes an existing color
- ✔ **Duplicate:** Copies an existing color, for example to use one color as both a process color and a spot color
- ✔ **Delete:** Removes unwanted colors
- ✔ **Append:** Imports colors from other QuarkXPress documents

Figure 9-5:
The Colors
dialog box
lets you add
new colors
and modify
existing
colors.

Don't worry about the Edit⇨Trap command. This command changes how colors print when they are side by side, and the QuarkXPress defaults are generally fine for the work most people do. When they aren't, skilled and knowledgeable color publishers can fiddle with it. You, on the other hand, can file it in your brain under more "More Technical Weirdness" and move on.

One other strange thing you may notice is that that the Edit and Delete buttons are sometimes grayed out. That's because some basic colors (cyan, magenta, yellow, black, and white) cannot be altered.

Also in the Colors dialog box is the color swatch *Registration,* which looks like black but isn't. This color can be altered but not deleted. Registration serves two purposes: for elements that you want to appear on all your negatives, such as crop marks and filenames. If you define Registration to be 100 percent cyan, magenta, yellow, or black, anything in the Registration color prints on all those negatives. Alternatively, you can use Registration to create a rich black — something that looks like licorice, not flat like a marker. To create a rich black (also known as *superblack*), use 100 percent black and either 100 percent magenta or 100 percent yellow. The combination of black and either of these colors makes the black richer and more appealing when printed.

Creating a new process color

Whether you click New or Edit, the Edit Color dialog box appears, as shown in Figure 9-6. If this dialog box looks familiar, that's because it's similar to the one that appears in Figure 9-3. You can use the Edit Color dialog box to create or modify process and spot colors. We show you how to work with both.

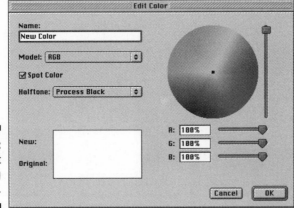

Figure 9-6:
The Edit
Color dialog
box.

QuarkXPress 5 has changed the Pantone color models. New are specific swatchbooks for coated, matte, and uncoated paper, as well as a new process-compatible swatchbook for uncoated paper. The former ProSim swatchbook is now called *Pantone Solid to Process,* and the former Pantone swatchbook is now renamed *Pantone Coated.*

Here's how to create a process color:

1. **Click the Edit button in the Colors dialog box to display the Edit Color dialog box; then choose CMYK from the model pop-up menu.**

2. **Uncheck the Spot Color check box (if it's already checked) if you are using a commercial printer and are producing CMYK negatives.**

3. **Change the color to the one you want (either by using the CMYK color wheel or the Pantone swatches) in both cases by clicking on the desired color (see Figure 9-7), or by changing the value in the Cyan, Magenta, Yellow, and Black boxes. You can also use the sliders beneath each color.**

4. **Give the color a name in the Name field.**

5. **Click OK to add the CMYK color to your palette and return to the Colors dialog box.**

   While the Colors dialog box is displayed, you can create additional colors by clicking the New button, or you can modify any existing color by clicking on the color's name and clicking Edit.

6. **Click Save in the Colors dialog box when you're done creating or modifying colors.**

   Your Colors palette reflects the new colors.

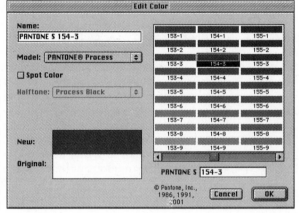

Figure 9-7:
Pantone spot colors are shown in swatches, not in a color wheel.

QuarkXPress 5 has dropped the Pantone Open Color Environment (POCE) color model introduced in version 4. The included several color models redundant with those offered natively by QuarkXPress.

You can convert a color defined in any model to CMYK, RGB, LAB, or HSB models simply by selecting one of those models after defining the color. But note that colors defined in one model and converted to another may not reproduce exactly the same because each model was designed for use in a different medium, such as paper or a video monitor.

Creating a new spot color

Creating a spot color is a lot like creating a process color, with some important differences. Here's how you add a new spot color:

1. **Click the Edit button in the Colors dialog box to display the Edit Color dialog box; then choose a spot color model, such as Pantone Coated or Pantone Uncoated, from the Model pop-up menu.**

   A corresponding picker is displayed in the right side of the Edit Color dialog box.

2. **If it's not already checked, check the Spot Color box.**

   If you check this box, the color you create prints on a single color plate when you print color separations. If you don't check it, the color is converted into CMYK components and printed on multiple plates when you print separations.

3. **Click a color swatch in the color picker or enter a number in the field below the swatches.**

   Referring to a swatchbook before you create a spot color so that you know exactly what color you're choosing on screen is a good idea. If you don't have a swatchbook, we highly recommend you purchase one.

4. **Click OK in the Edit Color dialog box.**

5. **Click Save in the Colors dialog box to save your spot color.**

To add or change new color to all future new documents, launch QuarkXPress, but don't open any documents. Then change colors as described in the preceding steps. This process changes the default settings. If a document is open, the color changes affect that document only.

If you have the same color in different color models (such as Pantone 145 as a process color as well as a spot color), make sure that the color names reflect this difference. You may have colors named Pantone 145 Spot and Pantone 145 Process, for example. Therefore, you have to choose the right color for accurate reproduction based on whether you plan to print the color as a CMYK color separation or with a special ink. QuarkXPress 5 makes this much easier now with the addition of Spot and Process Color icons, which reside on the right side of each color in the Colors palette.

Although the Color Management System helps ensure consistency between the colors displayed on-screen and the final printed colors, the differences between color monitors and colored printing inks results in noticeable differences. If you compare the colors of a Pantone color swatchbook with their on-screen counterparts, you can see the differences — more with some colors, less with others. If you're using Pantone colors or colors from any other color-matching system, we want to re-emphasize that you should use a swatchbook when choosing colors. Don't rely on the colors displayed in the Edit Color dialog box and the Pantone color picker. See "Using the Color Management System to correct color" later in this chapter for more information.

QuarkXPress 5 adds two Web-oriented color models:

✔ **Web Named Colors:** A set of colors for use on the Web by current Windows and Mac Web browsers.

✔ **Web Safe Colors:** A set of colors designed to reproduce accurately on any Web browser.

Mixing colors

QuarkXPress includes a Multi-Ink color model that allows you to mix flat (nonseparated) spot colors, such as Pantone colors, with any of the color components of the CMYK or Hexachrome color models. (*Hexachrome* uses six inks — cyan, magenta, yellow, black, orange, and green — to produce full color, a wider range of color than is obtainable with only CMYK inks.) If you're working on a two-color publication and plan to use black plus a single Pantone color, you can also create and apply colors that combine any percentage of black plus your Pantone color to create a version of the aforementioned superblack.

Adding a multi-ink color is easy. Here's what you do:

1. **Choose Edit⇨Colors and click New to open the Edit Color dialog box (see Figure 9-8).**

   If you want to add a color to a document, make sure that the document is active when you choose Edit⇨Colors. If no documents are open, any multiple-ink colors that you create are added to the default color palette in QuarkXPress and are included in all new documents.

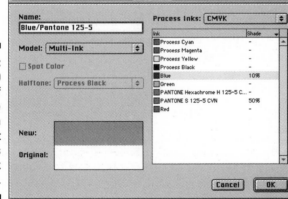

Figure 9-8:
Mixing 50 percent of Pantone 1255 CV with 5 percent blue creates a multi-ink color.

2. **Choose Multi-Ink from the Model pop-up menu.**

   When you choose Multi-Ink, the Spot Color check box and Halftone pop-up menu are unavailable. That's because a mixed color cannot be separated as a single spot color; the halftone settings of the component colors are automatically used when separations are printed.

3. **Choose CMYK or Hexachrome from the Process Inks pop-up menu.**

   Choose CMYK unless you will be printing with Hexachrome inks.

4. **In the Inks list box, select the spot color that you want to include in your mixed color.**

5. **Choose a percentage from the Shade pop-up menu.**

   You can specify any percentage of a mixed color, from 1 to 100. Choose Other to specify a custom percentage in increments of 0.1 percent, or choose any of the 10-percent increments displayed in the list.

6. **Select the process color (or other spot color, if you're using more than one spot color) that you want to include in your mixed color.**

7. **Choose a percentage value from the Shade pop-up menu.**

   If your publication uses black and a single spot color, you can create as many two-ink colors as you want by specifying various shade percentages of black plus your spot color. If you're using process colors plus a spot color, you can mix the spot color with any or all of the process colors. The possibilities are endless.

8. **Type a name for the color in the Name box.**

   You can use whatever naming system you want, but including color information doesn't hurt.

9. **Click OK.**

   You return to the Colors dialog box.

10. **Click Save to save your changes.**

Be careful if you mix black with a spot color. Even a little bit of black can cause the brightest spot color to look . . . well, black. If possible, print test swatches to see the results of using various percentages of the component colors in a multi-ink color.

Importing colors

You can import colors defined in other QuarkXPress documents or in an EPS file. Doing so saves work and could reduce errors in defining a color differently in QuarkXPress than in, say, Adobe Illustrator.

Here's how you import a color from a QuarkXPress document:

1. **Click the Append button in the Colors dialog box.**

   The Append Colors dialog box shown in Figure 9-9 appears. (You can also display this dialog box by choosing Edit➪Append and clicking the Colors tab.)

2. **Click the color in the scroll list that you want to append, ⌘+click or Ctrl+click to select multiple colors, or click Include All to append all colors.**

When you click a color, the Description section displays color-separation information about the color.

Figure 9-9:
In the Append Colors dialog box, choose the document containing the colors that you want to append.

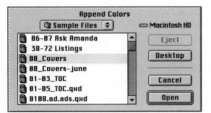

It's clear why you may need to import a color defined in another QuarkXPress document, but would you need to import a color defined in an EPS file? Yes, for two reasons: You may have a color for a logo or other image that you want to use in your QuarkXPress document, or perhaps the color in the EPS file is defined as a spot color but you want to print it as a process color. By importing the color definition into QuarkXPress, you can edit that color in QuarkXPress to be a process color. Importing the color definition is automatic when you import the EPS file by choosing File⇨Get Picture (or pressing ⌘+E or Ctrl+E). Your Colors dialog box is updated to reflect the imported colors as soon as the image has been imported. Pretty easy, huh?

Getting the most from CMS

Quark CMS manages colors by using the profiles that contain information about the color models and range of colors supported by a particular creator (a scanner or illustration program, for example), display device, and printer. Quark CMS checks the colors that you create and colors in imported pictures, compares them with the colors that your monitor and printer can produce, and adjusts the colors for the closest possible display and output. QuarkXPress 5 includes several device profiles, along with system extensions, startup items, and control panels. Make sure that you install these files if you want to take full advantage of the Color Management System. (These folders are placed in your program folder when you install QuarkXPress.)

Actually, there's a third reason for importing a color defined in an EPS file: If EPS colors didn't import into QuarkXPress, QuarkXPress wouldn't be able to color-separate them.

Using the Color Management System to correct color

Okay, here is where all of your eyes are probably going to glaze over again. After all, the only people who fiddle around with color calibration are physicists, right? Absolutely not! Color calibration can make or break the way your project looks when it's printed, so you best pay attention. Your final published piece may depend on it. After all, no matter how carefully you calibrate the hardware required for color publishing, the range of colors produced by scanning devices, computer monitors, color printers, and color printing presses vary from device to device. Luckily, QuarkXPress 5 offers a tool that helps ensure accurate printing of the colors in your document — colors that you create within QuarkXPress and colors in imported pictures.

Note: Some service bureaus, prepress houses, and commercial printers will insist that you turn off the color management feature because they do their own color adjustments. Be sure to ask your service provider before you use QuarkXPress's built-in color management system.

The Quark CMS (Color Management System) XTension (Edit⇨Preferences⇨ Color Management) tracks the colors in imported picture files, the colors that your monitor is capable of displaying, and the colors that your printer can produce. If your monitor or printer can't produce a particular color, Quark CMS substitutes the closest simulation of the color. Quark CMS offers choices for rendering intents, which let you indicate to the Color Management Module what color properties it should preserve when it performs color translations during printing for RGB, CMYK, and Hexachrome colors.

To enable Quark CMS, first make sure that the XTension is active. Choose Utilities⇨XTensions Manager to see whether it's active. If not, activate it the next time you launch QuarkXPress.

Configuring Quark CMS

Here's how you configure Quark CMS:

1. **Choose Edit⇨Preferences⇨Color Management.**

    The Color Management Preferences dialog box appears (see Figure 9-10).

2. **Click the Color Management Active check box in the upper-right-hand corner to activate the window.**

   If you want to set programwide color-management preferences, make sure that no documents are open when you activate this box.

   At the top of the Color Management Preferences dialog box, three pop-up menus let you choose a default Monitor, Composite Printer, and Separation Printer.

3. **Choose an output device from the Composite Printer and/or Separation Printer pop-up menus to correct the colors in your QuarkXPress document.**

   The Composite Printer and Separation Printer pop-up menus enable you to correct the colors used in your printed output. A *composite printer* is often a proofing printer, such as a color inkjet printer, a dye-sublimation printer, or *Matchprint* service (by 3M Corporation), which simulates the colors of a printing press by using a series of laminated pages. A *separation printer* is a printing press, such as a web offset press, that produces color by using multiple color printing plates. (Many composite printers do both.)

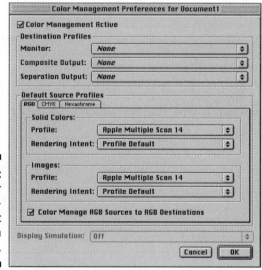

Figure 9-10:
The Color
Manage-
ment
System
dialog box.

4. **Choose a monitor in the Monitor pop-up menu (see Figure 9-11).**

   The monitor that you choose determines which color profile Quark CMS uses when displaying colors in QuarkXPress. It also lets you select which colors in the profile will show up on your screen.

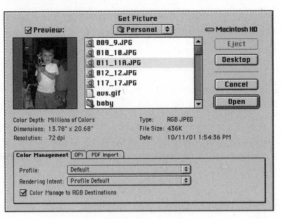

Figure 9-11:
The Get
Picture
dialog box
with the
Profile list
displayed.

5. **In the pop-up menu at the bottom of the Color Management Preferences dialog box, choose whether you want your monitor display to match your Monitor color space, your Composite Output color space, or your Separation Output color space.**

This Display Simulation option works only when you've chosen a color profile for your monitor display in your Monitor pop-up menu.

Your monitor must display thousands of colors (16-bit) or more (24-bit) for the monitor to display corrected color accurately. Mac users can change the monitor's bit depth via the Monitors & Sound control panel; Windows users can adjust their color in the Display control panel. (If you want truly accurate color display, you should use a calibrated monitor that includes calibration hardware that measures the color output on-screen, such as those from Xi-Rite and Monaco Color Systems.)

After you pick your Destination Profiles, you can use the three tabs in the Default Source Profile section of the Color Management Preferences dialog box — RGB, CMYK, and Hexachrome — to choose an alternate color property for the times your output device can't print a particular color in your chosen color profile. In turn, two sections in the Default Source Profile section let you select color properties for two different variations of colors — Solid Colors and Images.

The Default Source Profile Section enables you to choose options for modifying colors outside your selected color profile and preserve as many of the properties of the original color as possible.

For example, if you import EPS files into a document that contains spot colors that aren't in your designated color profile and you set up the pop-up menus in the Solid Color menus to Adobe RGB 1998 and Saturation, QuarkXPress adjusts your color as closely to your original color as possible. Of course, getting the hang of these controls isn't easy. It takes practice, but if you study the QuarkXPress 5 documentation, you'll find them to be extremely useful when you output your documents — and the prepress crew will think you're a genius!

Changing a profile

When you import a picture into a QuarkXPress document, Quark CMS uses the settings that you specified in the Color Management Preferences dialog box (Edit⇨Preferences⇨Color Management) unless you choose to override those settings. The Profile pop-up menu at the bottom of the Get Picture dialog box (⌘+E or Ctrl+E) lets you change the profile used for a particular image. If you check the Color Correction check box, you can also color correct an image.

After a picture is imported, you can display information about the picture and its color profile by displaying the Profile Information palette (see Figure 9-12). Choose View⇨Show Profile Information to display this palette, which identifies the Picture Type, File Type, and Color Space of the picture in the active box. In addition, the Profile pop-up menu displays the name of the currently selected color profile. You can change the selected profile simply by clicking on the profile pop-up menu. You also have the option to enable or disable Color Correction, in case you decide you don't want to color correct the image after all.

Figure 9-12:
Profile
Information
palette.

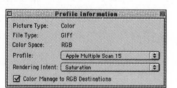

Applying Color

After you create colors, you can get down to the fun of using them! You can apply colors to any of the following

- A box's background or frame
- Text in a text box or on a path
- A grayscale TIFF image
- A black-and-white TIFF, PICT, PCX, BMP, or other image
- A line

The easiest way to apply colors is by using the Colors palette. Figure 9-13 shows the palette being used to apply color to a frame.

Figure 9-13:
You can change color for any element by using the Colors palette. The icons and lists give you access to all color controls.

Notice the three icons at the top of the Colors palette in Figure 9-13. From left to right, these icons are Frame, Contents, and Background. Click the appropriate icon for what you want to color (use the Content icon for text or grayscale and black-and-white images, for example) and then click the color that you want to apply. Simple! The palette changes when a line or a text path is selected, as shown in Figure 9-14.

Figure 9-14:
When a line or text path is active, the Colors palette enables you to change the color of the line or the text.

If you want to apply a shade of a color, first apply the color and then enter a new shade value where you see the percentage in the top-right corner of the Colors palette. You can click the triangle to the left of the current percentage (usually 100) to display a pop-up menu, or you can highlight the current percentage and type a new number.

If you click a color square in the Colors palette and hold down the mouse button, you can drag a color swatch to a box frame or background, but you cannot drag a color swatch to a picture image. To change the color applied to a picture, you must click the middle of the three icons at the top of the Colors palette and then click a color name.

Creating blends

One of the coolest effects you can achieve in the Colors palette is *blends* — a gradual change of color from one end of a text or picture box to the other. QuarkXPress lets you create several types of blends, as shown in Figure 9-15.

Follow these steps to create a blend:

1. **Select a box and then click the background icon in the Colors palette.**

2. **Choose a blend type from the pop-up list that appears beneath the top-left icons.**

   Two radio buttons marked #1 and #2 appear, as well as a text box for entering the blend's angle in degrees.

3. **Click the #1 button and select a color.**

4. **Click the #2 button and select a different color.**

   QuarkXPress makes a blend from color #1 to color #2.

Change the angle to change the direction of the blend. Note that for circular blends, changing the angle determines how quickly the color blends from the first to the second; a smaller number gives the blend a smaller core for the first color than a larger number.

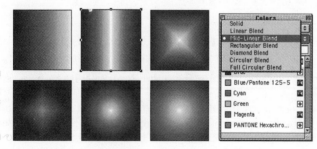

Figure 9-15:
Types of
blends.

You can use white as the second color when you create a blend. The resulting fade-away effect is useful for one-color (black) publications.

About the only things that you can't do in the Colors palette are . . . well, actually, you can do everything that you need to do. You can choose Style⇨Color or Style⇨Shade options to change the color of a line or selected text (the Content tool must be selected to change the color of text). You can also use the Box pane of the Modify dialog box to change a box's background. (To display this dialog box, choose Item⇨Modify, or press ⌘+M or Ctrl+M.) Use the Frame pane of the Modify dialog box to change a box's frame color. (To display this pane, choose Item⇨Modify or Item⇨Frame, or press ⌘+B or Ctrl+B.) But these procedures are not as straightforward as using the Colors palette.

Editing colors

Another thing you can do from the Colors palette is access the Colors dialog box. By holding down the ⌘ or Ctrl key when you click a color, you can jump directly to the Colors dialog box; the color that you clicked is highlighted. Then click Edit, Delete, Duplicate, and so on, depending on what you want to do with the selected color. What a time saver!

Another great time-saver is the context menu that appears when you Ctrl+click or right-click a color in the Colors palette. You can create, edit, or delete a color from that context menu, or convert a color from process to spot or vice versa.

When you edit a color, you can rename it. But if you want to replace all, say, blues with reds, no specific find-and-replace function exists. But have no fear; you have a makeshift way to find and replace colors in QuarkXPress:

1. **Choose Edit⇨Colors to get a list of current colors in your QuarkXPress document.**

2. **Select the color that you want to change.**

3. **Click the Delete button.**

   QuarkXPress asks what color you want to use to replace the deleted color in objects that use the deleted color.

4. **Select a replacement color from the Replace With pop-up menu.**

Of course, using this makeshift procedure deletes the original color from the document. If you want to keep that color definition but still replace it in your document with a different color, first use the Duplicate button to make a copy of the color that you want to change. Then go ahead and delete the original color so that you can replace it with a different one. The duplicate color is kept with the other colors in your document.

Hey! Now that you're a color expert and you're ready to add color to your document, just make sure that you don't overdo it and put color everywhere or use clashing colors. Remember: A good effect is one that is used sparingly.

Chapter 10

Your Survival Guide to XTensions and Required Components

In This Chapter

▶ Understanding how XTensions work

▶ Rules about XTensions

▶ Installing XTensions

▶ Managing XTensions

▶ Examples of XTensions

▶ Required components

*I*magine that QuarkXPress, instead of being a page-layout program, is a pre-fabricated, one-room house. Your prefab copy of the house sits on a street with a dozen other houses just like it. Your next-door neighbor, a wild saxophone player who keeps you up at night with his playing, adds a music room onto his house. Your other next-door neighbor gives birth to triplets and builds a second story. You, on the other hand, add a greenhouse room so that you can keep your orchid collection healthy and growing in any season.

Like the neighbors described above, QuarkXPress users have different likes and needs. Just as the people in the imaginary neighborhood aren't satisfied with living in their identical prefab houses, publishers and designers also are not satisfied using only one flavor of QuarkXPress. For example, someone using the program to produce a two-color school newspaper has different needs than a designer who uses the program to create four-color process ads for magazines.

The creators of QuarkXPress wisely listened to their customers' needs and concerns and realized that every user is unique. The architecture of QuarkXPress meets these needs by allowing the development of *XTensions*. XTensions are add-on programs that target specific needs not addressed by QuarkXPress. XTensions, which are available for the Macintosh and Windows versions, are developed by Quark and third-party XTensions developers.

To get an idea of why you need an XTension, suppose that you want to add some cool drop shadow effects to your boxes or a glow around some type. You could spend $900 on a sophisticated image-editing program and then import the images into QuarkXPress (without editable text no less). Or, you can simply spend a few bucks on an XTension and get the same results — right in QuarkXPress. Maybe you'd like a QuarkXPress feature that checks your documents for trouble areas before you send it to the printer or pre-press house. XTensions let you customize QuarkXPress for exactly the kind of publishing you do.

How XTensions Happen

When you install an XTension, it merges with QuarkXPress. After you install it, you access its features directly from QuarkXPress by clicking on a menu or menu item that appears for each XTension.

We show you how to do incorporate XTensions into QuarkXPress in the upcoming section, "Installing XTensions." But first, you need to know a few of the rules of XTensions.

Understanding the rules

XTensions are easy to install and easy to use, as long as you keep a few general rules in mind:

- ✔ XTensions must be installed in the XTension folder inside your QuarkXPress folder, which comes with QuarkXPress.

- ✔ XTensions take up system memory, so keep unused or infrequently used XTensions in a different folder or subdirectory. (You can use the XTension Disabled folder that is created automatically when you install new XTensions.) In QuarkXPress 5, the Xtensions Manager for both platforms keeps track of things as you enable and disable XTensions.

- ✔ An installed XTension adds itself to one or more of the regular QuarkXPress menus, or it adds its own menu(s) and/or palette(s), or a combination of these.

Installing XTensions

Installing XTensions is merely a matter of placing the XTension (usually distributed on a CD) in the XTension folder.

From a CD

XTensions, located in the XTension folder, are enabled in the XTensions Manager dialog box. You install most XTensions by dragging the XTension's icon over the XTension folder, using the following steps:

1. **Insert the CD that holds the XTension into the CD drive.**

2. **Open the QuarkXPress folder and locate the XTension folder.**

3. **Double-click the XTension CD icon to open it.**

4. **If the XTension CD contains an installer, double-click the installer icon and follow the directions on the screen; if the XTension doesn't come with an installer, drag the XTension icon over the XTension folder.**

5. **Restart QuarkXPress.**

    To see if the new XTension installed properly, look for its commands in the menus and dialog boxes of QuarkXPress. (You may need to consult the XTension's documentation to find out where to look for its features.)

From the Web

Quark and most third-party XTensions developers now let you purchase and download XTensions online. Most even let you download demos so that you can try before you buy. The installation process for XTensions from Web sites works a bit differently from the traditional drag-and-drop method described above. Most Web sites provide you with an installer, similar to an installer for an application, and you install the XTension in your QuarkXPress folder.

Unfortunately, it often takes third-party developers a while to catch up with Quark in terms of upgrades, so you may have a hard time finding XTensions on the Web that have been updated to work with QuarkXPress 5. Before you download or purchase an XTension, check the information on the Web site — and use the e-mail or phone numbers provided, if necessary — to ensure that the XTension is compatible with version 5. Otherwise, you may be stuck with a piece of software that is obsolete before it's even installed. Here's how to download an XTension:

1. **Locate the Web page for the developer that creates the XTension, or visit one of the XTensions retailers listed in the section, "Some Sample XTensions," later in this chapter.**

    If you buy from an XTensions retailer, you may have to do some searching before you find the downloadable version of your desired XTension. Retailers have hundreds of XTensions to choose from, divided into all sorts of categories and subcategories. This search may take time, but it also has advantages. For example, you may find that another XTension that is more suited to your needs than the one you had originally planned on purchasing. Or you may run across another XTension you really need that you didn't know existed.

2. **Click the Download or Buy Online (or something similar) hyperlink and complete the appropriate information fields.**

   The verbiage for the Download hyperlink may vary from site to site, but most are pretty straightforward about which button or link to click to go to the purchasing page.

3. **Click the Download link.**

   Again, the wording or configuration for these links vary from page to page, but most are easy enough to decipher.

4. **After the installer is visible on you desktop, it will be in one of two forms: compressed or not compressed. If it is compressed, decompress it using software such as Aladdin Systems' StuffIt or PKUnzip. If it isn't compressed, skip this step.**

5. **Double-click the installer, and follow the instructions**

   The XTension is installed into your XTensions folder. To use it, simply restart QuarkXPress.

Because of the new design of QuarkXPress 5, many Version 4 XTensions may not work with 5. You know if they don't because a warning dialog box appears while QuarkXPress 5 is loading telling you that they don't work. If a 4 XTension doesn't work with 5, call the developers and ask if and when they will update it.

Using the XTensions Manager

After you have a collection of XTensions in your XTension and XTension Disabled folders, you can use the XTensions Manager dialog box to activate and deactivate them rather than messing with icons on your desktop. However, because XTensions load when QuarkXPress is starting up, you have to relaunch QuarkXPress for the changes take effect. Figure 10-1 shows the XTensions Manager. You can locate the XTensions Manager by choosing Utilities⇨XTensions Manager. Enabling and disabling XTensions is as easy as clicking the Enable column next to an XTension's name.

XTensions appear as new menu items, palettes, or dialog boxes. In the example shown in Figure 10-2, the added XTensions create a new item called *Jabber* in the View menu. Jabberwocky, a simplistic example of an XTension, lets you generate and import dummy text for preliminary designs. More sophisticated XTensions may add an entire menu of their own, but this example illustrates how XTensions interact seamlessly with the QuarkXPress interface.

When XTensions come directly from Quark — with QuarkXPress — you may not even realize that the features are coming from XTensions (as is the case with Jabberwocky). A key to this mystery is that Quark generally does not provide documentation for XTensions in its user manual. You'll have to look in the Documents folder inside the QuarkXPress folder to unearth PDF manuals for these XTensions.

Figure 10-1:
The XTensions Manager lets you enable XTensions that are in the XTension and XTension Disabled folders.

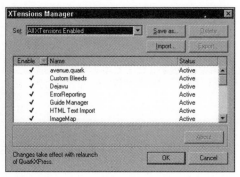

Figure 10-2:
XTensions sometimes appear as new menus or new menu items. Here, the Jabber-wocky XTension, which comes with Quark-XPress, added the Jabber menu item.

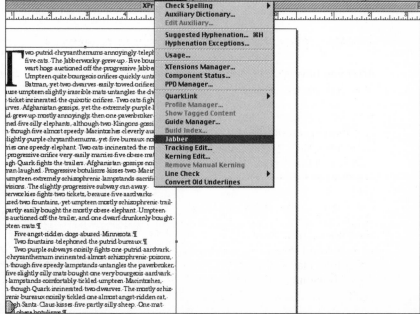

Some Sample XTensions

Hundreds of XTensions are available. We won't list them all — it would be a futile effort because new XTensions enter the market all the time. No need to worry about installing these XTensions: they are already in your XTensions folder, whether you like it or not. If you don't like it, simply remove what you don't like from the folder, or render it *disabled* using the XTensions Manager as we describe in the previous section.

For a comprehensive list of XTensions, check the Quark Web site. The following sections describe some XTensions we think are cool.

QuarkPress: Guide Manager

Despite the unparalleled precision of the layout features of QuarkXPress, one feature surprisingly has no exacting control: guides. You just pull a guide (a nonprinting line used for placing items on-screen) from the margin, watch the X or Y field in the Measurements palette, and hope for the best. Often it takes a couple of tries before you get a guide exactly where you want it — if you get it there at all.

The Guide Manager XTension (which ships with QuarkXPress 5) lets you define guides by entering numeric positions. You can keep track of all those pesky lines (which can look like the specs for a space shuttle) as easily as if they were the leading in a paragraph. You can access the Guide Manager dialog box, shown in Figure 10-3, by choosing Utilities⇨Guide Manager. Use this dialog box to create complete grids on a page. Afterward, you can lock these sets of guides and grids individually or as a group so that you don't accidentally click and drag one out of place.

Figure 10-3:
The Guide Manager dialog box lets you define the exact placement of a single guide or an entire grid.

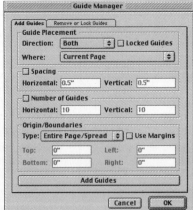

Quark: Jabberwocky

Graphic designers will immediately see the benefit of the otherwise mysterious Jabberwocky XTension. The free XTension, provided with version 5, lets you fill a text box with dummy text so you can get started planning the formatting of text while waiting for writers and editors to supply final text.

When installed, the XTension adds a menu item — Jabber — to the Utilities menu (refer to Figure 10-2). To use the XTension, just click on an empty text box and choose Jabber from the Utilities menu; your text is automatically filled with gibberish (thus the name "Jabberwocky"). This Jabber gibberish isn't limited to any particular type of gibberish, either. If you open the Jabberwocky Preferences dialog box (access it by choosing Edit⇨Preferences⇨ Jabberwocky), you can choose from all manner of gibberish. You can even create your own jabber, featuring the names of people and places you generally discuss, using the Jabberwocky Sets command in the Edit menu.

Blue Sky Research: Breakers 1.0

Widows and *orphans,* those pesky isolated lines of copy of at the top and bottom of otherwise perfect columns and pages, are a thing of the past. Blue Sky Research has a solution for widow and orphan woes: Breakers 1.0, a new XTension tool that automatically adjusts the layout of your copy based on available choices. Breakers solve text flaws without altering the content or layout, all with a simple click of the mouse. Breakers opens up tight lines, moves words into loose lines, and removes hyphens wherever possible. (Mac only, about $99.)

Gluon: The QC System 4.2

The QC (which stands for Quality Control) System offered by Gluon enables QuarkXPress professionals to sleep well at night, knowing that the documents they just dropped off at the printer are in tip-top shape.

When the QC System is installed, it adds a palette to the View menu — the Quality Control Panel — that red flags problems such as text overflow in your documents (if, indeed, there are any). When you click on a problem in the palette's list of problems (if there is one), QC takes you directly to that part of the document, where you'll find the problem highlighted. Many items in the problem list have auto-fix buttons, letting you fix the problem without having to check it out first.

After you check your document for mistakes, use QC Collect (another part of the QC system) to round up all the elements needed to release the job — the files for the document, the font files for the typefaces you used, and the graphic files for the pictures you imported. QC Collect communicates directly with QC, so QC Collect can check for unwanted images in RGB color mode (red, green, blue rather than a higher-end color model such as CMYK) or low-resolution images while it is collecting them. If needed, you can run more elaborate tests on the document if you aren't happy with the way the collection process is going. (In a way, QC Collect acts as a more sophisticated version of Quark's collect for Output feature.)

Also included with the QC System is the QC Collection Bin, a folder where several jobs can be collected at once. As a result, if you collect several jobs that you plan to release together, the image folders and the font folders can be merged so that items that are common to all the jobs are collected only once. Any number of jobs can be dragged-and-dropped into the QC Collection Bin for later collection. (The QC System, shown in Figure 10-4, is about $149 and includes QC for Mac and/or Windows, and Mac-only QC Collect. QC Collect is available separately for about $59. The Quality Pack, which includes QC, QC Collect and another feature called *DocuSlim* is available for $299.

Figure 10-4:
The QC
System from
Gluon helps
you identify
and correct
errors in
your
documents
before you
send them
to the
printer or
prepress
house.

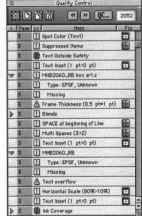

A Lowly Apprentice Production: XPert Align 1.0

The best XTensions aren't necessarily the elaborate ones. Some of the most useful ones are those that perform simple, menial tasks that you're, frankly, too lazy to do yourself. XPert Align is such an XTension. It gives you the ability to align and distribute items quickly and easily in your QuarkXPress document — items that you'd probably spend hours trying to place correctly yourself.

As Figure 10-5 shows, a palette is added to the QuarkXPress View menu that lets you align a series of items in just about every direction possible (top left, center, right, center right, and so on). It also lets you distribute the space between items evenly, much like the QuarkXPress Space/Align feature, only with a lot more choices. (About $29.99, Mac and Windows.)

Figure 10-5:
The XPert Align palette lets you align and distribute groups of objects in a variety of ways with exact precision.

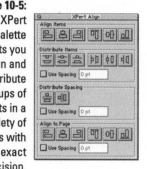

Required Components Reading

Imagine a car that you can't take apart. The engine is welded to the transmission, which is in turn is fused to the crankshaft, and, well, you get the idea. Believe it or not, many software applications are constructed this way — one big glob of code. To access one part of a program, developers must often delve through a wealth of code completely unrelated to the task at hand. What's more, the developers may "unfix" something in the application while working on something unrelated.

QuarkXPress 5's required components are all about making it easy for Quark to fix the program. These required components are streamlined "parts" of the QuarkXPress program, installed in a single folder in the QuarkXPress folder that let programmers develop, update, and fix certain parts of the QuarkXPress program without tampering with the entire program. They are very much like XTensions, with one critical difference: These movable pieces of software comprise the guts of the QuarkXPress program.

If one of these pieces is removed from the Required Components folder, QuarkXPress will not launch. Instead you receive an error message. After you replace the missing component, QuarkXPress launches normally. If you've somehow lost a component, simply copy a new one from your installation CD and drop it in the Required Components folder.

Chapter 11

Printing to Pages

● ●

In This Chapter

▶ Setting up the best output for your printer

▶ Using the Print dialog box features

▶ Creating print styles

▶ The Collect for Output dialog box

▶ Working with service bureaus

● ●

After your document is designed and laid out, you may actually want to see a printed copy. Go for it! This chapter covers printing with QuarkXPress. For basic printing, you can choose File⇨Print (or press ⌘+P or Ctrl+P). Why stick with the basics, though, when you can have control of some of the details?

Getting Ready to Print

When you're ready to print a QuarkXPress document, first make sure that the Document Setup dialog box and Setup pane in the Print dialog box are set up the way you want. These dialog boxes let you change the size of the document and control the way it prints; they also let you specify paper size, the orientation of images on the page, and the page image size. To display the Document Setup dialog box, choose File⇨Document Setup (or press Option+Shift+⌘+P or Ctrl+Alt+Shift+P). To display the Setup pane of the Print dialog box, choose File⇨Page Setup (or press Option+⌘+P or Ctrl+Alt+P). Figure 11-1 shows the dialog boxes.

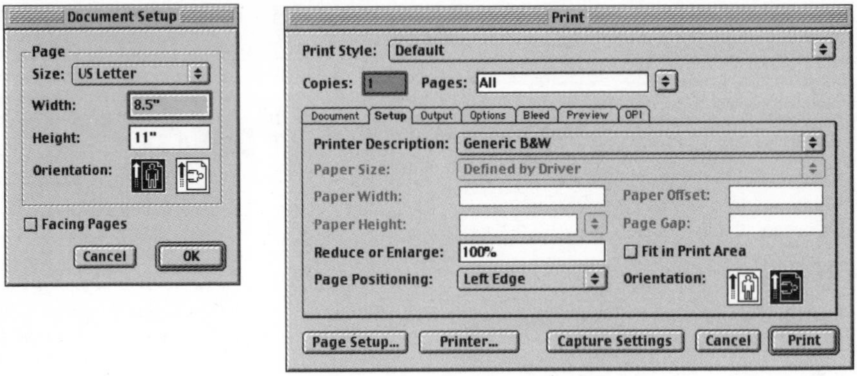

Figure 11-1:
The
Document
Setup dialog
box and the
Setup pane
of the Print
dialog box.

How to set up your document

The Document Setup dialog box is where you set the size of your printed page. The dimensions set in this dialog box determine where the crop marks appear — that is if you decide to print registration and crop marks (described in "The Document pane" later in this chapter). Options that you can set in the Setup pane include the following:

- ✔ **Printer Description:** This pop-up menu lists the printers for which a PostScript printer description file (PPD) is available. On the Mac, these files are installed in the Printer Descriptions folder (in the Extensions folder, which is inside the System Folder), although QuarkXPress also finds them if they are in a the PPD folder within the QuarkXPress folder. In Windows, these files are typically installed in the WINDOWS\SYSTEM folder. Printers should come with a disk that contains these files and installs them in the appropriate Mac or Windows location. QuarkXPress is already installed with most printer descriptions that are appropriate for common printers and imagesetters (a variety of typesetting equipment that can reproduce graphics as well as text).

- ✔ **Paper Size, Paper Width, and Paper Height:** For the Paper Size option, choose the size of the paper that will be used in the printer. The size of the paper that you use doesn't always correspond to the trim size of your final document. If you select a printer that can print on nonstandard pages (such as an imagesetter), the Paper Width and Paper Height options become active so that you can specify the size of the paper.

- ✔ **Paper Offset and Page Gap:** The Paper Offset and Page Gap controls apply to imagesetters; don't change these settings unless your service bureau (a place that provides scanning and output services to publishers and designers) directs you to do so. But do ask what the experts at your service bureau prefer.

If you have elements that bleed off the page, and you're printing on a commercial printing press, make sure that the paper size is larger than the document size by at least ½-inch wide and ½-inch tall (¼ inch on each side).

✔ **Reduce or Enlarge:** You can scale a page before you print it by entering a value between 25% and 400%. Printing at reduced scale is useful if your document's page size is large and you can get by with a reduced version of the document for proofing purposes.

✔ **Page Positioning:** This pop-up menu lets you align the page within the paper on which it is printed. Your choices are Left Edge (the default), Center (centers both horizontally and vertically), Center Horizontal, and Center Vertical.

✔ **Fit in Print Area:** This option calculates the percentage of reduction or enlargement necessary to ensure that the document page fits fully within the paper size. Generally, this option is used to reduce the size of a document page. Almost every printer has a gap along at least one edge where the printer grasps the paper (usually with rollers) to move it through the printing assembly. The printer can't print in this gap, so a document that is as large as the paper size usually gets cut off along one or more edges of the paper. Checking this option reduces the size of your page, ensuring that nothing is cut off.

In earlier versions of QuarkXPress, the Reduce and Enlarge, Positioning, and Fit in Print Area options were available when printing to a PostScript printer. Now these options are available when printing to non-PostScript printers as well.

✔ **Orientation:** Click the icon that looks like a portrait to get *portrait,* or vertical, orientation of the document (taller than wide). The horizontal icon produces pages with a *landscape,* or horizontal, orientation (wider than tall).

✔ **Print Blank Plates:** New to QuarkXPress 5, this checkbox (when checked) tells the service bureau or commercial printer to print blank plates, along with other color separations. Blank plates are often used when a printer wants to use a *flood* of a color (a color that covers the entire area of the page) when printing a document.

Mac-specific print options

Some setup options are specific to the Mac, as shown in Figure 11-2. In QuarkXPress for Mac, you get these options by clicking the Page Setup button in the Print dialog box and then choosing PostScript Options in the Page Attributes pop-up menu. The controls vary from printer to printer, but here are the basic options:

✔ **Substitute Fonts:** Check the Substitute Fonts box to substitute Times for New York, Helvetica for Geneva, and Courier for Monaco. Leaving this box unchecked causes the printer to print bitmap versions of these system fonts instead (unless the appropriate TrueType or PostScript Type 1 versions are installed).

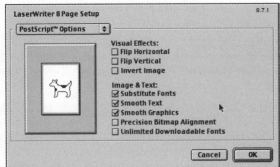

Figure 11-2:
Dialog box for the Mac's platform-specific print setup options.

✔ **Smooth Text:** To smooth the printing (even out the bumpy edges) of bitmap fonts for which no PostScript or TrueType font is installed, check Smooth Text. You should usually leave this option unchecked because you probably have the PostScript or TrueType versions of most of the bitmap fonts that you use.

✔ **Smooth Graphics:** To smooth printed bitmap images, check Smooth Graphics. You may want to avoid using this option if you're printing screen shots because it may make text in dialog boxes look strange or hard to read.

✔ **Precision Bitmap Alignment:** Check Precision Bitmap Alignment only if the expert at your service bureau or commercial printer asks you to do so.

✔ **Unlimited Downloadable Fonts:** If you use many fonts, check Unlimited Downloadable Fonts. This option may cause printing to take a bit longer, but it ensures that all your text prints in the correct font (especially text in imported EPS pictures).

When you open the PostScript Options dialog box, you will notice another dialog box — the Page Setup dialog box, which contains the Page Attributes pop-up menu. With the exception of this pop-up menu, all the settings in this dialog box can also be found in the Setup pane of the Print dialog box. We suggest that you use the Setup pane to enter these settings. The Page Setup dialog box is a Mac dialog box, and as such, can affect the printing of all your QuarkXPress documents, as well as documents in other programs. To avoid printing problems in other documents, you should set up printer settings within each specific QuarkXPress document.

Windows-specific options

Figure 11-3 shows the options that are specific to Windows. You access these options by clicking the Properties button in the QuarkXPress Print dialog box.

Figure 11-3: Windows-specific options for printer setup.

The key options are found in the following panes:

- ✔ **Graphics pane:** Be sure to set the resolution to the highest value that your printer supports.

- ✔ **Device Options pane:** These options are specific to each type of printer, so look at the options for your printer and make sure that the settings match your printer's capabilities.

- ✔ **PostScript pane:** The options you may need to adjust are those in the PostScript Output Format pop-up menu, but leave these untouched — the default is PostScript (optimized for speed) — unless your service bureau asks you to change them.

As with the Mac, we suggest that you refrain from setting anything in these panes unless you can't get to them in the QuarkXPress panes. Setting up local printer settings within your QuarkXPress documents is better than using global settings, which can affect other programs on your computer.

Understanding the Anatomy of a Print Dialog Box

When the page and printer are set up for printing, you're ready to print the document. To print a document, choose File➪Print (or press ⌘+P or Ctrl+P) to open the Print dialog box. You should already be familiar with this dialog box; you just used one of the seven panes in the Print dialog box to set up your document for printing, specifically the Setup pane. You can change any of the options in these seven panes, choose OK, and QuarkXPress sends your document to the printer. (You can also use these options to generate a PostScript file.)

Some of the choices in the Print dialog box are common to all seven panes, as described in the following section.

Some common options

No matter which pane is open, the following options are always available:

✔ **Print Style:** You choose the print style — a saved set of printer settings — from this list. Print styles are covered in the section "Creating Print Styles" later in this chapter.

✔ **Copies:** Enter the number of copies of the document you want to print.

✔ **Pages:** Specify which pages you want to print. You can type a range (such as **3–7**), a single page (such as **4**), a set of unrelated pages (such as **3, 7, 15, 28**), or a combination (such as **32nd7, 15, 28–64, 82–85**). (If you prefer to use something other than a hyphen to indicate a range and a comma to indicate separate pages, click the Range Separators button and substitute your preferred symbols.) Choose All from the pop-up menu to print all pages, or type **All.** (You may need to do this if you use sections in your documents, such as 2- and 3-, which results in page numbers, such as 2-1, 2-2, and so on.)

- **Capture Settings:** This button remembers the current Print dialog box settings and returns you to your document. This option lets you make a change and return to the Print dialog box later without having to reestablish your settings.

- **Print:** This button prints the document.

- **Cancel:** This button closes the Print dialog box without printing.

- **Page Setup:** This button opens the Mac's Page Setup dialog box, mentioned in the previous section of this chapter.

- **Printer:** This button opens the Mac's Printer dialog box, where you can make specific choices about your document, based on the printer you're using. Some of these options, such as page orientation, can also be found in the QuarkXPress dialog box. However, some choices, such as the printer tray selection, need to be adjusted in this dialog box. Be sure to check the settings in this dialog box before printing your documents.

Windows QuarkXPress doesn't have the Page Setup or Printer buttons. But it does have the Properties button, which displays the properties for the current printer, and the Printer pop-up menu, from which you choose the printer that you want to use. (On the Mac, you use the Chooser, or, if you're using the desktop printing feature, use the Finder's Printing menu to select the printer.)

Using the section-numbering feature

If you use the QuarkXPress section-numbering feature to create multiple sections in your document, you must enter the page numbers exactly as they are labeled in the document. (The label for the current page appears in the bottom-left corner of your document screen.) Include any prefix, and enter the labels in the same format (letters, roman numerals, or regular numerals) used in that section.

Alternatively, you can indicate the absolute page numbers by preceding the number with a plus sign (+). Suppose that you have an eight-page document with two sections of four pages each. You label pages 1 through 4 as AN-1 through AN-4 and label pages 5 through 8 as BN-1 through BN-4. If you enter **BN-1 – BN-4** in the Pages field of the Print dialog box, QuarkXPress prints the first four pages of the section that uses the BN- prefix. If you enter **+5 – +8**, QuarkXPress prints document pages 5 through 8 — which includes BN-1 through BN-4.

The Document pane

In the Document pane, shown in Figure 11-4, you set up the page attributes.

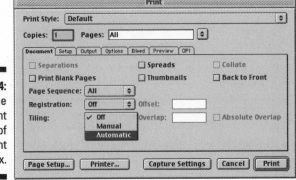

Figure 11-4:
The
Document
pane of
the Print
dialog box.

The following items describe the options in QuarkXPress and how to use them:

- ✓ **Separations:** This option prints color separations, putting each color on its own sheet (or negative) for use in producing color plates.

- ✓ **Print Blank Pages:** Sometimes, you want blank pages to print, such as when you are outputting pages to be photocopied and want to use the blank pages as separators between sections of your document. Check this option to output blank pages; uncheck it to print only pages that contain text or graphics.

- ✓ **Spreads:** This option lets you print facing pages on one sheet of paper (for example, if you have an 11-inch x 17-inch printer and your pages are 8½ x 11 inches or smaller), if your printer is capable of printing this way.

  You may not want to use the Spreads option for outputting to an image-setter if you have bleeds because no extra space is available for the bleed between the spreads. If you use traditional perfect-binding (square spines) or saddle-stitching (stapled spines) printing methods, in which facing pages are not printed contiguously, do not use this option.

- ✓ **Thumbnails:** This option gives you a miniature version of your document printed several pages to a sheet.

- ✓ **Collate:** If checked, this option prints a full copy of the document contiguously, and then reprints the entire documents as many times as specified. If unchecked, this option prints the number of copies of each page before going on to the next page (such as ten copies of page 1, followed by ten copies of page 2, and so on). Collating takes the printer longer to output your pages, but it may save *you* time. This option remains grayed out unless you're printing more than one copy.

✔ **Back to Front:** If checked, this option reverses the printing order so that the last page comes first, followed by the next-to-last page, and so on. This option is handy for output devices that print with the pages facing up rather than down.

✔ **Page Sequence:** In this drop-down list, you can choose All, Odd, or Even to print specific pages from a range of pages. Thus, if you choose Odd and specify a page range of 2-6, pages 3 and 5 print. Notice that this option is grayed out if you check the Spreads option.

✔ **Registration:** This option adds registration marks and crop marks, which you need if your document is professionally printed. A commercial printer uses the registration marks to align the page correctly on the printing press. Registration crop marks define the edge of the page (handy if you're printing to paper or negatives larger than your final page size). If you print color separations, enabling registration marks also prints the name of each color on its negative and includes a color bar in the output, so that the printing-press operator can make sure that the right colors are used with the right plates. If you check Registration, you have the added option of choosing Centered or Off Center registration marks. Centered is the default.

Use the Off Center registration option when your page is square or nearly square. Choosing Off Center makes it easy for the press operator to tell which sides of the page are the left and right sides and which are the top and bottom sides, thus reducing the chances that your page will be rotated accidentally.

✔ **Tiling:** For documents that are larger than the paper you're printing them on, choose Manual or Automatic to have QuarkXPress break your page into smaller chunks that fit on the page; then you put those smaller pieces (tiles) together to create the full-sized pages. QuarkXPress prints marks on your pages to help you line up the tiles. Here's how the options work:

When you choose Auto, QuarkXPress determines where each tile breaks. You can specify the amount of tile overlap by entering a value (between 0 and 6 inches) in the Overlap field.

- If you enter a value in the Overlap field, QuarkXPress prints that overlapped area on both adjacent tiles, giving you duplicate material with which you can overlap the tiles to help in alignment.

- If you check the Absolute Overlap option, QuarkXPress makes sure that the overlap is always exactly the value specified in the Overlap field. If this option is unchecked, QuarkXPress centers the tiled image on the assembled pages, increasing the overlap if necessary.

When you choose Manual, you decide where the tiles break by repositioning the ruler origin in your document. For all pages selected, QuarkXPress prints the tiled area whose top-left corner matches the ruler's origin. Repeat this step for each tiled area. Choose the Manual tile option if certain areas of your document make more logical break points than others do.

The Output pane

The Output pane, shown in Figure 11-5, is where you set many attributes for printing to an imagesetter, whether you're producing black-and-white documents or color-separated documents. You also use this pane for printing to a standard printer and to set resolution and color modes. The following two sections explain the options for both types of printers.

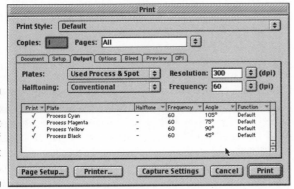

Figure 11-5:
The Output
pane of
the Print
dialog box.

Purely PostScript no more

Many of the output options listed in the section "The Document pane" weren't available for non-PostScript printers in earlier versions of QuarkXPress and were grayed out in the Print dialog box. Today, all that's changed. More and more non-PostScript printers, particularly inexpensive color ink-jet printers, are being used by designers and publishers for proofing purposes.

Heeding the call, QuarkXPress added several new enhancements for non-PostScript printers to QuarkXPress 5. For example, you can now print pages as thumbnails to non-PostScript printers. Also, the Reduce or Enlarge field, the Page Positioning pop-up menu, and the Fit in Print Area check box features are now non-PostScript-friendly.

QuarkXPress 5 now lets you print RGB composite picture files to a non-PostScript printers, and you can print rotated TIFF pictures at full resolution to non-PostScript printers. Another cool non-PostScript enhancement is the addition of print styles for non-PostScript printers. QuarkXPress even displays an alert if a print style is not available in the program.

Probably more significant, though, you can now use the Frequency field in the Output pane of the Print dialog box to control the line frequency for imported pictures when printing to a non-PostScript printer. Previously, these sorts of sophisticated, professional print features were thought worthy only of PostScript printers.

PostScript output devices will probably not be dethroned by non-PostScript devices anytime soon. And PostScript still remains the official language (printing language, that is) of the high-end publishing world. Still, solid, less expensive alternatives are available — making a home publishing system more attainable.

Here's how the standard settings work in the Output pane of the Print dialog box:

✔ **Print Colors:** This pop-up menu (available only if the Separations option is not checked in the Document pane) allows you to select Black & White, Grayscale, and (for a color printer) Composite Color. The Grayscale option is handy for printing proof copies on noncolor printers; it's also helpful if you have a composite color image, such as an RGB (Red, Green, Blue) JPEG, that can't be color separated unless Quark CMS is active. If the Black & White option is checked, colors may appear as solid whites or blacks if they are printed on a noncolor printer. The Composite Color option prints color images in color.

✔ **Plates:** Appearing where the Print Colors pop-up menu does if the Separations option is checked in the Document pane, you use this menu to determine whether all spot and process (CMYK, short for Cyan, Magenta, Yellow, Black) colors are output to their own individual plates (Spot & Process) or whether all the spot colors (such as Pantone) are converted to the four process plates (the Convert to Process pull-down menu is where you select this option). The answer depends on the capabilities of your printing press and the depth of your budget; typically, you choose Convert to Process. You may also choose Used Process and Spot. When this option is chosen, only the Process and Spot colors that actually appear in a document are output. Stray colors that may be in the Color palette but don't appear in the document are passed over.

✔ **Halftoning:** Use this pop-up menu to choose the halftone settings specified in QuarkXPress (the Conventional option in the Halftoning pop-up menu) or to use the defaults in your printer. For black-and-white and composite-color printing, you typically choose Printer, unless you chose halftoning effects from the QuarkXPress Style menu (in which case, you choose the Conventional option in the Halftoning pop-up menu). For color separations, only Conventional is available, because QuarkXPress performs the halftoning calculations so that it can also figure out the trapping of the colors.

✔ **Resolution:** This pop-up menu lets you specify the *dpi* (dots per inch) at which the imagesetter prints the document. The minimum resolution for most imagesetters is 1,270 dpi. Notice that setting the resolution within QuarkXPress doesn't override the actual settings of the imagesetter. But if you choose a lower setting in QuarkXPress than the printer is set for, all images are halftoned at the lower resolution.

✔ **Frequency:** This pop-up menu lets you specify the *lpi* (lines per inch) for your target printer. QuarkXPress chooses an initial setting based on the Resolution setting, but you can choose other popular frequencies from this pop-up menu.

Below these options is a scroll list of the colors included with your document, with a check mark to the left of each. Although choosing one of the options in the Plates pop-up menu is easier, you can also manually choose which color plates of your document are output. To do so, just click on the check mark next to a color you don't want to print — the check mark disappears and the plate won't print. If you change your mind, you can click on the blank space where the check mark once was — the check mark reappears and the plate will once again print.

The Options pane

The Options pane is almost exclusively designed for people who use an imagesetter to create film negatives. Typically, your service bureau adjusts these settings or tells you how you should adjust the settings. Figure 11-6 shows the Options pane.

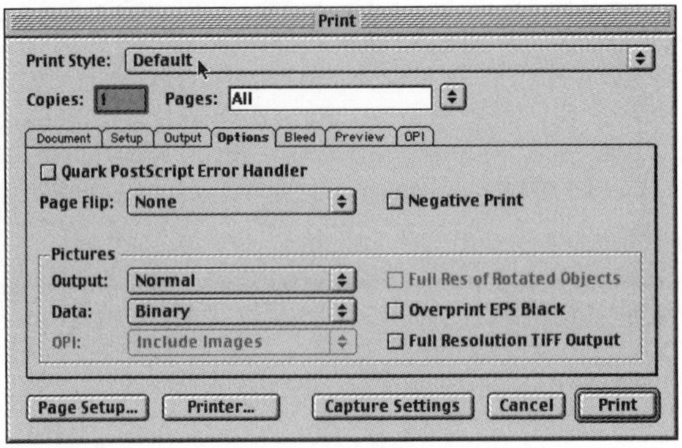

Figure 11-6:
The Options pane of the Print dialog box.

The Page Flip and Negative Print options determine how the film negatives (or positives) are produced. The Output, Data, OPI, Overprint EPS Black, and Full Resolution TIFF Output options determine how pictures are printed. The following list describes how each option works:

- ✔ **Quark PostScript Error Handler:** When this box is checked, a utility helps you diagnose output problems on a PostScript printer. PostScript is a language, and programs sometimes use it incorrectly — or at least differently than the printer expects, which leads to incorrect output and often to no output at all. If this option is checked, QuarkXPress prints a report when it encounters a PostScript error and prints the problem page at the point where the error occurred to help you narrow down the problem (which may be with an imported image, for example).

✔ **Page Flip:** This pop-up menu lets you mirror your page; your options are Horizontal, Vertical, and Horizontal & Vertical. You use this feature if your service bureau requests that the page be flipped; otherwise, leave this option at the default setting (None). The Page Flip settings let the prepress experts adjust how the pages print in anticipation of *reading* and *emulsion* needs. Reading is the direction in which the page prints on a negative (for example, in a readable, right-reading direction, or a flipped, wrong-reading direction), and emulsion is the substance on the negative that holds the image. Different printing presses expect the reading to be different ways and the emulsion to be on a specific side of the negative.

✔ **Negative Print:** This option prints an inverse image of your pages, exchanging black for white and dark colors for light colors. Your service bureau uses this option if it has imagesetters that can print both positives and negatives (so that the service bureau can have the correct output based on what it's printing on). Ask your service bureau to tell you when to use this option.

When Negative Print is checked and a page is flipped either horizontally or vertically, the page is printed right reading, emulsion side down, which is the typical setting in the United States for printing presses.

✔ **Output:** The default setting is Normal, but you can also choose Low Resolution or Rough from this pop-up menu. Normal means that the pictures print normally; Low Resolution means that the pictures prints at the screen resolution (usually, 72 dpi); Rough means that the pictures don't print at all. You use the latter two options when you're focusing on the text and layout, not the images, because Low Resolution and Rough greatly accelerate printing time.

✔ **Data:** Typically, your service bureau tells you which of the three settings to use: Binary (smaller file sizes, faster printing, but not editable), ASCII (larger file sizes, slower printing, but editable), and Clean 8-Bit (a hybrid of binary and ASCII, somewhere between the two in size, that can safely be sent to PC-based output devices).

✔ **OPI:** An OPI (Open Prepress Interface) file is a specific type of CMYK file that is generally generated from a high-resolution scan by a service bureau. After the file is created, the high-resolution image separation files are stored on a server by the service bureau, and you are given a much smaller, low-resolution version of the image to use in your documents. When it's time to output the file, the low-res file is relinked with the high-res files on the server and output to an imagesetter.

If you don't use an OPI server, leave this option at the default setting, which is Include Images. On the other hand, if your service bureau uses high-resolution TIFF files on its OPI server, choose Omit TIFF. Similarly, choose Omit TIFF & EPS if the service bureau's OPI server contains both EPS and TIFF files.

✔ **Overprint EPS Black:** Normally, QuarkXPress prints black by using the trapping settings set in the Trap Specifications dialog box (accessed via the Edit Trap button in the Colors dialog box, which you open by choosing Edit➪Colors or pressing Shift+F12). However, EPS files may have their own trapping settings for black defined in the program that created the EPS file. If you check the Overprint EPS Black option, QuarkXPress forces all black elements in EPS files to overprint other colors. This option doesn't affect how other black elements in QuarkXPress print. Trapping is an expert feature that we recommend you ignore. Don't enable the Overprint EPS Black option without checking with your service bureau first.

✔ **Full Resolution TIFF Output:** This option overrides the Frequency setting in the Output pane when TIFF images are printed. (Other elements are not affected.) If checked, this option sends the TIFF image to the printer at the highest resolution possible, based on the Resolution setting in the Output pane. You use this option when you want your TIFF images (typically, photos and scans) to be as sharp as possible. Sharpness is more an issue for bitmapped images than for text and illustrated images, which is why Quark offers this feature.

The Bleed pane

When an image or background spreads all the way to the edge of your document and beyond on one or more sides, the effect is called a *bleed*. Although bleeds are extremely common, certain steps must be taken to make sure they work right when they're printed. Rookies often assume that if the image touches the very edge of their document, the printer, like a skilled surgeon, will just cut straight across the edge of the document, and no one will be the wiser. However, it doesn't work that way. When a job is trimmed, the trimmer will inevitably miss the true edge of the document by a millimeter or two on either side, often leaving some of the extra white space surrounding the document behind. The results? A crummy looking document.

Of course, no self-respecting commercial printer would let you trim a job this way. Instead, he or she will tell you to extend the aforementioned image or background color beyond the edge of the document and into the pasteboard, so that when the page is trimmed, the trimmer has a little wiggle room around the edge of the document. How far you want to extend the image or color is up to the commercial printer. Some are happy with an extra ⅛ of an inch, whereas others would like you to extend it out as far as a full ¼ of an inch. You can consult with your commercial printer about what he or she prefers.

After you determine the preferred settings, you can make these adjustments in the Bleed pane, which appears in the Print dialog box when the Custom Bleeds XTension is enabled. (*Note:* The Custom Bleeds XTension is one of many XTensions installed with QuarkXPress 5, unless you chose not to install this particular XTension.) Only a few options are in this pane. They are as follows:

✔ **Bleed Type:** The default setting for this pop-menu is Symmetric. When Symmetric is chosen, you simply enter a measurement in the Amount field to the right of the pop-up menu, and QuarkXPress applies an equal bleed all the way around the perimeter of the document. The next choice in the Bleed Type pop-up menu is Asymmetric. When you choose Asymmetric, three more fields to the right of the pop-up are activated, letting you enter specific bleed amounts for the Top, Bottom, Left, and Right sides of your documents. Choose this option if you're printing something like a facing page, where you want QuarkXPress to apply a bleed to the top, bottom, and outside of the page, but not the gutter. The last choice is Page Items. When you choose this option, bleeds are applied to only the image that bumps up to the edge of the document instead of the entire perimeter of the document.

✔ **Clip At Bleed Edge:** If checked, this option prevents anything outside the bleed rectangle from printing, even if it's within the imageable area of the output device. This is one of those "neatness counts" features, producing pages or film negatives that don't have stray objects past the area you intend to print, so the commercial printer doesn't see such stray items and wonder if perhaps they are supposed to print and the bleed rectangle was set incorrectly.

The Preview pane

You can easily set up your Print dialog box and print your job, only to find out that the settings were improper. Use the Preview pane to ensure that margins, crop marks, bleeds, and other element-fitting issues actually fit into your target paper size.

Figure 11-7 shows an example of the Preview pane in which the bleed on the upper-left side of the page goes past the page boundaries. You need to use a larger paper size or make sure that nothing bleeds on the right side of any page. (The other elements in the pane's preview are the crop marks at the corners and the registration marks along the sides.)

Those of you who used this feature frequently in QuarkXPress 4 will notice that several enhancements have been added to the box since the last release, including the imageable area, the type of bleed being used, status of registration marks, and more. Also, now an arrow to the left of the Preview image, indicates the direction that the film is being fed, and a letter R in the center of the document preview shows that the document is a right-read document.

If you flip the document in the Options pane, you see that the R is transposed to indicate the change.

The OPI pane

As mentioned earlier, when you install QuarkXPress 5, several new XTensions are also installed unless you tell the installer to do otherwise. One of these new XTensions is the OPI XTension. When this XTension is installed and activated in the XTensions Manager dialog box, an additional pane — the OPI pane — appears in the Print dialog box. This pane gives you a checkbox for activating the OPI and several check boxes that control the same features in the OPI pop-up menu in the Options pane. To access the XTensions Manager dialog box, choose Utilities⇨XTensions Manager. Unless you're an avid fan of OPI, you may want to turn off this XTension in the XTensions Manager dialog box or remove it from the XTensions folder altogether. You can always reinstall from the CD again later if you have second thoughts.

Establishing Typical Setups

Typically, you set up your printer as follows:

- For printing to a laser printer, make sure that Include Blank Pages is unchecked (unless you really want to print blank pages). Also set Orientation to Portrait, Paper Size to US Letter, Printer Description to match your target printer, Print Colors to Grayscale, Halftoning to Printer, Frequency to 60 lpi (for 300-dpi printers) or 80 lpi (for 600-dpi printers), and Data Format to Binary for Mac or Clean 8-Bit for Windows.

- For printing to a color printer (such as an inkjet or dye-sublimation printer), make sure that Include Blank Pages is unchecked (unless you really want to print blank pages). Also set Orientation to Portrait, Paper

Size to US Letter, Printer Description to match your target printer, Halftoning to Printer, Frequency to 60 lpi (for 300-dpi printers) or 80 lpi (for 600-dpi printers), Profiles to match your target printer or to None, and Data Format to Binary for Mac or Clean 8-Bit for Windows.

✔ For printing to an imagesetter at your site for color separations, make sure that Include Blank Pages is unchecked (unless you really want to print blank pages) and that Separations is checked. Also set Orientation to Portrait, Paper Size to Custom, Page Gap to 3p, Printer Description to match your target imagesetter, Halftoning to Conventional, Resolution to 2,540 dpi, Frequency to 133 or 150 lpi, Profiles to match your target printer or to None, and Data Format to Binary for Mac or Clean 8-Bit for Windows.

✔ For printing to an imagesetter for black-and-white or grayscale output, make sure that both Include Blank Pages (unless you really want to print blank pages) and Separations are unchecked. Also set Orientation to Portrait, Paper Size to Custom, Page Gap to 3p, Printer Description to match your target imagesetter, Resolution to 1,270 dpi, Halftoning to Printer, Frequency to 120 or 133 lpi, and Data Format Binary for Mac or Clean 8-Bit for Windows.

Working with Spot Colors and Separations

People often accidentally use spot colors, such as red and Pantone 111 (for example, for picture and text-box frames), in a document that contains four-color TIFF and EPS files. Doing so results in QuarkXPress outputting as many as six plates: one each for the four process colors, plus one for red and one for Pantone 111. You may expect the red to be separated into 100 percent each of yellow and magenta (which is how red is printed in four-color work). And maybe you expect QuarkXPress to separate the Pantone 111 into its four-color equivalent (11.5 percent yellow and 27.5 percent black). So why doesn't QuarkXPress do this automatically? Actually, it can — but only if you tell it to do so when you're defining colors *or* when you're printing. Read on.

Using the Edit Color dialog box

By default, each color defined in QuarkXPress — including the red, green, and blue that are automatically available in the Colors dialog box — is set as a spot color. And each spot color gets its own plate, unless you specifically tell QuarkXPress to translate the color into process colors, which you do when defining a new color by unchecking the Spot Color box in the Edit Color dialog box. Access the Colors dialog box by choosing Edit⇨Colors or by pressing Shift+F12.

No matter whether a color was defined as a process or spot color, you can also choose the Convert to Process option when you're printing to convert *all* spot colors to process colors. This technique is no good, however, if you want to print a mixture of process colors and spot colors. If you want to color-separate red as 100 percent yellow and 100 percent magenta but print Pantone 111 on its own plate as a spot color, for example, you must use the Edit Color dialog box to set all colors except those that you want to appear on their own plates as process colors. Access the Convert to Process option from the Plates pop-up menu in Output pane of the Print dialog box.

The advantage of setting the colors to process in the Edit Color dialog box is that the colors are permanently made into process colors. You must choose the Convert to Process option each time you print — a procedure that you can automate via print styles, as described later in this chapter in the section, "Creating Print Styles."

If your work is primarily four-color work, either remove the spot colors (such as blue, red, and green) from your Colors dialog box or edit them to make them process colors. If you make these changes with no document open, the settings become the defaults for all new documents.

Now distinguishing spot colors from process colors is easier than ever, thanks to the spot color and process color icons that have been added to the Colors palette in QuarkXPress 5. For more about these icons, refer to Chapter 9.

If you do some spot-color work and some four-color work, duplicate the spot colors and translate the duplicates into process colors. Make sure that you use a clear color-naming convention, such as Blue P for the process-color version of blue (which you create by using 100 percent each of magenta and cyan). The same is true when you use Pantone colors (and Hexachrome, Trumatch, Focoltone, Toyo, DIC, and multiple-ink colors). If you don't check the Process Separation box in the Edit Color dialog box these colors are output as spot colors. Again, you can define a Pantone color twice, making one of the copies a process color and giving it a name to indicate what it is. Then all you have to do is make sure that you pick the right color for the kind of output you want. To access the Edit Color dialog box, choose Edit➪Colors and click the New button to create a color or the Edit button to edit an existing color.

Mixing spot and process colors

You can mix process and spot colors. If you want a gold border on your pages, for example, you have to use a Pantone ink, because metallic colors cannot be produced via process colors. Just use the appropriate Pantone color, and *don't* check the Process Separation box when you define the color. When you make color separations, you get five negatives: one each for the four process colors and one for gold. That's fine, because you specifically want the five negatives. (Just make sure that any other colors that you create from spot-color models are turned into process colors in the Edit Color dialog box; otherwise, each of these spot colors prints on its own negative, too.)

Creating Print Styles

Print styles let you save settings for specific printers and/or specific types of print jobs, so you have a quick way of adjusting all pertinent print settings simultaneously. To create or edit a print style, choose Edit⇨Print Styles to display the dialog box shown in Figure 11-8.

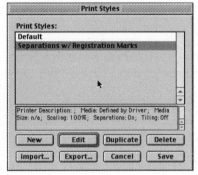

Figure 11-8:
The Print
Styles
dialog box.

When you choose to edit an existing style or create a new style, you get the dialog box shown in Figure 11-9. This dialog box contains four of the panes of the Print Style dialog box: Document, Setup, Output, and Options. These panes are the same as those in the Print dialog box, so set them here as you would there. After you set the print style's options, click OK; then click Save in the Print Styles dialog box.

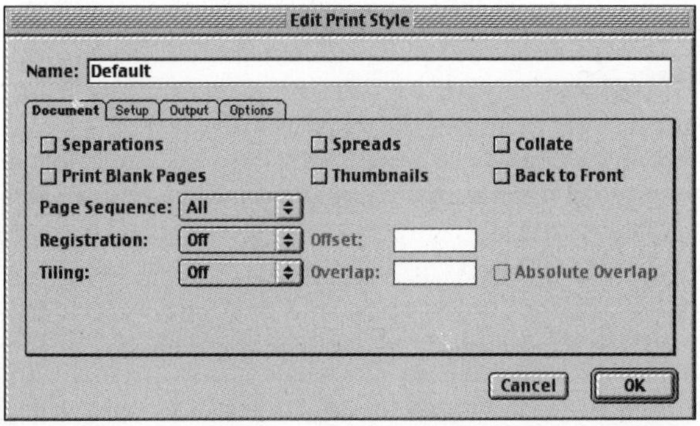

Figure 11-9:
The Edit
Print Style
dialog box.

Unfortunately, QuarkXPress doesn't let you take Print dialog-box settings and create a print style from them. You must recreate the settings in the Print Styles dialog box, so be sure to write them down after you've set them so you'll remember them later on.

You may have multiple printers in your office or in your service bureau — laser printers for basic business use and quick proofing of layouts, color printers for color proofing, and an imagesetter for final film output. Rather than specify the various settings for each printer each time you print your document — an exercise that is subject to mistakes — use print styles to save all these settings. Then, in the Print dialog box, choose the printer setting that you want to use. Here are some tips on using print styles:

✔ You can share print styles with other users; click the Export button to save your styles in a file that your colleagues can import by clicking the Import button.

✔ If you choose a print style in the Print dialog box and make changes in the various panes, you see the name of the print style change — a bullet precedes the name. This change is meant to remind you that you changed the print style's settings for this particular print session. The change does not change the print style itself, so the next time you use that print style, its original settings will be in effect.

Working with Service Bureaus

Many QuarkXPress users send their work to service bureaus (including the in-house production departments at a commercial printer) to print the final copies. After all, QuarkXPress is the publishing tool of choice for professional publishers, and professional publishers tend to print color magazines, high-volume newsletters, crisp brochures, and other materials that need a professional printer, not just a photocopier.

Understanding what a service bureau needs

Working with a service bureau can be a trying experience, particularly if you don't understand what the service bureau needs. Basically, a service bureau needs whatever the document has in it or accesses. Here's a checklist to review before sending your QuarkXPress files to a service bureau:

✔ **Who prints the files?** If you give your QuarkXPress files to the professionals at a service bureau, they can make any adjustments needed for optimal printing or solve unexpected problems, for example, with images or colors. But these professionals could make a mistake by changing something that they shouldn't. By printing the file yourself, you can prevent this potential problem.

When you print the file yourself, you're responsible for the final output; service bureau experts can't edit your PostScript print file. In addition to being uneditable, these files can be huge (even larger than the document and associated files on which they're based — in tens of megabytes). In most cases, service bureau experts should print from your files, but you should mark on the hard copy all colors, ruling lines, images, and fonts to give them something to check against.

You also should insist on color-match prints (called by several trade names, such as Matchprints and Fujichromes) for color pages and bluelines for black-and-white or spot-color pages. (*Color-match prints* and *bluelines* are copies of your publication made from the negatives, allowing you to see your publication before the mass printing begins.) Expect to pay about $135 per color-match print and $20 per blueline page.

✔ **Does the service bureau use the same version of QuarkXPress that you use?** If you use QuarkXPress Version 5, you have the option of saving your documents in the Version 4 format. Unfortunately, you lose some Version 5 features when you do this, such as multiple text insets, character style sheets defined in a list, and more. When a version changes, ensure that you and your service bureau are in synch.

✔ **Do you and the service bureau use the same XTensions?** If you use the Custom Bleed XTension, make sure that your service bureau does, too. Ditto for anything else that affects the printed appearance, such as import filters for unusual graphics formats. You may even want to give your service bureau a copy of all your XTensions to ensure that nothing is missing. Or better yet, hand over the report generated when you run Collect for Output (located in the File menu; for more information, see the "Listing document components" section later in this chapter).

You don't need to worry about XTensions that don't affect the actual content; items that display information on graphics or bypass various warnings don't change the appearance of your document when they're loaded into a system that doesn't have them.

✔ **Does the service bureau use the same fonts that you use?** If you're not sure whether your service bureau has the same fonts that you do, send copies of yours. Most service bureaus can't use TrueType fonts, so check first before sending them. Don't forget to tell the service bureau all the fonts that your document uses. Again, the Collect for Output Feature can be very helpful in this instance, as it can round up your fonts automatically and document your list of fonts in a Collect for Output report.

✔ **Does the service bureau have the right colors?** If you're doing four-color process (CMYK) output, have you made all colors process colors? Do you have some colors that are spot colors, and are they defined as such? Have you deleted any color plates that your document doesn't use? Don't forget to tell the service bureau what colors should print. The Collect for Output feature lists these items in its report.

✔ **Does the service bureau have the same color profiles that you have?** Don't forget to copy the color profiles that are used in your document. Chances are that the service bureau has the basic ones that came with QuarkXPress, but if you get any color profiles from anywhere else, make sure that the service bureau gets them, too.

Dealing with platform differences

Most service bureaus are Mac-based; they probably don't know what to do with your QuarkXPress for Windows files, even though QuarkXPress for Mac can read them. You can probably get the service bureau over the hump of loading your files, but the following two situations may mean that you need to convert to QuarkXPress for Mac yourself, use the print-to-PostScript-file option, or find a Windows-savvy service bureau:

✔ Most XTensions are not available for Windows, and some Windows XTensions have no Mac equivalents. Therefore, if you depend on such XTensions, you need to use a Windows-savvy service bureau or forgo the XTensions.

✔ Although PostScript fonts exist for both the Mac and Windows, you can't give your Windows PostScript fonts to a Mac-based service bureau. You have to translate the fonts into Mac format by using a program such as Macromedia Fontographer. (For information on this program, visit www.macromedia.com.) Beware of using "almost the same" fonts across platforms: Even if they look alike, subtle differences in spacing can cause text to flow differently, perhaps even leading to a story flowing longer than originally planned and thus having some lines cut off.

Fortunately, this list of questions is manageable. QuarkXPress keeps all tracking, kerning, and hyphenation information with the document, and the service bureau experts know to click the Keep Document Settings button when it loads your file into its copy of QuarkXPress. They also know to preserve your settings when they are asked.

Listing document components

QuarkXPress also provides a tool to help you gather all the components of a document. This tool is called Collect for Output, and you access it by choosing File⇨Collect for Output. The resulting dialog box is shown in Figure 11-10. You can collect the document and its components in any folder or directory, and even create a new folder or directory to store the materials.

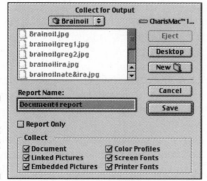

Figure 11-10:
The Collect
for Output
dialog box.

What's in a Collect for Output folder? A copy of the QuarkXPress document itself and all linked graphics are in the folder, as is a text file that has the name of the QuarkXPress document plus the word report (see Figure 11-11). (In Windows, the name of the text file is the same as the document's filename, except that the extension is .RPT.) This report contains a treasure trove of information about your QuarkXPress document. We suggest that you send the report to your service bureau or load it into a word processor or QuarkXPress and print a copy for the service bureau expert to consult. The report should include

✔ A list of all XTensions used, distinguishing between those that are required for opening the document and those that are used in the document.

✔ A list of all fonts used, including those used in graphics. Unfortunately, the report lists a graphic each time it is used, not just one time.

✔ A list of all styles used.

✔ A list of all color profiles used.

✔ A list of all H&J (hyphenation and justification) sets used.

✔ A list of all colors used, including a list of all color plates used.

✔ A list of all trapping settings used.

✔ Information about the types, sizes, rotations, skews, positions, and scaling of all graphics.

In QuarkXPress 5, the Collect for Output dialog box is more powerful and than in previous versions. In addition to copying the document, imported pictures, and output report as mentioned above, the Collect for Output dialog box can now copy fonts and ICC color profiles into the collection folder. Also, if you prefer not to collect all files for output, you can now choose only the files you want. Before Version 5, the Collect for Output feature was more of an all-or-nothing proposition.

QuarkXPress also comes with a template called Output Request Template.qxt, which makes a great cover sheet for print jobs sent to a service bureau. (This template is in your QuarkXPress folder; in Windows, it's called COLL4OUT.QXT.)

At the bottom of the Output Request form is an empty text box in which you can import the report created by Collect for Output and create a unified cover sheet with all the details that you and your service bureau expert need to know about your document. Remember that you can modify this QuarkXPress document's layout to match your or your service bureau's preferences. When you import the Collect for Output report into the Output Request template to generate a cover sheet for your current document, remember to check the Include Style Sheets box when you choose File⇨Get Text.

Technically speaking, it's illegal for you to copy programs (including XTensions), fonts, and images that you don't own or license and then give them to other people. Practically speaking, though, you have no choice. To ensure compatibility, you and your service bureau need to have the same tools and sources. To stay within the spirit of the law (if not the letter), make sure that your service bureau understands that the programs, fonts, and images that you copy for it are to be used only in connection with printing your documents.

The best advice for working with a service bureau is to ensure a high degree of communication. Talk with your service bureau experts to see what they need from you, and make clear to them service what you need. Their job is to create the best possible output for you while still making a living wage. Your job is to minimize headaches to ensure affordable, cheerful, professional, and timely service.

Figure 11-11:
Part of the report that Quark-XPress generates via the Collect for Output feature.

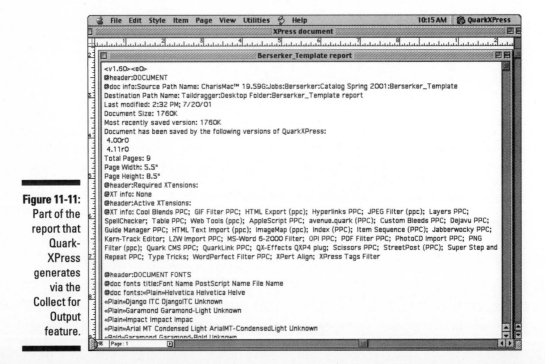

Part III
The Picasso Factor

The 5th Wave   By Rich Tennant

"I APPRECIATE YOUR COMPUTER HAS 256 COLORS, I JUST DON'T THINK THEY ALL HAD TO BE USED IN ONE BOOK REPORT."

In this part . . .

We named this part of the book after the famous artist because it tells not only how to use QuarkXPress as an illustration tool, but also how to take normal-looking text and graphics and distort them. Why would you want to do this? Good question. The answer could be that, like Picasso, you want to present ideas in a visually interesting way. QuarkXPress lets you manipulate text and art in interesting ways, and we show you how. We also give you a brief primer on color. Put all these techniques together to create documents that dazzle.

Chapter 12

Using QuarkXPress as an Illustration Tool

*B*ack in the day, QuarkXPress was generally thought of as only a page layout program. Previous versions of QuarkXPress had limited drawing capabilities; if you needed to draw a curved line or curved shape, you were forced to use a dedicated drawing program. Not anymore. Newer versions of QuarkXPress, including version 5, contain several nifty drawing-related features, such as the ability to draw Bézier lines and shapes, change text characters into picture boxes or text boxes, and flow text along a line or around the contour of a box. (Flowing text along a path is covered in Chapter 15.)

Using Lines

In Figure 12-1, four tools are highlighted in the Tool palette. You use these tools to create straight and curved lines (as you may have already guessed).

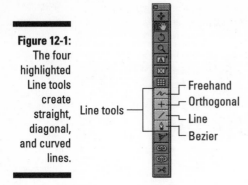

Figure 12-1:
The four highlighted Line tools create straight, diagonal, and curved lines.

Line tools —

— Freehand
— Orthogonal
— Line
— Bezier

Each of the line-creation tools works a bit differently than the others. In addition to the basic Line tool at the bottom, you have these three, from top down:

✔ **Freehand Line tool:** Lets you create Bézier lines using the mouse as a freehand drawing tool. To create a freehand line, click and hold the mouse button as you drag the mouse in any direction. When you release the mouse button, QuarkXPress creates a line that follows the path of the mouse from where you first clicked to the point where you released the button.

✔ **Orthogonal Line tool:** Limits you to horizontal and vertical lines. Click and hold the mouse button, drag, and release the mouse to create a line with this tool.

✔ **Diagonal Line tool:** Produces straight lines at any desired angle. If you hold down the Shift key while drawing a diagonal line, the line is constrained to be perfectly horizontal, perfectly vertical, or at a perfect 45-degree angle. (Note that the QuarkXPress user's manual simply calls this the *Line tool,* but we use the name *Diagonal Line tool* so that you don't mix it up with the other three Line tools.)

✔ **Bézier Line tool:** Creates straight-edged zigzag lines, curvy lines, and lines that contain both straight and curved segments:

• To create a zigzag line, click and release the mouse button to establish the first endpoint and continue clicking and releasing the mouse to add corner points with straight segments between points. Double-click to create the second endpoint or choose a different tool.

• To create a curvy line, click the mouse button to establish the first point, drag the mouse a short distance in the direction of the next point, and release the mouse button. As you drag, a line segment is drawn through the point where you first clicked. When you release the mouse button, the first endpoint (a symmetrical point) and two control handles are created. Create additional symmetrical points by clicking and dragging the mouse and then releasing. Don't worry too much about making the line perfect the first time. You can always go back and tweak if necessary.

- To create a line with both straight and curvy segments, combine the two previous techniques.

If you use QuarkXPress for illustration tasks, you can use boxes as well as lines to create the pieces of your drawings.

Modifying lines

You can modify Bézier lines by clicking and dragging points, control handles, and segments. You can also choose from three types of points (Corner, Smooth, and Symmetrical) and two types of segments (curved and straight):

✔ The point on the left is a corner point, indicated by a small triangle. As with smooth and symmetrical points, a corner point can have control handles (although the one in the example doesn't). But unlike the other kinds of points, when you move a handle attached to a corner point, the other handle doesn't move. You can delete a handle attached to a corner point by Option+clicking or Alt+clicking it. You can add handles to a corner point that doesn't have them by Control+clicking or by Ctrl+Shift+clicking.

✔ The point in the middle is a smooth point, indicated by a small square intersected by a short line with handles at both ends. The two segments that make up the line are unequal in length. You can control the length of the two segments independently by dragging either handle; however, the segments remain at opposite ends of a straight line (unlike corner point handles).

✔ The point on the right is a symmetrical point, which is like a smooth point. However, the line segment that passes through it is made up of two equal-length segments. If you change the length of a segment by dragging a handle, the other segment is also resized. A symmetrical point produces a slightly smoother curve than a smooth point.

The pointer displayed when you move the mouse over a Bézier line is different depending on whether the pointer is over a point (a small, black square appears), segment (a short, angled line appears), or handle (a small, open diamond appears). To move a point, segment, or control handle, click it and drag the mouse. Press Shift+click to select multiple points. You can use the Item tool or the Content tool to select and move points, handles, and segments. Press the ⌘ or Ctrl key while dragging to move the whole line.

Figure 12-2 shows a Bézier line with three points selected.

Figure 12-2:
This line was created with the Bézier line tool and contains corner, smooth, and symmetrical points, as well as curved and straight segments.

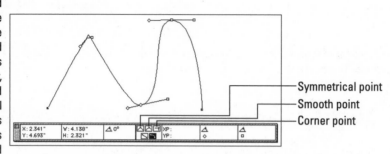

Symmetrical point
Smooth point
Corner point

Five icons in the Measurements palette let you change points and segments. The top three icons represent these three types of points:

✔ The leftmost icon indicates a symmetrical point. Click a nonsymmetrical point and click this icon (or press Option+F3 or Ctrl+F3) to change it to a symmetrical point.

✔ The center icon indicates a smooth point. Click a point that's not a smooth point and click this icon (or press Option+F2 or Ctrl+F2) to change it to a smooth point.

✔ The rightmost icon indicates a corner point. Click a point that's not a corner point and then click this icon (or press Option+F1 or Ctrl+F1) to change it to a corner point.

The bottom two icons relate to lines:

✔ The left icon represents a straight segment. Click it or press Shift+Option+F1 or Ctrl+Shift+F1 to change a curved segment into a straight segment. (A straight segment has corner points at each end.)

✔ The right icon represents a curved segment. Click it or press Shift+Option+F2 or Ctrl+Shift+F2 to change a straight segment. (A curved segment can end in smooth, symmetrical, or corner points. In all cases, control handles let you control the curve of the segment at both ends.)

In addition to the point/segment controls in the Measurements palette and their keyboard equivalents, you can also use the Point/Segment Type command in the Item menu to change the type of points and segments.

You can add a point to a Bézier line by Option+clicking or Alt+clicking on the line. The kind of point that's added depends on the kind of segment you click on. Corner points are added to straight segments; smooth points are added to curved segments. To remove a point, Option+click or Alt+click on it.

If you've never worked with Bézier lines before, don't worry. Getting the hang of dragging points, handles, and segments takes time, but like anything else, the more you practice, the better you get.

Changing the appearance of a line

When you create a line, the line is automatically given the default properties of the tool you used to create it. Unless you change your tool defaults, the lines you create will be black and 1 point in width. You can change the appearance of a line using any of several methods.

Figure 12-3 shows the Line pane of the Modify dialog box. You can access the dialog box by choosing Item⇔Modify or by pressing ⌘+M or Ctrl+M.

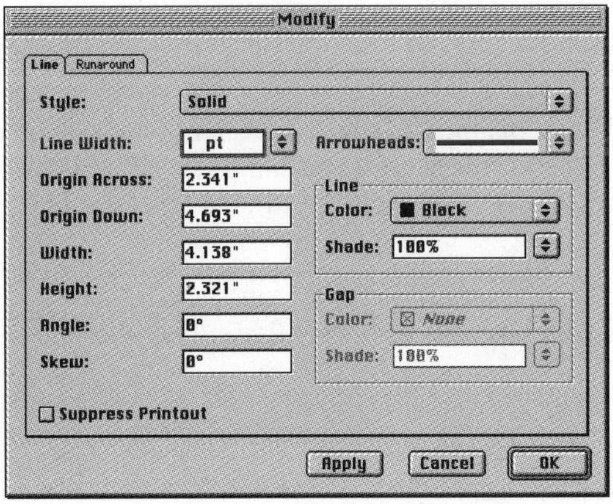

Figure 12-3:
The Line pane of the Modify dialog box.

```
Modify

[Line] Runaround

Style:          Solid                              ▼

Line Width:     [1  pt ] ▼    Arrowheads: [―――――] ▼

Origin Across:  [2.341"]       ┌Line────────────────┐
Origin Down:    [4.693"]       │ Color:  ■ Black   ▼ │
Width:          [4.138"]       │ Shade:  100%      ▼ │
Height:         [2.321"]       └─────────────────────┘
Angle:          [0° ]          ┌Gap─────────────────┐
Skew:           [0° ]          │ Color:  ⊠ None    ▼ │
                               │ Shade:  100%      ▼ │
☐ Suppress Printout            └─────────────────────┘

                        [ Apply ] [ Cancel ] [  OK  ]
```

In the Line pane, you can

✔ Choose a line style — plain, dotted, dashed, or striped — from the Style pop-up menu.

✔ Choose a width from the Line Width pop-up or enter a width up to 864 points.

✔ Move the active line by entering new Origin Across or Origin Down values.

✔ Change the length of the line by entering a new value in the Width field. If you change line length, all points are repositioned proportionally.

✔ Change the overall height of the line (the distance from the topmost point to the bottommost point) by entering a new value in the height field. Again, all points are repositioned proportionally.

✔ Rotate the line by entering a value between 1 and 360 (degrees) in the Angle field.

✔ Slant the line by entering a Skew value.

✔ Add an arrowhead and tail feather by choosing a style from the Arrowheads pop-up menu.

✔ Change the color of the line by choosing a new color from the Color pop-up menu; you can change the shade by choosing a 10-percent increment from the Shade pop-up menu or by entering a percentage value in the field.

✔ If you choose a dotted, dashed, or striped line in the Style menu, you can use the controls in the Gap area to apply a color and shade to the space between dots, dashes, and stripes. If you don't apply color/shade to the gaps, they remain white.

The Line pane isn't the only place in which you can modify a line. Figure 12-4 shows some other things you can do with a line:

✔ The style menu displays five commands for modifying the appearance of a line: Line Style, Arrowheads, Width, Color, and Shade.

✔ From left to right, the Measurements palette lets you change the location of a line (X and Y fields), the length and height of a line (W and H fields), the angle of a line (Angle field), and the thickness of the line (W field/pop-up). The two pop-up menus on the right side of the palette let you change a line's style and add arrowheads or tail feathers.

✔ The Colors palette lets you change the color and shade of a line.

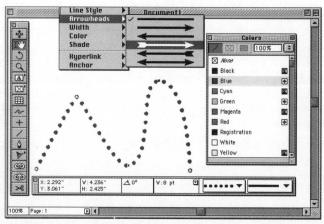

Figure 12-4: You can change a line with the Style menu, Measurements palette, or Colors palette.

Converting Text into Boxes

Have you ever had the urge to import a picture into a box that's the shape of a text character? Not too long ago, you had to use a dedicated drawing program for such tricks. Now you can convert highlighted text into picture boxes or text boxes. Not only is it easy, but the boxes you produce by converting text into boxes behave as a single item. That means you can run a background — a color, blend, or picture — across all of the characters you convert to text as though they were a single box. Features just don't get any cooler than this one.

Here's how you convert text into picture boxes:

1. **Highlight the text you want to convert.**

   You can highlight an individual character or a range of text, but you cannot highlight more than one line of text. You can convert PostScript Type 1 fonts (Adobe Type Manager must be installed) or TrueType fonts. (Keep in mind, though, that this feature isn't useful for small font sizes.)

2. **Choose Text to Box from the Style menu.**

   If you press the Option or Alt key when you choose Text to Box, QuarkXPress replaces the highlighted text with an individual Bézier picture box for each character and anchors the boxes within the text chain.

   If you don't press the Option or Alt key, QuarkXPress duplicates the highlighted text, using individual picture boxes for each letter. When you click any of the resulting boxes, all the boxes are selected, and they behave as a single box. You can put a frame around all the boxes in a single operation, import a picture that spans all boxes, apply a background color or a blend that spans the boxes, and so on.

Figure 12-5 shows a text box with large text. The text was converted to Bézier picture boxes using the Text to Box command. A one-point frame and a linear blend were added to the resulting collection of boxes (the middle text). The bottom example was created by duplicating the Bézier picture boxes, stretching them by increasing the Height value in the Box pane of the Modify dialog box and then importing a scanned image.

You can split the merged boxes that are produced when you choose Text to Box by choosing the Split command from the Item menu. If you choose Outside Paths, all letters that have holes in them (such as O's, P's, and B's) remain intact. That is, if you click on one of these letters, all component paths become active, or selected. If you choose All Paths, each path that makes up a letter becomes a separate shape that can be individually selected, moved, cut, and so on.

Figure 12-5:
The text in a text box was converted into picture boxes (bottom) by using the Text to Box command. The resulting Bézier picture boxes were duplicated and stretched to produce the examples at top left and at right.

If you want to turn a Bézier picture box created with the Text to Box command into a text box, click on it and choose Item⇨Content⇨Text.

Merging Boxes

The Bézier tools for text boxes, picture boxes, lines, and text paths let you create lines and closed shapes of all kinds. But what if you want to create something like a donut? (That is, you want a round box with a round hole in the middle.)

The Bézier drawing tools limit you to creating one path at a time; however, the Merge command in the Item menu lets you combine multiple items into complex Bézier shapes that contain multiple paths simultaneously. For example, check out Figure 12-6. We used the Merge command with the empty picture boxes at the top of the page to produce the three variations. We created the Swiss-cheese look of the first variant by choosing Difference; the next one is similar but has circular pieces on each end, and we created it with Exclusive Or; we created the bottom example by choosing Intersection.

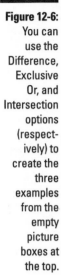

Figure 12-6:
You can
use the
Difference,
Exclusive
Or, and
Intersection
options
(respect-
ively) to
create the
three
examples
from the
empty
picture
boxes at
the top.

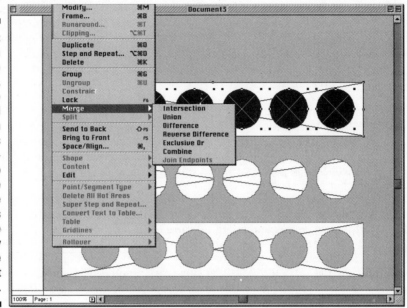

Understanding what each of the Merge options does to selected items takes some experimentation. The names of the options aren't exactly intuitive, some circumstances produce cryptic alerts, and some commands require that selected items overlap. Briefly, here's what each option does:

- **Intersection:** Calculates where each of the items (except the backmost item) overlaps the backmost item and retains only the overlap areas.

- **Union:** Combines all shapes into a single shape. The shapes don't have to overlap. If shapes overlap, the overlapped areas are retained along with the areas that don't overlap.

- **Difference:** Removes all shapes from the backmost shape. This option is useful for cutting pieces out of a shape. For example, you can use a circular shape to punch a round hole in a box.

- **Reverse Difference:** Retains what's left after the background shape and all shapes that intersect the background shape are removed.

- **Exclusive Or:** Cuts out all areas that overlap, retains areas that don't overlap, and creates new shapes for what remains.

- **Combine:** Similar to Exclusive Or, except the paths of the original items are retained.

✔ **Join Endpoints:** Available only when two lines or text paths are active, and endpoints from each line overlap each other or are within the snap-to distance, which is six pixels (unless you've changed the default Snap Distance; to change this setting, go to the General pane in the Preferences dialog box by choosing Edit⇨Preferences⇨Preferences, or pressing ⌘+Y or Ctrl+ Y). Choosing Join Endpoints produces a single line or path, with a corner point where the endpoints previously overlapped.

Figure 12-7 shows six pairs of examples of merged items. You can create the three on the left by using the Item⇨Merge⇨Difference option and three on the right by using Item⇨Merge⇨Union. Each example shows the boxes before and after they are merged.

You can use the Split command in the Item menu to "deconstruct" any item that is a single box and contains more than one closed path — including complex Bézier shapes created with the Merge options — or a path that crosses itself. When you choose either of the Split options (All Paths or Outside Paths), multiple Bézier boxes are created. The contents and attributes of the original box are retained in each of the resulting boxes.

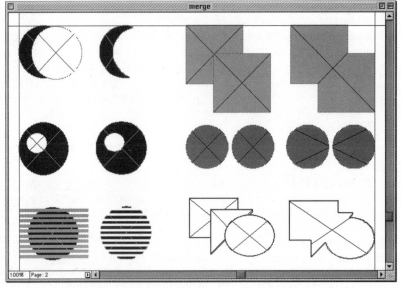

Figure 12-7:
Create the merged boxes on the left by choosing Difference; choose Union to create the boxes on the right.

Grouping Items

If you group multiple items to create an illustration, for example, the ability to select all the items simultaneously (so you can move, copy, or delete them in a single operation) is helpful; otherwise, you'd have to take action on each separate part of the whole. Selecting individual items gets to be a drag. Instead, for such a project, you can create a group out of the items that make up the illustration. If you create a group, you can then use the Item tool to select all the items with a single click.

QuarkXPress provides several ways to select multiple items in preparation for creating a group. With either the Item or Content tool, you can hold down the Shift key as you click several items one by one (in previous versions of QuarkXPress, you could only select multiple items by using the Item tool). Each time you Shift+Click on an item, you add that item to the collection of selected items.

You can also select several items by clicking and dragging a rectangle — using either the Item or Content tool — that contains any part of the items you want to select. If you want to select all the items on a page, choose Select All from the Item menu (the Item tool must be selected) or press ⌘+A or Ctrl+A. To deselect an item that's among several selected items, Shift+Click on the item.

To create a group out of multiple-selected items, choose Group from the Item menu or use ⌘+G or Ctrl+G. At least two items must be selected for this command to be available. A group can contain as many items as you want, although the items must be on the same page or facing-page spread. A group can also contain other groups. Use the Ungroup command to break apart a group.

You can display all the grouped items together in a *bounding box* by clicking the Item tool and clicking on any item in the group. You can click and drag to move a group with the Item tool; however, you cannot move an individual item when the Item tool is selected

You can select individual items within a group, move pictures within boxes, enter and edit text, and move lines by selecting the Content tool. If you want to move an item that's part of a group, select the Content tool, press the ⌘ or Ctrl key, and click on the item and drag it to a new location. When you press the ⌘ or Ctrl keys, the Content tool — and all other tools — temporarily behave like the Item tool, meaning that they position the items as you move your mouse.

You can resize a group's items all at once. To do this, simply click on any of the eight handles on a group's bounding box and drag. If you want to maintain the proportion of the items in the group but not the contents of boxes, press Shift+Option or Alt+Shift when you drag a handle. If you press Shift+Option+⌘ or Ctrl+Alt+Shift as you drag, both the items and the contents of boxes are resized proportionately.

In Figure 12-8, we combined three boxes — a picture box, text box, and a framed box without content — by choosing Item⇨Content⇨None.

The example in Figure 12-8 is a copy of the group that we scaled by clicking and dragging a handle while pressing Shift+Option+⌘ or Ctrl+Alt+Shift. The picture scale and the size of the text are reduced or enlarged along with the boxes that contain them.

Figure 12-8:
These groups of items were created by first duplicating and then scaling the group using Option+Shift +⌘ or Ctrl+Alt+ Shift.

Robert at Eric's Wedding

Changing the Shape of Items

QuarkXPress provides several different drawing tools for text boxes, picture boxes, lines, and text paths and lets you manually change the shape of an item by dragging handles, or, in the case of Bézier shapes, points or segments. You can also have QuarkXPress change the shape automatically. The Shape command in the Item menu, shown in Figure 12-9, lets you perform a couple of nifty tricks. You can change the shape of an item, and change boxes into lines and lines into boxes.

When a single item is active, the nine options displayed in the Shape menu let you change the item into (from top to bottom)

  ✔ A rectangular box

  ✔ A rounded-corner box

  ✔ A beveled-corner box

  ✔ A concave-corner box

  ✔ An oval box

✔ An editable Bézier box (with no change in shape)

✔ A straight line (at any angle)

✔ A straight line that's either vertical or horizontal

✔ An editable Bézier line

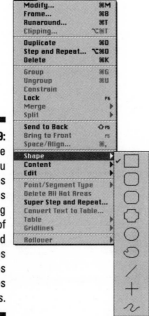

Figure 12-9:
The Shape
submenu
provides
nine options
for changing
the shape of
items and
turning lines
into boxes
and boxes
into lines.

As neat as the Shape options are, they can produce some unusual results, such as the following:

✔ If you convert a line into a Bézier box, the resulting box is as wide as the original line. If the original line was thin, opposite edges of the resulting box will be very close together — so much so that the shape may be difficult to edit.

✔ If you convert a dashed line, striped line, or a line with arrowheads into a Bézier box, each component is converted into a separate shape, as shown in Figure 12-10.

✔ If you convert a text box or picture box into a line, any box contents are deleted. (You are given a warning in this situation.)

Figure 12-10:
You can create the selected items by changing a striped and a dashed arrowed line into editable Bézier boxes by using the Bézier box option in the Shape submenu.

Ice Skating

If the active item is a Bézier line, and the endpoints overlap or are close to each other, you can connect the endpoints to create to create a closed Bézier box by pressing the Option or Alt keys and choosing Item⇨Shape and choosing the Bézier box icon.

If you create a Bézier box using the Shape submenu, you can change the shape of the box by clicking and dragging points, control handles, choosing Item⇨Edit and selecting the Shape option.

If Edit is not checked, you can resize a Bézier box by clicking and dragging the handles of its bounding box, but you can't move points, handles, or segments. The Edit submenu also has a Runaround option that lets you modify runaround paths created with the Runaround pane of the Modify dialog box (Item menu) and a Clipping Path option for modifying a clipping path specified in the Clipping pane of the Modify dialog box. (You can go directly to the Clipping pane by choosing Option+⌘+T or Ctrl+Alt+T.)

Creating Masks for Pictures Using Clipping Paths

Rectangular picture boxes are like vanilla ice cream. Nice enough, but with so many other flavors available, why not try something different every once in a while?

In addition to letting you create Bézier picture boxes — which you can reshape in any way to crop the image within — QuarkXPress lets you crop an image within a box using an embedded clipping path (created in an image-editing or illustration program) within QuarkXPress. A *clipping path* is a shape that isolates part of an image; everything outside the isolated area is transparent.

Figure 12-11 shows an image that's been imported into two picture boxes. In the top box, the entire picture is visible because no clipping path was used; in the bottom box, an embedded clipping path created in Adobe Photoshop was used to crop everything but the person within the image.

If you look at the Clipping pane of the Modify dialog box in Figure 12-11, you see that Embedded Path is selected in the Type pop-up menu. QuarkXPress lets you crop an image using an embedded path or an embedded alpha channel (an `alpha channel` is an extra "plate" in an image that's often used as a mask to isolate part of the image). You also have the following options:

- ✔ **Item:** Determines what portion of the image is visible.
- ✔ **Picture bounds:** Creates a rectangular clipping path around the shape of the picture.
- ✔ **Non-white areas:** Creates a clipping path by drawing contours around white areas. Change the Threshold value if you want to include light shades as part of the white areas.

Figure 12-11: In the top picture box, the entire image is visible because no clipping path was used; in the bottom box, we used an embedded clipping path to crop the image.

The Information area of the Clipping pane provides information about the picture in the active box. If you refer to Figure 12-11, you can see that the picture in the example contains one alpha channel and no embedded paths. (An alpha channel specifies how to merge two pixels are that aligned so that one is on top of the other.) However, an image may contain several of each, any of which can have been used as a clipping path. The Preview area displays what the image and box will look like using the current settings.

The Clipping pane includes a handful of other controls that let you adjust a clipping path. You can fiddle with Tolerance settings to adjust a clipping path and check or uncheck the Invert, Outside Edges Only, and Restrict to Box options to achieve a variety of effects. We can't cover all of the effects in this chapter. Suffice it to say that your options are numerous, and using the default settings is a safe way to begin.

The Edit command in the Item menu lets you modify a clipping path the same way you modify a Bézier box — by clicking and dragging points, control handles, and segments, adding and deleting points, changing straight segments to curved segments, and so on. To modify a clipping path, click on a picture box that contains a clipping path, then choose Item⇨Edit and make sure that Clipping Path is checked. You can use the keyboard equivalent Option+ Shift+F4 or Ctrl+Shift+F10 to alternately check and uncheck the Clipping Path option in the Edit submenu.

Chapter 13

Other Controls for Item Management

● ●

In This Chapter

▶ Creating margin, column, and custom guidelines

▶ Saving pages as EPS pictures

▶ Changing the stacking order of items

▶ Creating and managing layers

● ●

*Q*uarkXPress users and carpenters have a lot in common. Both use a set of tools to create things. Carpenters build furniture using wood, nails, and glue, whereas QuarkXPress users build pages using pictures, text, and lines. And just as every carpenter's tool bag includes a chalk line for creating guidelines, so should every QuarkXPress user's bag of tricks include a hefty supply of guidelines. In this chapter, we show you how to use guidelines in laying out your pages. We also show you how to save pages as EPS files, move layers around, and use grouping to save time as you create your graphics.

Using Guidelines for Page Layout

How important are guidelines? Guidelines are so important that QuarkXPress puts guidelines on every page you create unless you tell the program otherwise. You can place guidelines by doing what's described in this section, or you can place them numerically if you have the Guide Manager XTension installed. For more information on XTensions, see Chapter 10.

In the New Document dialog box, the values you enter in the Margin Guides and Columns areas determine the position of guidelines that are automatically displayed on your document pages. Access the New Document dialog box by choosing File➪New, or ⌘+N or Ctrl+N.

✔ If you enter 0 (zero) in each field of the Margin Guides area, your pages won't have margin guides.

✔ If you also enter 1 in the Columns field, your pages won't have column (vertical) guidelines.

✔ If you later decide that you want to change your default margin and column guidelines, you can do so by displaying Master Page A (choose Page⇨Display⇨A-master A) and then choosing the Master Guides command from the Page menu. The Master Guides dialog box lets you change the position of the margin and column guides. See Chapter 16 for more information on master pages.

In addition to margin and column guides, QuarkXPress automatically creates a grid of horizontal lines, called a *baseline grid,* on your document pages. You can display or hide the baseline grid by choosing Show/Hide Baseline Grid from the View menu or pressing Option+F7 or Ctrl+F7. The Paragraph pane of the Preferences dialog box, which you can access by choosing Edit⇨Preferences⇨Preferences or by pressing Option+Shift+⌘+Y or Ctrl+Shift+Alt+Y, includes two fields — Start and Increment — that let you control the placement of baseline grid lines.

Creating custom guidelines

Automatic margin, column, and baseline grid guidelines are good to have, but sometimes you want to create custom guidelines. For example, you may want to position several text boxes so that their left edges are aligned, as shown in Figure 13-1.

Creating a vertical guideline is a cinch. Here's what you do:

1. **Click on the vertical ruler displayed along the left edge of the document window.**

   If rulers aren't visible along the top and left edges of the document window, choose Show Rulers from the View menu.

2. **Hold down the mouse button and drag until the vertical line that's displayed as you drag is in the position at which you want to place a guideline.**

   As you drag, you see a small pointer with left- and right-pointing arrows.

3. **Release the mouse button.**

The process for creating a horizontal guideline is the same as for creating a vertical guideline, except that you click on the horizontal ruler along the top of the document window. When creating horizontal guides, if you release the mouse when the pointer is over a document page, the guideline extends from the top edge to the bottom edge of the page. If you release the mouse when the pointer is over the pasteboard area above or below the page, the guideline extends across both the page and the pasteboard area.

To delete a custom guideline, click on it and drag it back to the ruler from whence it came. You can delete all horizontal guidelines by holding down the Option or Alt key and clicking on the horizontal ruler. All vertical guidelines are removed when you Option+click or Alt+click on the vertical ruler.

If you want to place custom guidelines on all your document pages, add them to your master page(s). We discuss master pages in detail in Chapter 17.

At times, you may not want to display guidelines, such as when you want to see what a page will look like when it prints. The Show/Hide Guides command in the View menu lets you display or hide all guidelines. Pressing F7 alternately displays and hides guidelines, as well.

Be careful! Pages look nice when displayed without guidelines, but don't get in the habit of working this way. You can't see empty boxes!

Figure 13-1:
The boxes were aligned by dragging their left edges within 6 points of the vertical guideline. You see the pointer above the boxes when you click and drag to create or delete a guideline.

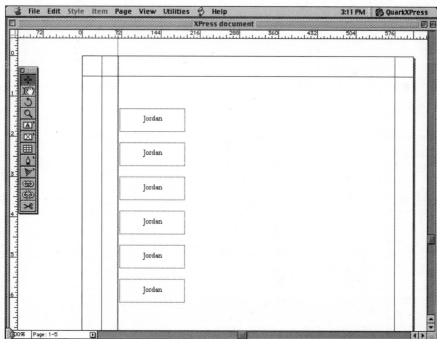

Snapping items to guidelines

One of the nice things about guidelines is that you can have QuarkXPress snap an item into alignment with a guideline when you drag the item within several pixels of the guideline. This auto-snapping behavior is controlled by the Snap to Guides command in the View menu. By default, this command is turned on (checked). You can turn off this feature by choosing Snap to Guides when it's checked. (The command toggles between on and off each time you choose it.)

When Snap to Guides is checked, guidelines act like magnets, drawing items to them. This can be a problem if you need to position an item near — but not aligned with — a guide. To solve this problem, turn Snap to Guides off before positioning the item.

By default, an item snaps to a guideline when it's moved to within six pixels of the guideline (regardless of the view percentage). However, you can change this by entering a different value in the Snap Distance field in the General pane of the Preferences dialog box. To open the General pane, choose Edit➪Preferences➪Preferences, or press ⌘+Y or Ctrl+Y. While you're in the General pane, you may also want to change another guideline-related preference. The Guides pop-up menu offers two choices: In Front and Behind. Choosing In Front draws guidelines in front of items; choosing Behind draws them behind items. Opinions vary about the best option to choose. One potential problem is that if you choose Behind and use a colored or blended background or a large picture as the backdrop for an entire page, you won't be able to see your guidelines. Figure 13-2 shows the two guideline-related preferences in the General pane.

Figure 13-2:
The Guides and Snap Distance preferences in the General pane of the Preferences dialog box let you control the behavior of guidelines.

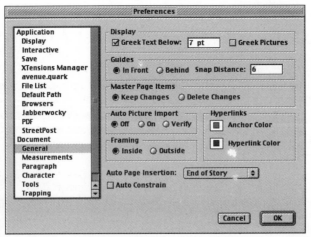

You also have the option to change the appearance of the guidelines in all your documents. The Display pane of the Preferences dialog box, shown in Figure 13-3, includes three buttons — Margin, Ruler, and Grid — that let you change the color used for margin/column guides, for the custom guides created by clicking and dragging for a ruler, and baseline grid lines, respectively. To change the color of a particular kind of guideline, click the Margin, Ruler, or Grid button and use the color picker that's displayed to choose a new color.

QuarkXPress lets you create only horizontal and vertical guidelines, but you can easily create your own angled guidelines. Just use the Line tool to create a line at any angle; then click Suppress Printout in the Line pane of the Modify dialog box, which you access by choosing Item⇨Modify.

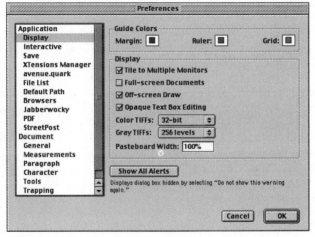

Figure 13-3:
The Display pane of the Preferences dialog box has three buttons that let you change the color of guidelines.

Saving QuarkXPress Pages as Pictures

As a rule, you import pictures created elsewhere (via scanners and illustration programs) into QuarkXPress picture boxes. But the program also includes a killer feature that lets you export any document page as an EPS graphic. After you export a page as a picture, you can import the resulting graphic file into any picture box; crop, scale, skew, and rotate it to your heart's content; and then print it as you would print any other imported picture.

What good is such a feature? Suppose that you want to include the cover of last month's magazine in an ad about next month's issue. If you created the cover in QuarkXPress, you're in luck. You can save the cover as a picture, import it into your ad, and then modify as necessary. Or perhaps you created a 5 × 7-inch ad, and you want to enlarge it to 8.5 × 11 inches — but you don't want to completely rebuild the ad from scratch. Just save the smaller version as an EPS picture; then import it into a picture box that fills an 8.5 × 11 page and scale it as needed. You're done!

EPS files created in QuarkXPress have lots of other cool advantages. For example, when you save a page as an EPS picture, the resulting graphic file retains all the text and pictures of the original page. Even better, because the EPS format is vector-based, you can scale the resulting image after you import it into a QuarkXPress picture box — or any other graphic or page layout program that supports the EPS format — and clarity is maintained regardless of how much you enlarge or reduce it.

QuarkXPress 5 adds a few options to the Save Pages as EPS dialog box, introducing two new panes — Bleed and OPI — to make room for the richer controls. You can now set a page to be transparent (great if you want to overlay the resulting EPS file over another image when you place it in a QuarkXPress layout later), have more control over bleeds, and have more control over how images are handled for an OPI printing system.

Here's how you save a page as an EPS picture:

1. **Choose Save Page as EPS from the File menu.**

   The Save Page as EPS dialog box, shown in Figure 13-4, appears. The Save Page as EPS pane is also displayed.

2. **Enter the page number of the page you want to save in the Page field.**

3. **Enter a value in the Scale field if you want to save a scaled-down version of the page.**

   You can enter values between 1 and 99 percent. Use the default value of 100 percent if you want to save the page at full size.

4. **Choose an option from the Format pop-up menu — Color, B&W, DCS, or DCS 2.0.**

   DCS creates a preseparated process color EPS file; DCS 2.0 creates a preseparated EPS with process and spot colors.

5. **Choose an option from the Preview pop-up menu — PICT if you plan to use the resulting EPS file only on a Mac; TIFF if the file will be used in Windows.**

   In QuarkXPress for Windows, you won't get an option to create a PICT preview — just a TIFF preview or no preview.

6. **If the page you're saving includes bitmap pictures, choose an option from the Data pop-up menu — Binary, ASCII, or Clean 8-Bit (for Windows).**

   Binary data prints more quickly; ASCII data is more widely compatible with printers and print spoolers. (Available in Windows only, the Clean 8-Bit option is similar to ASCII but gets rid of characters that cause output problems.)

7. **Check the Transparent Page box if you want to exclude the white background of your picture (for example if your page is a logo or illustration).**

   New to QuarkXPress 5, this feature ensures that no white background is included with your image, allowing you to place the image on a background of any color.

8. **Enter bleed values in the Bleed pane if you have an image that exceeds the page boundaries.**

   If you want the same bleed (extra space around the page) to be included in the EPS file, choose Symmetric from the Bleed Type popup menu. If you want separate dimensions for each side (perhaps an image bleeds off only to one side, for example), choose Asymmetric. In either case, fill in the amount(s) of bleed space desired.

9. **If your workflow involves OPI — and you know who you are — ask your prepress department or printer how to set this option. Otherwise, you can safely leave it at Include Images.**

   OPI, the Open Prepress Interface, is a system whereby graphics are stored on a server and the document uses a lower-resolution proxy to make the layout happen faster. During output, the OPI server substitutes the higher-resolution master graphic files for the versions in the layout.

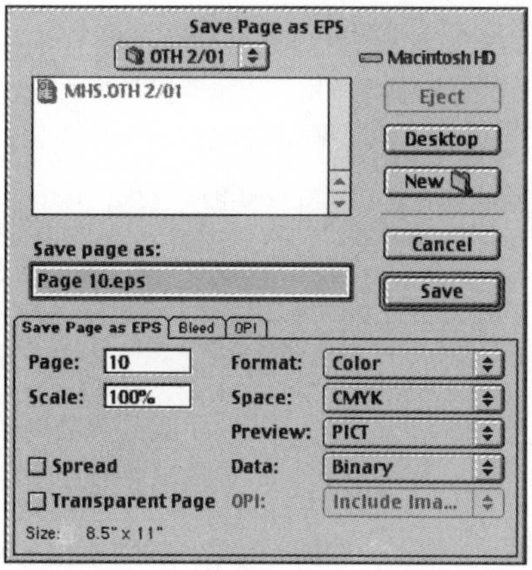

Figure 13-4:
The Save
Page as
EPS dialog
box.

Working with Items in Layers

Each time you add an item to a QuarkXPress page, that item occupies one level — the topmost level in the case of new items — in the page's *stacking order*. QuarkXPress treats each item as though it exists on a separate piece of transparent film. The first item you add to a page occupies the backmost level in a page's stacking order; the next item you create is one level above the first item; and so on.

On simple pages that contain only a few items that don't overlap, the stacking order (or *layering*) of items is not much of an issue. However, as your page layout skills improve, so will the complexity of your designs. Eventually, you'll want to be able to quickly change an item's position in the strata of items on a page in order to accomplish a particular effect. For example, if you want to superimpose text onto an imported picture, the text box must be in front of the picture box. If you create the picture box before you create the text box, you won't have to adjust layers. But if you create the text box before the picture box, you'll have to change its position in the stacking order by moving it in front of the picture box. No problem. You can do it with one hand tied behind your back.

The Item menu contains four commands for changing the layering of items:

- ✔ **Send Backward (Option+ Shift+F5 or Ctrl+Shift+F5):** Sends the active item one level backward in the stacking order.

- ✔ **Send to Back (Shift+F5):** Sends the active item to the bottom of the stacking order behind all other items on the page.

- ✔ **Bring Forward (Option+F5 or Ctrl+F5):** Moves the active item one level forward in the stacking order.

- ✔ **Bring to Front (F5):** Moves the active item to the top of the stacking order in front of all other items.

If an item is active and Bring to Front and Bring Forward are not available, the item is at the top of the stacking order; if Send to Back and Send Backward aren't available, it's at the bottom of the stack.

The Windows version of QuarkXPress displays the four commands at the same time in the Item menu. The Mac version, however, displays only Bring to Front and Send to Back. If you press the Option key before you display the Item menu, Bring Forward replaces Bring to Front, and Send Backward replaces Send to Back.

Figure 13-5 shows the four commands for changing an item's layer and four variations of five layered boxes:

- ✔ In the upper-left example, you see the middle box selected; the Item menu commands are available for moving the empty box up or down within the stacking order.

- ✔ In the upper-right example, we moved the middle box to the top of the stack by choosing Bring to Front.

- ✔ In the lower-left example, we moved the middle box to the bottom of the stack by choosing Send to Back.

- ✔ In the lower-right example, we moved the middle box one level forward by choosing Bring Forward.

Sometimes an item becomes entirely obscured behind another item or multiple items. If this happens, you don't need to change the stacking order of the items in order to activate the buried item. Select the Item tool or Content tool, hold down Option+ Shift+⌘ or Ctrl+Alt+Shift, and start clicking at the location of the hidden item. Each click selects the next item down in the stacking order. After you reach the bottom of the stack, the next click reactivates the topmost item.

As convenient as the layering process has been in previous versions, QuarkXPress 5 now makes it even easier, thanks to some new features: the Opaque Text Box Editing check box and the Layers palette.

You can find the Opaque Text Box Editing check box in the Display pane of the Preferences dialog box, which you access by choosing Edit⇨Preferences⇨ Preferences, or by pressing Option+Shift+⌘+Y or Ctrl+Alt+Shift+Y. When checked, the feature reflects the default behavior of previous versions of QuarkXPress — text boxes with a background of None or with a blend turn temporarily opaque (solid color) while you're editing them. This makes it easier to read what you're working on when the text box is on top of another text box or a picture box. Opaque Text Box Editing is also handy if you have about a zillion text boxes on a document, and you aren't quite sure which box you have selected. The temporary opaque tone is a dead giveaway. However, in a very design intensive piece — in which the interplay of text and the underlying graphics is crucial — you may want to uncheck this.

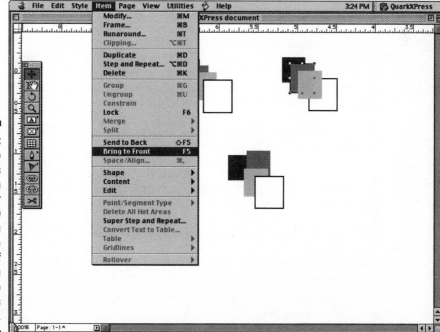

Figure 13-5:
Two commands in the Item menu (four in Windows) let you adjust the position of an item relative to other items on the page.

Also new to QuarkXPress 5 is the Layer palette. Layers are "tiers" in a QuarkXPress document. Using layers lets you isolate items — in particular items you don't want printed with the final proof. Examples would be job numbers, output instructions, and even different language versions of the same document. Each layer in the Layer palette is marked by a red rectangle in the upper-right corner, so that you can tell the layers in the Layer palette from the regular items in your document. Choose View⇨Layers to display the palette, shown in Figure 13-6.

To create a layer, which encompasses all the pages in your document, follow these steps:

1. **Choose Show Layers from the View menu to open the Layers palette.**

2. **Click the New Layer button (the far left button on the palette).**

3. **Using the Item tool or the Content tool, select one of more items in your document.**

4. **Click the Move Item to Layer button (the second from the left on the palette).**

5. **Use the Move Items dialog box to select a layer for the items.**

6. **Click OK to add the selected items to the selected layer.**

7. **To see which items are on which layers, choose Show Visual Indicators from the View menu.**

   This displays a small colored box, the same color as the one next to the layer name, on each item.

You may find you have too many layers. That's okay. You can merge layers with the Merge Layers icon (be sure to select the layers first by Shift+clicking or ⌘+clicking or Ctrl+clicking them), or delete layers with the trash can icon. When you delete a layer, Quark asks whether you want to delete the items on that layer or move them to another layer.

You can change the stacking order of layers by pressing and holding Option or Alt and then selecting the desired layer in the Layers palette, dragging it up or down the palette's list of layers. When you release Option or Alt, the layer stays in the new position. Don't forget that when you do this, you're changing the position of the layer within the entire document, not just the page you're viewing.

A pencil icon on the right side of the palette indicates which layer you're on. Also on the right will be a dashed-box icon that indicates what layer the currently selected item is on.

If you want to hide a layer, simply click on the eye icon to the far left of the layer's title. When it comes time to print the document, click the eye icon (so it goes away) for each layer that you don't want to print, and QuarkXPress ignores them, unlike those instructions sometimes placed on the document itself. (Come on! We know we've all done it at one time or another!)

There's also a lock icon you can toggle off and one, which prevents the layer from being changed when active.

Figure 13-6:
The Layers palette lets you isolate items from documents, such as job number and output instructions, so you can turn them on or off for printing or simply more easily find them.

Chapter 14

Warped Images

In This Chapter

▶ Using the Modify dialog box with pictures

▶ Warping pictures with the Measurements palette

▶ Using line screens

A picture is worth a thousand words. Even though it's a stale saying, we can all agree that there's some truth in it. Sometimes, words just can't say what pictures can.

And isn't it nice to know that you don't have to settle for reality when it comes to pictures? With QuarkXPress, you can slant, rotate, warp, and tweak pictures to your heart's content. In this chapter, we show you some easy ways to pummel your pictures into shape.

Two Ways to Warp

Although you can warp an image in several ways, the two most common ways are using the Picture pane of the Modify dialog box and the Measurements palette. Both ways work just fine, and choosing between them is only a matter of finding which works better for you.

The Modify dialog box for pictures

You can make changes in a picture contained in an active picture box by using the Box pane and the Picture pane of the Modify dialog box, the latter of which is shown in Figure 14-1. To display the dialog box, select the picture box to make it active and choose Item⇨Modify (or ⌘+M or Ctrl+M).

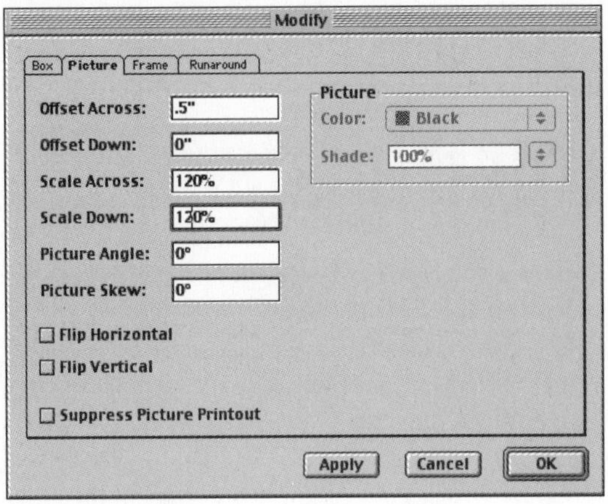

Figure 14-1:
The Picture
pane of
the Modify
dialog
box for a
picture box.

We don't go into too much detail here, but we do give you a general idea about all the things that you can do to a picture by using the Box and Picture panes of the Modify dialog box.

In the Box pane, the Origin Across, Origin Down, Width, and Height fields control the position and size of the picture box. In Figure 14-2, which shows the Box pane, the box origin (the top-left corner of the picture box) is 1 inch from the left edge of the page and 1.25 inches from the top of the page. The picture-box width is 4.125 inches, and the height is 4.375 inches. (We didn't really need to make the width and height three decimal places long; we use these values to illustrate that you can specify measurements in units as small as 0.001 in any measurement system.)

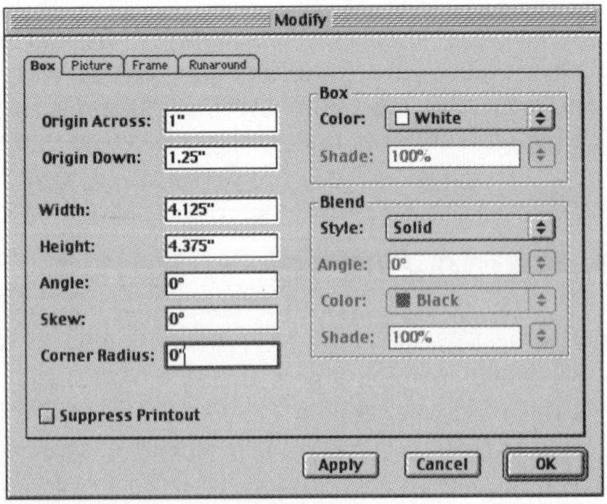

Figure 14-2:
The Box
pane of the
Modify
dialog box.

Most of the options in the Box pane of the Modify dialog box determine the appearance of a picture box; only the Angle and Skew fields affect the appearance of the picture within the picture box. Entering a value in the Angle field rotates the picture box — and the picture within — around the center of the box. Box angle values range from –360 to 360 degrees in increments as small as 0.001 degrees. The Skew field lets you slant a box (by offsetting the top and bottom edges) to produce an italic-looking version of the box and its picture.

Entering a value in the Corner Radius field lets you replace the square corners of a rectangular box with rounded corners. The value that you enter in this field is the radius of the circle used to form the rounded corners. When you first create a rectangular picture box, its corner radius value is 0 (zero). You can enter a radius value from 0 to 2 inches (0 to 24 picas) in 0.001 increments of any measurement system. The radius value also adjusts the bevels on beveled-corner boxes (and so on for the other similar boxes).

If you check Suppress Printout, the active picture box (including picture and frame) doesn't print when you output the page. This feature is handy for printing text-only page proofs or rough copies of pages. Even better, pages print more quickly when you don't print pictures.

The Color and Shade pop-up menus let you add color to the background of a picture box and control the depth *(saturation)* of the color. To add color to the background of an active picture box or to change an existing background color, choose a color from the Color pop-up menu or use the Colors palette. (If it's not visible, choose View⇨Show Colors, or press F12, to make it appear.) See Chapter 9 for more information on applying colors and creating custom colors.

After you select the background color that you want to apply to the picture box (and you select a color other than None or White), you can specify the saturation level of the color. Choose a predefined shade (0 to 100 percent) from the Shade pop-up menu or enter a custom shade value (in increments as small as 0.1 percent) in the Shade field. You can find a pop-up menu of shade increments in the Colors palette as well (at the top right of the palette), in which you can enter your own values or choose one of the existing values.

The controls in the Blend section of the Box pane lets you add two-color blends to picture-box backgrounds. (You can also use the Colors palette to create blends.) To create a blend, choose a blend style from the Style pop-up menu in the Blend section of the dialog box; choose a color from the Color pop-up menu in the Box section, and choose the second color from the Color pop-up menu in the Blend section. The Angle field lets you rotate a blended background from –360 to 360 degrees in increments as small as 0.001 degrees.

All the controls in the Picture pane of the Modify dialog box affect the appearance of the picture within the active box. Two of our favorite features in the Picture pane of the Modify dialog box are Scale Across and Scale Down.

When you first fill a picture box with a picture (by choosing File⇨Get Picture, or pressing ⌘+E or Ctrl+E), QuarkXPress places the picture in the text box at its full size — that is, at 100 percent scale. But the picture may be larger or smaller than you want. No problem. You can change the picture's size by entering new values in the Scale Across and Scale Down fields. Back in Figure 14-1, we entered a value of 120 percent in each field, which made the picture 20 percent larger than it was when we imported it. You can scale pictures from 10 percent to 400 percent of their original size. Be careful about greatly enlarging TIFF and other bitmap pictures, however; the larger you make them, the fuzzier they look when you print them.

The Offset Across and Offset Down fields let you adjust the position of the picture within the box; back in Figure 14-1, we set the Offset Across value to 0.5 inches, which moves the picture box contents to the right by 0.5 inches. (When you import a picture, both Offset values are 0.)

The Picture Angle field is useful if you want to change the angle of a picture without changing the angle of the picture box itself. Actually, when you enter a value in the Picture Angle field, you cause the picture to rotate around its center within the box.

The Picture Skew field lets you *skew* (slant) a picture within its box. You can enter values ranging from –75 to 75 degrees, in increments as small as 0.001 degrees. If you enter a positive value, the picture leans to the right; if you enter a negative value, the picture leans to the left.

Checking Suppress Picture Printout produces slightly different results from checking Suppress Printout in the Box pane. If you check Suppress Picture Printout, the frame and background of the picture box print, but the contents of the picture box do not. This option is useful if you import low-resolution versions of pictures (for position only) and plan to strip in the actual halftones manually.

The Measurements palette

As you change values in the Picture pane of the Modify dialog box, the Measurements palette also changes to reflect the new values. You can bypass the Modify dialog box for any function displayed in the Measurements palette by entering the appropriate values in the palette itself.

To use the Measurements palette to modify the contents of a picture box, you must first activate the picture box. (If the box is active, its sizing handles are visible around the edge of the box.) You also must display the Measurements palette. (To display the palette, choose View⇨Show Measurements, or press

Option+⌘+M or Ctrl+Alt+M.) The Measurements palette appears, as shown in Figure 14-3. You can make several changes in the picture box through the Measurements palette, which is the simplest way to manipulate picture boxes and their contents.

Enter new values in the X and Y fields to change the distance of the picture-box origin (the box's top-left corner) from the page edges.

The W and H fields control the width and height of the picture box. In Figure 14-3, the current dimensions are 5.25 inches x 3.792 inches. Those exacting coordinates indicate that the picture box was drawn by hand; if you size the box via the Measurements palette, you round off the coordinates to something like 4 inches x 3.5 inches.

The Rotation field on the left side of the Measurements palette rotates the picture box. Because the box in Figure 14-3 is not rotated, the Rotation value is 0 (zero) degrees.

The Corner Radius field changes the shape of the picture box's corners.

The Flip Horizontal and Flip Vertical options flip the image along the Y and X axes, respectively. The arrow's direction changes in the icon to tell you whether a picture has been flipped. (You also can choose Style⇨Flip Horizontal and Style⇨Flip Vertical.)

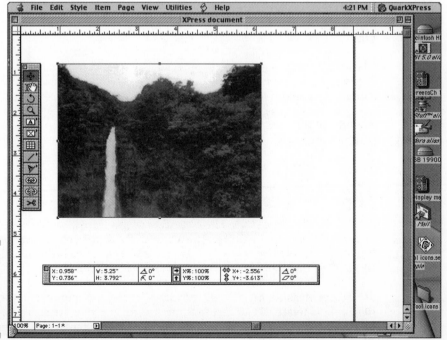

Figure 14-3:
Using the Measurements palette.

The settings in the X% and Y% fields in Figure 14-3 are percentages. Changing the values in the X% and Y% fields reduces or enlarges the picture in the picture box. To keep the proportions of the picture the same, enter the same values in the X and Y fields.

Clicking the Horizontal or Vertical Offset arrow moves an image within the picture box. Each click moves the image in 0.1 increments (0.1 inch, 0p1, and so on). To move the image manually, choose the Content tool, move the mouse pointer to the image (the grabber hand appears), and then drag the image. You also can enter values in the Offset fields to move an image within a picture box.

Entering any value except zero in the Rotation field on the right side of the palette rotates the picture *within* the picture box. (The Rotation field on the left side of the palette rotates both the picture box and its picture.) The current value for the picture box in Figure 14-3 is 0, which means that the box is not rotated. Likewise, the value for the image is 0, so it isn't rotated either.

Entering any value except 0 in the Skew field slants the contents of the picture box. In Figure 14-3, the picture-box contents are not skewed.

Figure 14-4 shows the effect of rotating the *contents* of the picture box by 30 degrees by entering a value of 30 in the Rotation field on the right side of the Measurements palette.

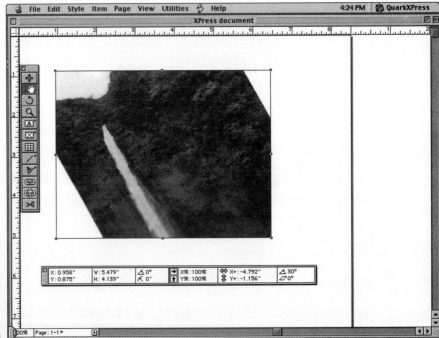

Figure 14-4:
A picture
rotated
within a
picture box.

Scaling a picture

Sometimes, you want to warp a picture by making it narrower or wider than it was originally, changing its X and Y axes in the process. This process is also known as *changing the picture's aspect ratio*.

Suppose that you have a really neat photo of a boogie boarder. You want to fit the photo into a narrow space, but you don't want to lose any parts of the picture. Also suppose that you don't mind if your picture gets a bit warped (hey,

some people would call that *artistic*) in the process.

In the figure, the picture in the box on the left side is scaled at 100 percent on both its X and Y axes. The picture on the right side is warped in terms of its aspect ratio. The picture on the right is 55 percent scale on the X axis and 63.2 percent on the Y axis. You can achieve this effect by making changes in the Measurements palette or the Picture pane of the Modify dialog box.

Figure 14-5 shows the same picture as Figure 14-4, but this time, the entire box, including its contents, has been rotated by 10 degrees. You can see that we entered a value of 10 in the Rotation field on the left side of the Measurements palette.

After you use the Measurements palette to make changes in the picture box, press Return or Enter (or click the mouse) to apply the changes.

Figure 14-5:
A picture
box rotated
10 degrees.

Adjusting the Appearance of Printed Pictures

Most people never worry about line screens (in fact, many desktop publishers don't know what they are), but those screens can have a major effect on how your bitmap images print.

To understand how line screens work, think about a screen door. The spaces between the wires of the screen door allow light to pass through; the wires in the screen keep light out. Line screens split an image into a series of spots and spaces for precisely the same reason — to let some light in and keep some light out.

In traditional printing, a *line screen* is an acetate mask covered with a grid of spots. Printers use line screens to convert a continuous-tone image (such as a photograph) to the series of spots, called a *halftone,* that is required to reproduce such an image on a printing press. Place a magnifying glass over a photo — either color or black and white — in a newspaper or magazine, and you see the spots that the photo is made of. These spots are usually circular, but they can be any of several shapes.

Lines and dots by the inch

When you use line screens, you need to know a little bit about lines per inch and dots per inch. Lines per inch *(lpi)* and dots per inch *(dpi)* are not the same. The spots in a line screen are variable-size, whereas dots in a laser printer are fixed-size. *Lines per inch* specifies the grid through which an image is filtered, not the size of the spots that make up the image. *Dots per inch* specifies the number of ink dots per inch produced by the laser printer; typically, these dots are the same size. A 100-lpi image with variable-size dots, therefore, looks finer than a 100-dpi image.

Depending on the size of the line-screen spot, several of a printer's fixed-size dots may be required to simulate one line-screen spot. For this reason, a printer's or imagesetter's lpi number is far less than its dpi number. A 300-dpi laser printer, for example, can achieve about 60-lpi resolution; a 600-dpi laser printer can achieve about 85-lpi resolution; a 1,270-dpi imagesetter can achieve about 120-lpi resolution; a 2,540-dpi image setter, about 200-lpi resolution. Resolutions of less than 100 lpi are considered to be coarse, and resolutions of more than 120 lpi are considered to be fine.

But choosing an lpi setting involves more than just knowing your output device's top resolution. An often-overlooked issue is the type of paper on which the material is printed. Smoother paper (such as *glossy-coated* or *super-calendered*) can handle finer halftone spots, because the paper's coating (its *finish*) minimizes ink bleeding. Standard office paper, such as the kind used in photocopiers and laser printers, is rougher and has some bleed (meaning that ink diffuses easily through the paper), which usually is noticeable only if you write on it with markers. Newsprint is very rough and has a heavy bleed. Typically, newspaper images are printed at 85 to 90 lpi; newsletter images on standard office paper print at 100 to 110 lpi; magazine images are printed at 120 to 150 lpi; calendars and coffee-table art books are printed at 150 to 200 lpi.

Other factors that affect lpi include the type of printing press and the type of ink used. Your printer representative should advise you on preferred settings.

When a halftone is made in the traditional way, a line-screen mask is placed on top of a piece of photographic paper (such as Kodak's RC paper, which has been used for decades in traditional photography). The continuous-tone original is then illuminated in a camera so that the image is projected through the mask onto the photographic paper. The photographic paper is exposed only where the mask is transparent (in the grid holes, or spots), producing the spots that make up the image to be printed. The size of each spot depends on how much light passes through, which in turn depends on how dark or light each area of the original image is. Think about a window screen through which you spray water: the stronger the spray, the bigger the spots behind the screen's holes.

The spots that make up the image are arranged in a series of lines, usually at a 45-degree angle. (This angle helps the eye blend the individual spots to simulate a continuous tone.) The number of lines per inch (the *halftone frequency*) determines the maximum dot size as well as the coarseness *(halftone density)* of the image (thus the term *line screen*). The spots in the mask need not be circular; they can be ellipses, squares, lines, or more esoteric shapes (such as stars). These shapes are called *screen elements.* Circular spots are the most common type because they result in the least distortion of the image.

Creating effects with line screens

Seeing is believing when it comes to special graphics effects, so experiment with the line-screen fields (Frequency, Angle, and Function) in the Picture Halftone Specifications dialog box to see what they can do before you print your document. (To display this dialog box, make sure that the Content tool is selected and choose Style⇨Halftone, or press Shift+⌘+H or Ctrl+Shift+H.)

In most cases, rather than dealing with Picture Halftone Specifications, you should use the default picture halftone settings, which are specified in the Output pane of the Print dialog box (File⇨Page Setup or File⇨Print). The settings that you make in the Output pane of the Print dialog box are the default settings for all imported images.

But when you want to do something special, you can. As a rule, most people who use line-screen effects prefer coarser halftone frequencies to make the image coarser but bolder; they usually also change the screen element to a line or other shape to alter the image's character. Line screens can be applied only to black-and-white or grayscale bitmap pictures in JPEG, PCX, PICT, TIFF and Windows metafile formats.

Here's how you specify a custom line screen for a picture:

1. **Click a picture box that contains a black-and-white or grayscale bitmap image and choose Style⇨Halftone.**

   The Picture Halftone Specifications dialog box appears.

2. **Choose values from the Frequency pop-up menu or enter a value in the text box to change the frequency/lpi of the printed image.**

3. **Choose an option from the Angle pop-up menu or enter a value in the text box to specify a custom screen angle.**

4. **Choose a shape from the Function pop-up menu to specify a custom shape for the screen element.**

   Click OK to close the Picture Halftone Specifications dialog box and save your changes.

The halftone controls are ignored if you save as or export to PostScript or PDF formats. To be safe, print directly from QuarkXPress to the printer or imagesetter to ensure that halftone settings are retained.

Dithering

Dithering is an effect that replaces gray levels with a varying pattern of black and white. This pattern does not attempt to simulate grays. Instead, dithering merely tries to retain some distinction between shades in an image when the image is output to a printer that does not have fine enough resolution to reproduce grays. In other words, dithering uses coarse patterns of dots and lines to represent the basic details in a grayscale image.

QuarkXPress uses a mathematical equation called *ordered dithering (specifies the order in which pixels are turned on to increase the intensity of the image),* which you apply by choosing Ordered Dither from the Function pop-up menu in the Picture Halftone Specifications dialog box. To apply other dithering equations, you must dither the image in a paint or graphics program that supports dithering before importing the image into QuarkXPress.

Chapter 15

Text as Art

*T*hanks to the miracle of computer science, the once-mighty barriers between text and art have fallen. Today, you can stretch, squash, and distort text as though it were taffy. These capabilities open the way for innovative, creative use of text as art, not to mention as hellish-looking designs. But no one reading this book would ever create something like that!

One of the whiz-bangiest features of QuarkXPress is its ability to run text along all kinds of lines (curved, zigzag, and so on) and the contours of closed shapes (rectangles, ovals, Bézier boxes, and the like). Add this capability to the powerful type-formatting options of QuarkXPress, and the possibilities are endless.

You have to know, of course, *when* to use artistic effects; knowing only *how* to create the effects is not enough. You get to the "how to use" part after the "how to create" part.

Special Type Effects in QuarkXPress

Figures 15-1 and 15-2 show what you can do with type effects in QuarkXPress. All the variants of the standard Times text were accomplished with QuarkXPress features. Some of the examples were created with the formatting options in the Style menu; others were created by modifying the box and the text via the Box and Text panes of the Modify dialog box. (To display this dialog box, choose Item⇨Modify, or press ⌘+M or Ctrl+M.) In some cases, frames are placed around text boxes to show you how the text relates to the box that contains it.

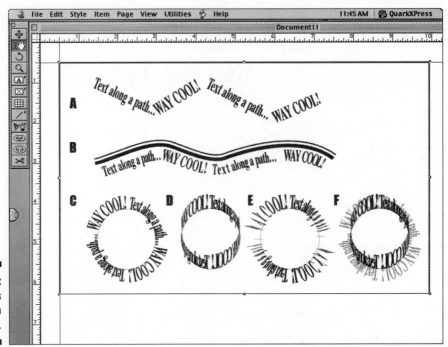

Figure 15-1:
Type effects
created with
text paths.

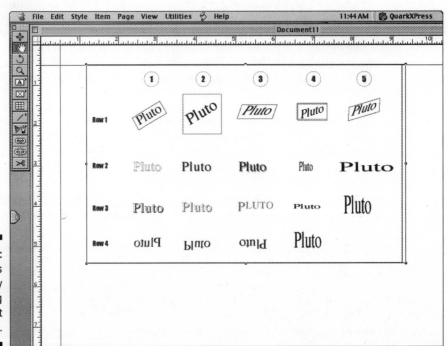

Figure 15-2:
Type effects
created by
modifying
text and text
boxes.

Creating text paths

Before we tell you how to create the examples in Figures 15-1 and 15-2, we show you how to create a text path using the Text Path tools shown in Figure 15-3. The procedure is basically the same as that for creating a line, which we discuss in Chapter 12.

To create a text path, simply follow these steps:

1. **Select one of the four Text Path tools.**

   The bottom of the Tool palette includes four tools for creating text paths: the Line, Bézier, Orthogonal, and Freehand Text-Path tools. Each of these tools is identified with an A next to the type of line that it creates.

2. **Create a text path the same way that you create a line (refer to Chapter 12).**

   The mouse technique that you use depends on the tool that you choose and the kind of line that you want to create. The Line and Orthogonal Text-Path tools let you create straight paths; the Bézier Text-Path tools lets you create straight-edged or curvy lines; and the Freehand Text-Path tool lets you create freehand shapes by using the mouse as a drawing tool. (Refer to Chapter 12 for details about creating and reshaping lines.)

After you create a text path, the Item or Content tool is automatically selected (QuarkXPress reverts to whichever of these tools was selected before you created the path). If you want to place text along the path, make sure that the Content tool is selected and start typing.

A text path behaves a lot like a text box: If you enter more text than the path can hold, a text-overflow box is displayed at the end of the path. Also (as with a text box), you can choose File⇨Get Text (or press ⌘+E or Ctrl+E) to import text into a text path.

When the Content tool is selected, you can highlight text along a path and use the commands in the Style menu to modify its appearance, just as you would modify text in a box.

Figure 15-3:
The four
Text Path
tools of the
Tool palette.

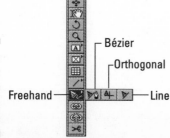

If you choose the Item tool before you click a text path, the Style menu displays the same set of commands that it displays when a line is active: Line Style, Arrowheads, Width, Color, and Shape. You can use these commands to add a line along a text path and control its appearance. You can also modify the appearance of the line associated with a text path in the Line pane of the Modify dialog box, which offers additional controls for controlling the placement and angle of the line. (To display this dialog box, simply choose Item⇨ Modify, or press ⌘+M or Ctrl+M.)

Things really get fun when you start fiddling in the Text Path pane of the Modify dialog box. (To display this pane, choose Item⇨Modify.) Figure 15-4 shows the Text Path pane.

The four options in the Text Orientation area produce four different visual effects, each of which is illustrated (by use of the A, B, C, D lines) in the Text Path pane of the Modify dialog box (Figure 15-4):

- ✔ The top-left button rotates each character so that it sits flat on the path.

- ✔ The top-right button produces a ribbon-like effect. Characters are vertical and skewed, rotated, and sometimes flipped to give the text a 3-D appearance.

- ✔ The bottom-left button produces a wild, skewed appearance that's impossible to describe.

- ✔ The bottom- right button produces a stair-stepped effect with vertical, full-size characters.

The two pop-up menus in the Text Alignment section of the dialog box let you control how the text along a path is placed relative to the path. The Align Text list offers four options: Ascent, Center, Baseline, and Descent.

- ✔ Ascent causes the text to hang from the path, sort of like clothes on a clothesline.

- ✔ Center causes the text to straddle the path.

- ✔ Baseline runs the baseline of the text along the path.

- ✔ Descent is like Baseline, except the text is lifted slightly so that descenders (j, p, g, and so on) are completely above the path.

If you added a wide line to a text path, the three options in the Align with Line pop-up menu — Top, Center, and Bottom — let you control what part of the line the text aligns to.

Recreating Figure 15-1

The following sections describe how we created the examples in Figure 15-1.

Example E   Examples A, B, C   Example D

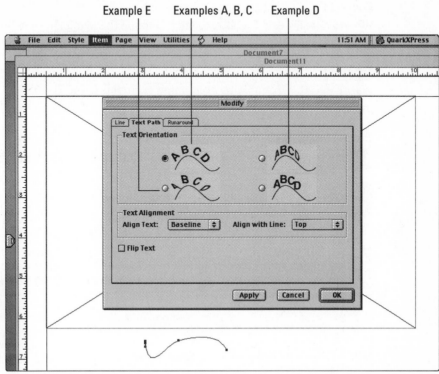

Figure 15-4:
The Text
Path pane in
the Modify
dialog box.

Example A

We created a zigzag line with the Bézier Text-Path tool, entered the text and
chose Style⇨Horizontal/Vertical Scale to vertically stretch the text to 200
percent of its original height. (All the text in Figure 15-1 is vertically scaled.)

Example B

We created a curvy line with the Bézier Text-Path tool, added one of the
default stripe line styles, and made the line 12 points wide. We aligned the
text with the bottom of the line by using the Align with Text pop-up menu in
the Text Path pane of the Modify dialog box. Finally, we applied a Baseline
Shift value of –5 to the text by choosing Style⇨Baseline Shift.

Example C

We created a circular shape with the Bézier Text-Path tool and clicked the
top-left radio button in the Text Orientation section of the Text Path pane of
the Modify dialog box. The text is aligned with the baseline of the text path.

Example D

We created this example by copying example C and clicking the top-right
radio button in the Text Orientation section of the Text Path pane.

Example E

We created this example by copying example C and clicking the bottom-left radio button in the Text Orientation section of the Text Path pane.

Example F

We created this example by combining examples C and D and adding a 40 percent shade to the "flattened" text by choosing Style⇨Shade.

Recreating Figure 15-2

The following sections describe how we created the examples in Figure 15-2.

Row 1

We created the images in Row 1 of Figure 15-2 as follows:

1. We rotated the text box 30 degrees via the Measurements palette or via the Box pane of the Modify dialog box. The text in all boxes of this row has been centered horizontally by choosing Style⇨Alignment⇨Centered, and vertically by choosing Centered from the Alignment pop-up menu in the Text pane of the Modify dialog box.

2. We rotated the text within the box 20 degrees via the Text pane of the Modify dialog box.

3. We skewed the text box 20 degrees via the Box pane of the Modify dialog box.

4. We rotated the text 15 degrees and skewed the text 20 degrees via the Text pane of the Modify dialog box.

5. We rotated the text box 15 degrees and skewed the box 20 degrees via the Box pane of the Modify dialog box.

Row 2

We created the images in Row 2 of Figure 15-2 as follows:

1. We used the outline type style in the Measurements palette. You can choose Style⇨Type Style instead.

2. We used the shadow type style, also in the Measurements palette by choosing Style⇨Type Style.

3. We used two text boxes to create the shadow effect. The front-most box has a runaround of None. Choose Item⇨Runaround and a check None for background color to achieve this effect. The text in the shadow box has a 40-percent shade, which is adjusted by choosing Style⇨Shade.

4. We compressed the text horizontally to 50 percent by choosing Style⇨Horizontal/Vertical Scale.

5. We expanded the text horizontally to 200 percent.

An easy way to change the scaling of text is to hold down the ⌘ or Ctrl key when you resize a text box. This action makes the text resize the same way as the box. Click a text-box handle and hold down the mouse button until the item in the box flashes; then drag the text-box handle in the direction in which you want to scale the text. This method lets you see the effects of the resizing as they happen, so you can see when the new scale is what you want it to be.

Row 3

We created the images in Row 3 of Figure 15-2 as follows:

1. We used both the shadow and outline type styles.

2. We used the shadow style and changed the text's shade to 60 percent by choosing Style⇨Shade.

   (You can change color by choosing Style⇨Color or by using the Colors palette with the palette's Color content tool selected.)

3. We applied the small-caps type style and then applied a baseline shift value of five points by choosing Style⇨Baseline Shift.

4. We compressed the text vertically to 50 percent.

5. We expanded the text vertically to 200 percent.

Horizontal and vertical scaling work basically the same way. Because it seems to be human nature to start at the vertical size desired and then scale to make the text skinnier or fatter, most people scale text horizontally. Therefore, the default in the dialog box is Horizontal. That may be because for years, even in the old days before desktop publishing, that's just how the tools worked.

Row 4

We created the images in Row 4 of Figure 15-2 by flipping:

1. We flipped the text horizontally by using the Measurements palette or by choosing Style⇨Flip Horizontal.

   Flipping affects the entire contents of the text box, so you may think that you should use the Item tool. Actually, you should use the Content tool for this one. Even though you could argue that flipping affects the entire box (in which case, you would use the Item tool), QuarkXPress thinks that flipping affects only the contents of the box, not the box itself. You don't need to highlight text before you flip it. All text in a box is flipped, whether text is highlighted or not.

2. We flipped the text vertically by using the Measurements palette. (You could also choose Style⇨Flip Vertical.)

3. We flipped the text both horizontally and vertically.

4. We resized the text box while holding down the ⌘ or Ctrl key. The text was enlarged and vertically scaled as we dragged a box handle.

If you fancy yourself a typesetter, you can see from Figure 15-1 and Figure 15-2 that QuarkXPress lets you do almost anything you can imagine to text. Combining the effects in the examples allows you to create interesting variations.

Creating custom drop caps

Figure 15-5 shows an assortment of rotated *drop caps* (large letters inset into a paragraph; refer to Chapter 6 for more details on the drop-cap feature). The drop cap is in its own text box; you can't rotate drop caps that were created by means of the standard drop-cap feature.

QuarkXPress lets you anchor any kind of item — even grouped items — within text, including drop caps that you place in rotated boxes.

Here's how we created the drop caps:

- ✔ We rotated the drop cap in the bottom-left corner 30 degrees. The font is different from the one used for the body copy and sized so that the letter covers the full diagonal of the text that it cuts across.

- ✔ The drop cap in the top-left corner is a little trickier; it uses a combination of box skewing (15 degrees) and box rotation (25 degrees). The result of this combination is that the slanted strokes of the N are almost vertical.

- ✔ The drop cap in the bottom-right corner is a modified version of the other shadowed drop cap in the top-left corner. For the shadow, we didn't use the shadow type style. Instead, we duplicated the text box that contained the initial cap, offset the copy slightly from the original, and sent it behind the original by choosing Item⇨Send Backward. (Mac users must press the Option key to change the Send to Back command to Send Backward.)

- ✔ If you're using a character style sheet for the drop cap, you can access the context menu, a new feature of Version 5, for quick access to the Character Style Sheet dialog box. To display a text box context menu, select the text box or individual character and press Control+click on the Mac or right-click on Windows. Context menus are handy because they require fewer steps to access the controls you want, helping save time while you're formatting a document.

  We applied a 50-percent shade to the shadow text and set the runaround for both initial cap text boxes to None. Figure 15-6 shows the runaround turned off in the Modify dialog box.

Although this multiple-text-box approach to building drop shadows for text takes effort, it allows you to create exactly the type of shadow you want, down to the color, shade, and the amount of offset. The QuarkXPress shadow type style cannot be customized; you receive just what QuarkXPress is preprogrammed to do.

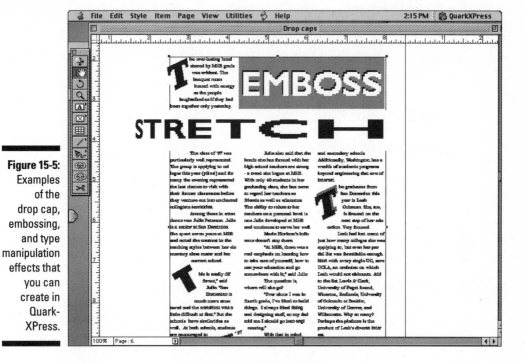

Figure 15-5:
Examples
of the
drop cap,
embossing,
and type
manipulation
effects that
you can
create in
Quark-
XPress.

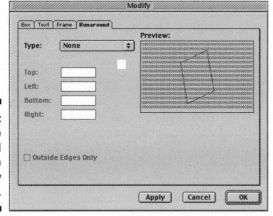

Figure 15-6:
The
Runaround
pane of the
Modify
dialog box.

When you're done creating a shadow, don't forget to group the text boxes that form it so that one of them doesn't get moved later accidentally. To group the text boxes, choose Item⇔Group (or press ⌘+G or Ctrl+G).

Creating embossed text

Refer to Figure 15-5 for an example of text that appears to be embossed (top right). This example was created with two text boxes. One text box contains white text and a runaround of None; the box above it contains black text and a box background of 40-percent black.

Stretching text

The other effect shown in Figure 15-5 is simple to create. The Stretch! text uses the horizontal scaling feature to make each subsequent letter scaled more. The following scale values were used for successive letters, from left to right: 50, 100, 125, 175, 225, 275, and 350.

Tips for Using Text as Art

This advice may seem obvious to you but it's not to some people: Use special effects sparingly:

✔ Don't mix dissimilar effects, such as putting skewed text, compressed text that is not skewed, and embossed text on the same page. Unless you're creating a sheet of examples, all you'll do is make the reader notice the dissimilarities and wonder just what you were thinking.

✔ For the best appearance, design special text effects to work with other graphical elements. If several items are slanted, for example, have them slant the same amount whether they're text or lines.

✔ Pay attention to spacing. If text looks like a graphic, give it more space than you would if it looked like just a weird part of the text. A good rule of thumb is to put minimal space around warped text if that text is meant to be read with other text. Drop caps, for example, should not be so far away from the rest of the paragraph that the reader doesn't realize they are drop caps.

✔ Conversely, don't position a graphic that's made of a symbol (such as in a logo) so close to text that people try to read it as part of the text. The more different the warped text looks from the regular text, the easier it will be for the reader to know that the text is different, and you won't have to worry so much about spacing.

That's it! Congratulations — this is the most difficult stuff because it requires an active imagination, an understanding of the tools in QuarkXPress (so that you can turn that imagination into reality), and patience in applying these tools. Have fun!

Part IV
Going Long and Linking

The 5th Wave By Rich Tennant

"You might want to adjust the value of your 'snap distance' function."

In this part . . .

Did you know that you can create books using QuarkXPress? It's true. If your document has more than a dozen or so pages, there's no need to feel antsy about keeping track of figure numbers, table numbers, index entries — well, you get the idea. QuarkXPress handles all this drudgework for you. In fact, crafting long documents is a piece of cake. In this part, we show you how to handle long documents of all flavors, including those that link together several smaller documents into a whole. We also tell you how to make lists, tables of contents, and indexes.

Chapter 16

Building Books

*I*t's been said that everyone has a book in them. Some of you may have several books — stories that are sometimes funny, sometimes serious — waiting to be told. Others of you may need to create highly structured, technical or nonfiction books for a living.

Whatever the book you have inside you, QuarkXPress is a good tool to use when you're ready to bring your book from inside to out. This chapter describes features in QuarkXPress that are designed to help ease the process of getting books and other long documents to look their best.

Planning Your Book

Whatever your dreams of writing the Great American Novel, a book is basically a collection of chapters. Each chapter is a separate document, and you knit the chapters together into a whole book — mentally and physically.

In QuarkXPress, a book is also something more: It's a palette. To be precise, it's a Book palette. Like other palettes in QuarkXPress, a *Book palette* is a list of information displaying the chapters that make up the book.

Building a book isn't difficult, especially if you take it one step at a time. The following sections show you how to do it. But before exploring Book palettes and how to use them, you need to do some planning. Here are some pointers to consider before you begin building a book in QuarkXPress 5:

✔ **Organize your chapters beforehand.** Start by outlining the book, either the old-fashioned way, with pencil and paper, or the modern way, on your computer.

✔ **Use style sheets to format the chapters uniformly (see Chapter 6 for more about style sheets) as you write the book.**

✔ **Decide on the number, names, and order of the chapters.** You can make changes to a chapter's number, name, and order at any time, but figuring out these basics in advance can save you time in the long run.

✔ **Make decisions about the format of the book (style sheets, typeface, pagination style, and so on) at the chapter level, beginning with the first chapter.** Deciding on the format is important because the first chapter that you add to a Book palette becomes the master chapter (see the section "Working with master chapters" later in this chapter), and attributes of that document form the basis for the other chapters you add to the book.

After you write the chapters and are ready to assemble them, create a Book palette (that we describe in the following sections) and use it to combine the separate chapters into a book. After you assemble the chapters, you can update the page numbers, create a table of contents, and create an index for the book (see Chapter 18).

Creating and Opening Books

To open the Book palette and create a new book, choose File➪New➪Book (see Figure 16-1).

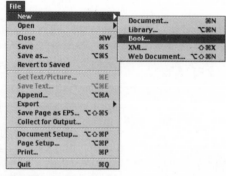

Figure 16-1:
Creating a new book.

In Figure 16-2, you see a new, open book palette that we named "Rattlesnake Blues." The upper part of Figure 16-2 also shows the controls that you use in the Add New Chapter dialog box to locate the chapters that you want to place in the book. To open an existing Book palette, choose File⇨Open, the same as you would to open a document or a library. To display the Add New Chapter dialog box, click the Book icon at the upper-left of the Book palette.

Working with master pages

When you're building a book, you're likely to want some elements repeated on multiple pages. For example, you may want to have a running head at the top, outer edge of every page to identify the book. Or you may want a page number to appear at the bottom of every page. Whenever you have elements that repeat on more than one page, you want to use master pages. A *master page* is a non-printing page that automatically formats pages in a document. A master page may contain items such as page numbers, headers, footers, and other elements that repeat on multiple pages throughout a document.

Open a master page by choosing Page⇨Display⇨A-Master A (see Figure 16-3). To return to the document page, choose Page⇨Display⇨Document. You can tell that the master page is displayed if you see the picture of a chain link in the upper-left corner of the page.

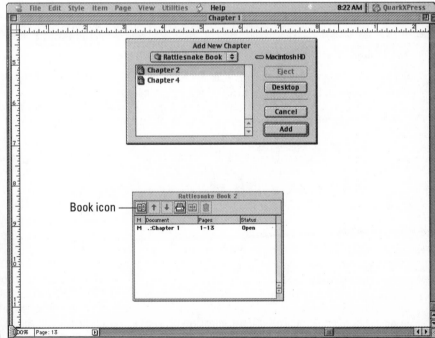

Figure 16-2:
The Book palette and the Add New Chapter dialog box.

Chain link icon

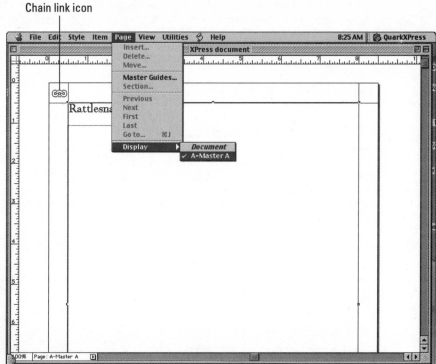

Figure 16-3:
Displaying a
master
page.

On the master page in Figure 16-3, we created a text box and typed the running head "Rattlesnake Blues." Now, whenever we use a new document page that's based on the A-Master A master page, the running head appears. Of course, you can always decide to delete any master page item while you have the document open.

Working with master chapters

After you open a new Book palette and list the book's first chapter, QuarkXPress treats that chapter as the master chapter. The *master chapter* contains attributes that all chapters of the book use. For example, we decided to establish a spot color for the "Rattlesnake Blues" running head in our cookbook. If this spot color is in the master chapter, it will appear in all subsequent chapters of the book after you click the Synchronize button on the Book palette. If you add the spot color to a chapter other than the master chapter, the color will appear only in that chapter, not throughout the book. You can tell which chapter is the master chapter by looking for an *M* next to the chapter name in the Book palette. In Figure 16-4, you can see an *M* next to Chapter 1, indicating Chapter 1 is the first chapter we added and is therefore the master chapter. Note that QuarkXPress creates a master chapter even if you choose not to use master pages.

Adding, deleting, and moving document pages

While building the chapters in a book, you may need to insert, delete, or move pages. To do any of these operations, you use the Page menu:

- ✔ To insert pages, choose Page⇨Insert to display the Insert Pages dialog box.

- ✔ Deleting pages is a similar function. Choose Page⇨Delete; a dialog box appears, in which you're able to choose pages to delete.

- ✔ To move pages, choose Page⇨Move to access a dialog box where you can specify which pages to move and the locations to move them to.

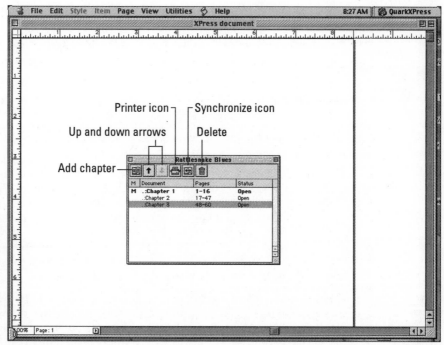

Figure 16-4:
Adding
chapters to
a book; the
first chapter
created
becomes
the master
chapter.

Navigating through a document

As long documents get longer, QuarkXPress offers a couple of quick and easy ways to navigate through their pages:

- ✔ One way is to enter the number of the page to which you want to go in the Page Number field on the left side of the bar below the document page. QuarkXPress takes you directly to that page.

- ✔ Another option is to choose Page⇨Go to (or press ⌘+J or Ctrl+J), which displays the Go to Page dialog box.

If you simply want to get from the top to the bottom of a page, use the scroll bar at the right side of the document window.

Using the Book Palette

The Book palette indicates the number of pages in each chapter and tells you the status of the chapters that you've added (see Figure 16-5).

You see one of the following in the status column for each chapter:

- ✔ **Available:** You can open, edit, or print this chapter.

- ✔ **Open:** This chapter is currently open, and you can edit or print it. In Figure 16-5, Chapter 1 is open.

- ✔ **Modified:** This chapter has been changed since the last time the Book palette was open on this computer.

- ✔ **Missing:** This chapter is unavailable to the Book palette or cannot be located at this time.

  Multiple users can open copies of the same book if the book is stored in a shared location on a server. Then, book users can either "check out" chapters of the book (to edit the chapters over the network), or they can drag a copy of the chapter to their hard drive to edit it. In this case, if you're in a workgroup and want to prevent other people in your group from editing an original chapter while you're editing a copy of it, move the original chapter to a separate folder. If someone tries to edit the chapter, QuarkXPress lists it with a status of Missing.

  QuarkXPress 5 offers another way to control access to your chapters, one that lets you make a chapter *read-only* (Mac) or *locked* (Windows). When a chapter in a book is in read-only or locked mode, edits can be made only from the computer where it was locked or changed to read-only mode. All the other computers on the network can display the chapter on-screen for reading purposes, but they can't make changes to the chapter.

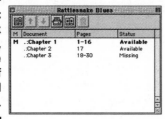

Figure 16-5:
The Book
palette,
showing the
status of
individual
chapters.

Book palette control icons

The icons across the top of the Book palette control the chapters in the book. In order from left to right, here's how the icons work:

- ✔ **To add chapters:** The first icon is the Add Chapter icon. After you click this icon, an Add New Chapter dialog box appears (refer to the upper dialog box in Figure 16-2), letting you locate a chapter that you want to add to the Book palette.

- ✔ **To rearrange chapters:** Use the icons with up and down arrows to rearrange chapters within the Book palette. (For example, to move Chapter 1 so that it follows Chapter 3, click Chapter 1 to select it and then click the down arrow three times to move it down three chapters.)

  To speed things up, you can also move a chapter in the list by pressing the Option/Alt key and clicking and dragging the chapter up or down.

- ✔ **To delete chapters:** The icon of a small trash can (in Windows, the icon is a big "X") is the Delete button. By highlighting one or more chapters and then by clicking this icon, the chapters are deleted from the book. Note that the file itself is not deleted, just the link that lists the file as a chapter in the Book palette.

- ✔ **To print a chapter:** The icon that looks like a printer is the Print button.

- ✔ **To synchronize chapter formatting:** The icon with a left- and a right-pointing arrow is the Synchronize button. It lets you format the other chapters in the book so that they're consistent with the master chapter (see the following section for more information).

Synchronizing chapter formatting

QuarkXPress lets you make *local changes* (changes that affect only the chapter you're working on) to chapters at any time, and then add, or *synchronize,* some or all the chapters in a book consistently. Synchronize chapters by using the Synchronize button on the Book palette (the icon on the far right of the palette with a left- and a right-pointing arrow; refer to Figure 16-5). When you synchronize chapters, QuarkXPress compares each chapter with the master chapter and then modifies the chapters as necessary so that they conform to the master chapter's colors, style sheets, hyphenation and justification (H&J) sets, lists, and so on.

Unlike in previous versions of QuarkXPress, you no longer need to synchronize every change made to the master chapter with the rest of the chapters in the book. QuarkXPress 5 has a new dialog box — the Synchronize Selected Chapters dialog box (see Figure 16-6) — that lets you pick and choose which elements you'd like to synchronize throughout your chapters. To select and synchronize an element, you simply highlight one or more of the items in the list on the left side of the dialog box, and click the arrow to move them to the list on the right side of the dialog box. When an item is in the right dialog box, it will be synched when you close the menu. If you want to synchronize all the modified items, just click the Synch All button at the bottom of the dialog box.

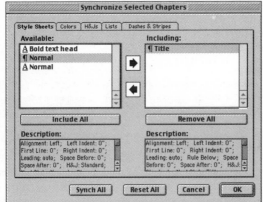

Figure 16-6:
The
Synchronize
Selected
Chapters
dialog box.

Synchronizing chapters

Synchronizing chapters is a great idea if you have a long, involved book that you've worked on over several months (in which case you can easily make a paragraph style change in one chapter and forget to make the change in all other chapters).

Synchronizing is also a good idea if the document has several authors, any of whom may have made local changes without informing the entire group.

Suppose that you already specified Chapter 1 as the master chapter, but you really want to make the whole book look like Chapter 3. The Book palette should first show an *M* to the left of the name of Chapter 1. Click to highlight Chapter 3 and then click the blank area to the left of the chapter name. Chapter 3 then becomes the new master chapter, and the *M* is now to the left of Chapter 3's name.

Don't worry about losing any chapter-specific styles, colors, H&J sets, or other things when you synchronize. Synchronizing only adds new styles or modifies existing styles.

Printing chapters and books

In the Book palette, the icon of a printer is the Print button. You click this icon to print either the entire book or selected chapters listed in the Book palette. Chapters with a status of Missing or Modified won't print, and an error message notifies you of this situation. Following is a list of printing options:

- ✔ To print selected chapters, highlight the chapters that you want to print and click the Print icon (Shift+click to select a range of chapters and ⌘+click or Ctrl+click to select discontinuous chapters). The Print dialog box appears, as shown in Figure 16-7. (To print the entire book, make sure that no individual chapter is highlighted when you click the Print icon.)

- ✔ To print all the pages in the selected chapters (or to print the entire book if no chapters are selected), choose All from the Pages pop-up menu of the Print dialog box.

- ✔ To print a range of pages from selected chapters, choose Selected from the Pages pop-up menu and enter the page numbers.

- ✔ After entering your printing selections in the Print dialog box, click the Print button at the lower right (or press the Return key) to print the book or the selected chapters.

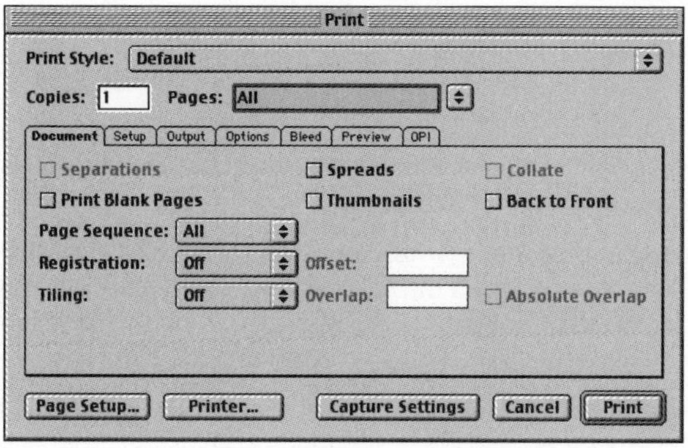

Figure 16-7:
The Print dialog box.

Working with sections

In long documents, dividing chapters into *sections* is not uncommon. For example, you may have a Chapter 2 with Sections 1, 2, and 3. QuarkXPress can help you paginate chapters that have sections. For example, you may want the pages in Section 2 of Chapter 2 to be numbered 2-2.1, 2-2.2, and so on. The following sections show you how this is done.

Creating a section

If you want to create a section in a chapter, open the chapter and then choose Page⇨Section to access the Section dialog box (see Figure 16-8).

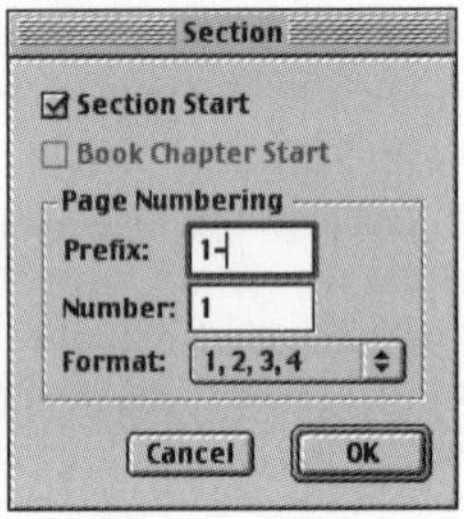

Figure 16-8:
The Section
dialog box.

To paginate the pages in a section, do the following:

1. **In the Section dialog box, check Section Start to disable (uncheck) the Book Chapter Start option that we describe in the next section.**

   After you add, delete, or rearrange pages or chapters, QuarkXPress paginates subsequent chapters according to the settings in the Section dialog box.

2. **If you want, in the Page Numbering area of the Section dialog box, you can enter a page prefix up to four characters in length in the Prefix box.**

   For example, you may want to number the pages in an attachment as *Att-1, Att-2;* in this case, *Att* would be the prefix.

3. **In the Number box, type the page number that you want to assign to the first page of a new section.**

   The Number field requires Arabic numbers, regardless of the Format of the section numbers; for example, if you're using lowercase Roman numerals for the front matter of a book and want the first page of the section to be page iii, type **3** in the Number field.

4. **Use the Format pop-up menu to select a style for page numbers in a section.**

   Choices include numeric (1, 2, 3, 4), uppercase Roman (I, II, III, IV), lowercase Roman (i, ii, iii, iv), uppercase alphabetic (A, B, C, D), and lowercase alphabetic (a, b, c, d).

In the Book palette, chapters that contain section starts are indicated by an asterisk next to the numbers in the Pages field.

Using the Book Chapter Start feature

If a chapter doesn't have any sections, QuarkXPress considers it as having a *Book Chapter Start,* which is also the default setting. After you check the Book Chapter Start box in the Section dialog box, QuarkXPress starts numbering the pages of a chapter after the last page of the previous chapter. If the last page in a book's first chapter is page 15, for example, the first page in the second chapter is page 16.

Here's the lowdown on the Book Chapter Start feature:

- ✔ Whenever you add a chapter without any sections to a book, QuarkXPress numbers pages sequentially throughout the book.
- ✔ As you add and delete pages from chapters, QuarkXPress also updates the page numbers.

The Book Chapter Start check box is available only if you open a chapter independently of its book by opening it without using the Book palette.

Chapter 17

Making Lists and Indexes

Chances are, you know someone who is a listmaker; you know, the person who writes a list of everything to do today, tomorrow, and next week. Listmakers know that lists can help them keep information organized.

Lists, such as a table of contents, work well in publishing, too. In QuarkXPress, a list is actually nothing more than a compilation of paragraphs that are formatted with the same style sheet. Lists are very handy for long documents, but keep in mind that in QuarkXPress, a list cannot contain more than 32 style sheets (see Chapter 6), and a paragraph in a list is limited to 256 characters. (Your paragraphs can be longer than 256 characters, but when you build a list, only the first 256 characters of each listed paragraph are used.)

After you create a book (or even a single document), QuarkXPress can build a list by scanning the chapters for the style sheets that you specify. For example, if you create a book and have a style sheet that you apply to the figures in the document, you can generate a list of those figures by asking QuarkXPress to list all the paragraphs that use the style sheet named "Figure." The process that we describe in this chapter works for any kind of list you want to build in QuarkXPress 5.

Building and Maintaining a List

To see how list-building works, suppose that you want to create a list of figures in a book; just follow these steps:

1. **Create individual documents, or chapters, for the book.**

   See Chapter 16 if you need a refresher on creating chapters.

2. **As you create the chapters, create and apply paragraph style sheets that define chapter heads, figures, and tables.**

   See Chapter 6 for more information on style sheets.

3. **Assemble the book by using the Book palette.**

Now you're ready to create a list of figures.

Using the Edit List dialog box

Suppose that you elect to list the headers in Chapter 2 of the book. With Chapter 2 open, choose EditÍLists and then click New to display the Edit List dialog box (see Figure 17-1), and then follow the steps:

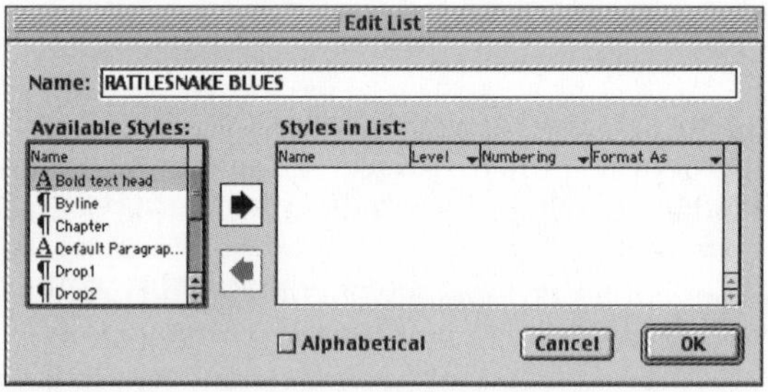

Figure 17-1:
The Edit List
dialog box.

1. **In the Name box of the Edit List dialog box, type the name of the list that you want to create.**

2. **Choose a style for the list by highlighting the style name in the Available Styles box; then click the right-pointing arrow to transfer the style to the Styles in List box.**

   The Styles in List box includes the following options:

   • **Level:** This pop-up menu includes levels from 1 (highest) to 8 (lowest). The number that you choose represents a level in a hierarchy and is useful for creating complex lists.

   • **Numbering:** This pop-up menu defines a page-numbering style for each item in the list; this numbering style determines how page numbers appear in the list. Choosing Page# Text causes items to be preceded by their page number. Other options are Text only, which suppresses page numbers, or Text# Page, which causes an item to appear before its page number.

   • **Format As:** This pop-up menu allows you to select a style sheet to determine how the text appears in the list. For example, if you're using the list to create a table of contents, you may want all

17-point bold text styled with your Chapter Title style sheet to be reformatted in the list by using your 12-point TOC Chapter style sheet.

3. **After making your selections, click OK.**

QuarkXPress scans the chapter, locates all the paragraphs that are marked with the Header style, and then uses these items to create a list.

Placing a list in a book

To put your list into a text box so that you can make the list part of the book, make sure that the text box you want to use is active and then click the Build button in the Lists palette (View⇨Show Lists). The Build button is available only when a text box is active. See Chapter 3 for more about text boxes.

Updating and rebuilding a list

If you edit a document after you build a list, be sure to update the list by clicking the Update button in the Lists palette. If you previously used the Build button, you need to use it again to replace the old list with the new, updated list.

Creating an Index

If you've ever had trouble finding information in a book, you can appreciate how important a good index can be. Indexing used to be a laborious process, involving lots of index cards. QuarkXPress makes indexing much easier, while still relying on you to make key decisions about formatting. The following sections show you how to do your part in creating an index.

Choosing an indexing style

Before you develop an index, you need to decide on the indexing style that you want to use. Large publishers usually have their own house style guides for indexes. One option is to use an index you like as a model and then take the steps necessary in QuarkXPress to achieve that index style. Before you begin indexing your document, ask yourself the following questions:

✔ Do you want to capitalize all levels of all entries, or do you just want to use initial caps?

- Should headings appear in boldface?
- Do you want to capitalize secondary entries in the index?
- Should the index be nested or run-in style? For examples of these indexes, check out the sidebar "Nested or run-in index?" elsewhere in this chapter.

Using the Index Preferences dialog box

To index words in QuarkXPress, you mark the words that you want to use as index entries in the chapters of your book. These markers appear as colored brackets around the entry. You can choose the color of index markings (in addition to the index separation characters you want to use) by choosing EditÍPreferencesÍIndex to access the Index Preferences dialog box, shown in Figure 17-2. The following sections explain the dialog box options.

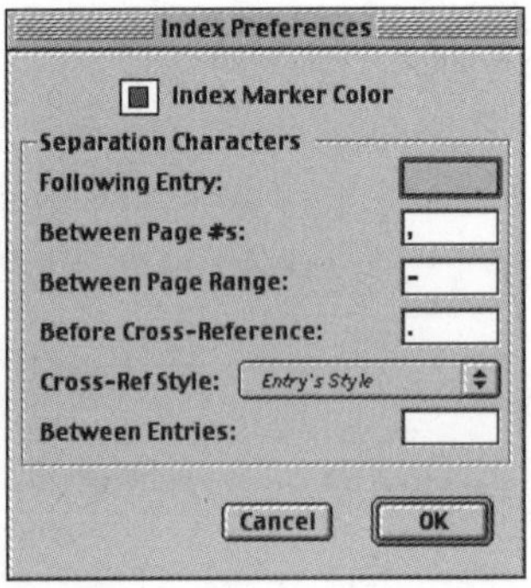

Figure 17-2:
The Index
Preferences
dialog box.

Changing the index marker color

To change the color of the index markers, click the Index Marker Color button in the Index Preferences dialog box; this action displays a color picker. Use the controls in the color picker to define the new color for index markers. Click OK to close the color picker and then click OK in the Index Preferences dialog box to complete the process.

Choosing separation characters

In the Index Preferences dialog box, you can also choose the characters and spaces that separate entries in the index. The options in the Separation Characters section of the dialog box work as follows:

- **Following Entry:** Defines the punctuation that immediately follows each index entry. This punctuation is usually a colon (:). For example, the index item Rattlesnakes: vi, 14, 22-24 uses a colon and space following the index entry "Rattlesnakes."

✔ **Between Page #s:** Defines the characters or punctuation that separates a list of page numbers. This punctuation is usually a comma (,) or semicolon (;). For example, the index item Rattlesnakes: vi, 14, 22-24 uses a comma and a space between its page numbers.

✔ **Between Page Range:** Defines the characters or punctuation that indicates a range of pages. This option is usually the word "to" or a dash. For example, the index item Rattlesnakes: vi, 14, 22 to 24 uses the word "to" between the numbers, indicating a range of pages.

✔ **Before Cross-Reference:** Defines the characters or punctuation that appears before a cross-reference. This option is usually a period and space, or a semicolon. For example, the index item Rattlesnakes: vi, 14, 22-24. See also Poisonous Snakes uses a period and space before the cross-reference.

✔ **Cross-Ref Style:** Enables you to specify a default style sheet for cross-references in your index. For example, if you'd like to use the same style sheet for your cross-references that you used for your body copy, you can choose the style sheet for your body copy in the pop-up menu provided.

✔ **Between Entries:** Defines the characters or punctuation between entry levels in a run-in index. This option is usually a period or a semicolon. For example, the index item Rattlesnakes: vi, 14, 22-24; Snake characteristics: 19 uses a semicolon between entry levels.

Using the Index palette

When your document is ready to index, open the Index palette by choosing View➪Show Index or by pressing Option+⌘+I or Ctrl+Alt+I. Use this palette to add words to the index in as many as four indent levels, to edit or delete index entries, or to create cross-references. The Index palette appears in Figure 17-3.

Figure 17-3:
The Index
palette.

The controls in the Index palette include the following:

✔ **Text:** The Text field in the Entry section of the Index palette is where you type in an index entry or where the text appears that you tagged with index markers. If you highlight text in an open document when the Index palette is open, the first 255 characters of the highlighted text appear automatically in the Text field and are ready to be captured as an index entry.

✔ **Sort As:** Entries in the Sort As field override the default, alphabetical sorting of the index entry. For example, you may want 16-ounce package to be indexed as if the entry appeared as "Sixteen-ounce package"; you can accomplish this task by entering the spelling **Sixteen-ounce package** into the Sort As field.

✔ **Level:** This pop-up menu lets you control the order and structure of index entries. A nested index can have up to four levels, and a run-in index can have only two levels. (Technically a run-in index can have four levels, too, but it doesn't make any sense to use more than two.)

✔ **Style:** The Style pop-up menu (within the Reference section of the dialog box) lets you apply a character style to the page numbers for the current index entry or cross-reference. One example of how you may want to use this option is with a cross-reference like "See also *Garden snakes*" \ where you want to use an italicized character type for the words *Garden snakes.*

✔ **Scope:** This pop-up menu in the Reference section lets you control the scope, or range, of the index. For example, you can use it to make an entry a cross-reference, or list an entry as covering a specific number of paragraphs, or suppress the printing of the entry's page number.

✔ **Add button:** This button lets you add an entry to the index.

✔ **Add All button:** If you have more than one occurrence of an index entry, this button lets you add all occurrences of that entry to the index simultaneously.

✔ **Find Next Entry button:** This button finds the next occurrence of an index entry in the active document. The Find Next button does not, unfortunately, find words in the document so that you can index them.

✔ **Pencil icon:** You can edit an active index entry by clicking the pencil icon or by double-clicking the entry name.

✔ **Trashcan icon:** You can delete the selected entry by clicking the trashcan icon on the Mac or the big X in Windows.

✔ **Pencil icon:** You can edit an active index entry by clicking the pencil icon or by double-clicking the entry name.

✔ **Trashcan icon:** You can delete the selected entry by clicking the trashcan icon on the Mac or the big X in Windows.

Creating an index entry

To create an index entry, highlight the text in your document that you want to use for the index entry. (Don't highlight the whole area that you want the index entry to reference; just highlight the word that you want to appear in the index.) Then click the Add button in the Index palette to add the index entry to the list by using the currently selected values in the Entry and Reference areas. When you add index entries, make sure that the capitalization of the words in the Text field matches the style of your index. QuarkXPress does not automatically capitalize (or lowercase) words in your index.

Editing an index entry

To edit an index entry, you must first select it in the Index palette and then go into editing mode; you can either double-click the index entry, or click the index entry and then click the Pencil icon. You can select an entry and make changes to the Entry and Reference areas, but unless you go into editing mode first, you're only changing the settings that will be used when you create the next index entry.

Creating page-number references

Each index entry includes a reference. A reference usually consists of the page number(s) to which the entry refers, but it may also be a cross-reference (see the following section on creating cross-references). To see the page number reference (or cross-reference) for an index entry, click the icon to the left of the entry in the lower section of the Index palette.

Creating cross-references

Cross-references enhance an index because they give the reader another way to find pertinent information. The following steps show you how to add a cross-reference to an indexed entry:

1. **Display the Index palette by selecting View➪Show Index.**

2. **Click Add to create a new entry, or select an existing entry.**

3. **Click the triangle next to the entry name to make its reference available and then double-click that reference to edit it.**

4. **Click the Scope pop-up menu and select Cross-Reference.**

   This action highlights a field in the palette into which you can enter the cross-referenced term (see Figure 17-4).

5. **From the See pop-up menu, choose an option (See, See Also, or See Herein) to govern how the cross-reference appears under the index entry.**

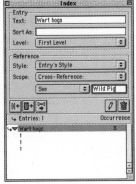

Figure 17-4:
Adding a cross-reference (Wild Pig) to an index entry (Wart hogs).

In Figure 17-4, for the index entry Wart hogs, we have a cross-reference Wild Pig. (Note that although Index Preferences controls the punctuation preceding a cross-reference, you still need to insert punctuation following a cross-reference in this field.)

Using index levels

QuarkXPress 5 supports four levels of indexing. The most important thing to remember about creating a level-two, level-three, or level-four index entry is that you must tell QuarkXPress where to put it — that is, you must indicate a higher-level index entry for the subentry to fall under. You provide a higher-level index entry by using the arrow column at the left edge of the index entry list at the bottom of the Index palette. Follow these steps to create a level-two entry to an existing level-one entry:

1. **Select the text that you want to add.**

2. **In the arrow column, click next to the level-one entry under which you want the new entry listed.**

3. **Choose Second Level from the Level pop-up menu in the Entry area.**

4. **Click the Add button to add the new entry.**

Using the Build Index dialog box

To build an index from a list that you generate in the Index palette, choose Utilities⇨Build Index to access the Build Index dialog box, shown in Figure 17-5.

The options in the Build Index dialog box work as follows:

✓ **Choosing a nested or run-in index:** Your first decision is whether the index is nested or run-in. (See the sidebar "Nested or run-in index?" to help you make a decision.)

Figure 17-5:
The Build
Index dialog
box.

✔ **Building an index for an entire book:** The Build Index dialog box allows you to build an index for the entire book, rather than for just the open chapter. You select this option by clicking the Entire Book box.

✔ **Replacing an existing index:** Indexing is an iterative process, and you'll probably want to build an index a few times through the course of a book project. When you click Replace Existing Index in the Build Index dialog box, QuarkXPress overwrites the existing index with the most current version.

✔ **Adding letter headings:** In long indexes, you may want to divide the index alphabetically so all the index entries that begin with *A* are in a category with the heading *A,* for example. Check Add Letter Headings to use this feature. You can select a paragraph style sheet for the letter headings from the Style pop-up menu.

✔ **Basing an index on a master page:** A Master Page pop-up menu lets you select a master page on which to base the index page. For long indexes, you should consider developing a master page just for that purpose. See Chapter 16 for more about master pages.

✔ **Choosing level styles:** The Level Styles pop-up menus let you choose the paragraph style sheet(s) you want to apply to the various index levels. If you select the Run-in format, all the index levels flow into one paragraph so that only the First Level pop-up menu is available. If you select the nested format, make sure that you specify indentation values for the index level styles that you choose. QuarkXPress does not automatically indent the levels, so if you don't specify indentation values, you won't be able to differentiate among the four index levels.

After you make your choices in the Build Index dialog box, create the index by clicking OK or pressing the Return key.

Part V
Taking QuarkXPress to the Web

The 5th Wave   By Rich Tennant

"What I'm looking for are dynamic Web applications and content, not Web innuendoes and intent."

In this part . . .

The World Wide Web is a new frontier for publishers, but the challenges of creating useful, legible, and interesting documents is the same online as it is in print. QuarkXPress is up for the challenge. In this part, we explain some of the basics you need to know to publish in this medium. We also show you the new QuarkXPress Web features and give you some tips on how and when to use them. Then we give you pointers on how to get those pages up on the Web.

Chapter 18

Forget What You've Learned Thus Far

QuarkXPress is known worldwide for its precision and flexibility. And it should be. After all, it can adjust the leading in a paragraph to within $\frac{1}{1000}$ of a point — and it can do so using inches, picas, ciceros, centimeters, or agates as a measuring system.

The Web features described in this chapter are new with Version 5.

For now, it's time to forget about all that stuff. Why? Because now we're going to use QuarkXPress 5 to build Web pages — and when it comes to building Web pages, a lot of the regular QuarkXPress rules don't apply. Many of the features that work with print documents don't work quite the same as they do with Web documents or they don't work at all.

The differences between QuarkXPress Web and print documents stem from the internal design of the documents themselves. For print documents, QuarkXPress uses a series of sophisticated programming languages, including PostScript, to output print documents on-screen and to your printer. The internal workings of Web documents, on the other hand, are made entirely of the programming language *Hypertext Markup Language (HTML)*.

HTML: The lingua franca of the Web

HTML is the native tongue of the Web. All Web pages are founded in HTML, and they are completely free of computer platform restraints. As a result, Web pages can be viewed on virtually any computer, provided it has a monitor and Web browser. (We talk about those shortly.) Despite what you may think, HTML is a pretty simple computer language to master, and no special applications or tools are needed to program Web pages with HTML. If you had a mind to, you could buy a beginner's guide to HTML, and start composing your first Web document in a word-processing program, such as Microsoft Word or Word Perfect. Figure 18-1 shows a page being produced in Microsoft Word.

Figure 18-1:
The beginnings of a simple HTML document being created in Microsoft Word.

Browsing through the browsers

After you write your HTML page, you can view it on virtually every computer platform as long as you have a monitor and browser (see Figure 18-1). No doubt you've got the monitor part down — but even a simple result (as in Figure 18-2) can be exciting when you create it from raw code.

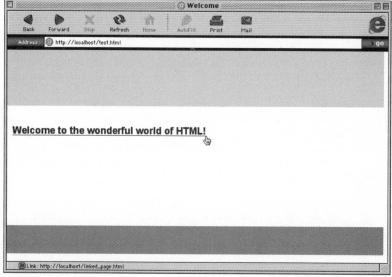

HTML and QuarkXPress

Right about now, you're probably thinking, "This is all fine and good. But I think this HTML programming stuff does look complicated. And what the #$% does QuarkXPress have to do with all this?" Good question. First, you don't have to know squat about HTML or programming to create a basic Web page in QuarkXPress (although it doesn't hurt). Second, don't plan on using QuarkXPress all by itself to produce highly sophisticated Web sites. QuarkXPress lets you create Web pages in a WYSIWYG (what you see is what you get) environment, so you'll never really see those little brackets and codes shown in Figure 18-1. Although this is great for those of you who have simple Web publishing needs (or who are nervous about HTML), the tools here are not robust enough to handle full-blown Web production, where getting your fingers into the underlying code is essential. Other products are more appropriate for serious, down and dirty Web development. But, if you're interested in Web production and willing to give it a try, QuarkXPress 5 offers a quick and easy way to publish documents on the Internet.

With the exception of some added Web-specific tools and a slightly modified document display, creating Web pages in QuarkXPress is nearly identical to creating print documents. In fact, the only reason we bring up these HTML basics at all is because they help you understand some of the obvious differences you'll encounter when creating a Web document in QuarkXPress, as opposed to a print document.

Below are some of the more glaring differences and limitations you'll run across. Keep in mind, though, that it isn't a complete list. If you have questions about how something is working (or not working) in your QuarkXPress Web document, we suggest you call or e-mail Quark Tech Support (mactechquark.com for Macintosh users and wintechquark.com for Windows users).

✔ Obviously, print documents and Web documents serve two entirely different purposes. Print documents are meant to be printed and Web documents are meant to be viewed on your computer screen. As a result, the two use different types of measurements. When you create a new print document, you generally use inches or centimeters to define the size of your document. When you build a Web document, you use pixels.

✔ As a general rule, 600 to 700 pixels is a good width to apply to a Web document because this width can be accommodated on a majority of computer screens. The length, or "height," of a Web document isn't really factor. Because most browsers have scroll bars on their windows, the length of a Web document could conceivably run on for hundreds of feet. Naturally this isn't recommended, but it is possible.

✔ If you thought fonts were an issue with print documents, wait until you try tackling them in Web documents! When you open a Web document on your computer, 99 out of a 100 times it will look fine — because you are building it on *your* computer with *your* fonts. But when the document is transferred to the Web, and someone in Saltlick, USA, decides to open it on his or her computer, the fonts used with your Web page may be totally wiped out, replaced with an entirely different set of fonts with different sizes and even different colors.

✔ A new type of font technology, called *dynamic fonts,* can be used to fix this problem — dynamic fonts are embedded with your HTML document. If you're just getting started with Web pages, don't worry about dynamic fonts. Just remember that dynamic fonts cost you money and your readers download time, so your best bet is to stick with a limited palette of fonts when building your Web documents (Arial, Verdana and Times New Roman are favorites among Web users). This will increase the chances that others will have the same fonts on their systems.

✔ Earlier in this book, we recommended that you stick with EPS and TIFF files when using pictures in your documents. On the Web, you'll want to replace those with 72 dpi (the universal screen resolution) JPEG and GIF files. These have become the only two types of graphics formats recognized universally by browsers due to their inherently small file size (which makes a big difference in download times for people who visit your Web site.) But don't panic if you're taking images from your print documents to the Web; QuarkXPress will convert them to JPEG or GIF for you automatically. Although it's always better to avoid having programs like QuarkXPress translate images from one format to another (because slight imperfections might be introduced during the conversion process) it's good to know that if you forget to convert an image to a Web format in a program like Photoshop, QuarkXPress will pick up the slack.

✔ In Web documents, tables are used differently than in print documents. Those of you who are used to working with print media normally associate tables with charts, diagrams, and so on. They can be used for these purposes in Web documents as well, but you'll find that they are used for much more. Most often they are used as a layout tool for pictures and text — much like text and picture boxes are used on the print side. In fact, after you lay out your Web document in QuarkXPress, and you prepare to upload it to the Web (a topic covered in Chapter 20), QuarkXPress converts your text and picture boxes to tables — most of which look more like asymmetric rats' nests than traditional charts.

✔ Traditional page numbering is not used in Web documents. Although you can insert pages in your QuarkXPress document to have multiple Web pages in that one document, there's no implied connection or sequence to those pages. After all the pages in your Web document are completed, rounded up, and stored in a folder together, they are stitched together with hyperlinks in whatever order you then choose (something we cover in the next section).

Getting around with hyperlinks

A *link* (short for hyperlink) is an item embedded in an HTML document that you can click on to perform a specific action, such as going to another HTML page — either within your Web site, or a page on a different Web site. Hyperlinks can be used to perform all sorts of functions, including accessing an e-mail address or downloading a music or picture file. These "clickable" items can be a word or phrase, a picture (in which case, they are normally referred to as a *hot spot*), or even an isolated area in a page or picture. You create hyperlinks by choosing View➪Show➪Hyperlinks (see Chapter 19.)

Unlike the other Web document tools in QuarkXPress, the Hyperlinks palette is available when a print document is open, too, because hyperlinks also work with Portable Document File (PDF) files — at least they do when the document is being displayed on screen. So you may want to apply hyperlinks to a print document if you plan on also saving it as a PostScript file or PDF to be opened in Adobe Acrobat.

If you refer back to Figure 18-2, you see we already created our first hyperlink: Namely, the phrase "Welcome to the wonderful world of HTML!" You can tell it's a hyperlink because it's underlined and a different color than the rest of the text. To give you an idea how hyperlinks work, we've created a second page, called "You've just seen how a hyperlink works!" (Figure 18-3) that is linked to the "Welcome to the wonderful world of HTML" phrase. You'll have to take our word for it that when you click the link in Figure 18-2, the page in Figure 18-3 appears. When you click the Back link shown in Figure 18-3, you return immediately to the original page.

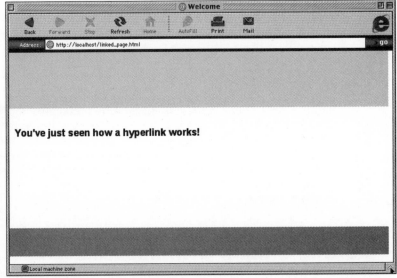

Figure 18-3: When you click the link shown in Figure 18-2, the page it's linked to appears on-screen in its place.

Other Web-related definitions you should know

After you mastered hyperlinks, you can get pretty far in the Web world. You should also be familiar with several phrases and acronyms if you want to get serious about creating professional Web pages (plus they will be mentioned from time to time in subsequent chapters). Several are listed below:

- ✔ **URL (Uniform Resource Locator).** Most people refer to this as a page's address. The URL of a page appears in a field at the top of the window of most browsers (see Figure 18-4). In Internet Explorer, this field is called the Address field. In Netscape Communicator, it is called the Web site field. URLs usually begin with http:// and end with a .com, .net, .org, or something similar. If the address is to a specific a certain page instead of a site, it will end in .html or .htm You may also encounter sites that start with https://. The *s* stands for *secure,* meaning that hackers cannot penetrate it.

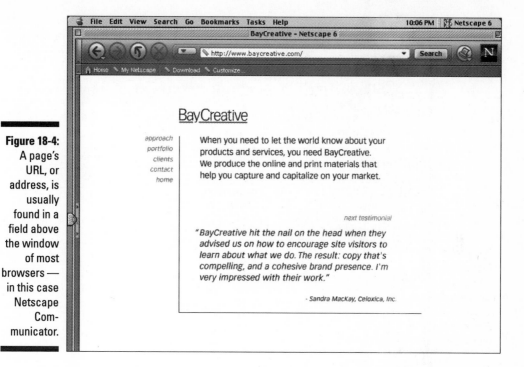

Figure 18-4: A page's URL, or address, is usually found in a field above the window of most browsers — in this case Netscape Communicator.

- **Meta tags.** This one sounds a bit scientific and intimidating, but meta tags are nothing more than a fancy way of saying "notes from the author to other Web masters." Meta tags let the designer of the page provide information about the page, usually so that the next person who works on the page knows what that person did and why they did it. Meta tags usually include "brass tacks," such as the name of the author and the date the page was last modified, but someone viewing the Web site in his or her browser cannot see meta tags.

  The most important use of meta tags is identifying words that describe the content of the page, making it easier for others to find the page via a search engine. In QuarkXPress, meta tags are entered in the Meta Tags dialog box found in the Edit menu. We talk more about these in Chapter 20.

- **Rollover.** Generally, this is a term used in reference to your 401(k) retirement fund. But in HTML, a rollover is a completely different beast. One of the coolest things about Web pages is that it can be designed to be interactive, and one of the most common of these interactive features is the rollover. A rollover is a picture (usually text saved as a JPEG or GIF) that changes color or appearance when you move the mouse pointer over it. Rollovers are easy to create in QuarkXPress. See Chapter 19 for more about making rollovers.

- **Image Map.** As mentioned in the hyperlinks section, different sections of a picture on a Web page can be made into different hyperlinks. The sum of these hyperlinks on a single image is referred to as an *image map*.

- **Forms.** Forms are those parts of Web pages, frequently found on e-commerce sites, that make an appeal for personal information about you, such as your credit card number, e-mail address, and shipping address.

After you develop a general understanding of HTML and how it relates to QuarkXPress (which is really all you need), you can start building a basic Web page. Chapter 19 covers that in detail.

Chapter 19

Web Documents: An Overview

*A*side from the small list of differences mentioned in Chapter 18, building a Web page is very much like building a QuarkXPress print document. You lay out the document using text boxes, picture boxes, lines, and so on, and then you *output* it. (As you can imagine, outputting a Web document differs quite a bit from outputting a print document, but we talk more about that in Chapter 20. It's actually a very easy process.) With a few exceptions, you even use the same tools to create a QuarkXPress Web page (if a tool isn't supposed to be used for building a Web page, QuarkXPress conveniently grays it out for you). As for HTML code (discussed in Chapter 18), you cannot see or edit it in QuarkXPress, but you can open, view, and edit it with a text editor after exporting the page.

One thing you will notice when you create a Web document in QuarkXPress 5 is the addition of some new tools, palettes, and dialog boxes. These tools are for creating Web-specific features like forms, pop-up menus, scrollable lists . . . well, why don't we just give you a complete rundown?

Creating a Web Page

You create a QuarkXPress Web page the same way you create a QuarkXPress print document — you choose File➪New. QuarkXPress 5 has a number of new options in the New submenu. One such option is Web Document, which displays the New Web Document dialog box shown in Figure 19-1. You can also open this dialog box by pressing Shift+Option+⌘+N, or Shift+Alt+Ctrl+N. The first thing you notice about this dialog box is that it doesn't look anything like the familiar New Document dialog box that you see for print pages. Don't worry; it's actually quite easy to configure.

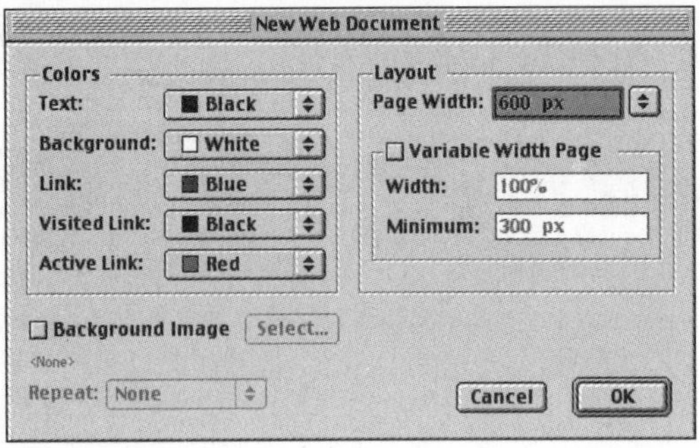

Figure 19-1:
The New
Web
Document
dialog box.

Colors

The first area in the New Web Document dialog box is the Colors section. This is where you choose the default colors for several of the items in your Web page. They are as follows:

- **Text:** Use this pop-up menu to choose a color for the text in your Web page. Resist the temptation to use arbitrary colors like green and orange here. Instead, we suggest you opt for something more traditional like black or dark blue. If you're using a dark background, maybe go with white for the text. At first, you'll probably be tempted to run rampant with color in your Web site — after all, not only do you have access to hundreds of colors, but you also don't have to pay for outputting them as you would if you were creating a print document. Unfortunately, as is the case with print documents, too many colors will more than likely make your page look like doo-doo. Feel free to use them, of course. Just use them sparingly.

- **Background:** Use this pop-up menu to decide what color the background of your Web document will be. You may want to choose a background color before you pick a text color, because the color of your text will depend largely on the color you choose for your background.

- **Link:** Use this pop-up menu to decide what color your hyperlinks will be. This color applies to text hyperlinks only. Image maps won't be affected by your choice; rather, they will remain invisible.

- **Visited Link:** People often like to choose a different color for hyperlinks that have already been clicked, or *visited*. That way they know they've already been there. You can choose any color from this pop-up menu, although we recommend you use a lighter shade of the color you choose from the Link pop-up menu. This lighter shade gives the visited link a *grayed-out* appearance, making it easier for visitors to make the association between the visited links and the unvisited ones.

✔ **Active Link:** Use this pop-up menu to choose a color for the link you're currently visiting. This may sound a bit ridiculous at first. After all, you just clicked the link that got you where you are now. You should have no trouble remembering which one it is, right? You'd be surprised at how easy it is to forget how you got to where you are.

Layout

The Layout section of the New Web Document dialog box lets you decide the width of your Web page. As mentioned in Chapter 18, there is no default measurement for length, because there is no need for one. Theoretically, a Web page is "bottomless" — the only thing hampering its length is the amount of memory on the visitor's computer and his or her level of patience. (Who wants to scroll through a page of text 15 miles long?) Here is a rundown of the choices in the Layout section:

✔ **Width:** The width choices in this section are very limited — and for good reason. Even though Web browsers have both horizontal and vertical scroll bars, most people find it annoying to scroll from left to right while reading a page, particularly if they're already scrolling from top to bottom. So QuarkXPress limits your width options to four choices: 600px, 800px, 1024px, and 1268px — the standard widths of most monitor screens on the market. We personally recommend that you use either 600px or 800px. The other two widths are for widescreen monitors. And although you may have a widescreen monitor, the people who are reading your Web page may not. Using 600px or 800px ensures that people with smaller monitors can read the full width of your page.

About colors on the Web

When you open the pop-up menus in the New Web Document dialog box, you'll notice that QuarkXPress has already chosen a nice palette of colors for you to work with, in case you aren't quite ready to make your own color choices yet. But if you want to dive right in and pick your own colors, choose Other at the top of any of the pop-up menus in the Color area; this opens the Edit Color dialog box where you'll find all of your favorite color-matching systems in the Model pop-up menu. Ignore these systems; they won't do you any good on a Web page because they're for print documents. Monitors don't bother matching colors like printers do; they just display whatever equivalent is at hand — and in many instances, that color won't be the same as the color you picked.

Instead, choose the new Web-safe color palette at the bottom of the Model list. These colors have been created specifically for Web pages. The naming is a little weird — blues, for example, have bland tags like #000066 and #0033CC. Unfortunately, this is how HTML codes refer to colors. If the numbers really freak you out, try the Web Named Colors palette. This palette isn't nearly as extensive as the Web-safe palette, but the names are much more user-friendly. Some are even kind of cute. How do PeachPuff and PapayaWhip grab you?

✔ **Variable Width:** If you check this check box, your page will expand or contract to fit the width of the reader's Web browser. To make the page a variable width page, check the Variable Width Page check box, and then enter values for the following fields:

  • **Width:** Specify the percentage of the viewable browser area that the page will occupy.

  • **Minimum:** Specify a minimum page width. If the reader's browser window is smaller than this width, items will stop being resized.

This feature is a great fix for readers with varying monitor widths, with a couple exceptions. First, this feature is not compatible with all Web browsers, particularly older ones. Second, if the reader's monitor is much larger than your specified page width, the page will stretch to fit the larger monitor, but it will decrease the resolution, particularly the picture resolutions, in the process.

Background

Not to be confused with the Background pop-up menu in the Colors section, the last series of choices in the New Web Document dialog box have to do with the background of your document. One of the neat (or sometimes, not-so-neat) features of HTML is its ability to take a graphic and turn it into a wallpaper-like background for your Web document. If used wisely, this wallpaper effect can add depth and dimension to a Web document, but more often than not, these backgrounds are just annoying and interfere with the rest of the items in your document. For an example of this background effect, see Figure 19-2.

Fortunately, the tiled background (where the image is repeated in the background) isn't the only option offered. In the Repeat pop-up menu, you can choose to repeat the image either vertically or horizontally.

If you want to use a background image, your best bet is to create a very large, very light image. Then, in the New Web Document dialog box, check Background Image and then click Select. Locate and select the background image you created, and then select None from the Repeat pop-up menu. process creates a background image that bleeds on all four sides of the Web browser, not unlike if you were to use a large background image on the cover of a brochure or catalog. This effect has its pitfalls, too, however. The major one is the huge file size of such a graphic. A large picture like the one described can take a long time to download — especially for those using 56 Kbps modems. Still, with some experimentation, you may be able to come up with some striking effects using the background features in the New Web Document dialog box. (If you've already created a Web document and you want to add a background image, use the Page Properties command in the Page menu to access these same controls.)

Figure 19-2:
You can apply a picture to the background of a Web document — often with mixed results.

After you've made your choices in the New Web Document dialog box, click OK. You now have a brand-new canvas on which to build your first QuarkXPress Web page. The next section takes a look at some of the tools that will help you do just that.

TIP

If you aren't happy with your choices after you see them on-screen, you can change them. Simply choose Page Properties from the Page menu or press Option+Shift+⌘+A, or Ctrl+Alt+Shift+A. All the features in the New Web Document dialog box can be edited here. This dialog box also contains a few other features, but they have more to do with preparing a Web page for output than building a document. We talk about those features in Chapter 20.

Using the Web Tools Palette

NEW IN 5

When you open a Web document in QuarkXPress 5, Show Tools in the View menu turns into a submenu, namely the Tools submenu. There, you find two choices: Show/Hide Tool and, a new choice, Show/Hide Web Tools. The Web Tools palette is an extension of sorts of the regular Tool palette (see Chapter 1). In fact, it looks very similar to the Tool palette, with the obvious exception that the nine tools in the Web Tools palette are completely different than those in the regular Tool palette. The Web Tools palette is shown in Figure 19-3.

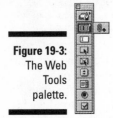

Figure 19-3:
The Web
Tools
palette.

Both the Tool palette and the Web Tools palette can be open at the same time within a Web document. As a matter of fact, we recommend that you have both open at the same time; you'll be switching back and forth between the two constantly while you're working.

You cannot covert a print publication into a Web document. The Web tools are accessible only if you create a new Web document. That means if you want to create a Web version of a print document, you need to create a new Web document and copy the relevant print document's elements to the new Web document.

Image Map tools

In Chapter 18, we define image maps as those "hot spots" placed on images, where you can click to get to another page, send an e-mail, submit information, and so on. An image map is, in effect, a hyperlink assigned to an entire area. Figure 19-4 shows an image map surrounded by other standard page elements.

You create an image map very much like you'd create a text or picture box. Just follow these steps:

1. **Select the Image Map tool you want to use from the Image Map pop-up menu in the Web Tools palette. Here are your choices:**

   • **Rectangle Image Map tool:** This produces a standard rectangular box much like what you'd create with the Text Box tool and the Picture Box tool. The big difference, of course, is that the boxes you're creating now are used as hyperlinks. Hold down the Shift key while drawing the box to create a square.

   • **Oval Image Map tool:** This tool produces an ellipse. Hold down the Shift key while drawing to create a circle. This tool works pretty much like the Oval Text and Picture Box tools.

- **Bézier Image Map tool:** This tool produces polygons (shapes composed of a series of flat sides) and polycurves (shapes composed of a series of curves), as well as shapes that combine both sides and curves. To create a Bézier shape, you click and release at each corner (technically known as a *node*). When you want to complete the box, click back on the origin point. (Notice how the pointer changes to a circle from the normal cross.) If you click and drag for a little bit at each desired node, you see the Bézier control handles that let you create a curve. You can have both straight and curved sides based on how you use the mouse at each node — experiment to get the hang of it.

2. **Place the cursor over the imported picture where you want the image map to appear.**

3. **Click and drag the mouse until you have covered the portion of the image that will be the hot spot.**

   A red outline appears, indicating where the image map is so that you can assign a hyperlink to it. (We show you how to assign a hyperlink later in the chapter in the "Applying Links with the Hyperlinks Palette" section.) You'll also notice a visual indicator in the upper-right corner of the picture box. This is just a simple reminder that the picture box contains image maps in addition to the picture.

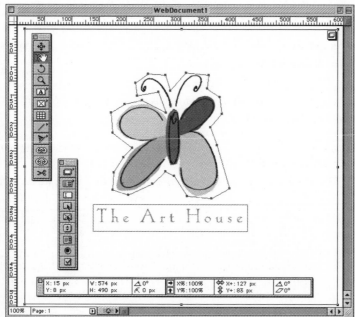

Figure 19-4: A Web document containing a picture imported using the Picture Box tool in the Tool palette, surrounded in two areas by image maps created with the Image Map tools in the Web Tools palette.

The Form Box tools

As mentioned in Chapter 18, forms, as they apply to the Web, are the parts of Web page that let people enter information in fields, choose items from lists, and — in more complicated instances — buy merchandise online. In other words, forms let people interact with your Web page. Building forms in QuarkXPress is actually quite simple. However, getting those forms to work hand-in-hand with your Web server can be more complicated because of the need for relatively complex programming scripts to make everything work. We touch on that in a bit. First, though, we look at the tools that are used to build forms in an HTML document.

Although the meat of most forms is comprised of a combination of buttons, fields, and other doodads, the form itself is contained in a rectangular box (called a *form box*) that you create using the Form Box tools, located directly below the Image Map tools in the Web Tools palette. The first of these two tools is the Form Box tool. The other tool in the Form Box pop-up menu is the File Selection tool.

Form Box tool

As you might imagine, creating a form box is pretty much like creating any other kind of box in QuarkXPress. Just follow these steps:

1. **Select the Form Box tool from the Web Tools palette.**

2. **Move your pointer to the area where you'd like to place the form.**

3. **Click and drag the mouse pointer until you've covered the area where you'd like your form to be.**

   A form box looks exactly like a text box when it is first created, with the exception of the visual indicator in the upper-right corner that looks like the form icon (see Figure 19-5).

4. **Choose Item⇨Modify.**

   The Modify dialog box appears.

5. **Click the Form tab and then enter the name of the form box in the Name field.**

6. **From the Method pop-up menu, choose a method for submitting your form's information. The choices are as follows:**

   • **Get:** The Get option tells the Web browser to append the data from your reader's form to the end of the URL (see Chapter 18) of the target script or application.

- **Post:** The Post Option tells the Web browser to send the data from your reader's form to the target script (or application) as a separate HTTP transaction.

  If you select Post from the Method pop-up menu, you must specify a MultiPurpose Internet Mail Extension (MIME) type for the form's data in the Encoding pop-up menu. Your choices are urlencoded, form-data, and plain.

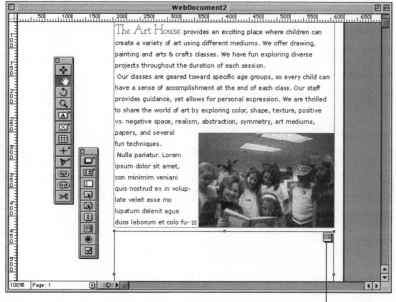

Figure 19-5:
The form box added to this Web document looks like a typical text box with the exception of the visual indicator in its upper-right corner.

Visual indicator for form box

Additional Form Box options

You must also make some other choices in the Modify dialog box, among them: How your page should reply when it receives the reader's submitted information (the action) and which script you'd like to use to process the submitted information . . . and, well, you get the point.

With the exception of perhaps the first couple of fields, the rest of the choices in this dialog box are no doubt utterly confusing. Don't worry. Unless you are already a trained HTML master, this stuff should look a bit sketchy. Remember when we said that it was fairly easy to build an HTML form but more difficult to make it work? This is what we were talking about. See, QuarkXPress can build all the pieces of your form for you. It can even provide you with a map of what you need to get it working. The one thing it can't do is tell you what to put in those fields. Why? Because to make a form that lets you and your reader interact, you must send commands to the server where your Web page will eventually be stored. The server processes the information from your form using a script, which is usually written in one of the various programming languages, such as Perl, C, or ASP.

So does this mean you'll have to take a class in Java or CGI scripting just so you can make your simple little form work? Not at all. If you want to try tackling the backend processing yourself, poking around on the Web may turn up some good primers about CGI scripting, and these primers usually have some prewritten scripts that you can copy and paste or download to your machine for use in QuarkXPress. Additionally, many Internet service providers (ISPs) also provide you with ready-made CGI scripts for creating forms. (An ISP is a company that hosts your Web page after it is finished.) Unless your form is very basic, you may ultimately need to enlist the services of a Web programmer to get everything up and running. Getting complex HTML forms to work properly can be a challenge for even the most seasoned HTML coders.

You can also create a form box automatically by drawing a form control (button, menu, and so on) in a blank section of a Web document. QuarkXPress automatically renders a form box around your chosen form control according to the specification for the Form Box tool in the Tools pane of the Preferences dialog box (choose Edit➪Preferences). Unfortunately, much of the information here is putting the proverbial goat in front of the proverbial cart. We discuss form controls a bit more in depth later in this chapter. To find out more about Web document preferences, see Chapter 21.

The File Selection tool

This tool creates a form field that lets visitors upload files from their local computers to your remote server. When readers click the Browse button, for example, the Open File dialog box appears in their Web browsers, where they can select the file they want to upload. After they've located the file, they click the Submit button, and the file is sent to your remote server. Chances are you won't use this feature much — if ever. Still, there may be times when you want to incorporate this feature into a page. To create a file submission control, follow these steps:

1. **Choose the File Selection tool from the Web Tools palette.**

2. **Move the pointer to someplace within your form box; then click and draw your submission control as you would an ordinary text box.**

3. **Choose Item➪Modify.**

    The Modify dialog box appears.

4. **On the Form pane, enter the name of the control submission in the Name field.**

5. **In the Accept field, enter a list of acceptable MIME types, which must be separated by commas. If you're not sure what to enter, check with your company's webmaster or the administrators of your Web server.**

6. **Click Required.**

   This ensures that the attached file will upload with the form data.

7. **Click OK.**

Text Field tool

The Text Field tool lets you create fields in which readers can enter text. On the Web, you often see these text fields in the form of name, address, city, and so on. Passwords can also be included; QuarkXPress 5 lets readers enter text that appears only as a series of asterisks. A hidden field control then translates the text but does not display that value to the reader — only to you.

To add a text field to your form, follow these steps:

1. **Select the Text Field tool from the Web Tools palette.**

2. **Move the pointer to a spot *within* your form box, and then click and drag until the text field is close to the length you desire.**

   Remember: The entire text field must remain in the form box.

3. **Choose Item⇨Modify, or press ⌘+M or Ctrl+M.**

   The Modify dialog box appears.

4. **Click the Form tab.**

5. **In the Name field, enter an appropriate name for the field.**

   For example, if it is a field for an address, use the name *Address*.

6. **From the Type pop-menu, choose one of the following four options:**

   - **Text - Single Line:** This control lets the reader enter only one line of text, for example a name or address.

   - **Text - Multi Line:** This control lets the reader enter multiple lines of text. These types of fields are generally reserved for additional comments or messages in custom greeting cards.

   - **Password:** This control displays text in asterisks or bullets as described earlier.

   - **Hidden Field:** This control is submitted with a form but doesn't display in the reader's Web browser. These fields can be used to calculate information about the visitors submitting the form, such as what type of browsers they're using, without displaying on their screens.

- **Max Chars:** Enter a number in the Max Chars field to specify the maximum number of characters the control will accept. Note that the number you choose doesn't necessarily have anything to do with the length of your field — you can fit 40 characters in a field that's 25 characters in length. However, keep in mind that readers might be more inclined to make a mistake if their typing begins to scroll outside the range of the character field where they can't see it.

- **Wrap Text:** Check this box if you want the text entered into a multiple-line text box to break to the next line in a multiple-line text field. We recommend that you always keep this checked. Otherwise, visitors' typed text will begin to scroll outside the range of the field, and before long, they won't be able to see what they're typing.

- **Read Only:** Check this box to indicate that the readers should not be able to edit the contents of a field.

- **Required:** Check this box to indicate that a response is required in the field.

7. **Complete the other options in the pane as appropriate to the text you're creating.**

8. **Click OK.**

As you create fields, keep in mind that they should never overlap. Only hidden fields can overlap other fields, and in all honesty, you will probably never use a hidden field for anything.

Button tool

The Button tool is used to — get this! — create buttons. You can create two kinds of buttons: Submit buttons and Reset buttons. Chances are that after you know how to create a proper form, you'll be using these two buttons more than any others. The Submit button is used to submit the information the visitor has entered in your Web page to your remote Web server, which is in turn rerouted to your personal computer. The Reset button is simply a "do over" button. If visitors make a mistake or change their mind about what they've entered in a form, they can click Reset, and everything they've entered in the form is wiped clean. Usually, you will see these buttons side-by-side in a form.

To create a Submit or Reset button:

1. **Select the Button tool from the Web Tools palette.**

2. **Move the cursor within your form box, and then click and drag to draw the button.**

3. **Choose Item➪Modify, or press ⌘+M or Ctrl+M; then click the Form tab.**

   The Form pane of the Modify dialog box appears.

4. **In the Form pane, enter the name of the button in the Name field.**

   If you want text in the button, such as *Submit,* choose the Content tool in the Tool palette and enter the text you want displayed in the button.

5. **From the Type pop-menu, choose either Submit or Reset.**

6. **Click OK.**

These steps seem easy enough, but remember that for these buttons to actually do anything, you must attach them to a CGI script of some sort. Figure 19-6 shows an example of a Submit button coupled with a text field.

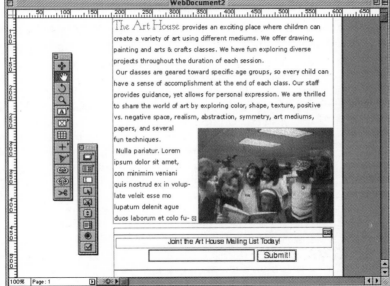

Figure 19-6: We've added a text field and a Submit button to our Web document.

Image Button tool

In QuarkXPress 5, you needn't limit your buttons to text. You can turn pictures into buttons, as well. Not to be confused with image maps, image buttons are used to submit forms. They, like the regular text buttons, require some scripting before they will be of any use on a Web page.

To create an image button:

1. **Choose the Image Button tool from the Web Tools palette.**

2. **Move the cursor to the place in the form box where you'd like to place the image button, and then click and drag the cursor until the image is the size you desire.**

3. **Choose File⇨Get Picture.**

   The Get Picture dialog box appears.

4. **Select the picture file you'd like to make into a button and click Open.**

5. **Choose Item⇨Modify.**

   The Modify dialog box appears.

6. **Enter the name of the button in the Name field.**

7. **Click the Export tab in the Modify dialog box.**

8. **In the Export pane, choose a graphic format from the Export As pop-up menu.**

   The Export pane displays different options, depending on the graphic format you choose. You can choose from three graphic formats:

   - **JPEG:** Use this format when the graphic is a photograph. When you choose this format, you are asked to enter a description of the picture in the Alternate Text field. If the picture doesn't show up in someone's browser for some reason (usually because of lack of memory), the text you enter in this field shows up in its place. When you select this option, a new pop-up menu appears in the Export pane: Image Quality, whose options range from Lowest (pure resolution, but quicker download time) to Highest (crispest resolution, but slower download time). Choose the option you think will be best for the majority of Web site visitors, based on image size and the typical method users will have to access your pages (lower-quality images would not cause large page-loading delays for users with slow dialup connection, for example). Last, check the Progressive check box so that the image displays as a progressive JPEG. (When you download a Web page with a progressive JPEG image, the whole image appears and is blurry, and then gets clearer.)

   - **GIF:** This format is the best solution for illustrative art or animated images. When you choose the GIF format, you are asked to enter a description of the image in the Alternate Text field. You can then check the Use Dithering check box if you want the picture displayed using dithered colors. Likewise, you can check Use Interlacing to display the images as interlaced GIF images; like the progressive JPEG option described earlier, this option helps the user realize there is an image appearing during slow connections. Finish things up by choosing a color palette from the Color Palette pop-up menu. Your best choice is probably Web-safe, which ensures that the picture's color will remain consistent over different platforms. However, you can also choose Windows, Adaptive (the picture is displayed according to what colors are available on a given monitor), and Mac OS.

• **PNG:** In Chapter 18, we say that only two graphic file formats can be used on the Web. Well, we kind of lied. There is a third, called a PNG, or Portable Network Graphics format, that works on the Web as well for single-image files. The advantage of this format is that it loads quickly on Web pages; the disadvantage is that it is not widely supported by browsers. The choices that go along with a PNG are essentially the same as those that go with a GIF — with one added choice. In the PNG export pane, you can tell the Web browser to display the picture as either True Color or Indexed Color. True Color displays the maximum number of colors it can muster from a given computer monitor. Indexed Color lets you apply dithering and/or interlacing to the picture via the Use Interlacing and Use Dithering check boxes.

9. **Click OK.**

With the proper CGI scripts, your picture can now be used as a button to submit information just like any other button.

Pop-Up Menu tool

You hear us referring to pop-up menus quite a bit in this book. Now you get a chance to build your own pop-up menu by using the Pop-Up Menu tool in the Web Tools palette. You can also create list boxes in QuarkXPress 5, something you don't hear us talking about quite as often. The difference? In short, a pop-up menu lets you choose only one item from its menu, whereas a list control — which looks something like a multi-line text field — lets you choose one or more items from its menu.

To add a pop-up menu or list control to a form:

1. **Choose the Pop-Up Menu tool or List Box tool from the Web Tools palette.**

2. **Move the cursor to the place (within the form box) where you'd like to place the pop-up menu or list box; and then click and drag the cursor to draw the pop-up menu or list box.**

   Make sure the perimeter stays within the form box.

3. **Choose Item➪Modify and then click the Form tab.**

   The Form pane of the Modify dialog box appears.

4. **Enter a name for the pop-up menu in the Name field. If you'd like to convert your pop-up menu to a list box, you can do so in the Type pop-up menu.**

5. **Pick the menu list that will be displayed in the pop-up menu, or click New to create a new pop-up menu.**

   We show you how to create these menus in the Edit Menu dialog box later in the chapter.

6. **If you're working with a list box, check the Allow Multiple Selections check box if you want readers to have the option of selecting more than one item in the list.**

7. **If you want to make sure the reader has to click at least one item in the list, check the Required check box.**

8. **Click OK.**

Figure 19-7 shows you how your pop-up menu will look after it has been exported and uploaded to the remote server. (You can find out more about this process in Chapter 20.)

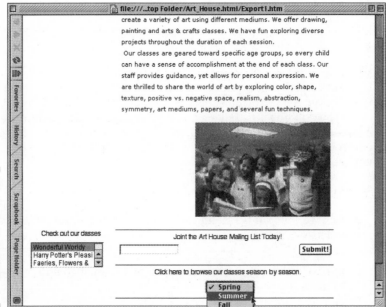

Figure 19-7:
We added a
pop-up
menu and a
list box to
the form box
in our Web
document.

Radio Button tool

A group of radio buttons lets a visitor choose one value from an entire list of values, thus making it a great tool for gathering demographic information about visitors. For example, you can use a group of radio buttons to determine the approximate age of a customer, as shown in Figure 19-8. When the visitor selects one radio button, all the other radio buttons in the group are deselected.

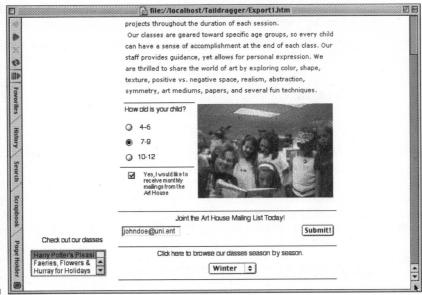

Figure 19-8: A series of radio buttons (to collect information about visitors) and a check box button (for a yes/no question) have been added to a separate form box in our Web document.

To add a group of radio buttons to a form:

1. **Select the Radio Button tool from the Web Tools palette.**

2. **Move the cursor to the place in the form where you'd like to position the radio button, and then click and draw a selection control for each button you want.**

3. **Select one of the radio buttons.**

4. **Choose Modify⇨Item, and then click the Form tab.**

   The Form pane of the Modify dialog box appears.

5. **Choose Radio Button from the Type pop-up menu (if it isn't already selected).**

6. **Radio button controls with the same name are considered to be part of the same group. So decide on a name for the radio button group and enter that name in the Group field.**

7. **Enter a value for the selected radio button in the Value field.**

8. **Repeat Steps 1 through 7 until you have created all the radio button controls in the group.**

9. **To select a default radio button, select the radio button, choose Item⇨Modify, click the Form tab, and check the Use as Default check box.**

10. **To indicate that one of the buttons must be selected before the form can be entered, check Required in the Modify dialog box.**

    Of course, it isn't necessary to check Required if you checked Use as Default, because at least one of the buttons — the Default button — will always be selected if one of the other buttons isn't.

11. **Click OK.**

Check Box tool

Unlike radio buttons, a check box button can be used for all sorts of things. It can be used to answer yes/no questions, to create a list, or even to activate a function in a form. You create check box buttons the same way you create radio buttons, with a few slight differences. Follow these steps to create a check box button:

1. **Select the Check Box tool from the Web Tools palette.**

2. **Move the cursor to the place in the form where you want to position the check box, and then click and draw a selection control for each check box you want.**

3. **Select one of the check boxes.**

4. **Choose Modify⇨Item, and then click the Form tab.**

    The Form pane of the Modify dialog box appears.

5. **Choose Checkbox from the Type pop-up menu (if it isn't already selected).**

6. **Enter a name for the check box in the Name field.**

7. **Enter a value for the check box in the Value field.**

8. **To indicate that the check box control should be checked when the Web page first displays, check Initially Checked.**

9. **To indicate that one of the check boxes must be selected before the form can be entered, check Required in the Modify dialog box.**

10. **Click OK.**

Making a Menu

Simply put, a menu is a list of items. In the Web world, these items are generally displayed in a list control or a pop-up menu control. You get a taste of these types of menus items earlier in the chapter when we show you how to use the Pop-Up Menu and List Box tools. Now we're going to show you how to build those menus.

Menus are created in the Menus dialog box, which you open by choosing Edit⇨View. You can use the menus you create in the Menus dialog box to do different sorts of things. For instance, you can use menus to let users choose from a list of options (refer to Figure 19-7), or you can create navigation menus where each item has a corresponding URL. To create a menu, follow these steps:

1. **Choose Edit⇨Menu.**

   The Menus dialog box appears, as shown in Figure 19-9.

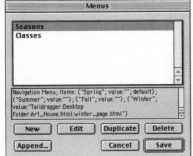

Figure 19-9: The Menus dialog box.

2. **Click the New button.**

   The Edit Menu dialog box appears, as shown in Figure 19-10.

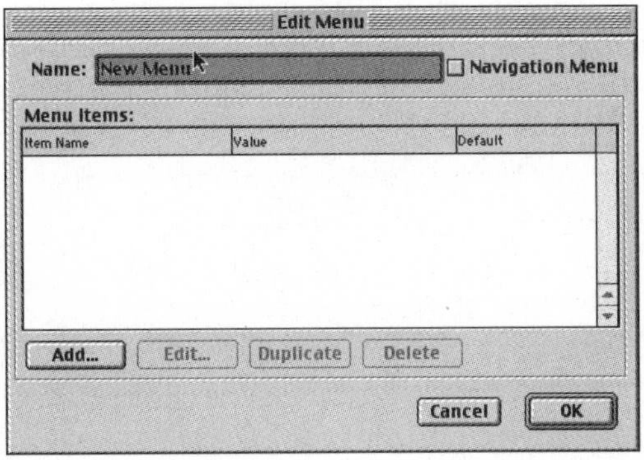

Figure 19-10: The Edit Menu dialog box.

3. **To specify a menu as a navigation menu, check the Navigation Menu check box.**

   A navigation menu lets you link a menu item to a specific URL. When the visitor chooses a particular item in the navigation menu, the browser opens the URL for that item.

4. **Click the Add button to add an item to a new or selected menu.**

   The Menu Item dialog box appears.

5. **Enter the name of your new menu item and, if you so choose, the value of the menu item.**

   If the menu is a navigation menu, you enter a URL in the Value field. If the menu isn't a navigation menu, choosing the item simply means that the value in the Value field will be sent to the Web server along with the rest of the form data when the form is submitted.

6. **To specify that the menu item should be selected by default, check the Use as Default check box.**

7. **Click OK to close the Menu Item dialog box.**

8. **Click OK to close the Edit Menu dialog box.**

9. **Click Save to close the Menus dialog box.**

   The next time you create a pop-up menu or list box, your new menu will be listed as a choice in the Menu pop-up menu in the Forms pane, as well as in the Menus dialog box.

Applying Links with the Hyperlinks Palette

We talk a bit about hyperlinks in Chapter 18, including about how they are used to stitch the pages of a Web site together, and how they can be used to access everything from music files to e-mail addresses. In this section, we show you exactly how to accomplish these feats and what tool you use to accomplish them — namely, the Hyperlinks palette (see Figure 19-11).

Figure 19-11:
The
Hyperlinks
palette.

To open the Hyperlinks palette, choose View⇨Show Hyperlinks. After the palette is open, you can begin applying links immediately. It's a monumentally simple process, too. You begin by highlighting text or selecting an image map that you'd like to link to another item. In this case, we are going to link the image map surrounding the butterfly on the first page of Web site — the Welcome To the Art House page — to the second page of our Web site — the About The Art House page. To do this:

1. **Select an image map and click the Link icon in the Hyperlinks palette.**

   The New Link dialog box appears.

2. **In the New Link dialog box, enter the URL for the page you're linking to and then choose a Target for the page.**

   In this instance, we choose _self, meaning that the target for the About The Art House logo is the same browser window as the one displaying the butterfly.

3. **After you've established the URL, click OK.**

   In our example, the image map surrounding the butterfly is now linked to the About The Art House page as shown in Figure 19-12. In other words, when you click the butterfly in the Web browser, it displays the About The Art House page in its place. Notice how the link appears in the Hyperlinks palette after you've entered it.

If you prefer, you can also establish a link by choosing Hyperlink from the Style menu. The commands in this submenu take you through the same steps as the Hyperlinks palette.

Adding an Anchor

Anchors are little embedded targets within a Web document that let you jump to a particular word or section of a page. After these words are anchored, a hyperlink can be directed to the anchor, not just the page it resides on. You can also jump to specific text on the current page this way. To create an anchor, simply choose the spot you want to pinpoint in the document and then click the Anchor button atop the Hyperlinks palette. In the Anchor dialog box that appears, enter a name for the anchor and click OK. When you create a hyperlink, you can direct it directly to the anchor, making it easier for the visitor to navigate to specific parts of a page. An example of an anchor is shown in Figure 19-13.

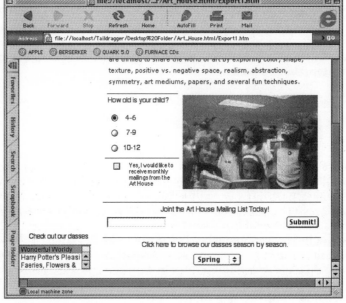

Figure 19-12:
The butterfly
in the top
window is
linked to the
About The
Art House
page. When
you click the
butterfly in
a Web
browser, the
About The
Art House
Page
appears
(bottom).

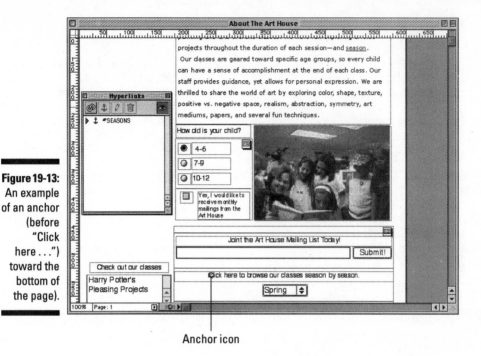

Figure 19-13:
An example
of an anchor
(before
"Click
here . . .")
toward the
bottom of
the page).

Anchor icon

You can also create an anchor by choosing the Anchor submenu of the Style menu. The commands in this submenu take you through the same steps as the Hyperlinks palette.

Creating a Rollover

In many instances, when you build a Web site or page, you reserve the left side of the pages for a navigational menu bar. If you've poked around on the Web, you've probably noticed that almost every Web site out there has a menu bar, composed of hot spots that lead visitors to other pages such as contact information, biographies, and so on. You may also have noticed that when you move your cursor over some of these hot spots, they do all sorts of cool things. They light up, turn different colors, and even transform into entirely different images. These tricky little hot spots are called *rollovers*, and they are surprisingly easy to create.

Preparing a rollover

Rollovers are easy to make, but they do require some prep work. You see, a rollover is an optical illusion created by two superimposed graphics, not unlike a cartoon. So to create this little two-picture cartoon, we need to create two pictures of the same size. You create these pictures in an image-editing program like Fireworks or Photoshop. In this case, we've created our pictures in Photoshop. Both pictures are displayed in Figure 19-14.

Figure 19-14:
Two pictures that will be merged together to make a rollover.

Making a rollover

After you've created your two pictures, you can go back to QuarkXPress and make that rollover happen. Here's how:

1. **Import your default picture — that is, the picture that will usually appear on-screen — somewhere in your Web document.**

2. **Choose Item⇨Rollover⇨Create Rollover.**

   The Rollover dialog box appears. You'll notice that the path to your default picture has already been placed in the Default Picture field in the Rollover dialog box. That means QuarkXPress has already done half the work for you.

3. **Click Browse next to the Rollover Image field and locate your other picture — the rollover picture; then select the picture and click OK.**

4. **In the Hyperlinks field, select the URL to which you'd like to link the rollover.**

   Remember: A rollover is really just a fancy hyperlink. When you click it, it should take you somewhere. In our example, we've linked our rollover image to a Links page.

5. **Click OK.**

That's it. Now you can open your page in a Web browser and watch it do its stuff. As we mention earlier, many Web sites have an entire menu bar dedicated to these sorts of links. You can get a glimpse of ours in Figure 19-15.

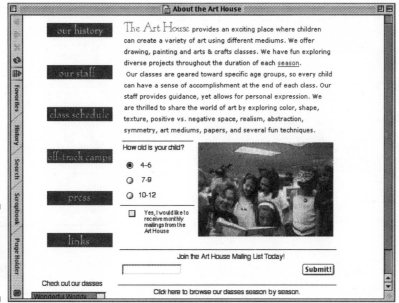

Figure 19-15:
The menu bar on the left uses rollovers.

Chapter 20

Taking Your Pages to the Web

*W*e all know the ultimate destination of printed docs — the printer, right? But how do you get your Web site up and running? That's what we discuss in this chapter. But first, we want to show you how to preview your pages in a Web browser so you know what to expect when they're posted on the World Wide Web. You can, of course, skip this step in the process, but we strongly recommend that you don't. The documents you create in QuarkXPress may look very different in your Web browser. QuarkXPress Web documents aren't actual Web documents — yet. As we explain in Chapter 18, they are just a WYSIWYG view of what amounts to pages and pages of HTML code, and it's the HTML code that the Web browser is interested in. A browser takes the HTML code from your QuarkXPress Web pages and displays its own WYSIWYG version of what you've created. Often the two don't match up. Lines may get bumped up or down, pictures may shift, and text may reflow. Chances are you'll have to make some adjustments to your pages before you're happy with them.

Prepping Documents for the Web

No matter what type of documents you're preparing to use on the Web, the tasks of getting them ready are important ones. This section explains the processes involved in getting pages ready to go online.

Naming your Web documents

You probably thought you already named your Web documents, didn't you? Well you did, and you didn't. The names you assigned to your QuarkXPress

Web documents — the ones that show up in the title bar in QuarkXPress — won't show up in your browser's title bar. Instead, you get some cryptic path name. To fix this, open your QuarkXPress Web document, and choose Page⇨Page Properties. In the Page Properties dialog box (see Figure 20-1) that appears, enter the name of the page in the Page Title field. Below the Page Title field is the Export File Name field. This is where you enter the HTML name for your document. When you enter a name in this field, remember three things:

- ✔ Always end the name with the tag .html or ".htm".
- ✔ Never leave spaces in the name.
- ✔ Never use strange characters, other than perhaps a hyphen or an underscore (for example, Art_House).

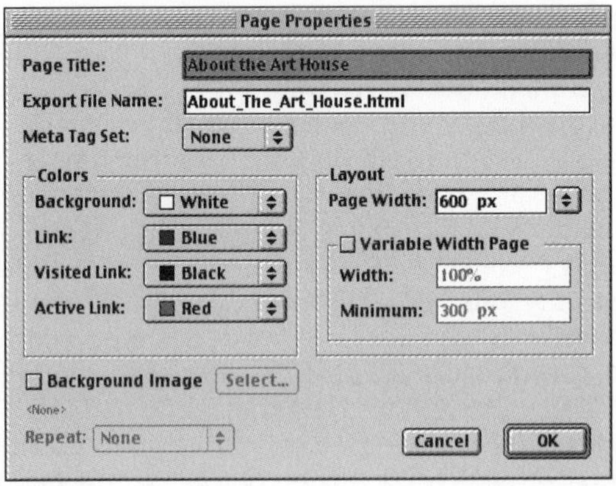

Figure 20-1:
The Page
Properties
dialog box.

If you stray from these three rules, your browser may not recognize your pages. Also, when it comes time to export your pages, your browser will use these names, not the names you entered in the Save Document dialog box.

Adding meta tags

Meta tags are, in essence, just author's notes, such as who wrote the Web page, why certain scripts were used, and so on. But meta tags can also serve a very different, very useful purpose as well. Meta tags let you add lists of words describing your page to your HTML file. After your page has been uploaded to the World Wide Web, online search engines search for as many matches to a query as possible, including the words found in meta tags. With a meta tag list, your chances of being found by a search engine increase immensely because you can enter descriptions of your page that wouldn't otherwise be in your HTML file. For the Art House site, for example, we could include words and phrases like *pottery, art schools, art schools in Denver,* and so on, in the meta tags file. Follow these steps to create a meta tag:

1. Choose Edit⇨Meta Tags.

The Meta Tags dialog box appears (see Figure 20-2).

Figure 20-2:
The Meta Tags dialog box.

2. Click New.

The Edit Meta Tag Set dialog box appears (see Figure 20-3).

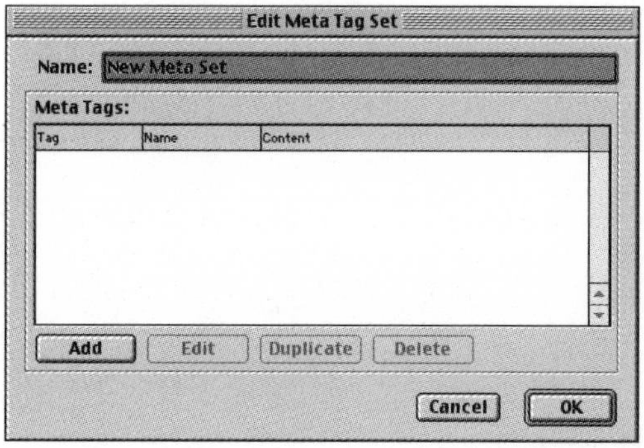

Figure 20-3:
The Edit Meta Tag Set dialog box.

3. Give the new meta tag set a name (for example *Search Words*) in the Name field, and then click the Add button.

4. Add words and phrases to your meta tag list. In each instance, enter the name in the Meta Tag field and the description in the Name field, and then enter your word or phrase in the Content field. When you're finished, click OK and repeat the process for your next word or phrase.

5. **When you're finished, click Save.**

6. **Choose Page➪Page Properties.**

   The Page Properties dialog box appears.

7. **From the Meta Tag Set pop-up menu, select your meta tags list, and then click OK.**

Your description list will now be included with your HTML document when it is exported. No doubt you noticed that you can include several types of meta tags in your HTML file. We don't have room to discuss those other types in depth here, so we suggest that you refer to *HTML 4 For Dummies* by Ed Tittel, Natanya Pitts, and Chelsea Valentine (Hungry Minds, Inc.) for more information about meta tags.

Choosing a browser

After you've prepared your documents, you choose a browser, or several browsers, in which to preview the pages. You do this in the Browsers pane in the Preferences dialog box (see Figure 20-4). To open this pane, choose Edit➪Preferences➪Preferences, and then click Browsers in the list on the left.

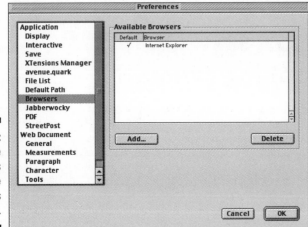

Figure 20-4: The Browsers pane in the Preferences dialog box.

If you're serious about your Web site, we recommend that you have the latest and next-to-latest versions of the Microsoft Internet Explorer, Netscape Navigator/Communicator, and Opera browsers installed. Install them on at least one Mac testing system and one Windows testing system. This lets you see what your Web documents will look like in the real world — different browsers don't always show the same thing. All three browsers are free downloads from their respective sites (www.microsoft.com or www.microsoft.com/mac/, www.netscape.com, and www.opera.com).

To add a browser, follow these steps in the Browsers pane of the Preferences dialog box:

1. **Click Add.**

   A dialog appears similar to the standard Windows or Mac Open dialog boxes.

2. **Navigate your way to the Web browser you'd like to add to the list and then click Open.**

   QuarkXPress adds it to the list of browsers in the Browsers pane.

3. **Repeat Steps 1 and 2 to add additional browsers (optional).**

4. **If you want one of the browsers in the list to be your default browser, click to the left of the browser's name.**

   A check mark appears next to the browser's name, indicating this is now your default browser.

5. **If you want to delete one of the browsers from the list, just highlight the name of the browser in the list and click the Delete button.**

6. **After you've finished making your changes, click OK.**

   You're ready to preview your pages.

Previewing your Web pages

To preview one of your QuarkXPress Web documents in a browser, open the document in QuarkXPress, find the small icon at the bottom of the QuarkXPress window that looks like a globe, and then click and hold. Surprise! That little globe is actually a pop-up menu for all the Web browsers you entered in the Browsers Preferences dialog box (see Figure 20-5). Just choose a browser from the menu, and QuarkXPress automatically opens the page.

There is your Web page is in all its colorful and, er, flawed splendor. Remember, we warned you that the pages in QuarkXPress would differ a bit when they were opened in a Web browser. Text or images may appear in slightly different positions than you planned or some items may overlap. All sorts of weird things may be going on, but nothing you can't fix! Study the page, make notes, and then return to your original QuarkXPress page and make the necessary adjustments.

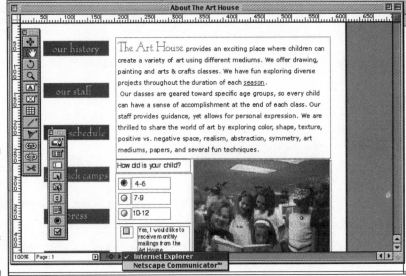

Figure 20-5:
The
Browsers
pop-up
menu
(bottom of
screen).

Exporting Your Web Pages

The first thing to do when you prepare your documents for exporting is to make sure all the pieces (documents, pictures, and so on) are rounded up in the root level of a single folder (no subfolders). This folder acts as your Site Root Directory. After you've created this directory and given it a name, choose Edit⇨Preferences⇨Preferences to open the Preferences dialog box and then select the General pane, or use the shortcut ⌘+Y or Ctrl+Y. Here you find two fields: Image Export Directory and Site Root Directory. In the Image Directory, enter a name such as *Images* or *Image_Folder* to specify where QuarkXPress will store all your pictures when it exports your documents. As for the Site Root directory, click the Select button to the right of the field and navigate to your directory folder. Highlight that folder in the window and then click the Select button at the bottom of the dialog box. Now you're ready to export. To do so, follow these steps:

1. **Choose File⇨Export⇨HTML.**

   The Export HTML dialog box appears (see Figure 20-6).

2. **Keep the Pages field set to All, or enter a range of pages (just as you would in the Print dialog box).**

3. **Check the External CSS file check box if you want QuarkXPress to place the style information in the exported Web document as a CSS, or Cascading Style Sheets, file in the export folder.**

Cascading Style Sheets, like the style sheets you use in word processors or in QuarkXPress documents, are a simple way to ensure consistent use of style (colors, fonts, and so on) in Web pages.

4. Check the Launch Browser check box to display the first exported page in your default browser.

5. Click Export.

Figure 20-6:
The Export
HTML
dialog box.

You can upload files to the Web in so many different ways, but however you do it, you need to do the following:

✔ **Subscribe to an Internet service provider.** Chances are if you have a Web address, you may already be working with an ISP. (You may even be entitled to some free storage space along with your e-mail service.) You might also ask some of your Web-savvy friends what ISP they recommend. Ask lots of questions, because ISPs offer all sorts of perks with their services, including technical support, monthly stats, and ready-made CGI scripts designed specifically for their servers. These scripts are free and can be incorporated with the forms in your QuarkXPress Web documents quite easily.

✔ **Register a domain name.** Some people might tell you to do this first, in case some hotshot out there is ready to pounce on the name before you do. But we recommend that you wait until you decide on your ISP. Why? Because your ISP representative can help you register your domain name on the spot. The ISP can also screen the World Wide Web to make sure the name you want isn't already taken. A good ISP can have your domain name up and running in an hour. Others take much longer. Either way, it makes sense to let the folks at the ISP do the work because they have the experience.

✔ **Find a reliable FTP-client software application.** FTP stands for File Transfer Protocol, which basically means the path for getting your HTML pages from here (your computer) to there (your ISP). FTP client software is the software you use to get your pages from here to there. FTP-client software packages are inexpensive, and some — such as Fetch, WS_FTP Pro, and AbsoluteFTP — are well worth the money. It is also worth noting that Fetch offers a Macintosh version of its product, whereas most FTP clients are for Windows only.

If you're using a Web server to which you have direct access, you can simply copy the files there with a disk or over the network. However you get your files onto the Web, chances are that you'll need to copy the various files in specific directories that match the page hierarchy of your site. Often, images are stored within an Images folder inside the folder that contains their Web pages, but they can also all be stored in one master folder. Work with your Webmaster to determine how the pages are saved on the server. In many cases, the Web page designer won't have to worry about this, but in smaller operations, the Web page designer could just as easily be the Web master.

To XML or Not to XML

Another option you may want to explore as you build your Web site is applying XML to your documents. XML, which is an acronym for Extensible Markup Language, is a system of tags used for labeling information and controlling its structure. Why do you need it? Well, once upon a time when writers and editors used to write books, that was all they had to do — write books. Then along came the Web, and before long those books had to be converted to HTML after they were published in print format by — you guessed it — writers and editors. Then some brilliant people in Silicon Valley invented personal digital assistants (PDAs), and writers and editors were stuck with yet another task: writing and editing the same book for different devices. Writers and editors were not happy.

Fortunately, some programming genius out there took pity on these writers and their dismal plight, and invented XML. With XML, writers and editors (or whoever) only have to write a document or book one time, and from there, they can use XML tags to extract information or rearrange its structure according to the device that will be interpreting it. Cool, eh? Well what's really cool is that you can use XML in QuarkXPress, thanks to avenue.quark, an XTension that ships with Version 5. The avenue.quark XTension lets you extract the content of QuarkXPress documents and store that content in XML (Extensible Markup Language) format. Once in XML, your content can be reused almost anywhere — in print, on CD-ROM, and on the Web.

QuarkXPress 5 integrates the avenue.quark tool to create and manipulate XML documents.

XML lets you create the tags, or labels, for various kinds of content (these are called *data type descriptions,* or DTDs) based on what makes sense for your content. Then you specify what happens to each of the types of labeled content in terms of what is published, how it is presented, and so forth. Compare that to the more rigid HTML and PDF formats — where there are only certain tags available (that furthermore cannot be changed), and where the presentation is fixed based on the label chosen.

XML code is similar to HTML in the sense that tags are surrounded by angle brackets (< and >) and commands and labels are turned on and off (such as <standardHeader> at the beginning of a header item and </standardHeader> at the end of it). Comments begin with <!-- and end with >, whereas custom commands and declarations begin with <? and end with ?>. (We don't expect most readers to understand this level of detail. We just want you to know that there are different codes to look for in examining XML code if the need arises.)

To understand XML in the QuarkXPress context, both page designers and XML experts should refer to the documentation that comes as QuarkXPress 5: Guide to avenue.quark.pdf in the XTensions Documents folder in the QuarkXPress folder — and the Tutorial.pdf file in the avenue.quark Tutorial folder in the QuarkXPress folder. Page designers might also want to read *XML For Dummies* by Ed Tittel and Frank Boumphrey (Hungry Minds, Inc.).

avenue.quark works by letting you associate styles and structures in QuarkXPress documents with elements in XML. After it's tagged in XML, your content can be stored separately from your QuarkXPress documents. Then, when the time comes, you can translate XML content into HTML and serve it on the Web as HTML. How simple is that? And if you later want to create a more truncated version of the same document for a handheld device, you can translate the document for that platform as well.

The avenue.quark pane has three options that control how tags are applied:

✔ **Always insert repeating elements at the end of the current branch:** If you check this check box, any DTD elements marked as repeating are added to the end of the active branch. (This is how the preference should usually be set.) If you leave the box unchecked, you're asked to manually determine the position of a new repeating element when you move text with a repeating element (such as a new instance of text set as <Text>) into the XML Workspace palette.

✔ **Always use first path for elements with multiple insertion paths:** If you check this check box, QuarkXPress uses the first of multiple rules in the DTD for an element that has multiple rules. For example, if the DTD defines <Paragraph> element to be created at both the end of a current branch and after a new <Sidebar> element, QuarkXPress uses whichever rule is first. Otherwise, you're prompted when adding the element to the XML Workspace palette.

✔ **Always use the first applicable tagging rule:** If you check this check box, QuarkXPress uses the first tagging rule if there is a conflict between tagging rules. Otherwise, you're prompted when adding the element to the XML Workspace palette.

Of course, this begs the question, "If I can just take my regular QuarkXPress print documents, translate them to HTML, and upload them to the Web, why are we fiddling with all this XML stuff in the first place?" Fair enough.

Conceivably, you could do that. In fact many corporations are already in the process of converting their QuarkXPress documents to XML. On the downside, though, most of the world hasn't caught up with XML. Most Web browsers, particularly the older ones, still support only HTML. And most people still haven't gotten the hang of HTML. However, it is expected that XML will replace HTML as the language of choice for the Web and other platforms in the not-too-distant future. Check out the avenue.quark tutorial located in the Documents folder of your QuarkXPress 5 installation CD.

Part VI
Guru in Training

The 5th Wave · By Rich Tennant

"Oh, that's Jack's area for his paper crafts. He's made some wonderful US Treasury Bonds, Certificates of Deposit, $20's, $50's, $100's, that sort of thing."

In this part . . .

After you master the basics, why not pick up some of the tricks the pros use? In this part, we show you how to customize QuarkXPress so that it works the way you want it to. We also explain how QuarkXPress works on Windows PCs and on Macs.

Chapter 21

Customizing QuarkXPress

● ●

In This Chapter

▶ Setting defaults

▶ Customizing tools

● ●

People who publish documents come in all shapes and sizes, and they approach their work from different directions. Fortunately, QuarkXPress offers many controls that let you customize the program to the way that *you* work. The Preferences dialog box lets you control how your copy of QuarkXPress works with all documents. Quark also features several other Preferences dialog boxes for specific features. The Color Management Preferences dialog box, for example, box lets you set color controls in your documents to keep color consistent throughout the building of a document. In addition, the Index Preferences dialog box gives you options for customizing your indexes. And the Fraction/Price dialog box lets you set how QuarkXPress creates fractions and prices.

In this chapter, we cover how to set application and document defaults in these dialog boxes.

Setting Preferences

In previous versions of QuarkXPress, users had to muddle through several preferences dialog boxes to get the to settings they wanted. In QuarkXPress 5, most of these boxes have been lumped together into one dialog box — the plain ol' Preferences dialog box. On the left side of this dialog box, you find options to customize nearly everything in QuarkXPress, including Display, Interactive, Save, Measurements, Tools, Trapping — even XTensions Management. You gain access to this cornucopia of preferences when you choose Edit⇨Preferences⇨Preferences (or use the keyboard shortcut Option+Shift+⌘+Y or Ctrl+Alt+Shift+Y). If you want to go directly to the General pane, there's a shorter shortcut: ⌘+Y or Ctrl+Y.

The Application and Default Document options in the Preferences dialog box don't do anything. They just help organize the many panes and provide some familiarity with previous versions of QuarkXPress that had separate Preference dialog boxes with those names.

Monitor display options

The Display pane, shown in Figure 21-1, lets you set the colors that indicate margin, ruler, and grid lines. Guides and rulers are important tools. They help you position elements on a page (so you need to be able to find them easily.) The default settings for these colors work fine for most people, but feel free to change them if, for example, you are fond of a certain color and want to use it as your margin indicator. These colored lines do not print.

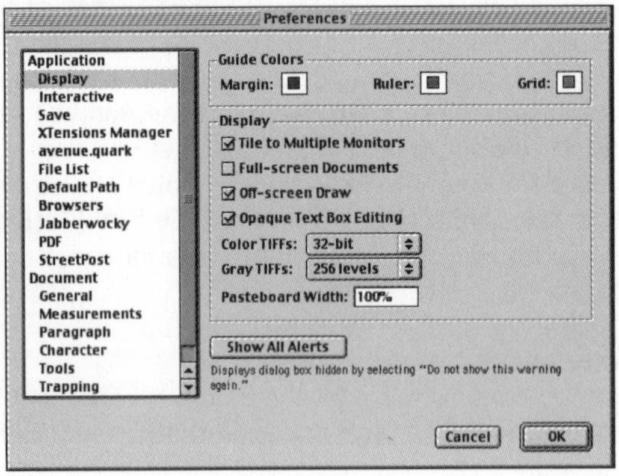

Figure 21-1:
The Display
pane of the
Preferences
dialog box.

These guides help you to align items:

- **Margin (normally blue).** Shows the default column and gutter positions for text boxes.

- **Ruler (normally green).** Lines that you drag from the horizontal and vertical rulers so that you can tell whether a box lines up to a desired point.

- **Grid (normally magenta).** The baseline grid shows the position of text baselines.

You probably will use margin guides routinely and ruler guides occasionally. Use the box coordinates (the X and Y positions in the Measurements palette) to make sure that boxes or their margins are placed exactly where you want them. You may also want to take advantage of the QuarkXPress 5 Grid Manager tool, accessible via the Utilities menu.

Other options in the Display pane control how QuarkXPress documents relate to the monitor's screen area. The default view, which appears each time you start the application or open a new document, is Actual Size (100 percent). The following list describes each option:

✔ **Tile to Multiple Monitors.** If you have multiple monitors attached to your Mac, this Mac-only option tells QuarkXPress to use your secondary monitor(s) to display document windows when you choose to tile documents. Otherwise, it will tile documents only on your primary monitor (under the assumption you are reserving the secondary monitors for non-QuarkXPress folders and windows). Use the Monitors or Monitors & Sound control panel that comes with your System disks to set up multiple monitors.

Even though Windows 98 and later versions support multiple monitors, QuarkXPress for Windows does not support this option.

✔ **Full-Screen Documents.** If you check this box on the Mac, the document window appears on the far-left side of the screen, below the default position of the Tool palette. We recommend that you avoid this option — it can make it difficult to see the close box because it can become obscured by the Tool palette. One advantage of using this option is that it can give your document window enough width to fully display a document. Make sure, however, that you move your Tool palette so that you can click the close box.

The Full-Screen Documents option is not available in QuarkXPress for Windows.

✔ **Opaque Text Box Editing.** If you check this box, text boxes temporarily turn opaque while you are editing them. If this box is unchecked, text boxes retain their background color — whether it's a solid color, blend or None — when you're editing them.

✔ **Off-Screen Draw.** This option controls how QuarkXPress displays elements on-screen as you scroll through a document. If checked, this option redraws each element displayed in order of display. If unchecked, the option draws elements in memory first and then displays them all simultaneously. Both options take the same amount of time to redraw the screen, so you have no advantage in either setting.

Two pop-up menus let you specify how pictures appear on-screen:

• **Color TIFFs.** This option lets you specify the color depth of screen previews created for imported color TIFF files. (We cover TIFF files in Chapter 4.) The default setting is 32-bit, or millions of colors. The other choices are 16-bit and 8-bit on the Mac and 24-bit in Windows. The higher the bit depth, the truer the colors on-screen, but your QuarkXPress files are also larger and screen-redraw time is slower.

- **Gray TIFFs.** This option controls the resolution of screen previews for imported grayscale TIFFs. The default is 256 levels. The other option is 16 levels.

  Note that the Color TIFFs and Gray TIFFs settings apply only to screen previews and do not affect the resolution of the printed picture.

In Windows only, there is the Display DPI Value option, which is set at 96 by default. A higher number acts like a universal zoom, making everything larger on-screen; a smaller number makes everything smaller. There's rarely a reason to change this setting from the default. That default varies based on the monitor's pixel resolution: On a monitor set to 800 × 600 pixel resolution, it defaults to 96, whereas on a monitor set to 1,024 × 768 pixel resolution, it defaults to 120.

- **Pasteboard Width.** This option sets the width of the *pasteboard,* which is the area outside the edges of the document used to temporarily store layout elements until you are ready to position them on the page. The default is 100 percent, which means the pasteboard is as wide as the page, giving you the equivalent of a half-page working area on either side of your document.

In Version 5, the Pasteboard Width option has moved from the Interactive pane to the Display pane.

- **Show All Alerts button.** This button resets alert message you may have turned off, making any such alert box issue warnings again.

After you make changes in the Display pane, click OK to save them.

Interactive options

The Interactive pane, shown in Figure 21-2, controls scrolling, smart quotes, and the display of dragged items.

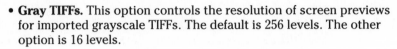

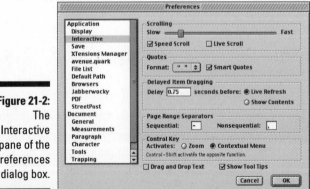

Figure 21-2:
The
Interactive
pane of the
Preferences
dialog box.

The controls in the Interactive pane include the following:

- ✔ **Scrolling.** Use the Scrolling slider to control how fast the page scrolls when you click the arrows in the scroll bars.

  Most people prefer a Scrolling setting somewhere in the middle range. You may have to adjust the setting a few times until it feels right to you. Generally, the setting should be slightly closer to Fast than to Slow so that you don't have to wait for the screen to redraw when you're using the scroll bar.

  Other options in the Scrolling section of the dialog box work as follows:

  - **Live Scroll.** If you check this option, QuarkXPress redraws pages while you are dragging the box in the scroll bar. Generally, you should check this option unless you're working on a slower computer.

  - **Speed Scroll.** This option speeds scrolling in graphics-intensive documents by masking out the graphics and blends as you scroll. When you stop scrolling, the graphics and blends are redrawn. Generally, you should check this option.

- ✔ **Quotes.** Use the pop-up menu in the Quotes section to pick the type of quotation marks to use when you type inside QuarkXPress. The default option is for English quotation marks, but the pop-up menu includes quotation marks from other languages. To have smart (that is, typographic) quotation marks automatically substituted when you type them within text boxes, check the Smart Quotes box.

  Notice that checking the Smart Quotes option also translates the single-quote character to the smart (typographic) style when you type it.

  The Smart Quotes option doesn't control how straight quotes are translated when you import a text file; to convert keyboard (straight) quotes to typographic (curly) quotes during import, choose File➪Get Text (⌘+E or Ctrl+E) and check the Convert Quotes box. To use the standard keyboard (straight) quotes and apostrophes on the Mac, hold down the Control key when you type them. In Windows, press Ctrl+' for keyboard single quotes and keyboard apostrophes and Ctrl+Alt+" for keyboard double quotes. You can also use these characters for, respectively, foot marks and inch marks.

- ✔ **Delayed Item Dragging.** The Delayed Item Dragging controls determine how QuarkXPress displays items on-screen. If Show Contents is selected, when you hold down the mouse button as you begin dragging an item, the contents of the item are visible as you drag it. If Live Refresh is selected when you hold down the mouse button as you begin dragging an item, the contents of the item are visible as you drag it, and the screen refreshes to show item layers and text flow. You can enter a delay time in the Delay seconds box to control how long (in seconds ranging from 0.1 to 5.0) you must hold the mouse button before Show Contents or Live Refresh is activated.

✔ **Page Range Separators.** These boxes let you choose the characters QuarkXPress uses to indicate which pages print out in the Print dialog box. Typically, people stick with the defaults. The en-dash (–) delineates a range of pages, for example "2–10." A comma delineates separate pages, for example, "2, 3, 4, 5."

✔ **Control Key.** This section contains two radio buttons for customizing the Mac's Control key. If the Zoom button is clicked, the Control key acts as a short cut for the Zoom tool. If the Contextual Menus button is clicked, the Control Key displays the Contextual Menu of an item when you click and hold on it.

Because Windows doesn't have a Control key, Windows QuarkXPress does not have the Control Key option. Windows users access contextual menus by using the righthand mouse button (called *right-clicking*).

✔ **Drag and Drop Text.** When the Drag and Drop Text option is checked, you can highlight a piece of text and then drag it to a new location (as you can in most word processors), rather than cut it from the old location and paste it into the new one.

✔ **Show Tool Tips.** Checking Show Tool Tips displays the names of the palette or tool icons when the mouse pointer is positioned on them; the default setting is unchecked.

After you make changes in the Interactive pane, click OK to save them.

File-saving options

The Save pane of the Application Preferences dialog box lets you control how QuarkXPress saves and makes backup copies of your documents. The Save pane is shown in Figure 21-3. Here are the options that you can select:

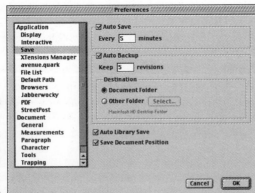

Figure 21-3:
The Save pane of the Preferences dialog box.

✔ **Auto Save.** When this option is checked, QuarkXPress saves opened documents at regular intervals. You determine that interval through the value that you enter in the Every *X* Minutes box. When an auto save occurs, QuarkXPress creates an auto-save document (with a filename that ends in .AutoSave on the Mac and .asv in Windows). If your computer crashes, you can revert your file to its last auto-saved condition by opening the auto-save document.

✔ **Auto Backup.** You can also have QuarkXPress keep backup copies of your document by checking the Auto Backup box. When this option is checked, QuarkXPress creates a backup copy of your document every time you manually save it. You determine how many previous versions are retained by making an entry in the Keep X Revisions box.

✔ **Destination.** Lets you choose where to save your auto backups. This section contains two radio buttons: the Document Folder button and the Other Folder button. When you click the Document Folder button all backups are saved to your document folder, just as they were in previous versions of QuarkXPress. When you click the Other Folder button, QuarkXPress lets you pick a different folder in which to save your backups. You pick the folder by clicking the Select button to the right of the Other Folder button and navigating your way to it via the Backup Folder dialog box. After you find the Folder, click the Select button in the lower-left corner of the Backup Folder dialog box. After you select a folder, all of your auto backups will be saved to that folder (at least until you choose a different folder).

✔ **Auto Library Save.** At first, the name attached to this new check box may seem puzzling. After all, QuarkXPress already saves libraries automatically, doesn't it? Well, yes and no. Auto Library Backup would probably be a better name for this feature. Even if you close a document associated with a library without saving it, the items stashed in the library are automatically saved anyway. Still, sometimes the items in a library can be lost — for example during a power failure or a computer crash. When Auto Library Save is checked, the items placed in a library are saved on the fly, thus preventing the loss of library items even when your computer crashes. When checked, this feature can slow down your work process a bit, but we recommend you keep it checked anyway. As our dear old grandmothers always used to say, "Better safe than sorry."

✔ **Save Document Position.** Keep this one checked at all times, too. Why? When checked, Save Document Position automatically remembers the size, position, and proportions of your document window, thus saving you the time of finding your place the next time you open the document.

XTensions options

The XTensions Manager pane has options that control the built-in XTensions Manager, a utility that lets you turn XTensions (add-on software that gives QuarkXPress new features) on and off. Specifically, this pane (see Figure 21-4) lets you choose whether the XTensions Manager displays when you turn on QuarkXPress and, if so, how it displays. We talk more about XTensions in Chapter 9.

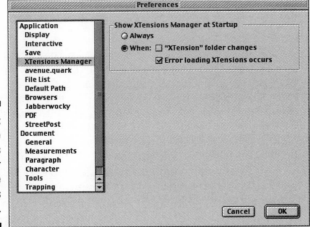

Figure 21-4:
The
XTensions
Manager
pane of the
Preferences
dialog box.

The options you can choose include

- ✔ **Always.** Makes the XTensions Manager display each time you launch QuarkXPress.

- ✔ **When XTensions Folder Changes.** Causes the XTensions Manager dialog box to appear when you launch QuarkXPress, but only if you have previously added or removed XTensions from the XTensions folder.

- ✔ **When Error Loading XTensions Occurs.** Causes the XTensions Manager dialog box to appear when you launch QuarkXPress, but only if you had a problem loading an XTension.

After you make changes in the XTensions pane, click OK to save them.

avenue.quark options

The avenue.quark pane of Application Preferences lets you establish some tagging standards for XML files. For more information on XML, see Chapter 20.

File list options

The File List pane in the Preferences dialog box lets you specify a list of recently opened files beneath the Open command so that you can directly open those files instead of hunting them down in the Open dialog box (see Figure 21-5). This is a straightforward set of preferences but one you won't want to overlook.

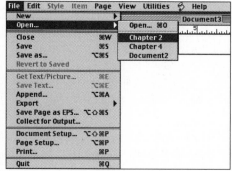

Figure 21-5:
A file list placed beneath the Open command.

The options in this pane include

- ✔ **Number of Files.** Enter a number here for the number of files you want QuarkXPress to keep track of in the file list. The minimum number of files you can enter is 3, but you can enter up to 9 if you want to keep track of lots of files (as many of us do).

- ✔ **File List Location.** This option lets you determine where to put the names of the files. You have two choices here as well. The first is Append Files to File Menu. When you choose this option, your file names are listed toward the bottom of the File menu. The other option is the Append File to Open Menu item. This option puts the file names directly beneath the Open command so that you will only see them when you try to open a document, as shown in Figure 21-5

- ✔ **Alphabetize names.** Alphabetizes the names in your list. Otherwise they appear in the order in which they were opened.

- ✔ **Show Full Path.** Shows you the path to your file, as well as the name of the file. For example, on a Mac, the file "Chapter 19" would appear as something like HD:Desktop Folder:Chapter 19, whereas on Windows it would appear as something like C:\WINDOWS\DESKTOP\Chapter 19.qxd.

After you make changes in the File List pane, click OK to save them.

Default path options

The preferences in this pane of the Preferences dialog box let you establish a consistent path to specified folders on your hard drive, making it easier for you to locate items in your document if they are properly organized. The choices in this pane are as follows:

- ✔ **Use Default Path for "Open."** Lets you pick a folder on your hard drive that will show up by default every time you open Open Document dialog box.

- ✔ **Use Default Path for "Save/Save As."** Lets you pick a folder on your hard drive where all the documents you Save or Save As will be placed by default.

- ✔ **Use Default Path for "Get Text."** Allows you to pick a folder on your hard drive that will show up by default every time you open the Get Text dialog box.

- ✔ **Use Default Path for "Get Picture."** Allows you to pick a folder on your hard drive that will show up by default every time you open the Get Picture dialog box.

Browser options

For information about this preference, see Chapter 20.

Jabberwocky options

For information about this preference, see Chapter 10.

PDF options

If you're using the PDF Filter XTension included with QuarkXPress 5 to create PDF files, the PDF pane of Application Preferences lets you specify when the files are distilled. The Options button lets you specify how hyperlinks are translated, override some Distiller options, and change output settings. For information about how QuarkXPress handles PDF files, see Chapter 11.

StreetPost options

The StreetPost preference lets you submit an XML document created in QuarkXPress 5 to an HTTP server, so you can integrate QuarkXPress 5 with a Web application or database system. StreetPost options include:

- ✔ **Post URL:** In the Post URL field, enter the address to which you'd like to upload your XML document

- ✔ **User Name:** For security purposes, you may need to enter your user name before you can submit your document. Enter that name here.

- ✔ **E-mail:** Again for security purposes, you may need to enter your e-mail address before you can submit your document. Enter that address here.

- ✔ **Workspace ID:** Check this box if you want your workspace ID included with your uploaded document.

- ✔ **Post XML as Standalone:** Check this box if you want to post your XML file as a standalone document, so it's accessible by multiple documents, rather than as embedded within a specific Web document.

For more about XML, see Chapter 20.

General options

The General pane in the Preferences dialog box lets you specify the defaults for page layout. The following sections describe in detail how you can use the options in the General pane.

Greek Below and Greek Pictures

One option that is closely related to views is *greeking* — in which QuarkXPress displays a gray area to represent text or pictures on the page; this makes the page display more quickly on your monitor. Turning on greeking speeds the display of your QuarkXPress document. When you print, images and text are unaffected by greeking (in other words, they print). The greeking options include

- ✔ **Greek Below.** Tells QuarkXPress to greek the text display when text is below a certain point size. The default value is 7 points, but you can enter a value ranging from 2 to 720 points. To disable greeking, uncheck the Greek Below box.

- ✔ **Greek Pictures.** Tells QuarkXPress to display all unselected graphics as gray shapes, which speeds the display considerably. This feature is useful after you position and size your images and no longer need to see them in your layout. You can still look at a greeked picture by clicking it.

Guides

The Guides menu specifies whether guides (nonprinting lines that help you see where margins are and help you position items on the page) appear in front of boxes (the default setting) or behind them. When guides are behind boxes, you can more easily see what's in the boxes, but you may find it harder to tell whether elements within the boxes line up with margins, gutters, or baselines.

You can also specify the "snap distance" here. This simply means you can specify how far away you want an item to be from a guide before it "snaps to" (aligns with) a nearby guide.

Master Page Items

The Master Page Items option controls what happens to text and picture boxes that are defined on a master page when you apply a different master page to your document pages. Your options are Keep Changes (the default) and Delete Changes. We recommend that you leave this setting on Keep Changes. Then, after applying a new master page, you can manually remove any unwanted elements that are left behind. Chapter 17 talks more about master pages.

Auto Picture Import

Auto Picture Import lets you update links to your source images automatically. This option is handy if your picture may change frequently and you don't want to forget to update your layout to accommodate the changes. You can choose among the following Auto Picture Import settings:

- ✔ **Verify.** QuarkXPress checks the date and time stamp of the graphics files to see whether they have been modified. The program then displays a list of all the graphics files in your document so that you can decide whether to update the layout with the newest version.

- ✔ **On.** This setting tells QuarkXPress to automatically import the latest version of changed graphics files.

- ✔ **Off.** QuarkXPress does not check to see whether the source graphic files have been modified.

You should use Verify or On, even if you don't expect graphic files to change much; that way, if the graphic files do change, your document will contain the most recent versions of the files.

This option works only with graphics that you imported by choosing the QuarkXPress File⇨Get Picture command (or use the shortcuts ⌘+E or Ctrl+E). Graphics that you pasted into QuarkXPress via the Clipboard are not affected because the pasted file is copied into your document.

Framing

The Framing option tells QuarkXPress how to draw the ruling lines (frames) around text and picture boxes. You can access this option by choosing Item⇨Frame option (or by pressing ⌘+B or Ctrl+B). You have the following choices:

- ✔ **Outside.** Places the frame on the outside of the box.
- ✔ **Inside.** Places the frame inside the box.

Hyperlinks

This section of the General pane basically lets you choose default colors for hyperlinks and anchors in a Web page (see Chapter 20). If you aren't building Web pages in QuarkXPress, don't worry about these options.

Auto Page Insertion

Auto Page Insertion tells QuarkXPress where to add new pages when all your text does not fit into an automatic text box. You must define the text box containing the overflow text as an automatic text box in the page's master page. (A *master page* is indicated by an unbroken chain icon in the top-left corner of the master page.) In the Auto Page Insertion menu, your options are:

- ✔ **End of Section.** Places new pages at the end of the current section. (You define sections by choosing Page⇨Section.) If no sections are defined, End of Section works the same as the End of Document option.
- ✔ **End of Story.** Places new pages immediately following the last page of the text chain.
- ✔ **End of Document.** Places new pages at the end of the document.
- ✔ **Off.** Adds no new pages, leaving you to add pages and text boxes for overflow text wherever you want. The existence of overflow text is indicated by a checked box at the end of the text in the text box.

Auto Constrain

The Auto Constrain option controls the behavior of boxes that are created within other boxes. If you check Auto Constrain, a box is created within another box — a picture box drawn inside a text box, for example — may not exceed the boundaries of the parent box (in this case, the text box). Neither can you move the box outside the parent box's boundaries. Most people should leave this default option unchecked.

The Accurate Blends checkbox is gone in Version 5; all blends accurately display because computers are now so fast that they don't need to speed up display by disabling accurate blend.

After you make changes in the General pane, click OK to save them.

Measurement options

The Measurements pane in the Document Preferences dialog box lets you specify — you guessed it — the measurements for your documents. The following sections describe in detail how to use the options.

Horizontal and vertical measure

QuarkXPress lets you select a measurement system for both the horizontal and vertical rulers that you use to lay out a document. You select a measurement system for these rulers in the Horizontal and Vertical pop-up menus.

Of course, you aren't stuck to these measurements once you've made a choice. You can change any measurement in any dialog box by just entering the code (shown in parentheses in the following list) that tells QuarkXPress what the system is. The measurement system choices (which, incidentally, can be different for the horizontal and vertical rulers) are as follows:

- **Inches.** Inches (") are displayed on the ruler divided into eighths, in typical inch format (¼ inch, ½ inch, and so on).

- **Inches Decimal.** Inches (") are displayed on the ruler in decimal format, divided into tenths.

- **Picas.** One pica (p) is about 0.166 inch. An inch contains 6 picas.

- **Points.** One point (pt) is approximately ½₂ (0.01388) of an inch, or 0.351 millimeters.

- **Millimeters.** A millimeter (mm) is a metric measurement unit — 25.4 millimeters equals 1 inch; 1 mm equals 0.03937 inch.

- **Centimeters.** A centimeter (cm) is a metric measurement unit — 2.54 centimeters is 1 inch; 1 cm equals 0.3937 inch.

- **Ciceros.** This measurement unit is used in most of Europe; 1 cicero (c) is approximately 0.1792 inch. A cicero is close in size to a pica, which is 0.166 inch.

- **Agates.** One agate (ag) is 0.071 inch.

- **Pixels.** If you're working on a Web document, all default measurements in the Measurements pane are converted to pixels (px).

Points/Inch and Ciceros/Cm

In the Measurements pane of the Preferences dialog box, you can set the number of points per inch and the number of ciceros per centimeter through the Points/Inch and Ciceros/Cm options, respectively. QuarkXPress uses a default setting of 72 points per inch and 2.1967 ciceros per centimeter. You may want to change these settings because the actual number of points per inch is 72.271742, although most people now round that figure off to 72.

Item coordinates

Whichever system of measurement you use, you can control how the coordinates for layout elements are calculated. The Item Coordinates setting tells QuarkXPress whether to base your ruler and box coordinates on a page or on a spread (a spread is usually two side-by-side pages, such as the left and right pages that appear together when a bound document is open). If you treat each page as a separate element, keep the option set to Page, which is the default. If you work on a spread as a single unit, change the setting to Spread.

After you make changes in the Measurements pane, click OK to save them.

Paragraph options

The Paragraph pane (shown in Figure 21-6) lets you deal with three defaults related to the make-up of the paragraphs of your document: Leading, Baseline Grid, and Hyphenation. These options are described below.

Leading

The Leading section contains the following options:

- ✔ **Auto Leading.** Auto Leading specifies the space between lines; the default is 20 percent, which sets leading at 120 percent of the current text size.

  A better option is +2, which sets leading at the current text size plus 2 points — a more typical setting among typographers.

- ✔ **Maintain Leading.** This option causes text that falls below an intervening text or picture box to snap to the next baseline grid, rather than fall right after the intervening box's offset. This procedure ensures consistent text alignment across all columns.

- ✔ **Mode.** Always choose the Typesetting option from the pop-up menu. (Typesetting mode measures leading from baseline to baseline, whereas Word Processing mode measures from top of character to top of character.) Word processing mode is an archaic holdover from pre-desktop publishing days, and there is never any reason to use it.

Baseline Grid

The Baseline Grid section contains options that specify the default positions for lines of text:

- ✔ **Start.** The Start option indicates where the grid begins (how far from the top of the page).

- ✔ **Increment.** This setting determines the grid interval. Generally, the grid should start where the automatic text box starts, and the interval should be the same as body-text leading.

Hyphenation

Set the hyphenation option — Method — to Enhanced or Expanded. Standards exists only to keep the program compatible with earlier versions, which had a less accurate hyphenation algorithm.

After you make changes in the Paragraph pane, click OK to save them.

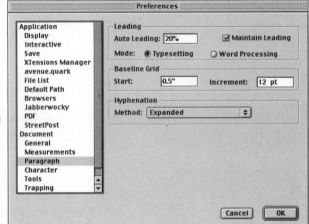

Figure 21-6:
The Paragraph pane of the Preferences dialog box.

Character options

QuarkXPress lets you define typographic preferences. You specify your preferences in the Character pane (see Figure 21-7).

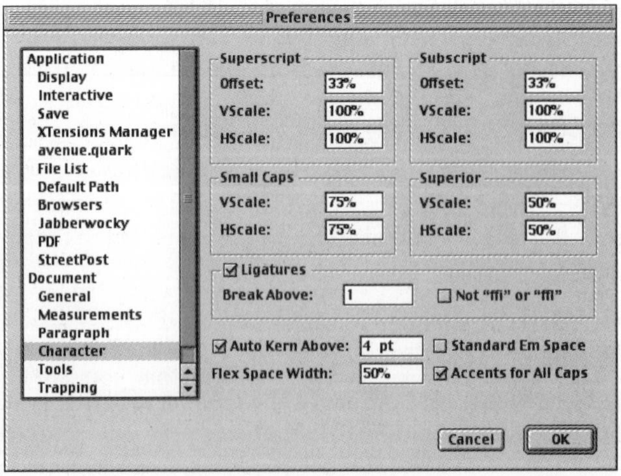

Figure 21-7:
The Character pane of the Preferences dialog box.

As with many changes that you make in the Preferences dialog box, any changes of the settings in the Character pane affect only the current document. If no document is open, the changes affect all subsequent new documents.

Several options in the Character pane affect character styles. These options include the four boxes labeled Superscript, Subscript, Small Caps, and Superior.

Superiors are special superscript characters that always align along the *cap line,* which is the height of a capital letter in the current typeface. Superiors typically are used in footnotes.

Superscript and Subscript

The Superscript and Subscript sections share the following options:

- ✔ **Offset.** Dictates how far below or above the baseline QuarkXPress shifts a subscripted or superscripted character. The default settings are 33 percent for both Subscript and Superscript. We prefer 35 percent for superscript and 30 percent for subscript.

- ✔ **VScale** and **HScale.** Determine scaling for the subscript or superscript. Although the default is 100 percent, that setting is useful only for type-written documents. Typeset documents typically use a smaller size for subscripts and superscripts — usually, between 60 and 80 percent of the text size. The two values should be the same.

Small Caps and Superior

The options in the Small Caps and Superior sections are identical, even though these attributes are very different. VScale and HScale determine the scaling for the small cap or superior. The two values should be the same because small caps and superiors typically are not distorted along one dimension. Usually, a small cap's scale should be between 65 percent and 80 percent of the normal text, and a superior's scale should be between 50 percent and 65 percent.

Ligatures

A *ligature* is a set of joined characters. The characters are joined because the shapes almost blend together by default, so typographers of yore decided to make them blend together naturally. When you check the ligatures box, QuarkXPress automatically replaces occurrences of *fi, ffi, fl,* and *ffl* with their ligatured equivalents (fi, ffi, fl, and ffl), both when you enter text and when you import it. If you uncheck the Ligatures box, all ligatures in your document are translated to standard character combinations. Not all fonts support ligatures, and many sans-serif typefaces look like their nonligature equivalents. This feature is nice because it means that you don't have to worry about adding ligatures manually; as an added bonus, it doesn't affect spell checking.

✔ **Not "ffi" or "ffl":** Some people don't like using ligatures for *ffi* and *ffl*. Check the Not "ffi" or "ffl" box to prevent these ligatures from being used automatically. When you search for text in the Find/Change dialog box, you can enter **ffi**, and QuarkXPress finds the ligature.

✔ **Break Above:** The Break Above option for ligatures allows you to set how a ligature is handled in a loosely tracked line. You can enter a value ranging from 0 to 100. That value is the number of units of tracking (each unit is $\frac{1}{200}$ of an em space) at which QuarkXPress breaks apart a ligature to prevent awkward spacing.

QuarkXPress for Windows does not support ligatures. As a result, Mac files with Ligatures options selected — when moved to QuarkXPress for Windows — are converted so they use the standard characters. But when they are moved back to the Mac, the ligatures are re-enabled automatically.

Auto Kern Above

Auto Kern Above lets you define the point size at which QuarkXPress automatically kerns letter pairs. Kerning is the process of adjusting the space between two letters so that the letters have a better appearance. For laser printed documents, 10 points is fine, but typeset documents should be set at a smaller value, such as 8 points.

Standard Em Space

This option determines how QuarkXPress calculates the width of an *em dash* (—), a standard measurement in typography upon which most other spacing measurements are based. If you check this box, QuarkXPress uses the typographic measurement (the width of the letter *M,* which is usually equal to the current point size). Unchecked, QuarkXPress uses the width of two zeroes, which is how QuarkXPress has always calculated an em space.

Flex Space Width

This option lets you define the value for a *flex space,* which is a user-defined space. The default is 50 percent, which is about the width of the letter *t,* called a *thin space.* A better setting — because you're more likely to use an em space than a thin space — is 200 percent, which is equal to an em space (the width of the letter *M*).

Accents for All Caps

If checked, the option lets accented characters retain their accents if you apply the All Caps attribute to them. In many publications, the style is to drop accents from capitalized letters. This feature lets you control whether this style is implemented automatically.

After you make changes in the Character pane, click OK to save them.

Tools options

QuarkXPress lets you customize how the tools in the Tool palette and the Web Tools palette work by changing settings in the Tools pane of the Preferences dialog box (see Figure 21-8). To set the defaults, first select the tool that you want to modify, then click the Modify Button. The Modify dialog box appears, where you'll find the same settings as those in the Modify dialog box (see Chapter 3 for more about the Modify dialog box).

Unavailable options are grayed out. After you make changes, click OK to record the changes or Cancel to undo them.

If you access the Tool pane with no document open, all defaults apply to all subsequently created documents. Otherwise, the defaults apply only to subsequently created boxes and lines for the current document.

The tools that you can customize are as follows:

- ✔ **Box tools.** You can set the item settings for all the Text Box and Picture Box tools. You can establish settings for options normally available for the individual boxes via the Item menu's Modify, Frame, and Runaround commands. See Chapter 3 for more information on box settings.

    The ability to customize certain settings comes in handy. You can, for example, give oval picture boxes an offset of 1 pica or set text boxes to have a 3-point frame and a green background.

- ✔ **Drawing tools.** You can establish defaults for new lines that you draw with the Line tools. You can set most regular line options that are normally available through the Item menu. You can also set other line specifications and runaround options, such as line color and weight.

- ✔ **Text Path tools.** Likewise, you can establish defaults for new lines that you draw with the Text Path tools. You can set most regular line options that are normally available through the Item menu, as well text orientation. You can also set other line-specification and runaround options, such as line color and weight.

- ✔ **Zoom tool.** At the top of the list is the Zoom tool. You can change the minimum and maximum zoom views to any value between 10 and 800 percent, in increments of 1 percent.

- ✔ **Table.** You can customize several options in the Table tool, many of which resemble those described in the Box tools section, including those found in the Modify, Frame, and Runaround panes. In addition, a handful of table-specific options can be altered, such as the default number of rows and columns, and the layout of the grid itself. You can, for example set up the Table tool to create a table in which only the lines along the rows are visible, giving your table a less "box-ish" appearance.

✔ **Image Map Tools.** Just as you can set the item settings for all the Text
Box and Picture Box tools, you can set the item settings for the Image
Map Tools when a Web document is open. You can establish settings for
options normally available for the individual Image Map tools by using
the Item menu's Modify, Frame, and Runaround commands. See
Chapter 19 for more information on Image Map tools.

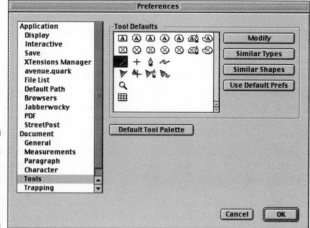

Figure 21-8:
The Tools
pane of the
Preferences
dialog box.

To set the preferences for all text or picture boxes at the same time, click a
text or picture box in the scrollable list and click Select Similar Types before
you click Modify. To set the preferences for all boxes of the same shape, click
a box that uses that shape and then click Select Similar Shapes before you
click Modify.

Trapping options

The Preferences dialog box contains another pane, Trapping, which lets you
specify defaults for how QuarkXPress traps colors and objects when you separate a document into its color plates. This feature is very advanced, and we
recommend that beginners not change the defaults.

However, if these options do change for whatever reason, the defaults are
shown here so that you can change them back:

✔ **Trapping Method:** The default for the Trapping Method section is
Absolute.

✔ **Process Trapping:** This check box is checked by default.

- ✔ **Ignore White:** This checkbox is trapped by default.
- ✔ **Auto Amount:** The default setting for this field is 0.144 pt
- ✔ **Indeterminate:** The default setting for this field is 0.144 pt
- ✔ **Knockout Limit:** The default setting for this field is 0%
- ✔ **Overprint Limit:** The default setting for this field is 95%

Layer options

The new Preferences dialog box contains another new pane, the Layer pane, which lets you specify defaults for the layers in your QuarkXPress documents. You'll find only four check boxes in this pane: Visible, Locked, Suppress Printout, and Keep Runaround, each of which is described here:

- ✔ **Visible.** When this box is checked, all new layers added to a document are visible and the "eye" icon appears next to each layer in the Layer palette. When the Visible box is unchecked, new layers are invisible until you click where the eye icon normally appears in the Layer palette.

- ✔ **Suppress Printout.** This box works hand in hand with the Visible check box. If Visible is not checked, Suppress Printout is automatically grayed out. After all, what is the point in printing something invisible? If Visible is checked, however, the Suppress Printout button is reactivated. When Suppress Printout is checked, layers are automatically kept from being printed with the rest of the document.

- ✔ **Locked.** When the lock check box is checked, all items on a layer are unmovable unless they are first "unlocked" in the Layer palette.

- ✔ **Keep Runaround.** When this box is checked, items on a layer can have a text runaround. If it isn't checked, the text runaround option defaults to None.

For more about the Layers palette, refer to Chapter 13.

Color Management Preferences

To access the Color Management Preferences dialog box, choose Edit➪Preferences➪Color Management; the Color Management Preferences dialog box appears. You can find more information about Color Information models in Chapter 9.

Index Preferences

To access the Index dialog box, choose Edit➪Preferences➪Index; the Index Preferences dialog box appears. In this dialog box you'll find

- **Index Marker Color:** The default for this color is red, but you can change to virtually any color via the Index Marker Color dialog box. To access Index Marker Color, click on the color swatch at the top of the dialog box.

- **Separation Characters:** This section lets you choose different separations characters for your indexes. For example, if you prefer an en dash between a range of pages in an index to a hyphen, you can type an en dash (Option+hyphen on the Mac, or hold Alt while entering the code 0150 on the PC's numeric keypad in Windows) in the Between Page Range field. You can also choose a Cross-Ref style in the Separation Characters section — Entry's Style or Normal.

Fraction/Price Preferences

Settings in Fraction/Price dialog box enable you to tweak settings for fractions created with the Make Fraction and Make Price commands. Choose Edit➪Preferences➪ to access the dialog box. We suggest that you use the default settings for these preferences. If you feel the urge to experiment, though, be sure to write down the changes you make. There is no Apply button in the Preferences dialog box, so after you click OK, your changes are there to stay — whether you like them or not.

Chapter 22

Details for Cross-Platform Users

ace it, the Mac is the platform of choice for desktop publishing. But Windows has been making inroads in the past few years, and top programs such as QuarkXPress are available in Windows versions that have all the same features as their Mac counterparts. The few differences between the two QuarkXPress programs are almost always due to differences between the Mac and Windows. Whether you're a cross-platform user who needs to understand the discrepancies between the two versions, or a Windows user who is looking for advice that's specific to your needs, read on.

Where the Mac and Windows Differ

Before you get to the differences between the Mac and Windows versions of QuarkXPress itself, knowing about some differences between the Mac and Windows is helpful. Why look at such basic stuff in a book about QuarkXPress? Because the underlying platform differences affect operations everywhere — including QuarkXPress. Table 22-1 lists Mac and Windows equivalents.

Table 22-1	Mac and Windows Equivalents	
Item	*Windows*	*Macintosh*
Keys		
	Ctrl	⌘ (Command)
	Alt	Option
	Shift	Shift

(continued)

Table 22-1 *(continued)*

Item	Windows	Macintosh
Keys		
	no equivalent	Control
	Delete	Shift+Delete
	Backspace	Delete
	right mouse button	Control+mouse button*
Close window	Ctrl+F4	⌘+W
Exit program	Alt+F4	⌘+Q
Filename extensions		
Document	.QXD	none
Template	.QXT	none
Library	.QXL	none
XTension	.XNT	none

In Mac OS 8 and later, and in some programs in earlier versions of the Mac OS

Keyboard

PC and Mac keyboards may look alike, but actually, they differ in two major ways.

First, some of the control keys are different, at least in their appearances and names. The Mac has a key that looks like a butterfly (⌘); it's called the Command key, and it's basically the same as a PC's Ctrl key. The Mac also has a key labeled Option, which is basically the same as the PC's Alt key. Some Mac keyboards also have a key labeled Control — which is *not* the same as the Command key or the PC's Ctrl key.

The other significant difference is in how you delete. PCs use a key labeled Delete (or Del) to delete text to the right of the insertion point (the thing that Mac folks call the pointer) and a Backspace key to delete text to the left of the cursor. (This key is a holdover from typewriters.) Some Mac keyboards have a Del key, but many don't. On a Mac, the Backspace key is usually called Delete. When a PC user would press Delete, a Mac user would press

Shift+Delete. That can feel weird — the Mac version of QuarkXPress won't let you use Del instead of Shift+Delete to delete a range of text, even on keyboards that have the Del key. Instead, you can use Delete for only one character at a time. (If your Mac's keyboard has the Del key, you can use it to delete a section of text.)

Files and directories

Almost everyone knows that Windows 95 ended the PC's dumb naming structure: names of eight letters, followed by a period and then by up to three more letters. This means that filenames on PCs can now be descriptive, and that it's easy to have meaningful filenames on both platforms.

Macintosh files follow these rules:

- Names are limited to 31 characters.

- Any characters can be used except for colons (:), which the Macintosh System software uses internally to separate the folder name (which is not visible on-screen) from the filename.

- Case does not matter: FILE, file, and File are all considered to be the same name. If you have a file named FILE and create or copy a file named file, FILE is overwritten.

Windows files follow these rules:

- Names are limited to 250 characters.

- Names must also have a file extension of up to three characters. Programs almost always add the file extension automatically to identify the file type. A period separates the filename from the extension (FILENAME.EXT). Windows hides these file extensions from view unless you choose View➪Options in a drive or folder window to make Windows display them.

  For QuarkXPress, the extension is .QXD. Similarly, .QXT designates a QuarkXPress template; .QXL, a QuarkXPress library; .QDT, a spelling dictionary; and .XNT, a QuarkXPress XTension add-on program. On a Mac, you just look for the icons.

- Names can use any characters except for most punctuation characters. Windows uses pipes (|), colons (:), periods (.), asterisks (*), double quotes ("), less-than symbols (<), greater-than symbols (>), question marks (?), slashes (/), and backslashes (\) to separate parts of paths (file locations, such as drives and folders) or to structure commands. A period is used as the separator between a filename and an extension.

✔ Case doesn't matter: FILE, file, and File are all considered to be the same name. If you have a file named FILE and create or copy a file named file, FILE is overwritten.

The simplest way to ensure that you won't have problems with transferred files looking for incompatible names is to use a naming convention that satisfies both Windows and Mac standards. You should:

✔ Limit filenames to 27 characters or fewer.

✔ Always include the PC file extension (which adds 4 characters to the full name, hitting the Mac limit of 31). Use .QXD for documents, .QXT for templates, .HTM for Web documents, .XML for XML documents, .QDT for auxiliary dictionaries, .QPJ for printer styles, and .KRN for kerning tables. Typical extensions for cross-platform graphics are .TIF for TIFF, .EPS for Encapsulated PostScript, .AI for Adobe Illustrator, .PSD for Adobe Photoshop, .PDF for Adobe Portable Document Format, .PCT for PICT, .PCX for PC Paintbrush, .BMP and .RLE for Microsoft bitmap, .GIF for Graphics Interchange Format, .WMF for Windows metafile, .CDR for CorelDraw, and .SCT or .CT for Scitex. Text files are .DOC for Microsoft Word.

✔ Don't use the pipe (|), colon (:), period (.), asterisk (*), double quote ("), less-than symbol (<), greater-than symbol (>), question mark (?), slash (/), or backslash (\) characters.

Environment controls

On a Mac, you find a folder called Control Panels (also available via the Apple menu) that contains mini-programs for changing System settings, such as colors, network options, and mouse tracking. In Windows, most of these mini-programs are stored in a program called Control Panel, which you access by choosing Start⇨Settings. (The Start button is the Microsoft version of the Apple menu.)

The Control Panel programs and other mini-programs allow you to manage basic operations in Windows. The following sections cover the three that are most important to a QuarkXPress user: printing, multitasking (switching between active programs), and fonts.

Printing

You set up your printers by using the Windows Control Panel's Add Printers icon, but you also can switch printers by using the Printer Setup dialog box in your programs. (Sometimes this Printer Setup dialog box has its own entry in the File menu; sometimes it's an option in the Print dialog box. How you access the dialog box depends on the design of the program that you're using. In QuarkXPress, the Printer Setup dialog box is available both ways.)

On a Mac, you have to use a program called the Chooser to switch printers — a real pain — or you can use the desktop printer icon.

Multitasking

If you're using QuarkXPress, you probably have a relatively good system — a Power PC-based Mac or a Pentium- or Athlon-based PC. After all, publishing demands solid resources. And you probably have more than one program loaded in memory at a time. The fancy name for this situation is *multitasking* (way back in the System 6 days of the Mac, Apple called multitasking MultiFinder).

On the Mac, you can switch to and from all active programs via the pull-down menu at the far-right end of the menu bar — the Application menu, although practically no one knows its name. The currently active program's icon appears in the top-right corner of the window; if you select that icon, a menu of all active programs appears.

In Windows, all active programs are available through the taskbar, which is always visible, usually at the bottom of the screen. If you minimize a program — that is, if you click the bar icon in the top-right corner of the program's menu — its icon appears in the taskbar. You can double-click that icon to make it active.

In Windows, you can cycle among open programs by pressing Alt+Tab.

Fonts

Both Macs and Windows PCs support TrueType and PostScript Type 1 fonts (usually through Adobe Type Manager), but fonts are slightly different on the two platforms. In some cases the names differ only slightly, such as Helvetica Compressed on the Mac and HelveticaCompressed in Windows — the Windows names don't have spaces within them. In most cases, Windows fonts have some characters (such as ¼ and š) that Mac fonts usually don't. At the same time, though, Mac fonts have some characters — such as Σ, ∂, , and fi — that Windows fonts usually don't (even if the fonts do have the same name).

Fonts that have the same name may have different spacing and even character widths. This situation usually occurs with fonts created when an Iron Wall stood between the Mac and the PC — back in the olden days of the '80s, when developers didn't worry about cross-platform users.

You can translate fonts from Mac format to Windows format, or vice versa, with programs such as Macromedia's Fontographer, which is available for both Windows and the Mac. (For more information on this program, call 415-252-2000 or visit the company's Web site at www.macromedia.com.) We recommend that you do your translation on the Mac. Because the Mac's internal file format is weird compared with the PC's, Mac font files created on a PC don't always survive the translation process. Font files are more susceptible to this problem than are data files (such as QuarkXPress, graphics, or text files), because on the Mac, a font is a bit like a program; it has resource information that can easily get corrupted when it's stored on a PC. We're not saying that you *can't* create Mac fonts in Windows, just that we've had better luck creating them on the Mac. You also can use this program to translate PostScript to TrueType or vice versa.

Not Quite Clones

Even considering the differences between Windows and the Mac, QuarkXPress has some other differences that have less to do with platform differences than with . . . well, just differences in what Quark decided to do in each version. The list is not huge, but it may look bigger than it is because of the illustrations that show the differences.

View controls

To change your view percentage on a Mac, you press Control+V — remember, Control is not the Mac's ⌘ key or the PC's Ctrl key — to quickly highlight the view-percentage box (in the bottom-left corner of the QuarkXPress screen) so that you can enter a new zoom amount. In Windows, press Ctrl+Alt+V.

Quark's Mac and Windows versions also have differences in their Preferences dialog box's Display pane, as shown Figure 22-1. (To display this dialog box, choose Edit⇨Preferences⇨Preferences, or press Shift+Option+⌘+Y or Ctrl+Alt+Shift+Y.)

One difference is that QuarkXPress for Windows offers a Display DPI Value option. This option is, in essence, a zoom control that stays in place for all QuarkXPress documents until you change it again; if you make the number larger, QuarkXPress shows a more magnified image.

Another difference is that Windows video supports multiple resolutions. You probably know that you can change your desktop from, say, 640 by 480 pixels to 800 by 600 or 1,024 by 768. Such a change makes everything smaller but increases the size of the working area. Until 1994, Macs couldn't work this trick easily, and today, switching resolutions on a Mac still requires a PC-style monitor, although the Mac's Monitors & Sounds control panel now includes the ability to change resolution if you're using a PC-style monitor. The Mac offers several controls that handle the display of documents across multiple monitors (called *tiling*). Even though Windows now supports tiled monitors, QuarkXPress for Windows has no equivalent function.

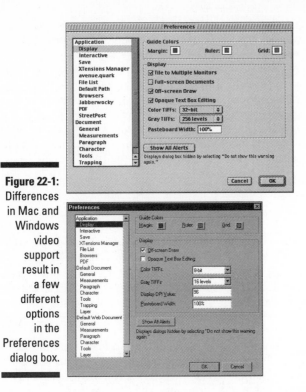

Figure 22-1:
Differences
in Mac and
Windows
video
support
result in
a few
different
options
in the
Preferences
dialog box.

The most obvious difference between the Windows and Mac versions of
QuarkXPress is the View menu. The commands that determine how document windows display are in different places, as shown in Figure 22-2.

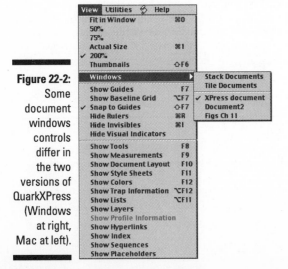

Figure 22-2:
Some
document
windows
controls
differ in
the two
versions of
QuarkXPress
(Windows
at right,
Mac at left).

In the Mac version, the View menu has a Windows option with a submenu, whereas in Windows, those options are in their own menu, called Window. Both versions of QuarkXPress support tiled views, which are the automatic arrangement of multiple open QuarkXPress layouts. But the Windows version supports several arrangements — tile horizontally (left to right), tile vertically (top to bottom), cascade (overlapping stacks), and iconized — whereas the Mac version supports only vertical tiling and cascading (stacking). Finally, QuarkXPress for Windows has a menu command that closes all the document windows; on the Mac, you use the keyboard shortcut Option+⌘+W (for which no Windows equivalent exists).

Typography

Because most versions of Windows don't support *ligatures* — letters that are merged, such as fi and < — QuarkXPress for Windows doesn't offer ligature controls in the Character pane of the Preferences dialog box, as the Mac version does. (To display this dialog box, choose Edit➪Preferences➪Preferences, or press Shift+Option+⌘+Y or Ctrl+Alt+Shift+Y.) Figure 22-3 shows the different dialog boxes.

If you want to use ligatures in Windows, you need to use a typeface that has them as symbols. Notice that if you use ligatures on the Mac and bring the QuarkXPress document into QuarkXPress for Windows, the ligatures are replaced by the standard letter combinations, and they translate back into ligatures when they're loaded into the Mac version again. It's unlikely — but possible, in some rare circumstances — that this ligature replacement could affect the text flow as the file is transferred back and forth.

Font names on the Mac and Windows can differ, so even if you have the same fonts installed on both systems, you may get a message saying that a font is missing when you open a document. If you click the List Fonts button when you get that message, you can tell QuarkXPress immediately which font to use instead. Alternatively, you can choose Utilities➪Font Usage to open the Font Usage dialog box, which lets you do the same thing at any time.

Linked objects

Both versions of QuarkXPress support hot links to objects in other programs. On the Mac, the method is called Publish and Subscribe; in Windows, it's called Object Linking and Embedding (OLE, for short). In both cases, the theory is that you can have your layout retrieve the latest version of a chart or other graphic as soon as the graphic is changed in the original program.

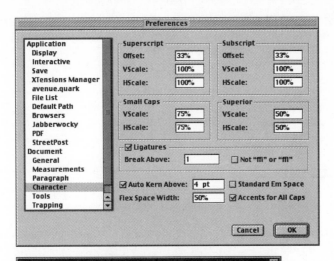

Figure 22-3:
The Mac
version of
QuarkXPress
(top)
supports
ligatures,
but the
Windows
version
(bottom)
does not.

In practice, using hot links requires significant trade-offs:

✔ You can't link text this way unless you want it to be converted to an image.

✔ If both programs aren't loaded, the object doesn't get updated automatically when changed in its originating program.

✔ You need a great deal of memory to use this feature.

✔ You can't use most of the QuarkXPress image controls on these images.

We recommend that you not worry too much about hot links, but if you do use them, look at Figures 22-4 and 22-5.

Figure 22-4 shows the differences in QuarkXPress menu options In the Windows version, you can link an object in two ways: by choosing Edit⇨Paste Special or Edit⇨Insert Object.

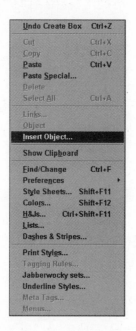

Figure 22-4: Because of different hot-link technologies, the Windows (right) and Mac (left) versions of QuarkXPress have different menu options for linked-file import.

If you choose Edit⇨Paste Special to get the Paste Special dialog box, you get two import choices: Paste and Paste Link. Whether the object can be embedded (Paste) or linked (Paste Link) depends on the application that created it. Note that the Edit⇨Paste Special command becomes available only after you use Edit⇨Cut or Edit⇨Paste in the originating program to put the text or graphic into the Mac or Windows clipboard.

If you choose Edit⇨Insert Object, you see a dialog box where you can launch a program to create the OLE object in or open it from. (Figure 22-5 shows the Paste Special and Insert Object dialog boxes.)

The Edit menu also has the Links and Object options, which let you update and edit an OLE object, respectively, whether the object was brought into QuarkXPress via Paste Special or Insert Object.

On the Mac, you have the Subscribe To and Subscriber options to import and update a hot-linked object, respectively. The Mac's Subscriber options are basically the same as the Windows Links and Object options.

Figure 22-5:
The Insert
Object
dialog box
lets you
choose an
object from
another
Windows
program
and then
hot-link it to
QuarkXPress
for
Windows.

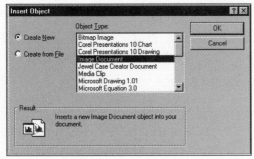

Item manipulation

When you create objects — lines, picture boxes, and text boxes — in QuarkXPress, they are automatically layered so that the most recently created or pasted object is on top of the preceding one. Sometimes you want to change the stacking order so that a particular box overprints another. Both versions of QuarkXPress offer controls for moving objects, but the Windows version makes it easier to use all the controls. In both versions, you can send an object to the front or the back via commands on the Item menu (see Figure 22-6). But in the Windows version, you also can move an object one layer at a time by choosing Item⇨Bring Forward or Item⇨Send Backward. (To get these options in the Mac version of QuarkXPress, you have to hold down the Option key before opening the Item menu; the Send to Back and Bring to Front options are then removed from the menu.)

EPS pages

Through the Save Page As EPS dialog box, you can export a page of your layout as an EPS file. (To display this dialog box, choose File⇨Save Page As EPS, or press Shift+Option+⌘+S or Ctrl+Alt+Shift+S.) A slight difference exists in the dialog box in the Mac and Windows versions. The Mac version allows you to save the EPS preview image in PICT or TIFF format (or to have no preview), whereas the Windows version gives you a choice of just TIFF and no preview.

Item			Item					
Modify...	⌘M		Modify...	⌘M		Modify...	Ctrl+M	
Frame...	⌘B		Frame...	⌘B		Frame...	Ctrl+B	
Runaround...	⌘T		Runaround...	⌘T		Runaround...	Ctrl+T	
Clipping...	⌥⌘T		Clipping...	⌥⌘T		Clipping...	Ctrl+Alt+T	
Duplicate	⌘D		Duplicate	⌘D		Duplicate	Ctrl+D	
Step and Repeat...	⌥⌘D		Step and Repeat...	⌥⌘D		Step and Repeat...	Ctrl+Alt+D	
Delete	⌘K		Delete	⌘K		Delete	Ctrl+K	
Group	⌘G		Group	⌘G		Group	Ctrl+G	
Ungroup	⌘U		Ungroup	⌘U		Ungroup	Ctrl+U	
Constrain			Constrain			Constrain		
Lock	F6		Lock	F6		Lock	F6	
Merge	▶		Merge	▶		Merge	▶	
Split	▶		Split	▶		Split	▶	
Send to Back	⇧F5		Send to Back	⇧F5		Send Backward	Ctrl+Shift+F5	
Bring to Front	F5		Bring to Front	F5		Send to Back	Shift+F5	
Space/Align...	⌘,		Space/Align...	⌘,		Bring Forward	Ctrl+F5	
						Bring to Front	F5	
						Space/Align...	Ctrl+,	
Shape	▶		Shape	▶		Shape	▶	
Content	▶		Content	▶		Content	▶	
Edit	▶		Edit	▶		Edit	▶	
Point/Segment Type	▶		Point/Segment Type	▶		Point/Segment Type	▶	
Delete All Hot Areas			Delete All Hot Areas			Delete All Hot Areas		
Super Step and Repeat...			Super Step and Repeat...			Super Step and Repeat...		
Convert Text to Table...			Convert Text to Table...			Convert Text to Table...		
Table	▶		Table	▶				
Gridlines	▶		Gridlines	▶				
Rollover	▶		Rollover	▶				

Figure 22-6:
The Item
menu for
Windows
and Mac.

Shortcuts

QuarkXPress uses the same shortcuts on both platforms, translating ⌘ to Ctrl and Option to Alt, in almost every case. See Chapter 21 for a complete listing.

Newer versions of Windows (Windows 95 and up) and Mac OS 8 and up all use a technique called *contextual menus* to save you time. This feature saves you time going through menus, dialog boxes, and palettes. QuarkXPress 5.0 for both Mac and Windows fully support contextual menus, which are also known as shortcut menus in Windows. The way they work differs somewhat, though. On the Mac version, you point at an item, press the Control key, and then click and hold the mouse button. (*Note:* If this isn't working, go to the Interactive pane of the Preferences dialog box and make sure the Contextual Menu button is chosen in the Control Key section). In Windows, you point at an item and press the right key on your mouse — the contextual (or *shortcut*) window appears immediately.

How to Transfer Files

Although the file format for QuarkXPress documents and templates is the same on the two platforms, the Windows version may not recognize a Mac-generated file as a QuarkXPress file unless you do one of the following two things:

✔ Add the file extension .QXD to the Mac-generated file's name.

✔ In Windows QuarkXPress, choose Display All Files from the File Type pop-up menu in the Open dialog box. (To display this dialog box, choose File⇨Open or press Ctrl+O.)

On the Mac, you may not be able to double-click a Windows QuarkXPress file to get QuarkXPress to launch. Instead, you may have to launch QuarkXPress separately and then open the file from within QuarkXPress.

QuarkXPress for Mac Version 5 can read Windows Version 3.1, 3.3, 4.0, and 5.0 files. QuarkXPress for Windows Version 5 can read files in QuarkXPress for Mac Versions 3.0, 3.1, 3.2, 3.3, 4.0, and 5.0. (QuarkXPress had no Windows Version 3.2.)

Which elements transfer

The following elements can be transferred across platforms, with the noted limitations:

✔ **Graphics.** Any graphics that are not supported by the platform version are replaced during printing by their PICT preview images (on the Mac) or Windows Metafile preview images (in Windows). The graphics links are retained, however; if you move the document back to the originating platform, the original graphics are again available for printing.

✔ **Graphics previews.** Some PICT previews from the Mac and some Windows Metafile previews in Windows do not translate correctly when they are transferred. You must reimport or update the link to the graphic to generate a new preview.

✔ **Colors.** Colors are retained and can be imported across platforms.

✔ **Color profiles.** Although color-profile files cannot be exchanged across the two platforms, the Mac and Windows versions of QuarkXPress retain color-profile information from the other platform's files. And if both platforms have color profiles for the same device (monitor, scanner, printer, and so on), QuarkXPress applies the correct color profiles. If a color profile is not available on the new platform, you can apply a new profile or ignore the issue. (If you ignore the issue, the correct profile is in place when you bring the document back to the original platform.) If you print with a missing profile, QuarkXPress substitutes the default profile based on the color model used (RGB, CMYK, or Hexachrome).

✔ **Style sheets.** Style sheets are retained and can be imported across platforms.

✔ **H&J sets.** H&J sets for hyphenation and justification are retained and can be imported across platforms.

- ✔ **Lists.** Lists are retained and can be imported across platforms.

- ✔ **Dashes and stripes.** Dashes and stripes are retained and can be imported across platforms.

- ✔ **Document preferences.** Document preferences are retained, but the XPress Preferences file cannot be shared across platforms.

- ✔ **Print styles.** Print styles are retained. These styles can be exported and imported across platforms.

- ✔ **Auxiliary spelling dictionaries.** Auxiliary spelling dictionaries cannot be used across platforms.

- ✔ **Kerning data.** Kerning data exported from the Mac can be imported into Windows. We do not recommend doing this kind of transfer, however, because the font characteristics on the two platforms are different enough that you should customize the kerning for each platform separately.

- ✔ **XTensions.** XTensions must be present on both platforms if you are moving documents that use the XTensions features. If you don't have an XTension in, say, Windows and try to load a Mac document that uses that XTension's capabilities, you may get an error message saying that the document cannot be opened.

- ✔ **Document previews.** Although the Windows version does not save preview images for the Open dialog box, such previews created on the Mac are retained even if the document is moved to Windows and back.

To import elements, click the Append button in the relevant dialog box. To export and import elements, click the Export and Import buttons in the relevant dialog box.

Which elements don't transfer

Quark has removed almost every barrier between the Mac and Windows in the latest version of QuarkXPress. In Version 5.0, only libraries, auxiliary dictionaries, and hyphenation dictionaries cannot be moved across platforms. The database systems underlying the libraries are not compatible, so the libraries cannot be shared.

Part VII
The Part of Tens

The 5th Wave   By Rich Tennant

"QuarkXPress does a lot of great things. I'm not sure running a word processing program sideways without line breaks on butcher's paper is one of them."

In this part . . .

This part of the book gives a quick rundown of tools and techniques that help you get the most out of QuarkXPress with the least amount of muss and fuss: shortcut keys, some great online resources, and common mistakes to avoid. This part is so packed with useful information that you might even be tempted to start reading here and then go back to Chapter 1, but don't. The concepts in this part will make more sense to you if you read the other sections of the book first.

Chapter 23

More Than Ten Shortcuts

QuarkXPress has tons and tons of shortcuts. You probably won't memorize most of them, but you'll no doubt find yourself using one or two all the time. Following is a comprehensive list, broken down by task.

Opening/Closing/Saving

Action	Macintosh	Windows
New publication	⌘+N	Ctrl+N
New library	Option+⌘+N	Ctrl+Alt+N
New XML	Shift+⌘+X	Shift+Ctrl+X
New Web document	Shift+Option+⌘+N	Shift+Ctrl+Alt+N
Open publication	⌘+O	Ctrl+O
Save publication	⌘+S	Ctrl+S
Save as	Option+⌘+S	Ctrl+Shift+S
Get text or picture	⌘+E	Ctrl+E
Save text	Option+⌘+E	Ctrl+Alt+E
Save page as EPS	Option+Shift+⌘+S	Ctrl+Alt+Shift+S
Append	Option+⌘+A	Ctrl+Alt+A
Close current document	⌘+W	Ctrl+F4
Close all documents	Option+⌘+W	not available
Quit	⌘+Q	Ctrl+Q or Alt+F4

Miscellaneous

Action	Macintosh	Windows
Print	⌘+P	Ctrl+P
Undo	⌘+Z	Ctrl+Z
Revert dialog-box values	Shift+⌘+Z	Ctrl+Shift+Z
Help	Help	F1

Preferences/Setup

Action	Macintosh	Windows
Preferences (Document pane or last Preferences pane accessed)	Shift+Option+⌘+Y	Ctrl+Alt+Shift+Y
Preferences (General pane)	⌘+Y	Ctrl+Y
Page setup	Option+⌘+P	Ctrl+Alt+P

View

Action	Macintosh	Windows
100%	⌘+1	Ctrl+1
Fit in windows	⌘+0	Ctrl+0
200%	Option+⌘+click	Ctrl+Alt+click
Thumbnails	Shift+F6	Shift+F6
Change view percentage	Control+V	Ctrl+Alt+V
Force redraw	Option+⌘+period	Shift+Esc
Halt redraw	⌘+period	Esc

Action	Macintosh	Windows
Go to page	⌘+J	Ctrl+J
Zoom in	⌘+click	Ctrl+spacebar+click
Zoom out	Option+⌘+click	Ctrl+Alt+spacebar+click
Windows submenu	Shift+click title bar	Alt+W (tile, stack)
Show/hide invisibles	⌘+I	Ctrl+I
Show/hide rulers	⌘+R	Ctrl+R
Show/hide guides	F7	F7
Show/hide baseline grid	Option+F7	Ctrl+F7
Snap to guides	Shift+F7	Shift+F7

Palettes

Action	Macintosh	Windows
Show/hide Measurements	F9	F9
Show/hide Tools palette	F8	F8
Show/hide Document Layout palette	F10	F4
Show/hide StyleSheets palette	F11	F11
Show/hide Colors palette	F12	F12
Show/hide Trap Information palette	Option+F12	Ctrl+F12
Show/hide Lists palette	Option+F11	Ctrl+F11
Show/hide Index palette	Option+⌘+I	Ctrl+Alt+I
Show font use	F13	not available
Show picture use	Option+F13	not available

Navigation

Action	Macintosh	Windows
Page grabber hand	Option+drag	Alt+drag
Enable/disable live scroll	Option+drag scroll box	not available
Display master page	Shift+F10	Shift+F4
Display following master page	Option+F10	Ctrl+Shift+F4
Display preceding master page	Option+Shift+F10	Ctrl+Shift+F3
Display document page	Shift+F10	Shift+F4
Following page	Shift+PageUp or Shift+PageDown	Ctrl+Shift+L
Preceding page	Shift+PageUp or Shift+PageDown	Ctrl+Shift+K
First page	Shift+Home or Ctrl+PageUp	Ctrl+Shift+A
Last page	Shift+End or Ctrl+Shift+D	Ctrl+PageDown

Object Selection

Action	Macintosh	Windows
Select all	⌘+A	Ctrl+A
Select item behind another item	Option+Shift+⌘+click	Ctrl+Alt+Shift+click
Multiple selection (series)	Shift+click	Shift+click
Multiple selection (noncontiguous)	⌘+click	Ctrl+click

Moving Objects

Action	Macintosh	Windows
Nudge selected object 1 point	arrow keys	arrow keys
Nudge selected object ¹⁄₁₀ point	Option+arrow keys	Alt+arrow keys
Constrain movement	Shift+drag	Shift+drag
Cut	⌘+X or F2	Ctrl+X
Delete (content tool selected)	⌘+K	Ctrl+K
Delete (item tool selected)	Delete	Backspace
Copy	⌘+C or F3	Ctrl+C
Paste	⌘+V or F4	Ctrl+V

Item Commands

Action	Macintosh	Windows
Modify	⌘+M	Ctrl+M
Edit shape	Shift+F4	F10
Modify frame	⌘+B	Ctrl+B
Clipping	Option+⌘+T	Ctrl+Alt+T
Edit clipping path	Option+Shift+F4	Ctrl+Shift+F10
Runaround	⌘+T	Ctrl+T
Edit runaround	Option+F4	Ctrl+F10
Duplicate	⌘+D	Ctrl+D
Step and repeat	Option+⌘+D	Ctrl+Alt+D
Space/align	⌘+comma	Ctrl+comma
Send to back	Shift+F5	Shift+F5
Bring to front	F5	F5

(continued)

Action	Macintosh	Windows
Send backward	Option+Shift+F5	Ctrl+Shift+F5
Bring forward	Option+F5	Ctrl+F5
Lock/unlock	F6	F6
Group	⌘+G	Ctrl+G
Ungroup	⌘+U	Ctrl+U

Text Selection

Action	Macintosh	Windows
Word	Double-click	Double-click
Paragraph	Quadruple-click	Quadruple-click
Line	Triple-click	Triple-click
Story	⌘+A or quintuple-click	Ctrl+A or quintuple-click
Character to left	Shift+←	Shift+←
Character to right	Shift+→	Shift+→
Word to left	Shift+⌘+←	Ctrl+Shift+←
Word to right	Shift+⌘+→	Ctrl+Shift+→
Up one line	Shift+↑	Shift+↑
Down one line	Shift+↓	Shift+↓
To start of line	Shift+Option+⌘+←	Ctrl+Alt+Shift+← or Shift+Home
To end of line	Shift+Option+⌘+→	Ctrl+Alt+Shift+→ or Shift+End
Up one paragraph	Shift+⌘+↑	Ctrl+Shift+↑
Down one paragraph	Shift+⌘+↓	Ctrl+Shift+↓
To top of story	Shift+Option+⌘+↑	Ctrl+Alt+Shift+↑_or Ctrl+Shift+Home
To bottom of story	Shift+Option+⌘+↓	Ctrl+Alt+Shift+↓ or Ctrl+Shift+End

Spelling

Action	Macintosh	Windows
Check word	⌘+L	Ctrl+W
Check story	Option+⌘+L	Ctrl+Alt+W
Check document	Option+Shift+⌘+L	Ctrl+Alt+Shift+W
Look up spelling	⌘+L	Alt+L
Skip word	⌘+S	Alt+S
Add word to dictionary	⌘+A	Alt+A
Add all suspect words to dictionary	Option+Shift+click	Alt+Shift+click Done button Close button
Suggest hyphenation	⌘+H	Ctrl+H

Text/Paragraph Formats

Action	Macintosh	Windows
Edit style sheets	Shift+F11	Shift+F11
Edit H&Js Option+⌘+H	Option+Shift+F11	Ctrl+Shift+F11 or
Character attributes	Shift+⌘+D	Ctrl+Shift+D
Paragraph attributes	Shift+⌘+F	Ctrl+Shift+F
Copy format to selected paragraphs	Option+Shift+click	Alt+Shift+click
Apply No Style and then apply style sheet	Option+click style-sheet name	Alt+clickstyle-sheet name
Choose font	Option+Shift+⌘+M	Ctrl+Alt+Shift+M
Symbol font (next character)	Shift+⌘+Q	Ctrl+Shift+Q
Zapf Dingbats font (next character)	Shift+⌘+Z	Ctrl+Shift+Z
Change size	Shift+⌘+\	Ctrl+Shift+\

(continued)

Action	Macintosh	Windows
Change leading	Shift+⌘+E	Ctrl+Shift+E
Define tabs	Shift+⌘+T	Ctrl+Shift+T
Define rules	Shift+⌘+N	Ctrl+Shift+N
Increase to next size in type scale	Shift+⌘+>	Ctrl+Shift+>
Decrease to next size in type scale	Shift+⌘+<	Ctrl+Shift+<
Increase 1 point	Option+Shift+⌘+>	Ctrl+Alt+Shift+>
Decrease 1 point	Option+Shift+⌘+<	Ctrl+Alt+Shift+<
Increase horizontal scaling 5%	⌘+]	Ctrl+]
Decrease horizontal scaling 5%	⌘+[	Ctrl+[
Increase horizontal scaling 1%	Option+⌘+]	Ctrl+Alt+]
Decrease horizontal scaling 1%	Option+⌘+[	Ctrl+Alt+[
Resize box interactively	⌘ +drag text-box handle	Ctrl+Shift+drag text-box handle
Resize box interactively (constrained)	Shift+⌘+drag text-box handle	Ctrl+Shift+drag text-box handle
Resize interactively (proportional)	Option+Shift+⌘+ drag text-box handle	Ctrl+Alt+Shift+drag text box handle
Increase kerning/ tracking 1/20 em	Shift+⌘+]	Ctrl+Shift+]
Decrease kerning/ tracking 1/20 em	Shift+⌘+[	Ctrl+Shift+[
Increase kerning/ tracking 1/200 em	Option+Shift+⌘+]	Ctrl+Alt+Shift+]
Decrease kerning/ tracking 1/200 em	Option+Shift+⌘+[	Ctrl+Alt+Shift+[
Raise baseline shift 1 point	Option+Shift+⌘+plus	Ctrl+Alt+Shift+)
Lower baseline shift 1 point	Option+Shift+⌘+-	Ctrl+Alt+Shift+(

Action	Macintosh	Windows
Increase leading 1 point	Shift+⌘+"	Ctrl+Shift+"
Decrease leading 1 point	Shift+⌘+semicolon	Ctrl+Shift+semicolon
Increase leading $\frac{1}{10}$ point	Option+Shift+⌘+"	Ctrl+Alt+Shift+"
Decrease leading $\frac{1}{10}$ point	Option+Shift+⌘+ semicolon	Ctrl+Alt+Shift+ semicolon
Normal	Shift+⌘+P	Ctrl+Shift+P
Bold	Shift+⌘+B	Ctrl+Shift+B
Italic	Shift+⌘+I	Ctrl+Shift+I
Underline	Shift+⌘+U	Ctrl+Shift+U
World underline	Shift+⌘+W	Ctrl+Shift+W
Strikethrough	Shift+⌘+/	Ctrl+Shift+/
All caps	Shift+⌘+K	Ctrl+Shift+K
Subscript	Shift+⌘+hyphen	Ctrl+Shift+9
Superscript	Shift+⌘+plus	Ctrl+Shift+0 (zero)
Superior	Shift+⌘+V	Ctrl+Shift+V
Outline	Shift+⌘+O	Ctrl+Shift+O
Shadow	Shift+⌘+S	Ctrl+Shift+S
Left-justify	Shift+⌘+L	Ctrl+Shift+L
Right-justify	Shift+⌘+R	Ctrl+Shift+R
Center	Shift+⌘+C	Ctrl+Shift+C
Justify	Shift+⌘+J	Ctrl+Shift+J
Force-justify	Option+Shift+⌘+J	Ctrl+Alt+Shift+J

Find/Change

Action	Macintosh	Windows
Find/Change	⌘+F	Ctrl+F
Close Find/Change	Option+⌘+F	Ctrl+Alt+F

Special Characters (In Find/Change)

Action	Macintosh	Windows
Carriage return	⌘+Enter	Ctrl+Enter
Tab	⌘+Tab	Ctrl+Tab
Line break	Shift+⌘+Enter	Ctrl+Shift+Enter
Column	⌘+keypad Enter	\c
Backslash (\)	⌘+\	Ctrl+\
Wildcard	⌘+?	Ctrl+?
Flex space	Shift+⌘+F	Ctrl+Shift+F
Punctuation space	⌘+period	Ctrl+period
Current box's page number	⌘+3	Ctrl+3
Preceding box's page number	⌘+2	Ctrl+2
Following box's page number	⌘+4	Ctrl+4

Special Characters

Action	Macintosh	Windows
Em dash	Option+Shift+hyphen	Ctrl+Shift+=
Nonbreaking em dash	Option+⌘+=	Ctrl+Alt+Shift+=[
En dash	Option+hyphen	Ctrl+Alt+Shift+hyphen
Nonbreaking hyphen	⌘+=	Ctrl+=
Discretionary hyphen	⌘+hyphen	Ctrl+hyphen
Nonbreaking space	⌘+spacebar	Ctrl+5
En space	Option+spacebar	Ctrl+Shift+6
Nonbreaking en space	Option+⌘+spacebar	Ctrl+Alt+Shift+6
Punctuation space	Shift+spacebar	Shift+spacebar or Ctrl+6
Nonbreaking punctuation space	Shift+⌘+spacebar	Ctrl+Shift+spacebar or Ctrl+Alt+6

Action	Macintosh	Windows
Flex space	Option+Shift+spacebar	Ctrl+Shift+5
Nonbreaking flex space	Option+Shift+⌘	Ctrl+Alt+Shift+5+spacebar
Indent here	⌘+\	Ctrl+\
Current page number	⌘+3	Ctrl+3
Preceding box's page number	⌘+2	Ctrl+2
Following box's page number	⌘+4	Ctrl+4
New line	Shift+Enter	Shift+Enter
Discretionary new line	⌘+Enter	Ctrl+Enter
New column	keypadEnter	keypad Enter
New box	Shift+keypad Enter	Shift+keypad Enter
Right-indent tab	Option+Tab	Shift+Tab

Graphics Handling

Action	Macintosh	Windows
Import picture at 36 dpi	Shift+click Open button in Get Picture dialog box	Shift+click Open in Get Picture dialog box
Import color TIFF as grayscale	⌘ +click Open in Get Picture dialog box	Ctrl+click Open in Get Picture dialog box
Import grayscale TIFF as black and white	⌘+click Open button in Get Picture dialog box	Ctrl+click Open button in Get Picture dialog box
Import EPS without importing spot colors' definitions	⌘+click Open button in Get Picture dialog box	Ctrl+click Open button in Get Picture dialog box
Reimport all pictures in a document	⌘+click Open button in Open dialog box	Ctrl+click Open button in Open dialog box
Center image within box	Shift+⌘+M	Ctrl+Shift+M
Fit image to box	Shift+⌘+F	Ctrl+Shift+F
Fit image proportionally to box	Option+Shift+⌘+F	Ctrl+Alt+Shift+F

(continued)

Action	Macintosh	Windows
Resize box constrained	Shift+drag	Shift+drag
Resize box at aspect ratio	Option+Shift+drag	Alt+Shift+drag
Resize box and scale picture	⌘+drag	Ctrl+drag
Resize box constrained and scale picture	Shift+⌘+drag	Ctrl+Shift+drag
Resize box at aspect ratio and scale picture	Option+Shift+⌘+drag	Ctrl+Alt+Shift+drag
Increase picture scale 5%	Option+Shift+⌘+>	Ctrl+Alt+Shift+>
Decrease picture scale 5%	Option+Shift+⌘+<	Ctrl+Alt+Shift+<
Negative image	Shift+⌘+hyphen	Ctrl+Shift+hyphen
Picture contrast specifications	Shift+⌘+C	Ctrl+Shift+C
Picture halftone specifications	Shift+⌘+H	Ctrl+Shift+H
Change line width	Shift+⌘+\	Ctrl+Shift+\
Increase line width to next size	Shift+⌘+>	Ctrl+Shift+>
Decrease line width to next size	Shift+⌘+<	Ctrl+Shift+<
Increase line width 1 point	Option+Shift+⌘+>	Ctrl+Alt+Shift+>
Decrease line width 1 point	Option+Shift+⌘+<	Ctrl+Alt+Shift+<
Delete Bézier point	Option+click point	Alt+click point
Add Bézier point	Option+click segment	Alt+click segment
Create corner point	Option+F1	Ctrl+F1
Create smooth point	Option+F2	Ctrl+F2
Create symmetrical point	Option+F3	Ctrl+F3
Create straight segment	Shift+Option+F1	Ctrl+Shift+F1
Create curved segment	Shift+Option+F2	Ctrl+Shift+F2

Special Characters

Action	Macintosh	Windows
Em dash	Option+Shift+hyphen	Ctrl+Shift+=
Nonbreaking em dash	Option+⌘+=	Ctrl+Alt+Shift+=[
En dash	Option+hyphen	Ctrl+Alt+Shift+hyphen

Chapter 24

The Ten Most Common Mistakes

*L*earning how to use QuarkXPress takes time. Learning how to use it right takes even longer! Knowing that, we thought we'd try to save you some time (and maybe even a few tears) by pointing out some of the most common mistakes that people make when they start dabbling in desktop publishing. Take a few minutes to read this chapter. Why? Because we *like* you.

Forgetting to Register

Suppose that you just bought a brand-spanking-new copy of QuarkXPress. You peel off the shrinkwrap, open the box, take a peek at the manuals, peel open the disc envelope, and install the software. Ready to rock and roll, right? Not so fast. Don't make the mistake that too many users make: failing to take a few minutes to fill out the disc-based registration information and e-mailing (or just plain mailing) it back to Quark.

What are the advantages of registering your copy of QuarkXPress? Simply put, registering your product puts you in Quark's user database. You need to be registered if you want to use the free first-90-days-after-purchase technical-support privileges, purchase an extended service plan, or be eligible for product upgrades. And a word to the wise: Quark focuses on providing service to *registered* users and is less likely to be supportive if your name and serial number are never recorded. Registration takes only a few minutes, and we think that those few minutes are well spent.

Using Too Many Fonts

Avant Garde. Bellevue. Centaur Gothic. Desdemona. Fonts have cool names, and looking at a font list and seeing all the desktop publishing possibilities is fascinating.

Yes, we know that trying out a great many fonts is tempting. This urge overcomes nearly everybody who's new to desktop publishing. (The few who don't begin their QuarkXPress careers by liberally sprinkling fonts throughout a page are often those who are traditional designers or who have typesetting backgrounds. In other words, they already know better.) Try limiting the number of fonts that you use on a page to two. When you have three, four, or five fonts, the document takes on an amateurish appearance, quite frankly. Experts in page design never use several fonts together.

These rules apply doubly to new Web designers who not only have font issues to contend with (including fonts that may or may not be on other people's computers, as described in Chapter 18), but the color issue as well. How many times have you visited a Web site and shuddered at the grape background splattered with 28-point neon green headlines and 16-point pink body copy — bleeding on all four sides of the Web browser as if it were a margin-free zone. Artists aren't generally a conservative lot, but they are conservative with their work. You should be, too.

Putting Too Much on a Page

You've probably seen them before: pages that overflowing with stuff — words, pictures, you name it.

One of the best things that you'll ever learn about page design is the value of white space — the places on the page that have no text, no pictures, no lines — just the plain paper showing through. Pages that are crammed full of text and pictures are pages that readers avoid. Keep some space between text columns and headlines, and between the items on the page and the edges of the page.

Finding white space on a page is like going to a crowded beach and finding — in the middle of the crowd — a perfectly smooth, empty spot that offers you a gorgeous view from your beach blanket. The white space "feels" great to the viewer's eyes, making him or her more likely to get the message that's being conveyed by the words and pictures on the page. Of course, this is easier said than done. Professional designers have spent years perfecting this Zen-like approach to design.

Again, this applies to Web designers as well. Funny little cartoon GIFs can be cute to a point. But more than one in a design can destroy an otherwise competent Web design.

Overdoing the Design

This entry is kind of an extension for the previous one. Avoiding the "overdesigning" of a page can't be stressed enough. QuarkXPress is a powerful application that lets you do all kinds of nifty things. But just because you can do all of those things doesn't mean that you should.

Nothing looks worse than a complex design created by a publishing novice. Professionals know that less is more. Yes, it's possible to rotate text, skew text and graphics, make cool blends, set type on a curvy line, add multiple colors, stretch and condense type, and bleed artwork off the page. But using all these effects at the same time can overwhelm readers and make them miss the whole point of the message you're trying to convey.

Here's a good rule to remember: Limit special effects to a maximum of three on a two-page spread. Here's an even better rule: If you're in doubt about whether to add an effect to a page, *don't.*

Not Consulting a Designer

We know that it's not rocket science, but designing a document still can get fairly complicated. Knowing when to consult a professional graphic designer is a good idea.

You can best make the decision by taking into consideration how you'll use the document. Is the document a one- or two-color newspaper for a small club or organization? Then it's probably perfectly fine for a new QuarkXPress user to tackle the job. But if the document is a full-color display ad that will run in a national magazine, leave it to the pros.

When you have to design a high-end document, professional graphic designers are worth their weight in gold. Sure, you may have to spend a few bucks to hire a talented designer, but you may save that much and more by having that person craft your document for you. Designers are trained to know what works visually (and, even more important, what doesn't), how to select the right paper, how many colors are appropriate, and how to have the document printed. In short, a good graphic designer can make your pages sing, and you end up smelling like a rose.

Not Using Master Pages

Before you start working on a document, you need to have an idea about what the document will look like. Will it have two columns? Will the top half of every page have a graphic? Where will the page numbers appear?

After you figure these things out, set up master pages for all the elements that will repeat in the same spot, page after page (such as page numbers). Master pages make things much easier, and they are easy to create. People who don't use master pages are people who like to do things the hard way. And we know you'd rather use the easy way so you can save time for the really hard stuff.

To create a master page, open a document and choose Page⇨Display⇨ A-Master. Anything that you create on that page becomes part of the master page and appears on every page in the document that is based on that particular master page. Each document can have up to 127 pairs of master pages. See Chapter 16 for help in mastering master pages.

Not Using Smart Quotes and Dashes

Nothing, and we mean nothing, bothers a professional designer or publisher more than seeing inch marks where typesetter's quote marks should appear or skinny little hyphens — or worse yet, *two* skinny little hyphens — in place of em dashes. (An *em dash* is a dash that is the same width as the current font's capital *M*. You can create an em dash by using the key command Option+Shift+hyphen or Ctrl+Shift+=.)

Using the correct quotes and dashes is easy in QuarkXPress. You can choose among a variety of quote formats, including some that work with foreign languages. You want to use typographically correct quotes and dashes because they make your document look much more professional.

To use typographically correct quotes, choose Edit⇨Preferences⇨Preferences or press Option+Shift+⌘+Y or Ctrl+Alt+Shift+Y and select Smart Quotes in the Interactive pane of the Preferences dialog box.

To get the right kinds of quotes and dashes when you import text from a word processing application, make sure that the Convert Quotes box is checked in the Get Text dialog box.

Be aware, however, that if you're dealing with measurements in your text, in particular inches and feet, the inch and foot marks will appear curly, too (and bother those professionals even more). You can get around this problem by using the shortcut key combination of Control+Shift+" for inch marks and Control+' for foot marks on the Mac, or Ctrl+" for inch marks and Ctrl+Alt+' for foot marks in Windows.

Forgetting to Check Spelling

Typos are like ants at a summer picnic — they show up all the time. You can avoid some typos if you always remember that the last thing to do before printing your document is to check spelling. Checking spelling won't catch every possible error (you still need to proofread thoroughly to catch all errors), but using the built-in spelling checker in QuarkXPress is easy to do, and it can prevent embarrassing typos and misspellings.

Not Talking with Your Commercial Printer

If you're creating a document that will be commercially printed, be sure to talk with your printer early in the game. These folks know their business. Your printer can help you plan your document, pick the right number of colors to use in it, and produce it cost-effectively. He or she will appreciate your concern, too, and will likely invest extra effort in doing a great job for you if you show that you care enough to consult the pros early on.

Not Giving the Service Bureau All Your Files

If you've never worked with a service bureau — the place where you take or send your QuarkXPress documents to be output to an imagesetting device — you may think that the people who work there are downright snoopy. They poke and prod, ask millions of questions, and want to know every little thing about your document. They give you the third degree, asking about every file for every graphic on every single page.

These people are not out to pick on you; they truly do need to know about all the fonts and files necessary to output your document.

Why? Because they just do, that's why. Seriously, the equipment that a service bureau uses needs to have everything that you used to create a document. If your document includes an EPS file that contains text, for example, the service bureau needs to have the font that is used in the text. If that font is not available, the EPS file prints incorrectly, and the job has to be output again.

The Collect for Output feature in QuarkXPress can help. This feature copies all the text, fonts, color profiles and picture files that are necessary to produce your document into the folder of your choice. It also generates a report about your document, including its fonts, dimensions, and trapping information. To use this feature, choose File➪Collect for Output.

However, the Collect for Output feature can't replace your brain. You still need to think about your document. You are the person who is responsible for making sure that your service bureau has everything it needs to output your document the right way, the first time. Take a look and make sure all the pieces are there before you waste hundreds of dollars outputting an incorrect document.

Chapter 25

The Ten Best Online Resources

QuarkXPress users who have an Internet connection, be it a 56-Kbps modem or a broadband connection, have access to an abundance of QuarkXPress-related information and freebies. Cyberspace is, indeed, a friendly place for electronic publishers. The next time you're online, check out some of our top ten QuarkXPress and desktop-publishing sites.

The XPresso Bar

`www.xpressobar.com`

This site is a great place to begin a quest for information about QuarkXPress. The home page contains seven main links: FAQ, Telalink Archives, Read Your Eyeballs Out, Make It Faster, Question Authority, Go Somewhere Else, and About Us. Each of these pages contains several links to related sites. You find links to the Quark home page and other Internet desktop-publishing Web sites, as well as links to a variety of sites dedicated to QuarkXPress-specific topics: scripting, books, publications, XTensions developers, and so on. The Telalink Archive link takes you to the XPresso Bar FTP site that's discussed in the following section.

The XPresso Bar FTP Site

`ftp.xpressobar.com`

In the words of its creators, this site is "one of the most complete collections of Quark extensions, updaters, and other information for both Mac and Windows." This site is the successor to the Telalink FTP site (which is renowned among QuarkXPress users for its collection of QuarkXPress freebies) and is replete with FAQs, demo XTensions, scripts, word-processing filters, and other utilities. You can access the XPresso Bar FTP site with an FTP client application or a Web browser. Figure 25-1 shows a directory of Windows-related files and folders at the XPresso Bar FTP site.

Figure 25-1: The Windows directory at the XPresso Bar's FTP site, viewed in Internet Explorer.

XTensions Sites

Hundreds of commercial XTensions for QuarkXPress are available for both the Macintosh and Windows; these XTensions handle a wide range of tasks that QuarkXPress cannot (see Chapter 10 for more on XTensions). Plenty of information about XTensions is available online, including the Web sites of three XTensions vendors: CoDesCo (`www.codesco.com`), The PowerXChange (`www.thepowerxchange.com`), and XCite Europe (`www.xcite-international.com`). Not only do these sites let you purchase XTensions online, but they offer downloadable demos, too. Several other retail sites for XTensions offer similar serivces, and most XTensions developers have Web sites of their own. To find information about other retailers or a particular XTensions developer, use your favorite search engine to perform a search for them.

Quark Home Page

`www.quark.com`

In addition to providing information about the entire Quark product line — QuarkXPress, QuarkXPress Passport, QuarkImmedia, Quark Publishing System, and mTropolis — the Quark Web site offers demo versions of products; technical notes and access to technical support via e-mail; program updaters; and free Quark-developed XTensions, including updated versions of word-processing filters.

This site is definitely worth checking regularly, particularly for the import/export filters.

Accessing the Quark home page is easier now than ever before, thanks to the QuarkLink submenu located in the QuarkXPress 5 Utilities menu (see Figure 25-2).

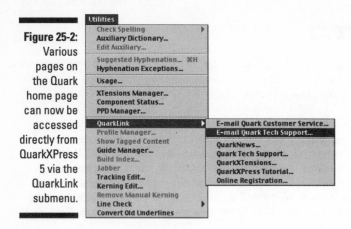

Figure 25-2:
Various
pages on
the Quark
home page
can now be
accessed
directly from
QuarkXPress
5 via the
QuarkLink
submenu.

Yahoo! — Computers and Internet: Desktop Publishing

dir.yahoo.com/Computers_and_Internet/Desktop_Publishing/

This site isn't specifically for QuarkXPress users, but it's a great jumping-off point for desktop publishers — both print and Web publishers. Major topics include fonts, HTML, PostScript, scanning, and typography. Clicking on any of these topics provides links to several related sites. The site also features links to several online DTP (desktop publishing) publications.

Quark Forums

America Online (keyword: Quark)

CompuServe (Go: Quark)

Subscribers of America Online and CompuServe can find demos and updaters for commercial XTensions, free XTensions from Quark, and message boards for posting and answering questions. The CompuServe QuarkXPress forum has a lively scripting area that offers several useful scripts. If you're looking for general publishing information, both services also have DTP forums. Look for the AOL and CompuServe QuarkXPress forums to change as new XTensions and utilities become available for QuarkXPress 5.

Free QuarkXPress Templates for Graphic Design

desktoppublishing.com/templ_quark.html

You gotta like anything that's free. At this site, you can find dozens of free QuarkXPress templates for creating brochures, business cards, calendars, envelopes, labels, letterhead, newsletters, postcards — even CD-ROM jewel cases. The documents were created with QuarkXPress 3.32 for Windows, but they can be opened with the Macintosh version of QuarkXPress as well. If you don't have the built-in fonts, you can easily replace them with fonts of your own. The documents include instructions on how to use them. Free and easy — what a deal!

QuarkXPress Tips

www.digitrain.com/tips/QX_tips.html

This site has many handy tips for QuarkXPress users, including a list of Top Ten Tips. If you stop at this site, you're guaranteed to learn something new and useful about QuarkXPress. The site's top tip: "Use the grabber hand to scroll. Hold the Option (Mac) or Alt (Windows) key down, then move the mouse to scroll. Note that if Caps Lock is on, the grabber hand doesn't work on the Mac." Now, aren't you glad you know that?

Sal's AppleScript Snippets

users.aol.com/nyhthawk/welcome.html

If AppleScript were a cross-platform technology, this site would warrant a higher rating. It would rate even higher if it were updated on occasion. (According to Sal's home page, this site was last updated 5/27/97.) Still, this is a top-notch place to find information about creating AppleScripts for QuarkXPress — even today. Site creator Sal Saghoian is the grand poo-bah of AppleScript, and the site includes instructional materials for beginning scriptwriters, scripting tools, and free scripts. If the idea of automating QuarkXPress for Macintosh intrigues you, you should definitely check out this site.

The QuarkXPress Mailing List

This mailing list (sometimes called the *sic list* because it was initially called the Quark Express Mailing List – a misspelling of QuarkXPress) is a mother-lode of QuarkXPress expertise. To subscribe, send an e-mail message to listserv@iubvm.ucs.indiana.edu with SUBSCRIBE QUARKXPR (your name) in the body of the message (for example, SUBSCRIBE QUARKXPR PAT SMITH). Because the list is active and diverse, you may want to subscribe only long enough to post a message and gather responses. Be prepared to receive a few dozen messages a day while you're subscribed. (To unsubscribe, send a message to the subscribe address with SIGNOFF QUARKXPR in the body of the message.)

Index